Bus Fare to Kentucky

Bus Fare to Kentucky

The Autobiography of Skeeter Davis

Skeeter Davis

A BIRCH LANE PRESS BOOK
Published by Carol Publishing Group

A Birch Lane Press Book
Published by Carol Publishing Group
Birch Lane Press is a registered trademark of Carol Communications,
    Inc.
Editorial Offices: 600 Madison Avenue, New York, N.Y. 10022
Sales & Distribution Offices: 120 Enterprise Avenue, Secaucus,
    N.J. 07094
In Canada: Canadian Manda Group, P.O. Box 920 Station U, Toronto,
    Ontario M8Z 5P9
Queries regarding rights and permissions should be addressed to
Carol Publishing Group, 600 Madison Avenue, New York, N.Y. 10022

Carol Publishing Group books are available at special discounts for
bulk purchases, for sales promotions, fund-raising, or educational
purposes. Special editions can be created to specifications. For
details contact: Special Sales Department, Carol Publishing
Group, 120 Enterprise Avenue, Secaucus, N.J. 07094

Manufactured in the United States of America
10 9 8 7 6 5 4 3 2 1

Library of Congress Cataloging-in-Publication Data

Davis, Skeeter.
    Bus fare to Kentucky : the autobiography of Skeeter Davis / by
Skeeter Davis.
        p.   cm.
    "A Birch Lane Press book."
    ISBN 1–55972–191–X
    1. Davis, Skeeter.   2. Country musicians—United States—
Biography.   I. Title.
ML420.D34A3   1993
782.42′1642′092—dc20
    [B]   93–8841
                                                      CIP
                                                      MN

This book is dedicated to the ones I love:
Mother, Daddy, Suzan and the kids—
Buddy, Poochie, Boze, Punkin, and Doozer

Contents

Contents

Acknowledgments

First and foremost, I thank God for His love, forgiveness, grace and salvation.

Thanks to my husband Joey Spampinato who makes me feel like Snow White—"happily ever after." And thanks to Linda Palmer, Dean Penick, Leigh Wieland, Phyllis Hill and Wanda Rose Guthrie for their unselfish labors of love in helping me with this book. Last, but not least, special thanks to Randall Medlock, counselor and friend, who was there to help me through the pain of opening up the memories so that I could write my autobiography.

To join Skeeter's fan club, write to: Fans and Friends Around the World, P.O. Box 92381, Nashville, TN, 37209–2381.

Bus Fare to Kentucky

THE DRY RIDGE YEARS

maryfrances

people meet maryfrances
she sings and she brings
home her friend from the city
named betty
she strums with a thumb
on a martin guitar
and sings like a bird
(songs that eddy and hawkshaw
and others have done)
and she nods at her harmony singer
named maryfrances
they sing and it rings
thru the hills of kentucky
and into ohio
if you listen real hard
maryfrances sings pretty

and granpappy says
maryfrances can make it
if she changes her name she can really go far
chester meet maryfrances
from dryridge and betty
they sing and they bring
a newfriend from newyork
named steve and he says
you can play your guitar
and they'll sing their new song
called "i forgot more"
and we'll press up some records
and maybe some more
cause this betty davis
and her friend maryfrances
can sing pretty good if you play your guitar
and granpappy says
maryfrances can make it
if she changes her name she can really go far
you'll love maryfrances
she sings and she brings
a tear to your eye
or a smile
her songs go a long
way from dryridge kentucky
but she's not a long way from home
her records sell so well
they sell millions
and she's in demand from portland to maine
she bows and now she gives others the credit
(steve and chester and felton and all)
but felton says kentucky soul
is what made maryfrances a star
so she sings and it rings
thru the hills of the country
and it brings a tear to granpappy's eye
and granpappy says
he knew she could make it
with her name changed to skeeter she had to go far

—Ronny Light

Eagle Creek

I know I'm just a country girl.
I hadn't seen much of the world
The day my bus pulled out of old Kentucky.
                    —"Bus Fare to Kentucky,"
                    by Skeeter Davis

Before Mother met my daddy, a guy named William Meadows had been calling on her. Mother had been looking for some nice way to tell him to stop coming around, because she didn't have the heart to tell him to his face that she thought he ought to bathe more often. She knew she did not want to spend her life with this man who smelled like the goats he raised.

Mother had heard the old wives' tale that if a young girl places a snail in an envelope just before sunrise on May the first, the snail will spell out the name of the man she will marry. So Mother got up bright and early the first morning in May of 1929, found a garden snail, and dropped it down in an envelope addressed to herself, Sarah Rachel Roberts.

Mother set the envelope down and left it, like she had been told to do, but then she got so anxious to know who her husband was going to be that she went and tore the envelope open too early. The poor snail had only had enough time to drool one word. But there it was, plain as day—*William*.

Mother threw the envelope down and stomped it until that poor little ol' snail was squashed flatter 'n a flitter.

"I don't care what you say," she told the gooey spot on the floor. "I ain't a-marryin' that blame ol' goat farmer William Meadows."

The snail could have saved its life by writing just a wee bit faster, because my daddy's name was William too. William Lee Penick. Everybody but Mother called him Will. She still calls him William to this day. Though you could never tell it now, Mother loved Daddy so much that one time she threatened to throw herself off the bridge into the deepest part of Eagle Creek if he wouldn't marry her—or so Daddy says. Mother denies this, however!

"Your daddy was a high-steppin' dandy," Mother told me. "That first day I met William on them railroad tracks he was wearin' a vested suit with a high-collared shirt. Why, Skeeter, that man looked like he just stepped off a page in the catalog. Every time he called on me he'd be dressed fit to kill, his shoes spit-shined like a new penny."

At this point in her story Mother started shaking her head disgustedly. "Well, as soon as we got married"—then she started laughing—"he let his beard grow out and took to wearin' overalls."

I was grinning by this time, because I could almost predict what was coming next. "Now look at him," Mother said, pointing over toward Daddy. "Since you bought that farm in Tennessee, Skeeter, he's even started raising goats and pigs. He makes me think of that William Meadows." She laughed. "Why, I'd been just as well off to have gone ahead and married that blame William Meadows."

Daddy just sat there while Mother cooked his goose. When he saw she was finished, he calmly said, "Now, Punzie, you know we were right in the middle of the Great Depression, and I lost my job the day after we were married. If you gonna tell it, tell it right."

"Well, William," Mother shot back quickly after taking a sip from her coffee, "I can't see where the Depression ever lifted for us. As far as I'm concerned, we're still right square in the middle of it."

My parents met one winter afternoon in 1931 on the railroad tracks in front of the depot at Glencoe, Kentucky. Mother was chasing the southbound L & N, and Daddy caught her just before she hopped on an empty flatcar. Part of his job was catching hoboes.

Picking cinders from the knees of his trousers, Daddy asked, "Where you headed, girl?"

"Where does that train go?"

"From here to Sparta, then Worthville, on to Louisville, then on to New Orleans."

"Well, that's where I was headed."

There's Gypsy in my soul, and I haven't got a doubt where it originated. It came from Punzie. For as long as I can remember, Daddy called Mother Punzie. He would tell us kids, "Punzie was runnin' that first day I met her, and she's been runnin' ever since."

It's the truth. In later years I got to see my mother between whistle-stops. Hers, not mine. I waited as late as April to exchange Christmas presents with her. One Christmas we decided to leave the tree up until she got home. It turned brown sometime in March. By April we decided it was too much of a fire hazard to wait on her any longer.

I think Mother knew the first name of every bus driver east of the Mississippi. One Fourth of July I gave her a music box for Mother's Day. (See what I mean?) When she opened it, I started singing, "There's nothing like Greyhound," while the little box plunked out the melody of "There's No Place Like Home." Everyone there was laughing, except Mother. She cried.

"What's the matter? Don't ya like it?"

"Oh...it ain't that I don't like it, Skeeter. But that's the song your grandpa used to fiddle every time I griped about having to stay home."

Once again I blamed myself with ruining Mother's homecoming. Because once again she had managed to find a way to bring up Grandpa Roberts. You see, her father was murdered when she was a little girl, and to bring his name up always cast a spell of gloom over the brief times I got to spend with Mother between her destinations.

I'm the entertainer, yet she was on the road more often than me. How I used to worry about her. I wished and prayed that Mother could settle down. But Lord knows, I'm not much better at settling down than she was.

It's not really fair of me either to pin all my hillbilly, Gypsy blood on Mother. Even Daddy ran away from home to join the circus when he was a kid. He wanted to be a trapeze artist, he said, but he ended up feeding and watering the elephants until Gramma Penick sent Poppy after him. To make up for it, Poppy and Gramma let him get a job with the railroad where he could travel all he wanted. He was working for the railroad, of course, when he ran into Mother.

Sometimes Mother made him sound like the Great Gatsby, claiming he had over twenty shirts when they met, but I don't see how that could have been possible, when I know for a fact he was dirt poor.

There has only been one side of my whole family tree that wasn't poor by nature. That was on Daddy's mother's side. Gramma Penick was originally a Colson. The Colsons had a plantation down near Williamstown with slaves, horses, a mansion—the works.

Rich as they were, nonetheless the Civil War left even that side of my family penniless. And they stayed that way.

Daddy didn't like for me to admit to anyone how poor we really were. Poverty and pride should be the Penick coat of arms. Most of my early childhood was spent in relief dresses, moving from one place to another while Daddy searched for work that would bring in enough money to feed us.

My father was born and raised in the hills of northern Kentucky like his father and grandfather before him. My great-grandfather, Robert Penick, was still living when I was born. One of the first things I remember was going to his funeral in a horse-drawn carriage. Mother spanked me for playing in the dirt mound while they buried my great-grandfather Penick. She stood me between her legs and forced me to watch as everybody else got to do what I had been spanked for—throwing clods on the box in the deep hole. I didn't think it was fair. I knew why I was crying. My bottom hurt. I couldn't, for the life of me, understand why all the big people were crying too. Who spanked them? I would learn later why big people cry.

Robert Penick had been a saw miller. I never saw the man. He traveled, Daddy told me, throughout the north Kentucky woods carrying his sawmill, as well as a portable hut for his wife and children to live in. His wife Rachel died shortly after giving birth to my granddaddy, Martin Luther Penick. That's my Poppy. I knew him, for sure. And next to my daddy, I loved him more than any man I have ever known.

When Poppy was old enough to be on his own, he settled in a little town called Dry Ridge and took up farming. Gramma Penick (Leona Naomi Colson) had twelve kids by him. My daddy was number two, or maybe I should say number one and a half. He has a twin sister named Lillian. Will and Lil were born June 13, 1910, and despite the fact that my father was born a hillbilly, always dependent on his back and hands for a living, he was one of the smartest, most sensitive men

I have known. He read every chance he got and always encouraged me to do the same. Mother, on the other hand, relied on her quick-wittedness and her cunning ways, like a fox.

I've got a touch of both of them in me. Either way, I'm just pure, but poor, Kentucky hillbilly.

On March 2, 1931, less than a month after they first met, Mother and Daddy eloped. Exactly nine months later I was born. Mother was just this side of seventeen. As soon as she discovered she was with child, Mother *ran* back home. So by the time I was born, they had settled in with my mother's parents in a two-room clapboard shack on the banks of Eagle Creek.

Eagle Creek carves a valley of tobacco through the northern hills of the Bluegrass State before she dumps her silt in the Kentucky River. Come summer, the creek winds green and deep beside my birthplace, two miles upstream from the little town of Glencoe. At times, I've seen rainwater push Eagle Creek clean up past the steps of the shanties hiding along her banks beneath the weeping willows. But in my mind's eye, I see Eagle Creek just lying there rather shallow, frozen and silent, five cold nights after Christmas Day of 1931.

That's when, so they tell me, Doc Eckler rushed over to Grandpa Roberts's tiny two-room shack, a little past midnight on the morning of December 30, 1931, and delivered me into the world.

I was the first of seven children born to William and Sarah Penick. Somebody told me one time that our family sounded to them like Snow White and the Seven Dwarfs, but my brothers and sisters haven't always gone by their nicknames—Buddy, Poochie, Boze, Punkin, Doozer, and Hoopers—and I haven't always been called Skeeter. My parents actually named me Mary Frances, the heroine in a book Daddy had fallen asleep reading the evening I was born.

I wasn't blessed with a big baby shower. As a matter of fact, I only got one present, the day Uncle Tom Tack Colson brought me a puppy. It was so tiny, Daddy told me, he brought it to me in a shoe box. The puppy was a white terrier whom I learned to call Snowball. Can you think of a better name for a white December dog? He looked like the RCA trademark. Snowball, my one and only gift as a baby, stayed by my side for the next thirteen years.

As soon as Mother felt strong enough to face the winter weather, they took me to church and passed me around. They claim I was a pretty baby, but I have honestly never felt like I was pretty in my life. Mother says she didn't get me back until church was over. I guess I must have been pretty at one time.

Once Mother had fully recuperated, Daddy moved me, Snowball, and Mother from Grandpa's two-room shack to another shack even smaller, a mile further up Eagle Creek toward Glencoe.

Things stayed peaceful though poor, so I hear, the first few years of my life as my parents scrounged here and there for food, clothing, and shelter. Little did either of them expect the bloody event awaiting us just around the corner—an event so shattering that it would cast its shadow across the rest of our lives.

Murder in Rising Sun

> We wandered today to the hills, Maggie,
> To watch the rising sun.
> The sounds were so sweet in the hills, Maggie,
> When you and I were young.
> —"When You and I Were Young, Maggie,"
> Old fiddle tune

Some folks don't dig up the roots of their family tree for fear of finding something bad, like a horse thief, or even a murderer. I've never had to dig.

When I was two years old my great-uncle Dilver Webster was convicted of murder in cold blood and sentenced to serve life and a day in the state pen at Michigan City, Indiana. That murder has upset me and the rest of my family for as long as I can remember. Because the man Dilver was convicted of killing just so happened to be my grandfather, Jim Roberts.

If you'll recall, it was Grandpa and Grandma Roberts's little two-room shack I was born in. Soon after I was born, my grandparents moved away from that little shack in Glencoe across the Ohio River to a large farm in Rising Sun, Indiana. The farm was owned by my great-grandfather, Billy J. Webster. Grandpa Roberts served as the foreman over my great-grandfather's tobacco crops and lived in the back side of the old man's farmhouse. The house had been split up like a duplex, with the Websters living in the front side with two of their sons (Grandma Roberts's brothers), Dilver and Estell.

Since raising tobacco was second nature to Grandpa Roberts, Grandma's brothers worked for Grandpa, even though it was their daddy who owned the farm. Grandpa Roberts had been a tobacco sharecropper all his life, renowned for drinking whiskey from a silver flask, kicking up his heels at square dances, and fiddling old ballads by the evening fire.

Grandma didn't like his fiddle playing near as much as everyone else, so I hear, 'cause Grandpa had a way of teasing her by fiddling and singing "When You and I Were Young, Maggie." She took it personally, I guess, since her name was Maggie—Maggie Ann Webster. She must have resented being reminded that she was getting older.

The Christmas I turned two, the Roberts' came back down to Glencoe to visit us, along with my mother's brothers and sisters, George, Marion, Hattie, Helen, and Jimmy, all of them younger than mother and as yet unmarried.

Grandma Roberts brought me a lamb's wool coat that she had made by hand. Grandpa fiddled Christmas carols while everybody sang. Everybody, that is, but me. I was too busy, so Mother said, eating the glass bulbs off the Christmas tree. She spanked me for it. And while I cried, Grandpa Roberts rode me on his knee and sang "she's my curly-headed baby," until I quieted down again.

After the celebration, my father and grandfather went out for a walk and a smoke. "Will, I'll tell you what," Daddy says Grandpa told him. "I done went twenty years before movin' in with my in-laws, and I guarantee you one thing—I'll wait another twenty before I do it again. That mother of Maggie's has come close to driving me as crazy as she is. Soon as the money off this year's tobacco comes in, I'm movin' back here to Glencoe. I went over today and paid advance rent on that ol' place where Mary Frances was born, so we ought to be back down here by the last of next month."

When Grandpa Roberts told Daddy that my great-grandmother Webster was crazy, he just may have been telling the truth. Mother told me that my great-grandmother accused Grandma Roberts of "laying" with my great-grandaddy, believe it or not, when Grandma wasn't but twelve years old. The old woman claimed that every time her husband yelled for a drink of water it was actually a signal for my grandma—his daughter—to meet him in the barn. As farfetched as that sounds, she beat Grandma with one of those old heavy, stove-heated irons for it. I later discovered that my great-grandma even accused one of her daughters-in-law, Christine, of having an affair with my great-grandpa. She must have been miserably possessed with suspicion. I understand that she would flare into a rage at the drop of a hat, and constantly badgered and belittled my great-granddaddy. Obviously she had managed to rattle Grandpa Roberts's nerves pretty bad too.

Everybody says Grandpa Roberts was a good man, very pleasant and easy to work for. That is, until the tobacco crop came in each year. Once the crop was in, he started filling that silver flask of his with whiskey and stayed drunk till the money ran thin. When he was drinking, they claim, there never has been a man on God's green earth more overbearing and rowdy than my grandpa.

On the day Grandpa was murdered, January 13, 1934, Mother and Daddy had taken me and my new little baby brother, Buddy, over to my other grandparents, Poppy and Gramma Penick. Back in those days it wasn't so uncommon to have aunts and uncles your own age or even younger. Gramma Penick had just given birth to a stillborn daughter who would have been my aunt, had she lived. They named her Frances Lou, after me and my older cousin, Mary Lou Cook. Mother was cleaning Gramma Penick's baby and dressing it for burial when Mother's brother Marion came across the ferry from Rising Sun with the horrible news that their daddy was dead.

Daddy left Poppy Penick in charge of me and little Buddy, loaded my trembling mother into Marion's Model A and drove, as fast as cars would go in those days, toward the house in Rising Sun. On the way Uncle Marion told them, the best that he could, what he thought had taken place.

I've compiled the following account of the murder from whispers that I overheard when I was supposed to be asleep and from the bitter stories I tried not to hear, year after year, told by Mother over coffee and whiskey to anyone who'd listen.

It seems Mother's uncle Dilver Webster had developed a fancy for her teenage sister, Hattie. Dilver had been taking his niece (my aunt) to some picture shows behind Grandpa's back. Their romance blossomed until, just a few days before the murder, Mother's oldest brother, George, caught Dilver and Hattie in flagrante delicto (as the law calls it, "in the act") out in the tobacco barn.

Figuring that George would squeal to Grandpa and that more than likely his brother-in-law wasn't going to cater to incest, Dilver got scared and drove to Rising Sun to borrow a gun from a friend.

That very same day, as Grandpa Roberts had hoped, the tobacco money came in. It meant freedom, as he had told Daddy, his way—to escape his in-laws and return to Kentucky. He laid out the bills on the kitchen table and made two stacks: his sharecropper's portion and Great-grandpa Webster's landowner's portion. Every tenant has to pay the help, so from his own stack Grandpa counted out the pay for Dilver and Estell.

Uncle George had been too scared to tell Grandpa about catching Dilver and Hattie in the barn. Supposedly Grandpa knew nothing about the incident at all, so he was unsuspecting of what lay ahead when he went knocking on the Websters' door to deliver Dilver's pay.

Dilver, meanwhile, was waiting for him. His arm propped on the table, the cocked revolver in his hand. When Grandpa stepped up on the front porch and knocked, Dilver unloaded all six shots from the borrowed firearm through the door glass.

Twenty minutes earlier, Dilver had sent Marion, Hattie, and Helen for a "nice country walk" with his brother Estell to get them away from the house. From about a mile up the dirt road, Marion and Mother's sisters heard what sounded to them like the echo of a hammer ringing from the rooftop of the farmhouse. *Kerblam— kerblam—kerblam-blam!*

They stopped and looked back toward the farm. Little Helen asked, "Uncle Estell, what's all that hammerin'? Is somebody fixin' up our barn?"

"That ain't hammerin'." Estell grinned. "That's Dilver shootin' your daddy." For some reason, they could tell Estell wasn't joking, and the three of them ran, screaming, toward the house.

Most of the bullets had hit Grandpa's head and neck. Grandpa Roberts stumbled from the porch and staggered to the roadside, where he sank to the ground beneath a maple tree. Bleeding to death but still living, he called out to Grandma, who came running when she first heard the gunfire.

"Maggie, hold me...God help...I'm dying!"

Grandma Roberts slid Grandpa's bullet-stung head into her aproned lap. Dilver stood above them on the porch, still slinging the revolver around. He commanded his sister, "Put his head back down, Maggie, or I'll have to kill you too."

My great-grandmother Webster, the crazy woman, danced around in the room behind Dilver, clapping and singing, "Do what he says, Maggie! You ain't gonna have to worry with that man no more."

So Grandma Roberts laid her husband's head back down in the dry leaves at the foot of the barren maple tree. And they say Grandpa was still begging Grandma to hold him as he drew his last breath.

Uncle George, Mother's oldest but frailest brother (only five feet and two inches tall), had been out in the fields working. Like everyone else, he came running toward the noise. When his eyes fell on what was going on, George started screaming, "Damn you, Dilver. I didn't tell Pa nothin' about you and Hattie."

"Shut up, George!" Dilver barked.

George tried to wrestle the empty gun from Dilver's hand, but Dilver slapped him down with the pistol butt and growled, "Listen, you little SOB, if I had a bullet left, you'd be next."

George didn't listen. He kept coming at Dilver like he was trying to stop what had already happened. Dilver pistol-whipped him until George fell unconscious beside his father.

By this time the girls and Marion had made it back to the farmhouse. They ran about the house gathering up bed sheets to stop their daddy's lifeblood from flowing away. Realizing it was too late, they turned their attention to their brother George and carried him wrapped in blood-soaked linen to a place near the kitchen wood stove.

Somebody called the Gallatin County sheriff. When he arrived to investigate, Dilver surrendered the gun and himself with no hesitation. Getting into the police car, Dilver glanced over his shoulder at Great-granddaddy Webster and said, "Now remember, Dad, you promised to get me out of this."

The sun was setting as Mother crossed the Ohio River. The sheriff had long since left with Dilver, and the coroner had come and hauled off the remains of her father. Her poor brother George was still there, however, nursing his wounds and weeping. He frowned and shook his head while Grandma lied to Mother about her heroic efforts to save Grandpa, but George refused to talk to anyone. At the coroner's inquest, he did talk enough to show just cause as to why Dilver should be bound over to the Gallatin County grand jury. But by the time of the actual trial, George was silent again. Dead silent.

Like Grandpa Roberts promised Daddy that he would, he came back to Glencoe as soon as the tobacco money came in. He crossed the ferry in a pine box on a wagon pulled by two mules. Despite the fact his mother-in-law literally danced on his grave, the *Grant County Kentucky News* carried a beautiful obituary:

> Everyone was sorry to learn of the tragic death of James Roberts, who one year ago moved to Rising Sun, Indiana. He had been a resident of this community for the greater part of his life, having lived on the Curtis Cullon farm for 10 years and on the Albert Couch farm for a number of years. He was married to Miss Maggie Ann Webster of Gallatin County in 1912, who along with 6 children survives him. They are Mrs. William Penick of Dry Ridge, Grant County, George, Marion, Hattie, Helen, and Jimmie, one brother William of St. Louis, Mo., two sisters, Mrs. Frank Roberts of Covington and Mrs. Cora Cooper of Rock-Castel County. The funeral was held at the Oakland Baptist Church where he was a member. Rev. McConnoll of Pleasant Ridge Christian Church preached an impressive discourse over the remains, after which they were laid to rest in the family plot in the church cemetery. Jim, as he was familiarly known, was an inoffensive kind of man, a good man, a good neighbor and a law abiding citizen. He was a kind father and husband and will be greatly missed by his family. Everyone extends their heartfelt sympathy to the heartbroken wife and children. He whose promise is to the widow and the orphan cannot forget His word.

Grandpa's grave had less than a week to settle before his "heartbroken wife" took her "orphans" and moved to the city of Covington, Kentucky, where, so it seems, she could be closer to the gambling halls and taverns. While living there in the ghettos of Covington, my uncle George developed pneumonia from the beating he had taken in Rising Sun. He stayed in a chair close to the stove for a month, trying to shake off the chills, sending Uncle Marion downstairs to fetch more coal.

Grandma Roberts told George, "Shame on you. If you need to be warmer, go get the coal yourself. Quit sending your little brother after it."

George threw his blanket off and went down the tenement stairs to the coal bin. He never returned. With the coal on his back in a burlap bag, Uncle George collapsed on the steps and died—one month and four days after Grandpa. The Gallatin County Court struck his name from their list of witnesses and wrote Grandma's in its place.

Although that is the story I've heard all my life and Dilver is the one who paid for the killing in terms of the law, through the years there have been countless disagreements among my kinfolks that lead me to believe the real story goes much deeper. I've often wondered, from what I know, if there was a conspiracy. For instance, it seems that Estell knew the murder would take place beforehand. Why else would he have said what he did to Marion and the girls: "That's Dilver shootin' your daddy"? Why was my great-grandmother Webster dancing and expecting Grandma Maggie Roberts to share in her joy? Why did Dilver remind his daddy, "You promised to get me out of this"?

I learned many years later that my great-grandfather Webster made a deathbed confession of the murder when he died at the age of ninety-one in 1956. Could he possibly have had reason to kill Grandpa? Did Dilver do it for himself or them or take the rap for someone else? Worst of all, at times the ugly notion has crossed my mind that even Grandma Roberts herself could have wanted Grandpa dead!

Because of all the unanswered questions, all the sick feelings it has caused my family, and all the contradictory bits and pieces told by other people, I became obsessed with finding out the truth about the murder in Rising Sun. I decided to go see Dilver Webster myself, talk to him, and get his side of the story. I wanted to see the house where my grandpa was killed and reenact the whole thing, as well as I could, in my mind.

Right before Halloween of 1978 I drove up to Rising Sun. I knew that Dilver's brother Everette (who was living somewhere else when the murder took place) now lived in the very house where Grandpa was killed. But I had no idea of how to get there. I looked for the ferry that would take me across the Ohio from Kentucky into Indiana. It had been replaced with a bridge. Driving around lost in the countryside, I decided to stop and ask somebody where I was. I pulled into the yard of the next farmhouse I saw and started toward the door just as a woman came out to meet me. "Skeeter Davis!" the lady said before I had a chance to open my mouth. "We've been hoping you'd come see us."

Out of the corner of my eye, I caught sight of the mailbox. The name Claude Webster was painted on it. Stunned, I asked, "Are ya'll kin to Everette Webster?" As if God had His hand in the matter, the lady turned out to be Pauline Webster, Everette's daughter-in-law.

She directed me to a house two doors down to the right—the haunted house where Grandpa was killed.

Everette and his wife, Christine, were as glad to see me as Pauline had been. Christine rushed out of the house to hug me, and Uncle Everette came lumbering up from the tobacco barn with a grin across his face wide as the Ohio. I wasn't nearly as apprehensive as I thought I'd be—at least not until we went inside. In the kitchen a stove stood over by the wall. Immediately, it triggered horrible visions of George huddled behind it, wrapped in sheets, oozing blood through the hardwood floor. I fought my imagination and waited for an opportune time to bring up the murder. The opportunity never arrived.

In a slow, hesitant way, Everette told me how a few years back he had caught "brain fever."

"Brain fever?" I asked. "I've heard of that all my life, but I've never known what it was."

"Encephalitis. Doctor said I ran the highest fever he'd ever seen in a human. Said I's bit by a mosquito that had bit a poisonous snake." When the fever subsided, Uncle Everette had been left with a slow manner and an impaired memory. I realized I knew more about the murder than he did, and it would make no sense at all even to bring it up.

My next stop, of course, would be Dilver's. After serving twenty years and six months of his life sentence, Dilver was released from the pen in 1954. One of the curious things I had heard rumored was that my Grandma Roberts had worked hard toward getting Dilver out of prison. I just couldn't understand that. It made no sense at all to me for Grandma to be testifying before a parole board on behalf of the man who killed her husband—even if he was her brother. Somehow that incriminated her in my eyes.

Grandma Roberts had never been what you'd call a real grandmother to me or any of us kids. I can remember asking her for a one dollar contribution toward my announcements when I graduated from high school and being refused. On the other hand, she never failed to ask me for money when the bingo parlors opened.

Mother used to say she was not a good mother either. While my Aunt Hattie was sick, Grandma didn't visit her at all. She was too busy tending to Dilver, who was in the same hospital. It seems she could never let go of her family long enough to take care of her own children. I had heard one other thing that seemed to implicate my grandma. On the day that Dilver went to Rising Sun to borrow the pistol that killed Grandpa, Grandma Roberts went with him.

Dilver was slowly dying of cancer. Dilver lived on a farm in Warsaw, Kentucky, with his warm, friendly wife, Frances, and their children. Since leaving prison, he had led a very responsible, respectable life. The people around Warsaw just loved him. I found that out as I asked around town how to get out to his farm. Friendly faces and hands directed me to a service station in Warsaw run by one of his stepdaughters and her husband.

The stepdaughter, Charlotte, told me, "Daddy's just gonna die when he finds out you're here, Ms. Davis. He talks about you all the time. We've heard about how he's kin to you since we were knee high."

I asked, bewildered, "You call him Daddy?"

"My real daddy died when I was eight. He's the only daddy I've ever known. Dilver's been so good to me you wouldn't believe it. Let me call him and tell him you're coming." Dilver told his stepdaughter to have me meet him halfway, at the Valley View Country Store, and he'd lead me from there to his farm. Driving down the highway from Warsaw, I was rehearsing just what I'd say. I was determined to ask him flat-out, "Dilver, did you kill my grandpa or not?"

Suddenly there he was. The way I'd pictured him in my mind. Tall, lean, and gray with a high forehead, but I expected him to be nervous and afraid of me. Instead he ran from his car and embraced me in the parking lot like I was a long lost friend.

"It really is you, ain't it, Skeeter?" he said. "You know I ain't seen you since you were less than three years old. I took you and your mama…"

I couldn't believe it. He was totally relaxed, more than ready to share his home with me. At the farm I learned from Dilver and Frances many interesting things, but as long as Dilver was in the room the murder went unmentioned. For some reason, I just couldn't muster the courage.

They told me how Frances's oldest son had accidently shot and killed himself while cleaning a gun, how my great-grandpa Webster had remarried after my crazy great-grandmother died, and how his new wife had run off to New York with all my great-grandfather's money. Then Dilver went outside, leaving me and Frances alone.

"I know what you'd like to know," she said as soon as he left the room. "There ain't no sense in asking Dilver. He don't talk about it. All I know I learned from his brother Estell."

I pulled closer to her not to miss a word and to let her know I wanted her to continue. "He says your grandpa, Mr. Roberts, had been mad about something for weeks. He was claiming around Rising Sun that he planned to 'clean out the ridge,' meaning he meant to harm the Websters and particularly Dilver." Frances hesitated for a second. "Well, so...on the day he's shot, your grandpa came into the Websters' side of the house and busted a chair over your great-granddaddy's head. That's when *whoever* shot him, shot him."

I shook my head in disbelief. Frances put her hand across mine like she was fixing to tell me something that was really going to hurt. "Estell says when him and the girls, you know, Hattie and Helen, heard the gunshots, Hattie said, 'Oh no! Daddy is shootin' Dilver.' Your grandma came around to the Websters' side of the house then and drug your grandpa's body out of the house, across the porch, underneath a tree in the front yard and wouldn't let nobody touch him till the sheriff came. The Websters were really upset with Maggie for moving Mr. Roberts's body out of the house, 'cause that's what made it seem like premeditated murder instead of self-defense."

I tried to say something, but I was totally speechless. Frances continued. "Your grandma lied on the witness stand and sent Dilver to prison, but he's forgiven her for it. Since he got out, he goes and gets her every month or so and lets her spend the week with us."

Just as I was getting ready to make a rebuttal, Dilver walked back in and Frances abruptly changed the topic of conversation. The more I studied Dilver, the more I realized that for some peculiar reason, I liked him. I decided to leave him his silence and not pry any further. But as I was putting my coat on to leave, I happened to notice that the index finger of Dilver's left hand was missing. I asked him how he lost it, and he told me about chopping it off by accident with an axe when he was cutting firewood.

Dilver held the absent finger up, as if it were still there, and said, "You know what the Bible says: 'If any part of your body offends you, cut it off.'"

Somehow I took that as a message with a hidden meaning. I left their farm that night wondering if Dilver was, by any chance, left-handed. But I had wondered and questioned enough. It will always be a mystery as to what really happened. What I was told by Frances just raised more questions. Why wasn't there blood on the floor?

Why was the door glass shattered? At that time only two people still alive knew the truth—God and Dilver. And Dilver wasn't talkin'. That was to be the last time I saw him, because the cancer took Dilver's life in 1983. Grandma Roberts died shortly after him, the same month.

Uncle George and Grandpa are buried side by side in Glencoe, somewhere close to those infamous railroad tracks where my mother and daddy first met. Their graves have been left unmarked all these years. It seems no one cared enough even to buy them a couple of cheap tombstones. When I offered to get them each a monument a few years back, neither Grandma Roberts nor anyone else could come to an agreement on exactly where the two men were buried.

I own two things that belonged to my Grandpa: his fiddle and his Bible. My sister Shirley knew how much I wanted that fiddle of Grandpa's, because I figure I owe a lot of my talent to that man. So she bought it for me from Uncle Jimmy, Grandpa's youngest son. Mother gave me Grandpa's Bible a long time ago. I keep a blue and white embroidered cross marking the blank page that separates the Old and New Testaments. I have no idea who wrote this, but in faded blue ink that yellowed page reads: "James Roberts departed this life January 13, 1934, age 50 years. George Roberts departed this life February 17, 1934, age 19 years. Be kind, one to another." If their graves are ever found, I think that's the epitaph I'll have carved on the headstones.

Mary Frances

I want love, love, love
More than anything in this world.
Just give me love, love, love, love
And you'll have one happy girl.
       —"Love, Love, Love,"
       Skeeter Davis

My mother became a bitterly depressed woman after her father was killed. Even years later she would still act as if she'd been dealt a raw deal. Whenever one of us kids threw her attitude up to her, though, she would come back with something like, "Well, if your daddy was killed, you kids would understand me. You'd feel like I feel."

We used to laugh about our family a lot to hide the very real pain and fear at the bottom of our hearts. I know a million unanswered questions plagued my mother since the Christmas of 1933 when she last saw Grandpa alive. Every Christmas after our family relived that pain with her. While other children sat beneath Christmas trees hearing the joyous story of Christ's birth, we sat around a Warm Morning heater hearing the story I've told you of Grandpa's death. Slowly the spirit of Christmas for us Penick kids would fade each year from the usual gay hues of red and green to gray edged in black.

Looking back over Mother's years of anniversary blues, I recall the times I kept her from committing suicide. I once slapped a bottle of

20

Clorox she was drinking out of her mouth and sat on her hands to keep her from reaching for a butcher knife. The most vivid memory I have of all her suicide attempts, however, is of the morning she was going to take me to heaven with her.

A short time after Grandpa died we moved to Cincinnati, Ohio, where Daddy found work at White's ice cream factory. I had passed three years old by then, and my brother Buddy had just turned one. He had gotten a sailor's suit just like mine for his birthday.

We lived in a three-story apartment in the heart of Cincinnati. I still can remember looking down out of the window on the heads of people walking the sidewalks below us.

One day Mother was holding me and Buddy, gathering the courage to jump out the window with us in her arms. She had us dressed fit to kill in our identical sailor's suits. I started raising such a commotion that the people on the street stopped what they were doing and started staring and pointing at the three of us sitting there on the window ledge. I wasn't raising havoc because we were going to jump; it was because I didn't want to leave without my sailor's cap. Luckily Mother had left it hanging on the dresser mirror. By the time she could grab the hat and get me to shut up, we had drawn such a crowd of people eager to see us splattered on the sidewalk that Mother changed her mind.

I've been drawing crowds all my life—from Carnegie Hall to Royal Albert Hall. But I guess that has to be the most important audience I've ever played. If it weren't for them and my sailor's cap, I certainly wouldn't be telling you the story of my life.

My sister Shirley was born while we lived in Cincinnati. She was the only one of the seven of us born in a hospital. Buddy and I were both sick with the croup while Mother was giving birth to Shirley. So Daddy doctored us by greasing our necks with Vicks salve, then wrapping an old itchy wool sock around our throats. Believe me, the cure was worse than the croup.

I just knew Mother was going to rescue me from Daddy's remedies when she returned from the hospital, but she didn't. Wishing I was getting the attention Shirley was, I went to bed crying rather than happy about my new sister.

Shortly after Shirley was born, we moved back to Kentucky to the little town I claim as mine, Dry Ridge. Sunday drivers snaking down the road that runs along the ridgetop could tell you one reason why

I've always claimed that town as my homeplace. It is beautiful. From U.S. Highway 25 you get a hawk's-eye view of the peaceful valleys and hollows of tilled farmland lying beneath the ridge on either side. It reminds me of a patchwork quilt, so soft it seems safe to drive on off the ridge.

West of Dry Ridge, the dark green ribbon of Eagle Creek runs through the valley past Glencoe, the town where I was born. Beyond the hollows both horizons become other ridges and rolling hills covered in tulip poplars, evergreens, and catawba trees. Nowhere are there bluer skies or cleaner air.

In the summer of 1970 the people of Dry Ridge honored me with Skeeter Davis Day. They gave me the town's city limit sign: "Dry Ridge, Population 1400." On *Hee Haw* I gave them a big "sa-lute." The sign hangs on my living room wall, and it's one of the things that makes my Brentwood house seem like home. It is a prized possession.

I started school at Dry Ridge in a one room schoolhouse with a pot-bellied stove. (That was the last year for the Skirvin Schoolhouse, as it was called. I would go from second through eighth grade at a new high school.) Inside the school were thirty-five kids in eight grades. I was the only five-year-old, as well as the only first grader. I cried a lot, wanting my mother. So while the other children took their naps, Miss Lottie Skirvin, our teacher, would cuddle me up in her lap and read to me from *Mrs. Wiggs and the Cabbage Patch* and *Uncle Remus*. I still love Brer Rabbit.

To get to school, I had to walk two miles down the dirt road we lived on just to get to the paved road, then another two miles down the pavement. In 1937 there weren't any school buses. At least not in those parts.

My dog Snowball was my only companion. He walked with me fall, winter, and spring. Now and then he'd leave my side to chase jackrabbits. I'd scold him, "If you don't quit chasin' Brer Rabbit, I'm gonna whup you, Snowball."

Snowball would hurry back with his tail tucked between his legs, pleading guilty and begging for mercy. He knew he was doing wrong, but he was so funny I never could really punish him. I loved him so much.

After walks through the winter snow, Miss Lottie would seat me and Snowball by the stove. She'd soak my hands and feet in cold water to thaw them out slowly, while my little dress made of flour sacks nearly scorched from the stove heat. Snowball would shake himself dry and curl up by the stove for the day. When my fingers loosened up enough, Miss Lottie would teach me my numbers and alphabet on the blackboard. I'd read to her from the primer very proudly, then little Snowball and me would head out through the snow for home.

The schoolhouse is gone now (drat it!). But before they tore it down, George Hamilton IV and I went by there on the way back to Nashville from a concert. We've been the best of friends for a long time, and I wanted to share with him where I was born, went to school, and so on. But the doors of the schoolhouse were padlocked.

As I stared through the broken windows, my mind flashed back to a scene I hope I'll never forget. There was Miss Lottie, pretty as ever, introducing me and this blond-haired boy from the second grade: "And now ladies and gentlemen, we present the Singin' Canaries..."

Suddenly I could see myself, little Mary Frances Penick, dressed in yellow crepe paper, singing to this boy a year older and a foot taller, "Reuben, Reuben, I been thinkin'/What a grand world this would be..." The older boy was singing back to me, "If the girls were all transported/Far beyond the Northern Sea."

Our classmates were all clapping, hooting, and hollering, and I was just glowing from all the attention. I guess I was born an entertainer, because I've lived for applause all my life.

That vision brought tears to my eyes and yet still another memory. I remembered the eighth graders picking little, first-grader me as their mascot and taking me with them on a class trip to the Cincinnati Zoo in the back of a cattle truck. At the zoo they gathered a crowd around and coaxed me into singing "Pop Goes the Weasel." The people in the crowd actually threw me money. The eighth graders took the money, but I got to keep the applause. The applause. The applause...

I stood on the steps of the school and thought about what a long, yet strangely wonderful journey it has been from those first public performances to the duets I've sung with George IV on the stages of Scandinavia, "far beyond the Northern Sea."

I never told George why I was crying, but he must have guessed. He found the latch on the broken window and pushed it up. The two of us crawled inside the condemned old school building.

"Look, George," I said, "here's the chair I think I used to sit in."

George looked at me and said, "Let's take it. You know it will just waste away." So we took the tiny chair and the lid from the outhouse john and left. I felt guilty at first but I'm glad I did it now. The next time I passed through Dry Ridge, they had torn the schoolhouse down.

My family lived in a two-story log cabin close to the end of a winding dirt road shadowed by cedars. It was so dark along the road that the ice in the puddles seemed to stay forever, long after it had melted everywhere else. My brothers, Buddy (James), Boze (Harold), and Punkin (Dean) were all born in that cabin.

Daddy handmade the furniture for the house. You should have seen him building our table. First he got the legs too long. When we sat down on the bench he had built for us earlier that day, the table came clear up to my chin. So he took the table back outside and sawed the legs a little shorter, then even a little shorter than that, until finally he got 'em too short. Daddy ended up having to saw the legs off the bench too.

Chopping and hauling the firewood and stovewood were two of my chores. When I was out gathering a load of stovewood, I would think about the reason the family that lived there before us had moved. Folks said that the daddy of that family had just gone out one day chopping wood; the next time they looked, he was gone, and they never saw him since. That worried me. I kept thinking, *What if he comes back and makes us move out of our house?* I just knew he was gonna show up any day and say, "Who are ya'll? Get out!" Then we'd be moving again.

Beyond our fence across the road in the corner of the tobacco field was the little cemetery where they buried Frances Lou, my stillborn aunt whom Mother was dressing the day her daddy was killed. Another one of Poppy and Gramma Penick's babies was laid to rest there with her.

That little cemetery seemed to call me. I used to walk in and look at the tombstones all the time. They told me, "Your aunts are buried there." I couldn't understand why the graves were smaller than me. How could my aunts be buried there?

At age six I was doing the same work in the tobacco field the grown people were. I know, looking back, that's what made me stoop-shouldered. It embarrasses me, if I let myself think about it, especially on stage. For a while I even tried wearing a back brace to correct my posture, but it didn't seem to help. Tobacco farming is hard work, even for adults.

First we would gather up brush and limbs to burn off a tobacco bed. The fire served two purposes. It got rid of the insects and left a fine ash that softened the soil for seedlings. We'd see fires burning all over the ridge, and it would be so pretty in the spring of the year with the smoke rising up above the blossoming trees. When the burn was done, we seeded the bed, and we waited until the little plants got about finger high before we transferred them to the field.

When it came time to plant the seedlings, I would be told either to carry a water bucket full of them or else to stoop over the rows setting leaves by hand each place somebody else dropped a plant—every three feet or so. The only thing I wasn't allowed to do was, of course, the thing I most wanted to do—cut the tobacco when the crop was ready to be cured. That really is a man's job. But I was young and wanting badly to please my daddy by proving to him that I could do everything he, Poppy, and my uncles could do.

One evening I went out to the field where they were cutting the tobacco and yelled that supper was ready. The men wiped their brows, washed their hands, and took long drinks from the water barrel before they left the field to go eat. At the roadside each of them playfully threw their knives where they'd stick up in the big oak tree by the cemetery. *Whoosh-tonk, whoosh-tonk.*

I watched them with so much admiration that they could just as well have been gods. An old tobacco knife, if you've never seen one, had a handle that ran at right angles to a kind of slanted square blade like a tomahawk's. As soon as the men were inside eating, I scooted up the oak, grabbed a knife, tried to cut a stalk of tobacco down, and sliced my thumb. Blood poured out. I still have a scar there. It scared me not just because the sight of blood always has, but even more so because I knew I had done something I was told definitely not to do.

I dropped the knife and ran around in circles for a minute before I headed down the road for Mrs. Stone's house. I knew her. She'd help me. Mrs. Stone's house was where they held square dances to which I followed Mother every Saturday night so I could hear the fiddler while she danced. I think Mother took me with her 'cause she was scared of the dark. When I reached Mrs. Stone's door, I cried, cried, and cried. "Oh, I know Daddy'll whip me."

"Why, your daddy ain't gonna whup you, chile." Mrs. Stone hugged me as she examined my bleeding thumb. "You've really hurt yourself, honey. Come on in here and let me see it."

She smeared the cut with salve and wrapped a rag around it. This salve was used for everything. It was for your dogs, your cows:

whatever got hurt, this salve cured it. It was brownish yellow and stunk like a polecat. I've seen folks use it on a cow's bag when she had raked her udder against briars or a barbed wire fence. Watkins liniment and Watkins ointment, that was the name of it. Their salesman would come up the road carrying a little black doctor's satchel to sell the farmers their year's supply of the stuff. Folks would say, "Here comes the Watkins man!"

I thought Watkins was his last name. Swinging on our gate when his Model A rolled up, I'd say, "How you doing today, Dr. Watkins? Nice day, ain't it? We don't need no salf. We ain't used up what you brought us last time yet."

Our old cabin was wide open. What I mean by that is there weren't any doors or dividing walls inside. It was just one big room with a stone fireplace and a hardwood floor. Steps led upstairs to the attic where I kept some baby chicks. I hand-fed them crushed corn until they were good-size hens roosting in the rafters. Mother and Daddy told me they were mine. Actually they were just my responsibility. I learned that the day the peddler's wagon came down the icy road toward our house.

I flopped a big, fat, flapping chicken down on Mr. Stephen's scales, and he gave me more money for it than I had ever seen. I stood there the longest time just staring at all that money.

The peddler grinned. "Now what are you supposed to buy with your money, little bit?"

"Candy," I answered.

"You mean all of it?"

"Yeah, all this in candy, please," I said, handing Mr. Stephen back the money.

"That's sure gonna be a pile of candy," the peddler said. "You positive your mama don't mind?"

"It's my chicken!"

"Okay, if you say so." He weighed out a bag of chocolates, peppermint sticks, Mary Janes, and B.B. Bats you wouldn't have believed.

I was the most popular girl at school that day, and when I got home, I still had enough left over to make me, Buddy, and Shirley sick at our stomachs.

That evening I discovered who the chickens really belonged to. Did I ever get spanked when my parents found out that I had swapped a good, solid supper for a half ton of candy! It was the first time I ever felt ripped off, but it was worth the spanking 'cause I can still remember how everybody at school loved me from then on. I won their hearts with that sack of chocolates.

Being poor made everything so hard to come by, especially anything fun. Christmas time might bring an orange and a couple of candy canes. That was, for the most part, the only store-bought treats we got. Recently, I read a book called *Sugar Blues* (by William Dufty, Warner Books) that tells how murderous refined sugar can be to physical and mental health. Since then I've really tried to curb my junk food habits. By and large I stick to honey and brown sugar as sweeteners. My body reacted like crazy when I first took the sugar away, and a cold RC Cola is still the most tempting thing in this world to me.

Walking home from school one day, I found a wonderful surprise. There were three sticks of Juicy Fruit chewing gum sent out as complimentary samples in our mailbox. I got halfway down the long dirt road before it occurred to me that three sticks wasn't going to be enough for our family. I ran back to the mailboxes and took our neighbor's samples too. Now Buddy, Shirley, Boze, and me could all chew!

One time up in the attic while I was tending *my* chickens, I found this little nest of baby mice among some papers. When I first found them, I could see right through their skins. They were so fascinating.

I started putting things up there for Mother Mouse to eat so she wouldn't starve, and her babies wouldn't die. I'd sneak her crackers or a piece of bread soaked in Karo syrup. Whatever I ate, I figured that mouse would eat. The babies grew until they were covered in little tiny hairs. I was so proud, I told on myself.

"Ya'll come up and see my mice."

"Your what?"

Mother came straight up the stairs. "Show me where those mice are, young lady!"

"What are you gonna do?"

She took the papers, the nest, the babies, and their mother outside and slung them over the barbed wire fence. I gathered up the little family and buried them near the tree where my aunts were buried.

Mother cooked kettles of beans and wild mustard greens in the open blaze of the fireplace and baked bread and berry pies in the oven of the woodstove. I grew up on potatoes. They didn't go as far when we baked them, so mostly they got skillet fried or mashed. We seldom had meat to eat, because at that time we couldn't afford any livestock. Just those few chickens.

What meat we did have was usually canned, of course, since we didn't have a freezer or refrigerator. Come to think of it, I don't guess anybody did. The first icebox I ever saw was in the city at Grandma Roberts's. She had to put a block of ice in the top of the box just to keep things decently cool, never cold.

Since we didn't have cattle or pigs yet, we made do the best we could. Daddy would take us down to Eagle Creek—usually on Sunday—and while we played beneath the railroad trestle where it was shallow and safe, Daddy would wade up the creek hunting.

There was no such thing as a bathing suit. We splashed around in our clothes, then laid down on the bank and let the sun dry us out. After a while Daddy would come wading back toward us carrying a turtle. "Boy-oh-boy, look at this!" he'd shout, lifting the turtle up so we could see from a distance how big it was. "We're gonna have some fine eating tonight."

I couldn't even eat a chicken if I saw Mother wring its neck. So the first time Daddy caught a turtle, I remember saying, "I ain't gonna eat no turtle."

Mother shrugged her shoulders. "Well, then I guess you don't eat. That's all we got."

She battered it in flour and fried the white slabs, and when it hit the table, it didn't last long. Believe it or not, they said it tasted better than chicken.

The same thing happened to me with groundhog and rabbit. I'd say, "I ain't gonna eat that." Mother would say, "Then you'll do without."

Me, Shirley, Buddy and Boze would wait near the fence when Daddy went hunting. They would hope he would bring home a mess of rabbits. Daddy always skinned them right there on the spot, then hung them from his belt. If we could see their little pink skins flopping around his waist as he came walking up the road, Buddy and Bose would go running to greet Daddy and Shirley and I ran to the house. "Mother, come look! He shot some rabbits!" I would cry. I started just eating biscuits, leaving my share of the rabbit to the others. (I stopped eating all red meat in 1974.)

All animals weren't good. At that time the woods of northern Kentucky were full of wild and dangerous creatures. Keeping a gun draped across the tenpenny nails above the bed was just good common sense. You never knew when a bobcat might want your chickens or your child.

Besides Snowball we had two old coon-hunting hounds named Sarey and Sally. When we got them, it seemed fitting to me that Snowball should be promoted to house dog. I was told, "No way. We ain't city slickers."

One night a rat ran across the headboard of the bed that Buddy, Shirley, Boze, and I slept in (crossways so we'd have enough room). The rat woke everybody up but me. Then I heard Daddy saying, "Mary Frances, be quiet and don't move." The gun was in his hand, but he couldn't shoot without hitting me. I looked up and saw that big ol' nasty rat snarlin' up at me from the headboard, and I wanted to jump and run, but Daddy kept saying, "Don't move. Don't move. I'll get the dogs."

Sarey and Sally bolted in the front door, and the rat scurried down the headboard. They chased it and chased it, but when it was cornered, the rat turned on them with its teeth bared. It was actually fighting the dogs off. I screamed, "Get Snowball!"

Daddy let Snowball in, and within seconds he had the rat down and dead. I was really proud of my dog. We crawled back in bed. Snowball crawled in among us. He was finally a house dog whenever he wanted to be and everybody's favorite dog!

A rumor spread that some folks had spotted a rabid dog on the ridge. All the farmers had been asked to stay armed at all times and keep an eye open for a mangy brown mutt with a white belly. Daddy told us after dinner one night in morbid detail the symptoms of hydrophobia and warned us not to pet any strange dogs until he told us otherwise. No dog was ever seen like the one described, so the rumor and fear slowly faded away.

One day when Daddy was away from home helping out a neighbor with his plowing, I took the kids to our hiding place in the shed where we hung tobacco. We were playing school when I heard Mother and Aunt Helen screaming from the doorway, "Get to the house, kids! For God's sake, hurry! Oh, Lord, Mary Frances, get them kids up here quick!"

We shot out the side of the shed through our secret door where some weathered tin had torn loose from the studs. Coming up the road was a slobbering dog. Shirley and Buddy had already reached the steps when I realized my little brother Boze wasn't with us. I heard him crying, "Mawey Fwances, help me. Don't wet the dawg get me."

Boze's overalls had snagged on the tin. His tiny feet were dangling in midair, running fast as they could run. I hurried back to Boze and yanked him loose just as the mad dog staggered up to the fence. His growl was lower and meaner than any sound I'd ever heard. *Oh no, I wish Daddy was home.* My mind raced, *where's Snowball?*

The rabid dog was pushing on the gate as I hauled Boze in the house and slammed the door. Inside the women were totally petrified, but out in the front yard Snowball was wagging his tail to greet the mad dog as if it were just another stray. Mother tried to hold me back, but I threw open the door and shouted, "Here Snowball! No! Come here now!"

Suddenly I saw my granddaddy sneaking out from behind the old tree at the edge of the cemetery. He had a chair in one hand and his shotgun in the other.

"Dog!" Poppy yelled. The brown, mangy killer turned toward him, its head weaving like a drunk. It leaped from our gate back out into the road, and I heard the first barrel of Poppy's gun go off. *Ba-loom!*

The blast slapped the dog up against our fence, but it just got up and charged Poppy again even crazier. The other barrel exploded, and the dog dropped in its tracks. It was still rearing its ugly head and growling, however, as I knelt in the yard to pet Snowball. Poppy raised the chair and beat its slobbering head until its skull was crushed. I looked at Poppy's face when he finished. There were tears rolling down his cheeks. "You kids all right?"

I ran out in the road and gave him my biggest hug. Still I stayed as far from that dead dog as I could. *It may bite even after it's dead*, I thought, *and not let go 'til it thunders*.

Poppy lived just down the road from us. Before my family could afford its own radio, we'd spend Saturday nights at Poppy's listening to "the Solemn Ole Judge" from WSM. Poppy could remember the memorable evening George D. Hay first announced, "For the past hour we have been listening to music taken largely from Grand Opera, but from now on we will present the Grand Ole Opry."

On weekdays, when we would drop by Poppy's on our way home from school, Buddy, Shirley, and I would listen to *The Shadow Knows* and *Inner Sanctum*. Shirley would always get scared. It seems like Lipton Tea sponsored one and Blue Coal the other. Poppy would fuss at us, "You kids are gonna run them batteries down listening to them spook shows, and we'll end up having to miss the Opry Saturday night."

As much as me and Buddy liked those horror stories, we would flick the radio off, because nothing compared to the warmth and joy we felt when the whole family gathered in Poppy's living room to listen while Bill Monroe sang "Put My Little Shoes Away" and "I Traced Your Little Footprints Through the Snow."

Even though we didn't have a radio at home, we had our own music. Mother had learned all kinds of songs from Grandpa Roberts. And she'd sing them while she cooked and worked. Sometimes her sister Hattie would come down to our cabin to visit. She and Mother would sing, "When there's moonlight on the Colorado/That's when I'll come back to you..."

Aunt Hattie sang low alto harmony. It was the prettiest sound I'd ever heard. Prettier than the radio. If I happened to be studying by the kerosene lamp, or in the winter by the glow of the fireplace, I'd close my books when Aunt Hattie came because I knew she knew something I wanted to learn more than reading and writing. "Please sing," I begged them. "Sing 'Moonlight on the Colorado.'"

I picked it up quick. By the age of eight or nine, I could sing alto harmony too. I would listen to the Grand Ole Opry, as well as the other musical programs, and practice until my voice blended with whoever was singing.

When Buddy was walking to school with me and Snowball, he'd throw rocks at the trees, or chase some farmer's cows back into the pasture for him. To pass the time on the long walk, I'd write poems in my head and jot 'em down as soon as we reached the schoolhouse. It's funny how things stick in our minds, especially when they don't mean anything. For instance, I can still remember one of my nonsense poems:

> There was an old man from Kentucky.
> They all called him "Batch-ler Bucky."

He sits 'round and chews,
Like he's got chewin' blues,
This ol' bachelor man in Kentucky.

I wrote it for this man I actually called Uncle Mose. He could tell us stories that would make the hair on the back of our necks stand up.

One night Uncle Mose told us about this horse from the Civil War that just kept galloping over our ridge despite the fact a sword had slashed his head off. The story goes the horse was looking for a dead Confederate captain who once rode him into battle. Uncle Mose even knew where the ghost of Cap'n Bones lived. "He's down thar under that bridge ya'll cross going home tonight. Zackly whar the Yankees left him with a lead ball twixt his eyes."

Uncle Mose whittled on a stick of cedar as he told us the story, so matter-of-fact. "I'd be right careful going home tonight, if'n I'd be ya'll. Someday that ol' horse and Cap'n Bones is gonna find each other, then they won't be near as restless and mean as they have been lately."

Before we knew it, Shirley was in absolute hysterics, begging to spend the night at Poppy's. "I ain't never gonna cross that bridge again." Shirley stayed with Poppy while me and Buddy headed down the dark, winding road by ourselves.

The shadows from the trees moved by the wind beneath the moonlight made some of the most ghastly creatures you could imagine. By the time we reached the bridge where Cap'n Bones laid waiting with his sword drawn for his restless, headless horse, our little hearts were clapping like hoofbeats crossing the wooden bridge. We both screamed bloody murder and broke into a run faster than any ghost could have traveled until we safely stood out of breath, pounding at our cabin door. "Let us in! Let us in! He's here!"

The door swung open. Daddy stood there dangling a kerosene lantern under his chin, throwing shadows across his face. "Boo!" he yelled.

Buddy and I left our skins laying out there on the doorstep that night. But we really loved it. It was so exciting to get scared by one of Uncle Mose's stories.

Near sunset on a summer's day I was darting around Poppy's house playing tag with my aunts and uncles. As I cut a quick corner around a rose bush, Poppy reached out to grab me and give me a hug. I tore loose from him, shouting, "Don't let 'em catch me, Poppy."

Poppy commanded, "Come back here, Skeeter, and give Poppy a hug." I giggled, raced back to Poppy, squeezed my arms around his overalled legs, looked up at his face, and asked, "Why'd you call me that name, Poppy?"

"'Cause you're just like a little ol' water bug, Skeeter. Skeeting here and there. Why, you won't even slow down long enough to let your ol' Poppy hold you."

Gramma overheard him. "Don't you start calling that little girl some silly name. It's liable to stick and she'll never get shed of it. Her name's Mary Frances, and she's gonna stay Mary Frances."

Poppy paid no attention to Gramma. Every time I passed there walking home from school, I'd hear him call out from the porch, "Hey there, li'l Skeeter," or "What you know, there's ol' Skeeter-bug." Before long Daddy was calling me Skeeter too. Then Mother started calling me Skeeter. In no time everybody in Dry Ridge knew me as Skeeter. Except Gramma; she stubbornly kept calling me Mary Frances. She was the only person I knew that ever did. She lived to be ninety-five years of age, and I was Mary Frances to her until she died.

But Skeeter became the name I went by to everyone else from then on out. To be proud of being dubbed after a silly water bug may seem stupid to some, but I love it, mainly because I loved and still treasure every memory of the man who first recognized me for what or who I really am—Skeeter.

I ain't the only one Poppy named either. When Punkin was born, Daddy shook me, Buddy, Shirley, and Boze awake in the middle of the night and had us walk with him down to Poppy's. I guess they did not want us kids to hear Mother scream from the painful delivery. At sunrise the next morning, Poppy drove up to our little cabin in his rumble seat, two-tone, yellow and green Ford to see his new grandson. He was tickled to death. Poppy stopped playing gitchy-goo with Punkin long enough to ask, "Have you named this'un yet?"

"Not yet," Mother answered.

"Then name him Meryle Dean."

"Well, how in the world do you spell that?"

"I ain't got the foggiest notion," Poppy said, "but that's gonna be the boy's name." M-e-r-y-l-e Dean became Punkin's real name. Even though none of us knew how to spell it, it sure beat John Henry. There were enough of them running around the ridge already.

When all the neighbors came calling to see our new baby Dean, I helped Mother entertain the ladies. One neighbor lady even brought her own baby with her. I thought I was being a complimentary hostess when I told her, "Oh, how wonderful! Your baby looks just like Charlie McCarthy."

Edgar Bergen and Charlie McCarthy were only voices on the radio, so I had actually never seen them. But in the department store windows of Covington, I had seen a Charlie McCarthy doll. I wanted one like it desperately. I was so envious of the neighbor lady having a real, live Charlie McCarthy doll. "Well, I never!" The neighbor lady blushed, grabbed her kid up, and left our house fuming at the gills. I really meant no harm by what I said, but I guess she thought I must have meant that she had given birth to a dummy.

In mid-March of 1939, a month after Meryle Dean was born, my family moved in with Poppy and Gramma. Poppy had purchased a big old farmplace. Since times were definitely hard for us, Poppy decided if he let us move upstairs, it would ease Daddy's burden somewhat.

I remember the horses, Jack and Tony, standing in snow a foot deep, hitched to haul a huge wooden sled loaded with the handmade furniture from our cabin. I was excited as a person could be to be moving into Poppy's big white farmhouse. "Let me ride with you," I begged Daddy, pulling on his trouser leg. Daddy lifted me by the shoulders onto the bed of the sled, and I climbed right to the top of our heap of furniture as Buddy, Shirley, and Boze lined up at the cabin door.

"Let me go."

"Me too, Daddy."

"Wet me wide," little Boze pleaded.

"Not this trip," Daddy said. "You kids stay here an' take care of your mama and the baby. I'll be back to get you in no time." Daddy spanked the reins against the two workhorses and hollered, "Giddup Jack, giddup Tony!"

I felt so grown-up and special sitting atop our whole world. The snowflakes stung my eyes; the air was cold enough to give me an instant earache, but I didn't mind. *How could anything but fun lay ahead*, I thought, *with us moving in with Poppy?*

Poppy's Place

Ever since I was a little bitty baby
All I ever wanted was love
My memories of my childhood I recall
As the very most favorite times of all
Sittin' and rocking on my daddy's knee
Mother made a new dress for me
Dear old Poppy sang with me
And Gramma baked a berry pie for me
      —"All I Ever Wanted Was Love,"
      Skeeter Davis

Poppy was a very successful farmer, particularly as years went by, and my daddy always dreamed so desperately of making it as a farmer, but it seemed he forever had to settle for some city job in order to make ends meet.

That same gnawing urge was passed on to my brothers Buddy and Boze. Buddy has a farm in Dry Ridge even now, close to Poppy's old place. Until his heart attack in 1988, he drove every day over eighty miles to a job in Ohio. Boze farmed for me at one time and now has his own place outside of Chapel Hill, Tennessee. Even me and my sisters caught a strain of farming fever. All of us but Mother, I think, dreamed of recreating a place like Poppy's where we all could pitch in and make a go of it. That's why I bought the three-hundred-acre Holy Ghost Farm down below Nashville at a little railroad crossing called

35

Thompson Station. I hoped it would become a homestead where my brothers and sisters could live and farm in harmony, but some dreams just don't come true. Farming is hard work, dependent on too many things besides simple desire.

I know now Poppy must have really had a knack for it. During my teenage years, he became the champion tobacco grower of our area. Some men even came from a Lexington radio station to do a remote broadcast interview with Poppy about his agricultural methods. They gave him a beautiful bronze plaque, which he proudly displayed by hanging it over his favorite old chair.

When we moved in with Poppy in 1939, however, he wasn't anywhere as prosperous as he later became. Still we had sheep we sheared, hogs we butchered, and cows we milked right there on the farm. We raised our own wheat, corn, and soybeans, as well as hay for the livestock. The big money crop was always tobacco. And of course we had our own vegetable garden. It was a lot fatter-style living than the cabin days, but not too fat, now mind you. Food was easily come by, but extravagant things like clothing and toys were not.

Like I said, we lived upstairs above Poppy and Gramma and my aunts and uncles who weren't married yet. For a while we had as much fun at Poppy's place as I expected we would. Whenever Jack and Tony weren't being used to plow or pull a hay wagon, we got to ride either one we chose. Besides the two workhorses, we also had a pony named Ol' Bird.

One Sunday Poppy got drunk and started showing off for us kids. He led Ol' Bird right into the house. Gramma started fussing at Poppy about it and chasing Ol' Bird around the living room with her broom trying to run them both back outside. So Poppy jumped up on Ol' Bird and rode her straight up the stairs. Me and the kids stood watching all this at the top of the banister and went crazy laughing, of course. Halfway upstairs, Ol' Bird got scared, raised her tail, and shoo-shooed right square on the steps. Gramma like to have fainted.

If there ever was a fun drunk, Poppy was it. I never saw him violent or mean. In his earlier days, he may have been, but as far back as I can remember, I never heard him even say a cuss word.

He did have one really bad habit when he was drinking, however. Trading things. Poppy and Daddy would go out drinking one night and the next day some guy would show up at the farm to collect his newly won pig, sheep, horse, cow, or plow. Of course once he'd sobered up, Poppy never wanted to let go of whatever the man had come after.

"Look, I'm sorry 'bout last night, Buddy, but I's drunker 'n Cooter Brown when I asked you if you'd trade a milk cow for that case knife of yours." I would hear Poppy in the morning, leaning against the slab board fence bartering with some friend or stranger. "You think I'm crazy enough to even suggest somethin' like that if I'd been in my right mind? ... Yeah, I understand but look here, I wouldn't hold you to a deal like that either if you'd been as drunk as me."

They'd usually end up shaking hands, then I'd hear Poppy start in again. "You wouldn't consider takin' a layin' hen for that whittlin' knife, would ya?"

Sometimes he'd win; sometimes he'd lose. Regardless, Poppy was always a good sport when he was horsetrading. Some folks weren't. For instance, one morning Poppy woke up with an unbearable toothache. He complained about it half the day before Gramma finally persuaded him to go to the dentist. The Dry Ridge dentist just happened to be one of Poppy's horsetrading and drinking cohorts, so when Poppy got there he told his old friend that he was quite definitely going to need something for the pain before the tooth could be extracted. The dentist pulled a fifth of Kentucky bourbon from underneath the sink, and Poppy took himself a big swig, then another. Pretty soon, his old buddy decided that he'd join Poppy and reached under the sink for yet another fifth. Once both men were two sheets in the wind, they happened to remember why Poppy had dropped in to begin with, so the dentist staggered over to the chair, straddled Poppy, and wrenched the tooth from his mouth. The dentist threw the wretched tooth over in a porcelain pan and then told Poppy he now needed an antiseptic mouthwash, so Poppy and his dentist buddy courteously joined each other in still one more fifth.

Poppy came strolling up to the farm that evening just beaming and singing. He proudly showed all of us the new hole in his mouth. Everything was fine until the liquor wore off; then Poppy realized his old horsetrading buddy had pulled the wrong tooth. And that's the truth!

Poppy was always trying to hide his bottle from Gramma. When he came home drinking, he would look around for her, then wherever she was, he wasn't. Gramma knew he drank. Have mercy! How can anyone hide it? But all the same, he'd sneak in through the kitchen door and hurriedly toss his whiskey bottle over in this great big green flour barrel. Flour flew everywhere. Gramma used to laugh. "Luther thinks I don't know where he puts his whiskey. Why, it would take a fool to miss it. All you got to do is trace them flour tracks."

As a kid I never knew a time when my daddy wasn't drinking either. And he could often be as funny as Poppy. Earlier, when I was three, Daddy had come in drinking one night, swooped me off the floor, tossed me in the air, and said, "How's my girl?"

He caught me, gave me another toss in the air, and caught me again. He tossed me up one more time, and I went straight through Aunt Lizzie's plasterboard ceiling—and stuck! I dangled there a second before their astonishment wore thin enough for them to grab a chair and get me down. Needless to say, Mother made sure that was the last time I got tossed in the air.

It wasn't Daddy's last time to get drunk, however. And a time would come later on in my life when his drinking was no longer funny. Even when we were living with Poppy, Daddy's drinking had grown more serious and was beginning to scare me, especially when he drove.

Daddy had to buy a car soon after we moved to Poppy's so he could drive into Cincinnati to his job as an apprentice to a one-eyed electrician who supplied Daddy with a laugh a minute by shocking himself every time he turned around. I didn't like Daddy being away from home all day, but I didn't particularly like riding up to the city with him either.

Along Highway 25 toward Covington to visit kinfolks of a weekend, Daddy would have to stop outside of Walton and get himself a beer. He'd always ask Mother, "Can I get you something, Punzie?"

"A Big Orange'll do fine, William," she'd always say. Mother didn't drink at this time. She sat in the car with us kids and waited for Daddy to get his liquor. My first little prayers were about that. *God, please don't let us have a wreck*, I'd pray, as we went weaving on toward Covington, dodging ditches and oncoming traffic.

In Covington I saw my first porcelain bathtub. What a difference from our old galvanized tub. I always wanted to take a bath as soon as we hit the door at Aunt Naomi's.

"Afterwhile," Mother would say.

In a few minutes, I'd run back to see, "Is it afterwhile yet?"

"Afterwhile—I told you. Now be quiet. Afterwhile."

I thought afterwhile was a certain specific time, but I learned afterwhile never came. *Afterwhile* means never.

They had toothpaste in the city too. On the farm we used a washcloth caked in baking soda, but Aunt Naomi had a real toothbrush and Colgate toothpaste. Toothpaste was the best stuff I had ever tasted. First time I tried it, I liked it so much I ate a whole tube. *This is the neatest stuff,* I thought, *like flavored chalk coming straight out of a squirter. Wait till my teacher hears about this!* I took Aunt Naomi's other tube and smeared some words on her mirror and windows, playing like they were blackboards.

Seems like I was always doing dumb things whenever we went to the city. That same day, for example, I was playing with Cousin Betty's doll and the squeaker popped out of its back. I picked the tiny whistle up off the floor and blew on it. Much to my delight, it squeaked. So I put it up to my nose, being funny, so that I'd squeak like a doll when I breathed. I pushed the air out of my stomach like I was a rubber dolly. And sure enough, I squeaked. I got so tickled doing this, however, that I sniffed one time when I should have snuffed, and the whistle went right up my nose.

"Whoops—*squeak!*"

I blew hard, trying to blow it back out, but the harder I blew, the louder and longer I squeaked. "*Squeeeeeeeeeek!*" It was stuck. I started crying and racing around Aunt Naomi's house in an absolute panic. I just knew I was gonna be a Betsy Wetsy for the rest of my life. "Whaa-*squeak,*" I was crying, "Whaa-squeak!"

Mother caught me, held me down, and tried to pry it out with her bobby pin. It wouldn't budge. Then Daddy tried, and all he could do was push the squeaker further up my nose. I kept squeaking and crying, crying and squeaking. Finally Daddy got so disgusted he turned me over his knee and gave my behind a good wallop. The little whistle shot out of my nose and went rolling across the floor. He claimed he knew it would do that, but I never believed him.

Even with its huge bathtubs, delicious toothpaste, and dolls, I never liked the city all that much. I especially hated leaving the farm if it was early morning. Sunrise had taught me the natural meaning of that old proverb, the early bird gets the worm. At daybreak the woods, streams, ponds, and fields came alive. Daddy told me that he thought at one time I would grow up to become a regular Madame

Curie because I was so curious about what made things tick. Mainly I was interested in wildlife.

Long before breakfast was ready, I would wake up and go searching for spiders, snakes, and insects. I never hurt them or killed them, just stored them in jars to study their designs. I remember being particularly amazed by and fond of the praying mantis and a peculiar insect called a walking stick, or darning needle. Both these odd gentlemen seemed to be from the same bizarre family, and they camouflaged themselves well among our weeds and our trees. I prized them because they were hard to find. They had one other value too—much less scientific: they scared the devil out of my brothers and sister.

During my days of exploration I had a new puppy named Fuzzy that always accompanied me on my morning safaris. I loved him almost as much as Snowball, who really belonged to all of us by now.

Every morning they would have trouble pulling me away from my mason jar zoo, but this one particular morning I remember vividly, because on the way to Covington we had a wreck. A public works crew had left a sawhorse in the road, and in the fog, without warning, we hit it.

I hung on to Fuzzy and rolled to the floorboard of that old gray Ford with my puppy tight in my arms. Everybody was concerned about everybody else, except me. I was saying, "Oh, little Fuzzy, are you alright?"

Everybody, including Fuzzy, was okay. So we left the scene of the accident and drove on to Covington. Daddy dropped us off at Grandma Roberts's house, then headed on into Cincinnati to work.

Grandma always had Ritz crackers. They were so much better than the plain old soda crackers we had at the farm. I was sitting on the stoop of Grandma's house, sharing my Ritz crackers with Fuzzy, when these three guys came swerving and backfiring down Philadelphia Street. Slamming on the brakes, they stopped their old wreck on the sidewalk in front of me.

"Hey, sweetheart, let's see your doggy," one man said, leaning out the window while slapping the side of the door.

I held Fuzzy up.

They asked, "How much you want for your puppy? We'd like to buy him."

"Fuzzy ain't for sale," I said.

"Aw come on now, little girl. Why, we'll give you some money for your dog," the man in the back seat said. He pulled out his wallet and thumbed through the bills like a card deck. "Bring him here."

"No!" I shouted, leaving the Ritz crackers on the stoop, and running with Fuzzy for the door. I told Mother there were some men outside trying to buy my dog.

"I'll bet they are," Mother said sarcastically as she stared out the window.

Knowing what I know now, I doubt seriously it was my doggy they were after. Mother must have known that too. "Just stay inside awhile, honey. Let the men go away."

Naive as I was, I still felt scared even then. There were always things like that in the city that frightened me. I couldn't wait to get back home to Poppy's farm and safe things like black widow spiders and rattlesnakes.

My dog Fuzzy grew up. And I grew up a little bit too. Fuzzy became a fantastic sheepdog, and I became a fair-to-middling hay baler. I worked hard every summer in the hayfields hauling hay-shocks. We would pile the hay in good-size stacks, back Jack or Tony toward the stack with a long pole and chain rigged behind them, then we'd drape the chain across it and let the horse drag the hay either to a much bigger stack or to the hayloft. Backing a horse with a pole attached behind took a great deal of skill, but Uncle Gerald yelled at me till I got it right.

One day I was working the hayfields gathering shocks, when the man who owned the A&P store in Dry Ridge, Mr. Eric McBee, and his son came cutting across our field in their black sedan. They pulled up to me and got out. "You want to help us catch that sheepdog, honey?"

"You mean Fuzzy?" I asked. "What for? He ain't done nothin'."

They laughed. "Of course he ain't, sugar. We just bought that dog from Mrs. Penick."

"My mother?" I stood there trembling. I couldn't understand it. It had never been discussed with me or even mentioned, but I could see they were telling the truth. I had to do what I was told. I called Fuzzy to me and walked him over to the gentlemen's car, but Fuzzy wouldn't get in. He just stood there beside me swishing his tail and panting.

Mr. McBee said, "Well, it looks like you're gonna have to get in the car first." I got in. When I got in, Fuzzy got in. When I got out, Fuzzy got out. We repeated this ridiculous parade four times before the men finally slammed the door fast enough to keep Fuzzy in. It was just breaking my heart, but I held back my tears until the strange men rode away with my dog. (Maybe I should say *strangers*. There was nothing strange about them: they were just buying a good sheepdog). I waved goodbye to Fuzzy, who was fogging up their sedan's back window as he watched me, then walked back to Tony and his long pole and chain.

"Mother must really hate me to sell Fuzzy like that," I told Tony while I stroked his nose. Then I burst into tears. "Why? Why? Why?"

Tony just snorted, as if he was as disgusted as me, then hoofed at the ground as if to say, "Get back to work, Skeeter. There ain't a thing you can do about it." Mother told me that afternoon she had to sell Fuzzy to get grocery money. I would have starved to keep my dog!

Fuzzy came home to me three days running. But each time the McBees came and caught him again. Then one day Fuzzy didn't come back. We drove past their farm in Crittenden, later, on our way to Cincinnati. Then I saw why Fuzzy hadn't come back. I started crying and kicking the seats. The men had chained Fuzzy to their back yard fence.

Every time we drove to Covington from that day on, I had to look at Fuzzy tied like a mongrel to keep him from running back to Poppy's place and me. At first I would yell, "Hey, Fuzzy," out the window. But I soon realized, as he tugged against his chain barking, that to keep doing that was pure torture for him and for me.

I begged Mother to let me ask the A&P man if I could have him back. I just knew they'd let me buy him. "They bought him as a stock dog," I argued, "so he ain't good for nothin' to them on a chain."

"Skeeter, we ain't got a bit more money now," Mother argued back, "than we did then."

Fuzzy wasn't purebred. Neither was Snowball, nor Sarey and Sally, for that matter. In fact, I didn't even know what *purebred* meant until Poppy's half-sister, Ruth Poleman, came to visit us from her home in Washington, D.C.

Aunt Ruth drove a brand-new convertible and had a pedigreed German shepherd named Pal that sat up in the front seat with her. Ruth Poleman worked for a government agency, and she was quite rich compared to us, and certainly influential. Later on Aunt Ruth was mysteriously murdered, but while she was living, she invariably came to Poppy's every summer vacation. Around Independence Day each year Ruth Poleman would roll through Dry Ridge in her roadster with a silk scarf fluttering from her hair and her dog Pal sitting by her side in his spike-studded collar.

When Aunt Ruth got ready to ride around sightseeing through the hollows, she'd whistle for her German shepherd and shout, "Come get in this car, Pal Poleman!"

Pal would tear across the field like his tail was on fire, fly clean over the car door, and land in the passenger seat of the roadster. A soldier at attention, Pal Poleman would sit catching his breath, patiently staring out the windshield, waiting obediently on Aunt Ruth's next command. He didn't move till she said move, and he didn't stop till she said stop.

Ruth Poleman was one of those sophisticated sorts that held her little finger away from the cup, smoked cigarettes through a tortoise-shell stem, and drank unheard-of things like martinis. She always brought her own supply of fresh lemons and ice, which she stored on her stay in our cellar. Whenever she needed a "twist of lemon" or "just a chip of ice," she would flip a kid a quarter to "be a sweetheart and run to the cellar for me." Believe me, we gathered around Aunt Ruth and waited as patiently and obediently on her as her purebred Pal Poleman. A quarter could buy a lot of candy.

Another purebred dog I saw belonged to my cousin, Todd Lawrence, one of Aunt Lil's sons. Todd was always into something exciting. He was a great basketball player and an even greater acrobat. On the school playground he'd gather a crowd by doing tricks on the slide or the swings and on the monkey bars. I mean dangerous things like monkeyshines or tightrope walking the pole at the top of the swings.

The younger kids would run to squeal on him. The teacher would come out yelling, "Moreland Todd Lawrence, you come down from there right now!"

"What?"

The teacher would repeat herself. "And don't waste another second, young man!"

Todd would come flying off the top of the swing every time, doing a somersault in midair and landing feet first right in front of the teacher.

"Yes, ma'am," he would say with a twirling-hand bow. The teachers never were able to scold him. They'd just shake their heads, *What's the use?* and smile. It thrilled us to death. The kids only told on him, I'm sure, to get to see him do his grand finale. He was really slick.

Anyway, about the dog. Todd went off somewhere on a trip and came back to Dry Ridge with a huge Alaskan husky. Other than Pal Poleman we hadn't seen nothing that refined. In fact, I didn't see another dog like it until Sergeant Preston's Yukon King on TV.

Todd brought this monstrous dog over to Poppy's to show it off. He fixed a rope harness for the husky and hitched it to the red wagon Santa Claus had brought us the Christmas before that summer (our one and only present, by the way). However many kids we could fit in the wagon, that's how many that big husky pulled. We couldn't believe it. We yelled, "Daddy, come out here and look at Todd's dog."

When Daddy came out on the porch, we started working on him. "Oh, get us one. Get us a dog like Todd's."

But the next thing we knew, while we were still begging for a husky, that big dog grabbed Snowball for no apparent reason and started shaking him like a dishrag. We were screaming, trying to get him to stop. Todd pulled with all his might to get the husky off Snowball, but it didn't quit until my little white terrier seemed to have no life left in him. Todd felt terrible. He yanked the dog by the rope harness over to a tree and tied it up. We all ran to Snowball.

There wasn't a place left on my dog that didn't have a hole from that husky's teeth. He laid there whimpering, torn to shreds. "Don't die, Snowball," we cried. "Daddy, please don't let Snowball die."

Daddy looked him over, then without a word, he walked in the house and got the gun. "No, Daddy." I ran toward him screaming. "Don't shoot Todd's dog. It didn't mean to."

Daddy shook his head, knelt down, and put his arm around me. "Listen, Skeeter, it ain't Todd's dog I've got to shoot. This is gonna just kill ya'll, I know, but I've got to put Snowball out of his misery."

All of us kids were screaming and crying. "Oh, no, no, no, no!" I held Daddy's neck and trembled.

"I've got to, Skeeter. You don't want to see him suffer, do you?" He pulled me from his neck and said, "You kids get in the house. Go on now."

Daddy was crying. We got away from Snowball into the house, and from the window we watched Daddy tenderly pick Snowball up and cradle him in his left arm, then head for the hills. We silently wept and waited for the gun to go off. We were all gathered around Mother in tears.

About an hour later, we heard Daddy stomping up on the front porch. "Punzie, bring me the Mercurochrome!"

"You didn't kill him?" I shouted, swinging open the front door screen.

"Nah." Daddy shook his head. "Ol' Snowball wouldn't let me."

"Whatcha mean, *wouldn't letcha?*"

"Ah, the little rascal would look me straight in the eyes every time I raised the gun up. I tried three times. So finally I said to him, 'Look, Snowball, if you don't cooperate, I don't know if I can do this or not.' Snowball went 'Uhmm-mmm.' And that did it. I just couldn't shoot him."

We doused Snowball with Mercurochrome, then rubbed some of that old Watkins salve on him, and that little white December dog turned bright orange but stayed alive another five years. He developed a bad limp and went deaf and blind before he finally died, but right up to the end he remained as faithful as anyone or anything has ever been. I guess he was a purebred after all. He sure was special. When he died, we buried him in a special spot by the garden and had a funeral for him. Buddy, Shirley, Boze, and me all still think about Snowball.

I'm sure Gramma Penick thought at times that me and the kids were just out to see if we could drive her crazy. Can you imagine five kids, ages ten through one, living above you while you're going through menopause? Besides that, add the fact that Gramma had a change-of-life baby of her own named Bobby (who was Boze's age), plus she had to keep Poppy straight, as well as her own teenage sons and daughters.

Gramma used to yell at us to be quiet all the time, so sometimes we saw her as mean. But looking back, I see us five barging in and out of her house like we owned it, stomping up the stairs, slamming doors, and bouncing on the beds above her. It's a wonder we didn't drive her crazy.

One day, as the routine soon became, Mother had gone to Covington and left me to babysit the kids. Daddy, of course, was at work in Cincinnati. I had my hands full, needless to say. Well, while I was tending to baby Punkin's diapers, little Boze sneaked off downstairs. As soon as I realized he was gone, I took off after him. I got to Boze just in time to see him reach up on Gramma's bric-a-brac shelf and knock off the prize ashtray Aunt Dorothy and Uncle Gerald had won at the Halloween masquerade.

Gramma reached Boze at the same time I did. She took the palm of his little hand and slapped it. "No, no, Boze."

Boze started squalling. When he started, I started. Then of all things to do, I slapped my grandmother. I'd never done anything like that in my whole life. Oh, mercy! As soon as I did it, I knew it was wrong. I got scared. Gramma looked a hole through me. "I'm gonna have to tell your daddy that you hit your grandma."

Gramma never had a chance. As soon as Daddy's car rolled in, I told on myself. "Daddy...I hit Gramma."

"You did what! You hit Gramma?"

"Yeah." I sniffed. "'Cause she hit Boze." I told him the whole story.

Daddy said, "No matter what happened, you should never hit your grandma. Now, go tell her you're sorry, and you shouldn't have let Boze go downstairs in the first place." Here I was eight, maybe nine, years old and left in charge of Buddy, Shirley, Boze, and Punkin. Why? Because Mother had gotten to the point where she was always gone. It was already more than I could handle, and I could tell by looking at Mother's stomach we had another one on the way.

There was a good period in my life when Mother was what I expected a mother to be. I can still envision her, even today, when we lived in the cabin—her bent over a scrub board washing my clothes, making sure I got off to school on time, stirring the beans over the kettle in the fire, taking me with her to church or the dances at Mrs. Stone's, trying her best to teach me right from wrong. I was proud of her too, because she was pretty.

But Mother started changing after Punkin was born and we moved in with Poppy. I've often tried to pinpoint what exactly caused the change, but I just can't figure it out. Maybe it had to do with us moving in with Poppy, or maybe it was caused by her depression over Grandpa's death. Maybe she decided I was old enough to take care of things by myself. I only know that at first she would take us with her if she went to Covington; then all of a sudden, she stopped. She started leaving the kids with me and running off by herself or with one of her sisters, Hattie or Helen.

She would come home from Covington or wherever and nearly always tell us what good things people up there had to say about her. "Oh, did I tell ya'll? I saw so-and-so today, and they said I just look too young to have five kids."

Maybe she was too young to have that many kids, but so was I. I was insecure myself, and I wanted to get love, not to be having to give it all the time. For instance, in the middle of the night I'd get out of the bed where all us kids slept and sneak into the bed with Mother and Daddy. I would slip in beside Mother and tangle my fingers in waves of her hair; or I would sometimes lie at the foot of their bed and snuggle around her feet, trying to get as close to her as possible—to get her back. I felt like she was slipping away from me forever. I was much too old to be sleeping with Mother, but much too young to be Mother. For all practical purposes, nevertheless, that's what I became.

Church is where I got the love I didn't feel like I was getting at home. What made me decide to go there is still a mystery. My family had long since quit going. Often I was the only one in the whole house who went to church. Occasionally Poppy and Gramma took me, but most of the time I either walked or caught a ride with one of the neighbors.

At the Dry Ridge Christian Church (Disciples of Christ) people loved me and I felt it. I also felt loved by the God they talked about. And especially loved by His Son, Jesus, who, they were telling me, had died to keep me from having to die because He loved me so much. I didn't understand at that time why He had to do that, but I knew it would take a lot of love for me to do something like that for somebody.

There was a picture of this wonderful man they were talking about hanging right there in the Sunday school room. He was surrounded in the picture by an ocean of kids, and in His lap He held a little blond-headed girl with long hair. I'd say to myself, *That's me on his knee*, as we sang "Jesus Loves Me." And, for some reason I'd think, *I'm special to Him.*

Had it not been for those and later experiences, I'm sure I would be an old, bitter woman by now.

I knew God loved me, but still I kept trying to win my own mother's love. I wasn't sure she loved me anymore. Several things led me to believe this. In late summer, just before I entered fifth grade, I was complaining that my hair was too long. It was sweaty and hung to my waist. Every time it was braided it pulled and hurt because of the weight. I wanted it trimmed before school started.

"If you don't shut your mouth about it," Mother said, "I'll cut it all off for you."

Later that day I said something else about it being too hot. "Okay, that did it," she said and grabbed a pair of pinking shears. I ran from her. I made it to the snowball bush in Poppy's front yard before she caught me. "You've been fussin' 'bout that hair long enough, young lady."

I tried to climb through the bush to get away from her, but she held on and started whacking. While I struggled among the branches, crying, Mother cut my hair off with the shears in every which direction. When she finished, it was jagged and stupid looking, the length of a boy's.

Embarrassed is not the word for what I felt when school started the next week. It was totally humiliating to sit there while the photographer took our school pictures. He looked at my head and shook his. "What in the world happened to your hair, little girl?" What could I say? He waited until I quit crying before he snapped the picture.

In October of that year, 1941, Doozer (Carolyn Sue) was born. While Doozer was still nursing, Mother would run off up to Aunt Hattie's or Grandma Roberts's. Doozie would cry and cry and scream. I couldn't get her quiet. I would rock her, then lay her on the bed and try to softly blow her eyelids shut, figuring if I could get her eyes closed, she'd go to sleep.

It was exhausting 'cause I was having to holler at all the other kids too. I even tied Buddy to the bedposts because he was big as me and wouldn't help. I have to laugh remembering that. Gramma Penick came up the stairs when she heard all the commotion and discovered the predicament I was in. "Lord help, child, why don't you fix that baby a sugar teat where she'll be quiet?"

"What's a sugar teat?"

She took me down to her kitchen, and, while I held Doozie on my hip, Gramma fixed the baby her first sugar teat. "I ain't gonna show you but once," she said, "so watch close."

Gramma took a piece of fine cloth like Poppy used to strain milk at the dairy. She got a wad of fresh butter, rolled it in sugar, then wrapped the straining cloth around it. "Here, put this to her mouth now," Gramma said, "and see if she'll hush up."

Doozie took to that sugar teat like there'd be no tomorrow. The butter drooled from her mouth and went rolling down her chest. When she finished that one, I fixed the next one myself. Doozie got suddenly content—sticky but quiet.

Mother came in that evening late. Her breasts were hurting her something awful. Immediately she tried to get Doozer to nurse, but she wouldn't do it. I'm sorry to say, it tickled me. *Now maybe she'll stay home.*

Mother was getting more and more frustrated. She kept squeezing Doozie's cheeks to press her mouth open. "Take it!" she half-pleaded, half-ordered. "Come on now, take it."

"She ain't gonna do it," I said. "I've got her taking cow's milk." It had seemed only fair that if I was going to be left with the chore of Mother, this should be the price Mother paid. But when I saw the pain she had to go through because I had converted Doozie to milk, my glee over what I had done changed to feelings of sadness for Mother. Her milk caked. She waited too long and ended up having to buy a breast pump. It was a shame. Mother stayed home for a while, however. But Doozer had even grown accustomed to being carried on my hip, so Mother gradually returned to her running.

Sing Pretty for the People, Skeeter

Roses on my shoulder,
Slippers on my feet.
I'm my daddy's darlin',
Don't you think I'm sweet?
—"Roses on my Shoulder,"
  Skeeter Davis and
  Joe Spampinato

Christmas was coming. The kids in my fifth-grade class at Dry Ridge School were getting more and more restless as vacation time approached. We all had big ideas about what we wanted from Santa Claus. My best friend, Corine Ford, and I were talking about dolls when a group of the older kids came racing down the hall sticking their heads in the classroom. "They bombed Pearl Harbor. The Japs have just bombed Pearl Harbor."

Mrs. Landrum, our teacher, put her hands to her mouth and shook her head, "Oh, no!"

Corine looked at me quizzically and I shrugged my shoulders. "Mrs. Landrum, oh, Mrs. Landrum." Corine raised her hand. "What's Burl Harbor?"

Then I asked, "What's a Jap?"

50

Mrs. Landrum must not have heard us; she just kept shaking her head in shock. Finally she said, "Well, I guess ya'll know what this means. It means we'll probably go to war, kids. The Japanese have bombed Pearl Harbor!"

It was so utterly confusing. I thought she meant us personally, and I got all excited. *It'll be like the "Silver War" Uncle Mose fought in. 'Cept this time we'll win. That'll be great, we'll win!*

That afternoon I realized from listening to Poppy and Daddy that it wasn't going to be so grand after all. That evening we listened to FDR, and it wasn't one of his fireside chats followed by the usual, "I thank you, Eleanor thanks you, and our dog Fala thanks you." The President's voice seemed sadly urgent.

"I don't see how we can expect Germany and Italy to stay out of this thing, Will," Poppy said.

"I know what you mean, Pop," I heard Daddy say. "It looks like the whole world's fixing to be at war."

"Hard times never seem to end," Gramma interjected.

Poppy walked over and cut off the radio. "Yeah," he said, "but we got to do what we got to do."

"Yep."

"Yeah."

"That's right."

Like nearly every other American family, ours was ready to make whatever sacrifices were necessary to beat those Japs and Krauts— the Axis, as they were called. In my mind, I pictured them fighting with axes. *If any of them get near me*, I reassured myself, *Daddy'll shoot 'em.*

Years later I went to see the movie *Tora! Tora! Tora!* with a Japanese friend of mine. Throughout the movie, I kept thinking about when I was ten and didn't know what the devil was going on. I've been to Pearl Harbor since then, of course, to sing for the G.I.'s stationed in Hawaii, and I know a wee bit more than I did then. Like I know where "Burl" Harbor is, what happened there and afterward. And I know it was anything but swell. On the other hand, I've seen the ruins of Hiroshima and Nagasaki too, done concerts in Tokyo and Kyoto, where the people kept thanking me for not bombing their sacred city.

School let out for Christmas. Daddy took me, Buddy, Shirley, and Boze up in the hills to cut a tree. I wanted to make sure they got a cedar, because I've always loved the smell of cedar. Mix the aroma of oranges and apples with cedar, and you've got my favorite fragrance. It's called Christmas. If Max Factor would create it, I swear I'd wear it.

We strung popcorn chains and hung the tree with bright glass bulbs. Mother stuffed the bare holes with angel hair, then we all stood back and admired our work of art. We didn't have any Christmas lights, but the kerosene lamplight dancing on the glass bulbs made the prettiest sight I'd seen.

"Oh, how I wish my daddy could see this," Mother said. Then it started. She sank lower and lower. She started recalling first one thing and then another about "the last Christmas I saw ya'll's grandpa."

We sat by the stove and listened while Mother told various parts of the murder story, about me eating the glass bulbs and about Grandpa bouncin' me on his knee to make me stop crying. Then the funny, sentimental parts of the story were over.

Melancholia spread like chicken pox. But still the high expectations of Christmas morning can help any kid fight the blues, and I could always drift off to sleep dreaming about the doll and new dress I was gonna find beneath the tree.

Christmas morning finally came, and the kids and I raced each other down the stairs to see what Santa Claus had brought. "Look, Skeeter!" Buddy said. "Santy left you a letter."

I was so excited. I had been wanting him to write me ever since I started writing him. I ripped the letter open just as fast as I could. It read: "Dear Skeeter, I'm sorry, but I ran out of toys. Love, Santa. P.S. I know you'll understand."

What a hurting letter! I never understood. I said I did, of course, but I didn't. My parents asked me, "You do understand, don't you, Skeeter?"

"Oh, yeah, of course," I said, choking back the tears. I sneaked away from the tree, out the back door, and headed to the woods where I could be alone to cry.

Maybe I should have understood. I was in the fifth grade, a pretty big girl by then. But at ten I had no reason to believe that Santa Claus wasn't real. Two dozen of them weren't lining the streets of Dry Ridge. There was just one Santa Claus, and he was as real to me as God or the ground I walked on. Nobody could have told me, "Hey, Skeeter, Santa ain't really real. Your mama and daddy didn't have enough money to get everybody something this year; and since you're the oldest, well…"

Nobody could have told me that and made me believe them. For some reason that I didn't understand, Santa Claus had just run out of toys when he got to me, the last and least important kid in the whole world.

During and after the war years, motion pictures became very important to me. However, the very first time I ever went to the movies turned out to be one of the scariest experiences of my life. I couldn't have been more than three or four at the time. I remember clutching Mother's hand so tight as she led me down the dark aisle to a seat in the front row. "I'll be back to get you later," she said, and left me alone in the darkness.

The cartoon began, and I laughed till the tears went away. Throughout the newsreel, I kept looking behind me to see if Mother had come back yet. Then the main feature started. A huge lion, bigger than life, came out from behind the silver wall and roared at me so ferociously that I jumped clear out of my seat and ran lickety-split up the aisle screaming, "Oh no! Help me!"

An arm reached out and grabbed me. I fought it. I just knew the lion had caught me and was fixing to swallow me with one bite. "Don't be scared, little girl," the lady who owned the arm said. "It's not real. The lion's just a picture. Where's your mama?"

The lady pulled me onto her lap. I struggled against her for a while. She held me throughout the movie, but I kept my eyes buried in her shoulder and refused to watch. She kept saying, "Your mommy'll be back soon."

During the war the movies became the place to drop us kids off whenever we did get to town with Mother. Liberty Theatre in downtown Covington sure saw its share of us Penicks.

One day Mother and her sister Helen left us at the Liberty with me in charge of our brood plus Aunt Helen's—Shirley Ann, Jerry, and Doc—while the two of them went to the Madison Avenue Chili Parlor to play the slot machines. When they came to pick us up, Mother did a head count and asked me, "Where's Boze?"

I looked the bunch of kids over and shrugged my shoulders. Mother had a conniption. "You've lost Boze! You've lost little Boze!" she screamed. "If Boze is lost, Skeeter, there ain't no tellin' what I'll do to you."

We searched the theater, looking under every seat, told the manager and waited on the sidewalk over an hour, hoping that just maybe Boze would casually wander up. All the time I thought and thought. "I just can't remember Boze even being with us, Mother. Honest, I can't."

The lady at the ticket box helped me out. "What's the matter? Did you lose a kid? These six is the only ones I seen go in."

Finally Mother decided that we'd go back to Aunt Helen's house before we called the police. And there, of course, was Boze playing in the neighbor lady's children's sandbox.

It was the musicals I enjoyed the most, and most of the wartime movies were musicals—films like *Stage Door Canteen* and *I'll Be Seeing You*. I would memorize the songs from them: "Over there, over there, say a prayer," or "I'll be seeing you in all the old familiar places/That this heart of mine embraces all day through," or "Don't sit under the apple tree with anyone else but me..." The song and dance routines were often light and comical, and I loved to imitate them too. One particular scene I recall had the dancers dressed in Aunt Jemima bandanas and overalls. These were the years when women began to take over the jobs once held by the men in the factories. While the chorus line danced around constructing an airplane part by part, they sang a song called "Rosie the Riveter." Their tap shoes went *rat-a-tat-tat-rat-a-tat-tat* in time to the music. I loved it.

Betty Hutton is one lady I had down to a tee. "My Rocking Horse Ran Away." Wow! What a song! All the zang-bang-booey of Betty Hutton was just the thing for me. I like anything energetic, dynamic, animated, and alive—like June Haver's "Be my little honey bumblebee./Buzz around, keep a buzzing 'round." June Haver wore a bee costume, fluttering her wings while she sang. I wanted a costume wardrobe so badly. I had all those songs and dance routines down pat. I would seat the kids on Karo syrup buckets in rows like a theater in Poppy's backyard, and I'd give 'em a show as good as the movies.

Preparing for my little backyard performances, I'd roll my hair up in a pageboy like one of the movie stars. For rollers, I had to use coffee can strips wrapped in catalog pages to keep the tin from cutting through my hair. Can you imagine how I looked and felt running around with a half ton of metal on my head? Yet when the homemade rollers came out, here would be this little kid with a Betty Grable hairdo. I never got into makeup, since we couldn't afford it, but I'd change hairstyles overnight and become whatever star I needed to be for the next day's show.

The kids loved it. They stayed happy and obedient as long as I promised to put on a show for them. I learned quickly that this was the best way to take the pressure out of motherhood.

My brothers and sister Shirley particularly liked a skit I had learned not at the movies, but at church.

> I don't want to *march* in the infantry,
> *Ride* in the cavalry, *shoot* the artillery.
> I don't want to *fly* over Germany.
> I'm in the King's *arm-eeeeeeeee.*

For those that think protest songs were a product of the sixties, that little Christian ditty should prove surprising. It was an audience participation song. You were supposed to go through the motions of what the song said as you sang it. I'd get the kids off their buckets following along like Simon says, but they were forever shooting when they were supposed to fly or flying when they were supposed to march. We'd get so tickled at each other's awkwardness, we'd end up rolling in the grass, laughing until we couldn't get our breath.

Another way I learned to entertain the kids was by telling ghost stories. After the radio left the air at night, I'd gather everybody under the quilts and tell some tale I'd heard from Uncle Mose, or better yet some gruesome story I had made up myself. One of the most horrid characters I ever invented was a bogeyman named Mr. Nobody. When I couldn't get the kids to behave, Mr. Nobody could.

"If you don't hush and get to sleep, Mr. Nobody'll *getcha!*"

Surprisingly, after their bedtime horror story the kids would be ready to snuggle up around me and go to sleep. That is, everybody but Shirley. Her heart would beat so loud against the bed that it even kept me awake. If Daddy had come home by then, I'd call out, "Daddy, come in here and make Shirley's heart stop. It's beating so loud, I can't get to sleep!"

Daddy would come and check on us. Tucking the cover around us, he'd whisper, "Skeeter, if you'd quit telling her them awful stories, we could all get some sleep." Gradually I caught on to the fact that Shirley was a nervous child and started looking for other ways besides horror stories to get the kids to sleep.

Shirley was scared of other things too, particularly storms. She got that fear from Mother. I love storms. But still to this very day they scare Shirley to death.

Late one afternoon Mother was going to the movie in Dry Ridge, leaving the kids with me. A Gene Autry movie that I was just dying to see was playing. It was *South of the Border,* and all the kids at school had been talking about how good it was. It wasn't funny to be left at home with Gene Autry playing the Dry Ridge Theatre, because I knew I would be the only kid at school who missed it.

As Mother crawled into the back seat of the car with Corine Ford and Corine's brother Claude, however, dark clouds began to form along the horizon toward town. I warned her, "Mother, it sure looks like a storm's coming."

"There ain't gonna be no storm, Skeeter. You're just sore 'cause you ain't goin'," she said. "You have them kids in bed when I get home, ya hear?" Claude backed his Chevrolet out of Poppy's yard, and the three of them set out for town to see Gene Autry.

No sooner were they out of sight than the sky got deathly black and thunder rolled across the early darkness like a trainload of war-bound soldiers. The wind began to slam the barn doors open and shut. We were still out in the front yard waving goodbye to Mother when the first bolt of lightning cut through the blackening sky. Shirley started screaming like there would be no tomorrow.

I told all the kids to get to the house, and everybody ran but Shirley. We yelled from the porch. "Come on, Shirley. Let's get inside, 'fore the rain hits." Shirley couldn't move. She was petrified, staring down the road where Claude's car had disappeared and screaming, "Mother, Mother!"

I ran back out and grabbed her. In the house I lit a lantern to show Shirley there was nothing to be afraid of. But she screamed and screamed and just kept screaming until she was gasping for breath. Nobody was home but me and the kids. *I've got to do something,* I thought. Then it dawned on me.

I was so embarrassed about what I had decided to do that I went off by myself to the kitchen. I could still hear Shirley screaming in the living room, louder each time the thunder roared. *They said at church that all you have to do is believe,* I remembered. *God will do anything you ask Him to do if you really believe it.* Like any child, I had been given no reason to doubt. I had never had much reason to call on Him before. I felt like He probably didn't have time for my little problems, but right then and there I desperately needed Him to help me.

I knelt on the kitchen floor and prayed out loud, "God, please listen. Send the lightning down and make Mother turn around and come back home, 'cause my sister Shirley's scared and I can't do nothin'. Thank you, and oh yeah, in Jesus' name I pray. Amen."

Ten minutes did not pass. There stood Mother in the doorway drenched from head to foot. She, Corine, and Claude were trembling like leaves. Shirley ran to Mother and wrapped her arms around Mother's legs. "You won't believe what happened," Mother said. Her eyes were white with fright. "The lightning just kept dancing in front of Claude's car, and we couldn't move."

I clapped my hands in joy and shouted, "God did it! God did it!"

"What do you mean, 'God did it'?"

"I prayed for God to send the lightning to make you come home 'cause Shirley was so scared." I thought Mother would turn her attention toward Shirley and bring her out of her hysterics, but instead she unclasped Shirley's grasp from around her legs, came across the room, and slapped me so hard that I went tumbling back into the kitchen. I lay on the floor sobbing; then I thought, *at least I've found someone I can count on—God!*

Since I couldn't seem to win my mother's respect and affection, I turned my attention toward Daddy. In doing so I brought myself into direct competition with my brother Buddy, because most of Daddy's attention was rightfully going toward his boys. They got to hunt with him, ride horses with him, and work by his side. I was determined to show Buddy up, however, and land myself a gold star from Daddy.

At the Penick family reunion in 1941, everybody came down to Poppy's place. There were two big events that day besides the usual picnic and horseshoes. Boze and my Uncle Bobby had real long hair. All the kinfolks gathered around and watched them get haircuts. Then came the main event—a boxing match between me and Buddy.

Buddy had gotten a set of boxing gloves for Christmas that year, and the men had fashioned a ring of sorts in the front yard out of rope. Daddy gave us a lecture before the fight, telling us not to hurt each other, not to go for the eyes or bust any lips or anything. We were going to have regular rounds just like Madison Square Garden. People were already grouping around the ring at least a half hour before we stepped through the ropes to duke it out.

When Buddy crawled into the ring, all the men and boys cheered. The women and girls were all for me. We warmed up by sparring our shadows and bouncing up and down on the hay mat. Then we went to our respective corners to be announced. Like I said, it was all set up like the big time.

Somebody hit a wooden soup ladle against the cowbell and round one began. I had really practiced before the fight at putting my left arm up to protect myself and jabbing with my right, just like on the radio. Buddy and I danced around amidst the cheers for a couple of rounds without causing too much damage, but in the middle of the third round Daddy shouted, "Get 'er, Buddy! Get 'er!"

I remember looking straight at Daddy in shock. I couldn't believe he was rooting for Buddy. Gosh, it hurt. While I was busy staring at Daddy, Buddy caught me off guard and busted my lip. I staggered back against the ropes. I tasted blood, then I went for blood. I tore into him like a swarm of hornets.

I was really hurt more by what Daddy said than by Buddy's fist. But I was determined to make Buddy pay. I wasn't worried about protecting nothing then. I smacked Buddy in the stomach a couple of times with my left, then I just squashed his eye. I banged him right in the face. This time he staggered back.

Daddy stopped the fight! That's right. As soon as I got Buddy in the eye, Daddy stopped the fight.

Buddy's eye was all puffed out. My mouth was swollen, yet they were still having to hold me down in my corner while I was yelling, "More, more! Let me at him."

Somebody rushed out of the kitchen with a slab of bacon to take the swelling from Buddy's eye. I don't even remember getting to raise my hand as the champion or nothing. They were all too busy making such a big fuss over Buddy.

I came across the ring pouting. I was still hurt.

"Daddy, how come you told Buddy to *get* me?" Mother even came to my defense, telling Daddy he was wrong. Daddy never did explain. I figure it's just a man wanting his son to be better than his daughter. I still felt like the winner anyhow, even when it wasn't announced. But I never ever picked up a pair of boxing gloves again. You might say I retired undefeated. I was Joe Louis for a day—even if I was a girl!

The following winter we were hanging tobacco up in the barn roof.

One man handed the tobacco up from the wagon to another man who straddled the rafters, sliding them down, and packing them in. The man up top had to reach down and take the tobacco from the man on the wagon; the whole enterprise resembled somebody hanging clothes while they were doing situps. It was high up in the barn and dangerous.

Daddy had sent Buddy up into the rafters to be the hanger. My job was to hand the tobacco sticks up to Daddy for him to hand up to Buddy. The dust from the leaves fell in my face. It burned my eyes and made me sneeze. I hated my job because of that. Maybe that's why I still dislike cigarette smoke. Anyway, Buddy was at the top, and all of a sudden, he got to shaking and calling for Daddy, "Come and get me."

I got scared too, because Buddy was really trembling. He couldn't come down, and he couldn't stay up there either. "Don't fall, Buddy!" I yelled.

Daddy said, "Keep steady, Buddy. Just be calm and I'll climb up and get you." Daddy got Buddy around the waist and carried him down the ladder. Buddy was so embarrassed.

"Well, I guess that's it for the day," Daddy said, looking at me. "You ain't quite tall enough to hand me the sticks."

"I'll get up there," I volunteered. Daddy laughed.

"Watch me," I said, and while he was still laughing I climbed up the ladder to the rafters. "Okay. Hand me one." They started handing me the sticks and by nightfall we hung that whole wagon load of tobacco.

I felt real pride. I was so glad I could do the job. Seems like I honestly always did good at whatever job I had. Stripping tobacco or whatever. It's because I wanted approval—that good pat on the back. Somebody to say, "Boy, Skeeter, you're really doing good." But it seemed like, no matter how hard I tried, it was never coming from Mother or Daddy.

One day Daddy came home from work early and without my knowing it, silently watched me entertaining the kids in the back yard with one of my routines I had stolen from the movies. Instead of my usual Betty Hutton stuff, however, I was singing a new song by Jeanette MacDonald. "Sweetheart, sweetheart, sweetheart, say you'll love me ever..."

It was almost operetta, nothing like most of the pop songs at all. To my knowledge Daddy had never bragged on me before, but when I finished singing I heard his applause coming from behind me. "Bravo, Bravo."

I wheeled around, blushing. "How long you been standing there?"

"Through most of your show," Daddy said and laughed. He could see that getting caught being a show-off was embarrassing me, so Daddy came over and messed up my hair with his hand. "Hey, you did fine, kid."

I heard him telling Poppy as he went in the kitchen door, "You wanta know somethin'? That kid of mine can sing."

My pride puffed up like a yeast roll. *Gosh, I like Betty Hutton's and June Haver's songs the best*, I thought, *but if that kinda singing impresses Daddy, then I'll put my heart in it.* I know Daddy had all these aspirations for me to become a great opera singer someday, but it turned out that I was to become an Opry singer instead.

Late at night when I couldn't get to sleep, Poppy would sing with me. Our favorite song was "Leaning on the Everlasting Arms." I'd sing the lead, holding out the word *leaning* as long as I could while Poppy sang in deep bass harmony, "I'm leanin' on Jesus, I'm leanin' on Jesus, I'm leanin' on Jesus." I didn't know to call it harmony back then, so I'd ask my fifth grade classmates if they knew how to sing the "other part."

"What do you mean?"

"Well, when I sing this part...," I'd say. "No, I'll tell you what. You just sing the song and I'll show you."

But nobody could do that either. They'd do fine until I came in on harmony, then they'd get off key and start singing my part. Finally one day in the cloakroom during lunch period, Corine Ford, Wanda Littrell, Mary Lee, and I were singing "The Battle Hymn of the Republic," and I discovered Mary Lee could do it.

Wow! We had ourselves a duet. I was so happy. She stayed on her part, the basic melody, while I sang alto harmony. When we finished, I heard this applause come from the doorway. There was our teacher, Marie Landrum, and the sixth grade teacher, Georgia Hinage Conrad.

Mrs. Conrad looked at Mrs. Landrum and said, "You better pass that little blonde. I want her in my class." It was a good feeling. I was getting those pats on the back that I needed so desperately. I remember the last day of school that year, Mrs. Conrad came in our room and asked, "Well, do I get my little girl?"

Mrs. Landrum smiled. "Oh yes, regretfully."

From then on, I seemed to get the lead role in school plays whenever it was a singing part. Always it was lead singing though, no more duets. I played anything from an angel to a pickaninny.

I remember when I was getting ready for my first school play, I was nervous as a cat. Daddy called me over to his car that morning as he was leaving for work. I had my costume draped across my arm and I was walking out to the main road to catch the bus with the rest of the kids.

"It's gonna be a big day for you, ain't it?"

"Yeah, I guess so."

"I sure wish I could be there to see you."

"That'd just make me more nervous," I said.

Daddy cranked the old gray Ford and answered, "Well, just sing pretty for the people, Skeeter. You'll do alright."

He always said that. If I called him before I left for the Opry, or went off on the road, he'd always say, "Sing pretty for the people." And since so many singers wear blue jeans on stage, he added a new phrase, "And be sure to wear a dress. Them fans done seen all the blue jeans they want to see. Wear a dress."

Mrs. Conrad let me go get her lunch for her every day across the street at her mother's house. That was the only time in my life I was ever the teacher's pet, and I sure did enjoy it. I was still so insecure at the time, nevertheless, that I'd think on the way over to get her lunch, *Is she doing this 'cause she likes me or is she just making me run errands?*

I wanted somebody to love me so bad that I finally decided Mrs. Conrad did love me and was letting me love her back by going after her lunch. I still believe that's not far from the truth. Love is such a strange combination of giving and receiving that we can easily get to feeling used if we don't watch it.

I remember Mrs. Conrad's mother's house distinctly, because her mother let me change out of my wet clothes there the night I was first baptized. I don't count that first baptism, and I seriously doubt that the Lord does either.

This preacher came by the playground one afternoon and yelled at us, "Did you kids know that you're all going to hell?"

Boy! We just stood there trembling, thinking about devils, horns, pitchforks, and fiery furnaces. We looked around at each other, then back at him. All we had been doing was playing drop the handkerchief, blindman's bluff, and hide 'n' seek. Even when we played spin the bottle, the boys never let it stop on me. I hadn't done nothin', but I freaked out like the rest of 'em. We were all asking each other out the corners of our mouths, "Have you been bad?"

"I ain't been bad," we whispered back and forth. "I ain't stole nothin'." We tried to figure out what we'd done, but this preacher convinced us anyhow that we had best get ourselves down to the church that night and get baptized. Nobody bothered to explain to us ideas like "born in sin" or even the story of salvation. No, instead it was, "Ya'll get down to the church tonight. There's a revival going on."

When I was younger, as I've explained already, I had convinced myself that Jesus loved us. This man was making me have doubts. He was stopping by every house and yelling at the kids. He never once went inside to discuss what he was doing with our parents.

"There'll be a school bus come pick you up this evening. So you best be on the road and ready."

I couldn't wait. I thought the bus would never show up. I stood out in front of Poppy's place for an hour before I finally spotted it coming. *Thank God, here comes the bus.*

When we got to the church, I wanted to get up there fast. I had no idea when they were gonna call us up there, but I wanted it done quick like a dose of castor oil. Take it and get it over with. At least seven of the ten kids in my group got baptized that night.

As soon as I came up from the water, I remember thinking, *Whew, I'm glad that's over. The devil can't get me now.* Then I hightailed it over to Mrs. Hinage's house to change clothes.

Later on, when I really came to Christ, I came to Him because I loved Him. He's *my* way, *my* truth, *my* life. Of course I fear Him, but it's the same way as we mind our daddy. I know He'll reprimand me if I've done wrong, but the sort of thing I went through that evening is ridiculous. Scaring children is not the way.

I don't think the Lord ever meant to have Himself shoved down the throats of children. I know the Bible says, "Suffer the little children to come unto me for of such is the kingdom of God." That's a lot different from "Suffer, little children, suffer," like some evangelists must have read it. I tell you one thing: they sure scared the devil out of me.

One weekend in the spring of 1942, when I was visiting Daddy's sister Naomi in Covington, Daddy got off work early and came over and got me. I was so tickled 'cause he told me he was taking me to see the movie of all movies, *Gone With the Wind*. When the little girl, Bonnie, got thrown from the pony and killed, I cried so hard that Daddy had to let me borrow his handkerchief.

On the way back home we stopped in Erlanger at a girl's shop with a green canvas awning where Daddy bought me two little silk undershirts and a couple of pairs of flannel bloomers. I don't think I've ever liked anything any more than I did those undergarments at that particular moment. Before that, if I wore any underwear at all, it was like longhandles with the cotton stockings.

"You're getting to be a big girl now," Daddy said.

I felt big. My heart was overflowing. I was so thrilled that right then I loved him more than Santa Claus.

When we got back to Poppy's farm, Daddy told Mother, "Well, I took my favorite girlfriend to the movies today, Punzie."

Aunt Stella was there, and before Mother could say anything, she said, "William! I think that's terrible." Aunt Stell looked over at me with a look that said, *This is just too horrible for your young ears to hear*. "You don't mean you've been out with another woman?"

Daddy just grinned, 'cause Daddy had a sense of humor that not everybody quite got off on. He said, "Yeah, I did."

Aunt Stell was flabbergasted. "I think it's terrible for you to come in here and tell Sarah you took another woman to a movie."

I felt good all over because I picked up on what he'd said, "My favorite girlfriend." Daddy started laughing. I laughed, then told them proudly, "It was me!"

Of course Mother knew it all along. She knew Daddy. He never pulled nothin' on her.

A few weeks later my joy at being Daddy's favorite girlfriend ended. I overheard Daddy talking to Mother. From the very first of the conversation I could tell it was something I certainly didn't want to hear, especially at the point in my life when I was just beginning to feel loved by my father. The something was that he was leaving us.

"What kinda fool thing have you done, William? Joined the army?"

"Well, not quite," Daddy answered. "I tried to get in the Seabees, but my impacted tonsils kept me out." He himmy-hawed around.

"Well, it just so happened there was this government man there, and when he found out I was an electrician, he offered me a job in east Tennessee I couldn't refuse. It pays better than you can imagine."

Mother asked the same question I wanted to ask, "But why can't we go with you?"

"Because the job is in a little town outside of Knoxville under military command. It's some kind of top secret project and it's heavily guarded."

"What will you be doing?"

Daddy hesitated a moment. "I couldn't tell you if I knew, Punzie."

Things happened fast after that. The following week we bought a house right next to the Dry Ridge High School. There was gonna be plenty of money, but there'd be nothing to spend it on and worst of all, no Daddy. After we moved into our new little house and were squared away, we drove Daddy up to Covington to catch the train for Tennessee. Just seeing how easily Daddy was allowed to board the train let me know his work was as important as a soldier's.

When everybody had said their goodbyes and the train prepared to pull out, Daddy hugged me and said, "Be a good girl. Do what your Mother tells you. And if you get to be in any more school plays," he smiled, "sing pretty for the people, Skeeter."

He kissed Mother and my brothers and sisters. We stood there on the ramp waving goodbye and crying, as the train hauled Daddy away to the heavy water of the Clinch River near a little town called Oak Ridge, Tennessee.

The World Peace Queen

I'm a lover, not a fighter,
I kinda like it that way.
If you want a fighting partner,
Go live with Cassius Clay.
—"I'm a Lover, Not a Fighter,"
   Ronny Light

The September after Daddy left for Oak Ridge, I entered the seventh grade. Assuming that being in junior high made me mature enough to quit going by a nickname, I started demanding to be addressed as Mary Frances—and only as Mary Frances.

Habits, needless to say, are not easily broken. So even after constant stubborn reminders from me, my schoolmates seemed unwilling to budge. It was still Skeeter this and Skeeter that. I decided if I could just manage to rehabilitate one of the teachers, from then on I would have myself a proper name. After the last class one afternoon I finally gathered the courage to confront my seventh-grade homeroom teacher.

"Mrs. Abernathy," I said. "If you really don't mind, I'd prefer to go by my real name, Mary Frances."

"Why of course, Skeeter. I can understand that," she told me as she hurriedly put her things away in her desk drawer for the day. "I'll do my best to make sure that starting tomorrow I call on you as Mary Frances."

The next day in Government, sure enough, Mrs. Abernathy called on me right at the first of class. I can vividly remember hearing the question because I had studied hard the night before. "Mary Frances, could you please tell us who was responsible for having the Bill of Rights attached to our Constitution?" Not used to being called by my proper name, I just looked around the room to see who it was she was calling on. Everybody else was looking back at me and giggling. Mrs. Abernathy coughed. "Oh, Mary Frances."

She paused for a second or two. For some strange reason she seemed to be staring directly at me with a scowl across her face and shaking her head. I straightened myself up in my desk and started nervously tapping my pencil.

"Mary Frances, can you hear me?"

Finally Mrs. Abernathy walked over to my desk and flipped me right square on the head with her knuckle. Towering over me with her hands on her hips, she said, "Look, Skeeter. I thought you wanted me to call you by your real name, Mary Frances. Now do you, or don't you?"

I know I must have turned beet red as I exploded in embarrassed laughter. After all the rigmarole I'd been through, I was so used to Skeeter myself that when somebody actually did call me Mary Frances, I flat forgot who I was.

Poppy played daddy as much as possible while Daddy was off working at Oak Ridge. For instance, one night Poppy came over and took us all to a live stage show, the WLS Barn Dance. The performers had come all the way from Chicago, Illinois. It was the biggest treat imaginable—real live hillbilly singers.

I remember they also showed a movie that night, featuring Roy Acuff, called *Smoky Mountain Melody*. After the movie a comedy act came on stage that I'd never heard of before or since, Aunt Ida and Little Clifford. But boy, they had the funniest routine I'd ever seen.

Aunt Ida pushed Little Clifford out in one of those plush leather carriages like rich folks used back then to stroll their babies. Little Clifford was a full-grown man sucking on a gigantic baby bottle, dressed in a pale blue bonnet, white dress, white shoes, and pale blue baby socks. His hairy legs dangled out of the baby buggy almost to the ground.

Ida wore a wide brim hat like Minnie Pearl's, except Aunt Ida's was completely engulfed in apples, oranges, clusters of grapes, and bananas. The audience just went ape. We thought it was artificial fruit, of course, because we all had seen real people wearing those tacky cornucopian hats around downtown Covington.

That impression didn't last long. While Aunt Ida told her one-liners, Little Clifford was reaching out of the buggy, plucking fruit off the fruit basket hat and eating it. We were amazed. Then all of a sudden Clifford threw a real banana sailing out of his buggy onto the stage floor. Aunt Ida started to scold and whip him, so he jumped out of the buggy and ran off the stage with Aunt Ida close behind. The "baby" in the buggy became bigger than Aunt Ida and she couldn't catch him. That's how the act ended.

Excitement and memories from that night at the Williamstown Theater had to be put aside quickly. Early the next morning, coming back from the outhouse, I happened to notice there was blood trickling down my leg. I tried to think of how I could possibly have cut myself. Nothing seemed to be hurting, so I went back to the outhouse to find out what part of my body was cut. I wasn't cut, but what I did discover scared me absolutely to death. I tore out screaming toward the house, "Oh, Mother! Something up inside me broke."

I pulled up my dress to show her what I meant. The blood was just pouring out of me. "There ain't nothin' in you broke," was all Mother said, so nonchalantly. She tore a piece of linen rag from an old bed sheet. "Here, put this in your panties. It'll soak up the blood. You'll be alright in a few days."

Neither she nor anyone else had forewarned me about a woman's period. Neither did she bother to tell me what was going on when I started that day. I had to learn what to call it at school from other girls just as scared and naive as myself.

When Daddy went away to Oak Ridge, it was the farthest he had ever been away from home. Once a year for only two weeks was all he got to come see us.

The train didn't make a scheduled stop in Dry Ridge. There was no depot. But as a favor the engineer would throttle down enough, as the northbound train came through town, to allow Daddy a chance to throw off his suitcase and bail out behind it.

Gosh, were we ever glad to see him! But Daddy had changed. He had become very reserved and silent, a completely different kind of man from the daddy I had known. I noticed he drank a little more than usual. He seemed preoccupied and distant. Daddy had always been a reader, like I've said, but during the whole two week visit he never seemed able to take his nose out of a book long enough to give us any attention. Mother told him, "William, your nose is always in a book. Why can't you talk to us?" And the books he was reading were as strange as he was. They were nothing but page after page of diagrams and numbers. They made absolutely no sense at all to me, yet Daddy was skimming through them of an evening as if they were simple as the *Saturday Evening Post*.

We begged him to tell us what he was doing down in Tennessee, but he kept such a silent air of mystery around it that he might as well have been the cherub guarding the Gates of Eden. We bribed him. "Oh, come on. Tell us what's there, and we'll tell you what's been happening here."

We told him all about the public health nurse who had given Shirley her smallpox vaccination three times in a row and it never would take. Other kids were complaining about theirs not taking either. Well, come to find out, we told him, our public health nurse wasn't a nurse at all. One morning the Louisville paper had a picture of her on the front page standing between two FBI agents. They had broken into the basement of her Williamstown home and found a wireless transmitting system along with several blueprints from a Cincinnati airplane factory. "Get it? She was a German spy!" we told him excitedly.

"That's all the more reason I can't tell you what I'm doing," Daddy said, and calmly returned to his reading.

While Daddy was home I asked him to write something to me in the autograph book I'd received for my birthday. Everybody else had written the usual "Roses are red, violets are blue" stuff, but my daddy wrote: "A quitter never wins, and a winner never quits." He signed it, "Your Daddy," and dated it. It impressed me to no end. It was so different from First comes love, then comes marriage, here comes Skeeter with a baby carriage.

I asked him, "What does it mean, Daddy?"

He just grinned. "You'll know someday."

I had finally gotten a Christmas doll and was told it would be the last 'cause I was a big girl now. Dolls are the only things I collect that I know I am possessive of. I know it's because I was so doll-poor earlier. Now I've got walls full of china dolls, stuffed animals, Madame Alexander dolls, and every other kind of doll you can think of. I love my dolls!

What a contradiction I was—a seventh grader already having her monthly period, yet so attached to this new doll I'd finally gotten that it was hard to get it out of my hands. It had a painted china face, a cloth body dressed in gingham, and china hands and feet. I thought she was the loveliest thing I had ever owned. I called her Suzie.

Aunt Hattie and her kids came to visit us while Daddy was home and my cousin Nancy begged to play with Suzie. Even though I told her no, after they left, my doll turned up missing. Filled with frustration, I tried to decide if Nancy had taken Suzie home with her or just misplaced her somewhere. I looked everywhere I could think of around the house and down the street toward the school.

Daddy was out back plowing our garden, and I heard him call out to me while I searched frantically for Suzie, "Skeeter! Come get your doll."

Oh boy, he's found her, I thought and got that wonderful rush you feel when something you love isn't lost after all. In the back yard Daddy stood holding the reins of Poppy's mule and pointing at the plowshare. There in the freshly furrowed field lay Suzie, all dirty and scarred. I grabbed her up, squeezed her, and brushed her off. Then Daddy said the most hurting thing: "Thought you'd take better care of that doll. I told you it would be your last."

It killed me that he thought I would do that to something I loved, but he wouldn't take any of my excuses. I ran to my bedroom. After a good long cry, I buried the remains of Suzie in a little grave beside Snowball.

We were required to take agriculture in the seventh grade. The teacher's name was Clarence Cobb. He had been discharged early from the service. People around town said he was "shell-shocked." It's so funny. It seems if anybody came out of World War II with anything the least little bit peculiar about them, they were all "shell-shocked." I imagine the war did mess a lot of folks up, but they could have found another word for it. As far as us kids were concerned, Mr. Cobb was just plain crazy.

Clarence Cobb used to teach us this one thing all the time. With so much emphasis on the letter *p*, we thought he was going to spit all the way over his desk. Mr. Cobb would say, "Planning is the parent of progress." Every day we had to recite that after him before class could begin. Behind his back we raised outstretched palms and muttered "Heil Clarence!" underneath our breath.

To get to the agriculture class we had to leave the main schoolhouse and go to a temporary concrete building behind the school. It was so cold in that place. In winter everybody that took agriculture huddled around the steam heat register for a minute to knock the chill off before we went to our desks.

One day it was so cold that I asked Mr. Cobb if I could run back to the schoolhouse and get my little gray coat. When I got back to agriculture, I stood by the register for a minute or two with Nancy Gibson and a few other people.

About two weeks before, Nancy had worn to school some artificial daisy combs in her hair. Mr. Cobb grabbed Nancy during class that day and shook her so hard that those daisy combs went flying across the room. We all agreed, even then, that Mr. Cobb was a little bit strange. We asked Nancy if she had told her daddy about the incident; she said she hadn't because she was afraid her father would come up to school and whip Mr. Cobb. She didn't want to start nothing, she said. We suggested to Nancy that maybe she ought to tell her daddy anyhow. We were right.

I kept on shivering even after a couple of minutes by the radiator. Finally I said, "I'm sorry I'm staying here so long, Mr. Cobb, but I'm freezing."

He said, "What are you complaining about?"

I repeated, "I'm freezing."

"I'll warm you up." Mr. Cobb grinned. And with that, he picked me up under my arms, making my coat, dress, and everything else ride up past my thighs. Then he set me down on the steam-heat radiator. It literally cooked me. I was so shocked, I couldn't even scream. As I tried to fight him to get off, he pushed me even harder down against the hot register. "You warm enough now, girl?"

Finally I got my breath and screamed loud enough to break the window glass. I pressed my shoes against the pig iron tubing of the radiator and leapt away from the heater with every ounce of strength in me. I had to grab Mr. Cobb around the neck. It was the only way I could get myself up and off the register.

"My God, Mr. Cobb." One of the boys shuddered as he pointed to the register. "Skeeter's skin is stuck to the heater." I looked back and saw layers of my skin bubble, then shrivel up on the steam heater. I still hurt even thinking about it.

"Go to your seats!" Mr. Cobb commanded the class. "I don't want another word out of anyone."

Without a word, everybody else raced like mad for their desks. I kept standing. I said, "I've got to go home, Mr. Cobb."

"You take your seat with the others, young lady."

"But, Mr. Cobb," I pleaded, "I've got to go home. I'm hurt bad."

"You take your seat, Mary Frances Penick."

I took my seat, but no matter how hard I tried, I could only sit on the very edge. I whispered across the aisle to Wanda Littrell, "I can't stand it; I'm burning up. I've got to get out of here."

"If you want to go," Wanda said, "I'll go with you. Let's go show Miss Day."

We got up to go to Miss Day's home ec room back in the main building. Mr. Cobb shouted, "Just where the devil do you two think you're going?"

We just kept walking out of the agriculture building to Miss Day's room. She asked her home economics class to step out in the hall. And while I laid across a table, she examined the back of my thighs and my bottom.

"Good Lord, Skeeter, what happened?"

We told her the whole story, and she sent Wanda to get Principal Miller immediately. When Mr. Miller came in the room, Miss Day said, "Skeeter is burned really bad. She needs a doctor. I just can't believe what these girls tell me could be true, but I think you need to have a word with Clarence Cobb right now."

Mr. Miller called Mr. Cobb over to the home ec room. Of all things, the teacher's defense was "I'll have to see it to believe it."

Mr. Miller shook his head. "I think we can take Miss Day's word for it. The girl is burned. I'm afraid, Mr. Cobb, the school board is going to have to meet about this."

Across the eight-party telephone lines that night, Mr. Cobb and I were the talk of the town. "Did ya hear about Will Penick's girl?"

The board of education met hurriedly that afternoon and decided the school would pay my doctor's bills and ask Clarence Cobb to hand in his resignation and leave Grant County as soon as possible.

Everything was done real quick, except for me getting well. I lay on my stomach in bed for weeks before I could return to school. Even then I had to sit on a cushion.

Mother carried my last sister, Suzan, either ten or eleven months. I know it was a long time because we all expected the baby to be walking by the time she got here. Mother was outrageously pregnant, and she kept having to go back and forth to the doctor's. I guess Suzan must have been waiting for Daddy to get home from Oak Ridge before she decided to come out of hiding.

Daddy came home for good in the summer of 1945. This time the train actually stopped in Dry Ridge to let Daddy off, although it was not a scheduled stop. We were all there to meet him.

We were so glad to finally have him back with us. To make things even better, he got a job as the projectionist of the Dry Ridge Theatre, which meant, of course, free movies. I got to watch some of them five or six times before they left town.

Even with Daddy back home and away from Oak Ridge for good, what had been going on down there remained a well-kept secret. No matter how much we badgered him, Daddy kept his mouth shut. All we knew was that the liquor seemed to flow through the streets of Oak Ridge like rainwater. According to Daddy, it was smuggled into the barracks daily by some wheelin'-dealin' cook who was getting rich off the bootlegged whiskey and cigarettes, yet losing his wealth back to the guys every evening in the camp crap games. Daddy had drunk his share of the bootlegger's booze and won none of his money, and we could tell. His habit had increased to an almost nightly need.

One August night Daddy got enough to tell us that he had witnessed the arrests of several German espionage agents who had infiltrated the project, and that he himself had almost had his head blown off while building a radio broadcast system for the camp. He accidentally interrupted the broadcast of KNOX one night, and fifteen minutes later an M.P. was standing at the barracks door pointing an M-1 rifle at his face. The guard laughed when he realized the innocence of Daddy's experiment but went ahead and took the transmitting tube with him just to be on the safe side.

What in the world, I asked myself, *could possibly be that important?* I found out the very next day.

Corine had come over for a slumber party and she listened to Daddy's tale too. I remember she was there because we got to sleep in Mother and Daddy's big bed that night, instead of with the kids. That is, we slept part of the night. A little past midnight Daddy came in and sent Corine to the kid's bedroom. He had Mother with him and

she was bent double in pain. Daddy told me to run up to the McCoys'
house and call Doc Harper.

I walked up the dark lane and woke Mrs. McCoy up. "I need to call
the doctor," I told her, "to come for Mother to have the baby."

"Well, thank goodness," Mrs. McCoy said. She let me do the
calling myself. "How close are the pains?" Doctor Harper yawned.

"I don't know," I told him, "but Daddy said for you to hurry up
'cause he's already chopping wood for the hot water."

Suzan was born that night. Amid screams and periods of long
silence, me, Corine, and the kids waited for word to come from the
bedroom. Boze and Buddy claim we watched through a crack in the
door, but I honestly don't remember doing that. I do remember the
talk of the afterbirth and how Doc Harper had to cut Suzan loose
from Mother's womb. During the nearly year-long pregnancy, Suzan
had grown attached to the uterus, and the delivery left a birthmark at
the point of attachment in the shape of the number seven. Ironically,
Suzan was the seventh and last child my mother and daddy had. We
almost lost Mother that night.

Suzan's real name, by the way, was Leona Ann after both my
grandmothers. I nicknamed her Suzan after my doll, and sometimes
we called her Hoopers. Confused?

The day after Suzan was born, Daddy came racing into the house
with the morning paper, yelling, "Here it is! Here it is! They've used
it!" The big black headlines read, "A-Bomb Falls on Hiroshima."

"I was sworn to secrecy until it was used," he told us. "That's what
I've been doing. I've been helping 'em build that thing."

When school started the following month, we were told to write an
essay entitled "My Biggest Surprise This Summer." Needless to say, I
wrote about my father's well-kept secret and made myself a big fat A
for the A-Bomb.

Many years later Daddy, Shirley, and I went to see the movie *The
China Syndrome*. Throughout the show Daddy kept describing in
detail what was happening inside the nuclear plant, but driving him
back to the farm that evening, I noticed he seemed awfully quiet. So I
asked, "What's the matter, Daddy?"

"It breaks my heart," he said, "to know I was in on that. I've
regretted it more than anything I've ever done in my life."

Daddy didn't want to see any more breeder reactors come into the
Tennessee Valley. For that matter, neither do I. I have faith we can

find some better, safer way for our children and their children to have power. If we don't, I wonder if their children will be able to have children at all.

The war ended, so we had this big parade from Dry Ridge all the way to Williamstown. I was chosen to walk at the very front of the celebration. I had on a crescent moon cardboard crown sprinkled in glitter. It wasn't a queen's crown at all, but you couldn't have proved it by me. I sure thought I was the queen. I had a yellow satin ribbon across my chest with WORLD PEACE stenciled on it. Beneath the sash, I wore a gown cut from an old sheet that made me look like the Statue of Liberty.

We used sheets for everything back then. If you were Julius Caesar in the school play, an angel or wise man at Christmas, or a ghost or witch at Halloween, you always wore a sheet. A sheet miraculously turned you into whatever it was you were supposed to be. My sheet, sash, and crown turned me into Miss World Peace. And did I ever act the part.

I was so proud of myself. People lined the roads, mile after mile, waving, shouting, throwing shreds of cut-up newspaper, holding up current ones to show the headlines: "V-J Day." We had won the war; but you'd have thought I had done it single-handedly, if you'd been there that day. From the crowd along the road, I suddenly heard somebody scream, "Der's Skeeter! Der's Skeeter! Hi, Skeeter, hi!"

I looked over in the ditches of Highway 25, and there was Mother holding my little brother Punkin up to wave at me. I raised my nose and tossed my head right back around to the other side of the road, just as snobbish as I could get.

Punkin kept hollering, "Hi Skeeter! Skeeter, look, it's me." I just kept my nose up, hoping nobody would think I was Skeeter. *I'm Mary Frances*, I guaranteed myself, *the World Peace Queen*.

When I got home from Williamstown that night, Punkin met me at the front door. "I saw you, Skeeter. Why didn't you wave at me?" He was rubbing tears out of his eyes. "You didn't even wave at me."

"I didn't see you," I replied and slipped toward the kitchen for something to eat.

Mother looked across the room at me, "You saw him, Miss High-falutin." I lowered my eyes. "I'd be ashamed of myself too, acting that way to my little brother. He just yelled and waved. He was so proud of you. And you! You wouldn't even wave back at him."

I really felt ashamed of myself. If I could have sunk through the floor to China, I would have. From that day to this, when folks call me Skeeter, it's perfectly all right with me. My days as Mary Frances were over.

When I first decided to audition before the whole school for cheerleader that year, Daddy told me he didn't want me to. It was one of the few times I remember ever disobeying him.

As soon as I heard the results I ran home and left a note on the kitchen table. "I won. I won." Then I got ready to leave on the school bus for the first game. I didn't need any practice. Though I was just an eighth grader, I already knew all the cheers from watching last year's girls.

We were the Dry Ridge Cardinals. Our colors were red and black. I borrowed a black velvet skirt from Aunt Helen, slipped into my red letter sweater, then hopped on the basketball bus bound for Williamstown. I was so thrilled!

Uncle Gerald and my cousin Todd Lawrence played for Dry Ridge, and they both were really good ball players. Despite having a Coke bottle thrown at him from the angry Williamstown stands, Todd went ahead and sank the winning free throws that evening. Everybody in Dry Ridge was celebrating. Daddy didn't say a word about me cheerleading. In fact, he and Mother ended up coming to all the home games. It was one of the most fun times of my life.

My creativity was coming to the surface because I got to make up most of our cheers. You want to hear one? Well, first you have to remember these were still the war years. Instead of the wolf whistle, the soldiers and sailors went "hubba-hubba" when they spotted an attractive female. So here's one of my cheers:

> "Hubba-Hubba-Hubba
> Choo-Choo-Choo
> Take a look at our team
> Woo-Woo-Woo.
> Well you may have the rhythm
> And you may have the jazz
> But you haven't got the team
> That Dry Ridge has.
> *D-D-D-R-Y*
> *R-I-D-G-E.* DRY RIDGE!

I would do a handspring, then come down in a split. I'll have to admit right here and now, I was the best cheerleader I've ever seen. Better than a Dallas Cowgirl, I was a much better cheerleader than I am a singer.

But one night I went up in the air shaking my pom-poms, threw my arms out wide at the end of the cheer, and—*twang*—like a guitar string, my bra busted. My face turned red as our letter sweaters as I hit the floor on the run for the bathroom.

I wouldn't come out of the bathroom. The girls came in after me, but I wouldn't move.

"Nobody knows what happened," they argued. Finally one of them went to get my mother.

"What's the matter with you?" Mother asked as she stormed through the bathroom door. I told her.

"Aw, that ain't nothin'," she said. "Get yourself back out there, before this team loses." I went back out and yelled my cheers, but I did no more handsprings that night.

That evening when we got home, I asked Daddy, "How come you didn't want me trying out for cheerleader?"

"Oh, I just didn't want you to be disappointed, Skeeter. That's all."

I thought about that for a while, then I went to my room and dug out my little autograph book. I sat down on Daddy's lap and pointed to the words he had written there two years before.

"Quitters never win, Daddy. You said it yourself."

He grinned, slapped my behind, and said, "Get to bed, smart aleck."

The Curse of
the Locked Hearse

I know you're sad and lonely
Since your mother went away,
But think of little sister,
You can't leave Lula Fae.
So please don't talk of dyin'
And please try not to cry.
I know you long for Heaven
But you're just too young to die.
Yes, I know you miss your mama
But you're too young to die.
     —"Too Young to Die,"
     Skeeter Davis

Since I was a grade ahead of Elsie Mae Osborne, she was more my friend out of school than in. Besides, she missed classes a lot taking care of her mother, who suffered from tuberculosis.

Elsie Mae and I would meet on the playground in the afternoon to swing the kids. Like me, she lived on the same street as the school, and both of us had babies to tend. I was still mothering Doozer and sometimes Suzan, and Elsie Mae had a little sister Doozer's age named Lula Fae that she looked after because their mother was bedridden. Every few hours Mrs. Osborne needed injections of streptomycin and morphine sulfate. One for the illness, one for the pain. Elsie Mae was the one who had to administer them. Mrs. Osborne had a brass bell she would ring to call Elsie Mae from the playground. When it rang, Elsie Mae would tell me, "Whoops, gotta go. There's Mom." Then she'd tear off toward her house across the street from the playground.

Elsie Mae's house faced the main road of Dry Ridge and was less than a hundred yards from our house. Ours was on the same side as the school, and hers was on the same side as the church. Wisteria hung in clumps from the arched entrance to the Osborne's front-door path. Behind the house was a champion flower garden filled with hybrid tea rosebushes. Quite out of place, their outhouse stood in the middle of that beautiful garden and it had *real* toilet paper. That, in itself, was unheard of because everybody else used either old newspapers or pages from the Sears and Roebuck Catalog.

They were well-off, in other words. Mr. Osborne was either a prosperous farmer or else he had collected an immense amount of insurance. Perhaps both. He had been married three or four times previously, and each wife had, in turn, contracted tuberculosis and died. As a matter of fact, Elsie Mae's mother had been the live-in nurse for Mr. Osborne's last wife. Why Mrs. Osborne wasn't placed in a sanitarium instead of endangering Elsie Mae, I don't know. It seems to me they could have afforded it.

I worried constantly about my friend being so close to her mother, afraid she might possibly catch the disease too. At school each year they gave us the Mantoux test to determine whether we had tuberculosis. It was widespread then, so widespread in fact, that we even made up jokes about it, like people do nowadays about the bomb, cancer, pollution, or anything they fear and have no control over. "T.B. or not T.B., consumption be done about it?" Not much could be done about it back then. Quite often "galloping consumption" took yet another friend to heaven, and everyone feared and hated it.

The year I met Elsie Mae, my first test showed a positive red splotch. And it scared me to death. *I'll be like Elsie Mae's mother,* I thought. *I'll turn into an invalid and die real young.* The second test, however, came back negative. I remember stopping by the church and thanking God on the steps for that little favor.

Usually I kept Lula Fae whenever the bell clanged from the window, signaling Elsie Mae to come give her mother a shot or help her use the bedpan. But one day Elsie asked me, "Come with me, Skeeter."

I went, stood at her mother's door, and watched. *Ooh! How can she do that?* I thought. Without so much as a grimace, Elsie took this long needle and huge syringe and gave her mother the injection. The room smelled of creosote and turpentine. A bag hung from the bedside for Mrs. Osborne to cough up in. Either prolonged use of streptomycin had left Mrs. Osborne deaf, or she was just too weak to speak to me when Elsie Mae introduced us. She limply lifted her left hand to acknowledge that she saw me. Then she seemed to smile faintly.

Elsie Mae took a sponge of cool water from a porcelain basin by the bedside and wiped the sweat from her mother's forehead. Then we quietly closed the door and left the room.

Despite her daughter's constant care and devotion, after I saw her that first and only time, the woman hemorrhaged to death during that night. It tore Elsie Mae's heart to pieces.

I tried my best to console her with the few verses of scripture I'd been able to memorize. I even gave her the cross a boyfriend had given me. I spent the night with her as often as I could throughout her grief, but in doing so, I learned that I didn't like Elsie Mae's father at all.

Elsie's sister Lula Fae had a little pillow she carried for security, like a Linus blanket. And she especially seemed to need it after Mrs. Osborne passed away. Instead of a doll, like most kids, Lula Fae lugged the little pillow around all the time. She loved it. Mr. Osborne, however, was continously grabbing the pillow from Lula Fae whenever he caught her with it.

"Dad, please!" Elsie Mae would say. "Don't do that to her. She ain't got no mama now."

"It's stupid, Elsie. She's too old for that sort of thing. It's worse than thumbsucking."

Lula Fae couldn't have been more than two years old. But one night when I was over there, Mr. Osborne took the beloved pillow from Lula Fae and threw it in the fireplace. Her pillow went up in instant flames. Elsie Mae and I held Lula Fae back from running into the fireplace after it. She screamed her head off. It made me mad as a wet hornet too. But I kept my mouth shut. I figured I'd better stay the night, for Elsie Mae's sake.

In the middle of the night, Elsie Mae shook my shoulder to wake me up. She lit a kerosene lamp and propped her pillow against the headboard. She was all excited about something. I struggled to wake up while she kept pleading, "Oh, Skeeter, you've got to wake up and listen to this. I've had the strangest, most beautiful dream."

I yawned, pulled the covers up around me, and sat up to listen. She told me, "I heard Mother's voice calling me. Then I saw her standing on a staircase waving for me to follow. I told her, 'Mother, I can't leave. Who'll take care of Lula Fae?' Then Mother said to me, just clear as I'm talking to you now, 'She'll be okay. Just come, Elsie Mae.'"

She coughed and hesitated. "So, Skeeter...I started climbing up these beautiful golden stairs and at the very top I saw my mother standing there beside Jesus."

Gooseflesh covered my forearms. I was wide awake then. Elsie squeezed the cross I had given her in the palm of her hand and continued with the dream. "I asked Mother, 'But, what about Dad?' 'He'll take care of himself,' she told me. 'It's you I'm worried about. I don't want you to be sick, Elsie Mae. See, I'm not sick here and neither will you be.'"

I didn't know what to say to Elsie Mae at that moment, but I asked, surprised, "I didn't even know you were sick, Elsie."

"Oh yes, Skeeter, I am," she said. "Sometimes a pain will shoot across my head from one temple to the other; then again, it may start on the other side and go across. I know if they ever come at each other at the same time and meet in the middle, well, it'll kill me."

Even then it seemed absurd to me, but I nodded as if I understood. Before I fell back to sleep, I said, "I don't know what your dream means, Elsie, but I know me and you are both just too young to die. So go on to sleep and don't be scared."

"I ain't scared, Skeeter. Honest." She laughed. "Sometimes I think I want to die."

"Don't be crazy," I told her. All the same, I made sure she was awake the next morning before I left. She had me spooked.

The summer of that year we left Dry Ridge for a little community a few miles south of there called Mason. We all cried when Daddy sold the house next to the school. I had hoped that's where we'd stay, but Daddy wanted to be a farmer so bad. That's why we were moving to Mason. He had rented a tobacco farm there. It meant back to the fields for all of us old enough to work. It meant saying so long to

Corine Ford, Wanda Littrell, Elsie Mae Osborne, and cheerleading. It meant starting high school among mostly strangers.

In Mason we lived on the highway close to the Mason Christian Church and close to the railroad tracks, two things that still mean a lot to me. When the train rolled past our house, the conductor threw candy out the window for us kids. It was a daily ritual to gather by the railroad tracks and wave as the train raced by. Rod McKuen says in one of his poems, "I never met a train I didn't like./I wish I could say the same for people./But I keep on looking." I couldn't put it any better myself.

Not long after we moved to Mason, Mother's sister Helen and her husband, Jeston, came to visit us. Daddy and Uncle Jeston took us kids and dropped us off at the moviehouse in Mason. When they came back to get us, somebody had called the law on 'em. Just as we walked out of the theater, we saw the sheriff's car pull up to the curb. Daddy and Jeston weren't being mean or anything, just funny, hardly drunk at all.

For no apparent reason, this policeman started beating Daddy and Jeston over the head with his billy club. Me and the kids started screaming and squalling. People were gathering around to watch. Another lick from the billy club and I saw my daddy's knees buckle. He collapsed in the street. Daddy pulled himself up with the car door handle, but the cop just knocked him down again. Blood was oozing from his head. The deputy sheriff started kicking him in the side like a dog, yelling, "Try and get up again, you#*%!"

The deputies threw Daddy and my uncle in the back seat of their sedan despite the pleas of us kids, "Please don't do this. That's my Daddy." They hauled 'em down to the city jail. The kids and I walked up the highway back to the house, crying.

We told Mother and Aunt Helen what had happened, and they called Poppy. He came down the next day and bailed them out of jail. When Daddy got back to the house, his head was all bandaged; believe it or not, he was even drunker than he had been on the street the day before. Daddy and Jeston told us that their cellmate just happened to have brought a fifth of bourbon with him.

I told my cousin, Betty Lawrence, to save me a seat the first day of school, but she didn't do it. I ended up having to sit by a girl named Helen Eibeck, whom I did not know. So I was in a new school, sitting by a stranger who was even shyer than me. I was hurt that Betty had not saved me a seat beside her. This was all done as if to be some joke on me.

Helen's attitude, compared with that of the rest of the people in the class, made me feel honored to have her as a deskmate. Later that year, after I had gone out for the cheerleading squad and made it, I was popular enough around school to sit by anyone I wanted to, male or female. Yet I chose to continue sitting with Helen. I became her friend, and she became mine. Years later, I heard that she's one of my most loyal and dedicated fans. A disc jockey in the Louisville area once told me at the Country Music Association convention, "Skeeter, you've really got a fan up around Williamstown. Not a day goes by, Helen Eibeck doesn't call in requesting one of your songs."

I was the first cheerleader at Mason never to miss a game. The Mason Blue Devils didn't take cheerleading near so seriously as the Dry Ridge Cardinals. The girls were always calling in sick or coming up with one excuse or another. I'd never be able to talk the next day, but I made every game at home or away.

We even played Dry Ridge. It felt so strange to be cheering against my cousins and friends that I had been rooting for only a year before. But with the same fervor with which I had yelled for Dry Ridge, I learned to yell for Mason.

Cheerleading made me feel important for the first time in my life. It was my first real accomplishment. I felt Mother and Daddy both were proud of me, because they'd tell me they overheard somebody bragging about how good I was. They came to nearly every game. They looked happy and seemed to be drawing closer to each other.

Mother and Daddy started letting me go roller-skating about that time too. Usually I went with Daddy's sisters Helen and Dorothy and my cousin Mary Lou. Helen was dating N.B. (Napoleon Bonaparte) Neal, and Mary Lou was going with his brother Randall. The Neals also had a brother my age named Jackie.

Their father, Mr. Neal, was a very interesting old man who reminded me of an Indian chief. He had a wisdom beyond his years. For instance, I had a wart on one of my fingers that constantly irritated me when I was milking cows. Folks told me that Mr. Neal could remove warts, so I went to see him. He took my hand in his and began rubbing his finger round 'n' round the wart, saying some sort of words over it. His mouth was moving, but I couldn't tell what the words were, so I asked him, "What are you saying?"

"I can't tell you that." He laughed. "But I'll tell you one thing, little girl. That wart's gonna go away this week and you won't even be able to tell when it leaves your finger."

Sure enough, two or three days later, I was milking cows when it dawned on me, "Hey, my wart's gone." I went running for the house just yelling out the good news. It was completely gone off my finger and there wasn't even a scar where it had been. That has always fascinated me.

They say Mr. Neal was a seventh son. He could take burns out of children and stuff like that. People used to bring their children to him; he'd touch them and the burn, infection, whatever would leave their bodies.

Anyway—back to skating. When I came home from the roller rink one night, Daddy was propped up in bed reading the Sunday paper that came, oddly enough, on Saturday nights. He put the paper down and said, "Alright now, Helen was with N.B. and Mary Lou was with Randall. Who does that mean you were with?"

"Nobody, Daddy." I blushed.

"Now don't tell me you didn't skate with some boy, Skeeter," he teased me.

"I really wasn't *with* anybody."

"Okay. Who else was there?"

"Well," I said, "their brother Jackie was there."

"I bet you skated with him. Did you hold his hand?" Daddy's ribbing embarrassed me. I really had been skating with Jackie and I really had held his hand. I hadn't kissed him though.

Believe it or not, the first boy who ever kissed me was at Sunday school. They played this game where you called out a name, then called out a number. The name and the number then got to go in this dark room together. I guess it was a cute way to tell us that it's okay to kiss, in a holy way!

The first serious kissing I ever did, however, was in the ninth grade classroom there at Mason. Ward Evans, this junior, took me back in the cloakroom one day during lunch break and French-kissed me. Boy, that was strange. I'd always seen my mother and daddy kiss like cartoon characters, you know, just a little smack on the lips and that's all. When Ward kissed me that way, I remember thinking, *Uh, what's he doing that for?*

In those days, being bad, having sex, getting in a "family way" was a shame and disgrace. There were seven of us girls that ran around together in the freshman class. One of those girls told me one day, "It's something else, that out of the seven of us, you and Maxine are the only ones who haven't been with a boy."

"You've been with a boy?"

"Yes," she answered and started to cry, "two boys."

It aroused my curiosity. "Well, where do ya'll go to, you know, do it?"

"To the lumberyard at Williamstown."

I said, "Really?"

"Yeah, but don't do it, Skeeter," she said and broke down right there in front of me. What hurt her was that one of the guys had kissed and told.

"Don't do it, Skeeter. They just run and tell, then laugh behind your back."

I didn't figure I needed to worry about that. Nobody had tried anything. If I'd kissed Ward Evans back like he kissed me that day, I don't know what would have happened. But, thank goodness, I didn't.

Most people at that time didn't have sanitary napkins yet. We used rags. One day after the last bell rang, I was getting ready to board the bus for home when I noticed blood trickling down my leg. I was overflowing from my discharge. There was nothing, absolutely nothing, I could do about it. I ran for a seat on the bus, crossed my legs and stared out the window. I sobbed all the way, knowing that everybody had seen me and knew what was going on. I got off the school bus as fast as I could and ran for the house. It was terrible—the worst possible thing that could happen to a teenager.

When Sissy Spacek was in Nashville filming *Coal Miner's Daughter*, I told her how much I related to the opening scene of *Carrie*, where the girls in the locker room began to taunt Carrie, throwing tampons and Kotex at her for not having knowledge of what was happening when her period started. Sissy and I agreed that if someone were to write a book about women and their periods, it would be both eye-opening and bizarre to find out everything we've been through with those monthly cycles. I think it's wonderful that we now have sex education in schools. There is still much, even in this day and age, that we don't understand about ourselves and our bodies. If the parents don't tell the kids, like mine failed to tell me, then at least they've got a chance to learn it at school—the right way.

It's like grass. A friend of mine said he was going to try marijuana.

I told him to learn everything he could about it first. Education can sure spare us some humiliating experiences caused by some hurtful things. I think to myself, nowadays even, that if I remember that day on the bus, those other kids probably remember it too. I turn red just thinking about it.

I used to be embarrassed when Mother wrote an excuse for me missing school. I'd beg her to write that I was sick, instead of having to stay out to work the tobacco crop. She'd say, "Ain't no use in tellin' 'em you're sick when every other kid is out working tobacco too."

How many times did I hear Mother say, "This is what I get for marrying a farmer," as we stooped over the rows, working the tobacco crop together? But I wasn't thinking, *I'm gonna get married and get away from this place.* No, I was thinking, *I'm going to finish school. I'll get me a diploma and find my own way out.* At that time that was my ambition. I never dreamed of furs, or diamonds, or being a millionaire.

All I knew I wanted at this time in my life was not to be a wife. Every farmer's wife I knew, as well as their kids, were working the fields. I wanted to finish school, because all my relatives were saying, "Well, Skeeter is just the right age. Some boy'll be coming home from the service any day now to grab her up and marry her."

That was my frame of mind when Ronald McGee came home from the service. Besides being good-looking, he was good to me. He bought me presents: a red heart box of candy for Valentine's, a dresser set that I just thought was something grand. *Romantic* is not even the word for the way he talked to me. He told me how he had thought about me the whole time he was in the service, hoping that he'd make it back home alive to see me once again. I darn near melted.

He really courted me. It almost scared my folks to death. I was pretty young, fourteen, and he was older, a soldier. Gramma Penick was saying, "That kid'll get married, but she ain't never gonna want nary a kid 'cause she's done raised so many already."

I was thinking just the opposite, *I want a baby, but I don't want to get married.* I made up my mind to tell Ronald where things stood. On a double date with Mary Lou and Randall, he let me know how much he liked me. We were at the movies watching a war picture. (Movies had taken a turn toward the dramatic.) Ronald couldn't understand when I told him that I didn't want to go out with him anymore. I never really gave him a reason; it was just that I was so stubbornly determined to finish school. I was not ready for a husband and a baby.

Mother was forever warning me about guys getting fresh with me, but none of them ever did. I asked her why the guys never tried anything with me. I was beginning to feel left out. I wanted an opportunity to say no.

Charlie Kinman was a senior the year I was a freshman. He invited me to the senior class party with him. We went with another couple. After the party was when everybody, I guess, headed for the Williamstown lumberyard. But that night, Little Purity herself spoke out: "We ain't going to no lumberyard."

"That's alright with us," the boys agreed, as we headed out a long, deserted dirt road.

I had on a pretty little dress I'd borrowed from the girl who was with the other guy. It had a round, ruffled neck, sort of like the country things you see nowadays. But back then the zippers weren't in the back of dresses. They ran along the side of the dress up under the arm. You loosened the dress just enough to slip it over your head. Some European designs are still like that.

We had decided earlier that I would stay all night with the other girl. That way the boys could just take us to one house. I was in the back seat with Charlie in the other guy's car.

"Okay," the guy up front said to Charlie when we pulled off along the country road, "you call it."

"Heads," Charlie said, and the other boy flipped a quarter. Charlie leaned up over the seat to watch and exclaimed, "Hey, hey, alright. We win."

"Win what?" I didn't know what was going on. "What does that mean?"

"It means we get the car, dummy," Charlie said.

I asked, "Well, what are they gonna do?"

"They have to take a walk."

The other boy and girl got out of the car and headed off down the road toward a wooded area. The moon wasn't near bright enough. As soon as they were out of sight, Charlie started working on the side of my dress, trying to get the zipper down. I pressed my arm against his hand and demanded, "What on earth are you doing?"

"What do you think I'm doing?"

"It seems to me you're trying to get in my dress," I said, biting my lips and pouting.

Charlie was quiet for the longest time; then he asked me so pitiful like, "Well, what did you think all this was about? If we had got tails, then we'd have to take a walk."

"Well, you might as well take that walk too," I said, wiping my eyes, "'cause we ain't gonna do nothing bad, and you better not try anything else."

I knew right then what Mother was talking about. He didn't even hug or kiss me or put his hand on my knee; he went straight for my zipper! As soon as the other couple got back to the car, we went right to my house. I never dated Charlie again.

The first time Mother ever got drunk was while we lived at Mason. It was on a Sunday afternoon, so I know it had to be bootleg. Before that day, she always drank Orange Crush. I remember it as if it were today. When she went out the door with Daddy and Uncle Howard, she looked at me and said, "I'm gonna show your daddy what it's like to put up with a drunk."

The three of them drove off together and in less than two hours they came back. I looked out the window. The kids were all standing around in the front yard with their fingers in their mouths, watching Uncle Howard and Daddy carrying Mother to our door. One had her by the arms, the other by the feet. Her dress had ridden up her legs to where it exposed her panties. I ran out of the house crying and tried to hold her dress down as the men hauled her into the bedroom and dropped her on the bed.

It hurt me to see my mother drunk. I could smell on her that smell I'd always associated with Daddy. All afternoon I kept going into her bedroom to check on her, wondering if she was dying.

Daddy was sober. Uncle Howard was sober. So apparently when they got her wherever it was they went that day, she kept her word to me and right away got drunk. She was going to show Daddy; for many years afterward, she was never able to quit. I used to wish she still drank nothing but Orange Crush.

I was over visiting at Wanda Littrell's house the day Mother came to tell me that Elsie Mae Osborne was dead. I asked the Littrells to run me over to Elsie's house immediately.

The usual crowd of well-meaning mourners stood out in the rose garden smoking. Inside, the table was spread with everything to eat imaginable. Elsie's crippled brother, Buck, her other brother, Junior, Mr. Osborne, and little Lula Fae were all in the parlor receiving guests. In the living room, Elsie Mae's body was laid out for the wake.

She had on a real pretty blue dress that seemed to blend with her pale skin. My little cross hung around her neck. Though I had been to my grandfather's funeral at an early age, I had never seen him dead. Elsie May was the first dead person I'd seen, and she was my age.

Buck limped over to the casket and stood beside me. "Ain't she pretty?" He was crying. "Elsie seen that dress in the store window and wanted it so bad. It was sold when we went to get it for her, but the people who bought it let us have it to bury her in. Folks sure are kind, ain't they, Skeeter?"

I was standing there shivering, shocked, staring at her through my tears. "What happened, Buck?"

"Well, I really don't know. She started complaining about these really strange headaches—" My expression must have changed to fear, because Buck asked, "What's the matter, Skeeter?"

"It's nothing," I said.

Buck went on, "Junior had been teasin' her that she wasn't sick, but I believed her. I's making biscuits in the kitchen this morning, and Elsie Mae came in, then went out to our rose garden. When she came back I said, 'How ya feelin, Sis?' She says to me, 'Oh, Buck, I don't feel good at all. I've been thinkin' about this dream I had.'"

A chill ran from the top of my head down my spine to the heels of my feet when Buck said that. I shook my head, remembering the dream she had had that night, but I didn't say a word. It was too crazy to be real.

"Elsie propped herself against Lula Fae's high chair," Buck continued, "and I just kept making my biscuits. I heard her whisper, 'Oh no! They're gonna meet this time.' Then she just chomped right down on her finger so hard that the blood came." Buck pointed at Elsie's hand to show me he was telling the truth. "Her eyes got wide open, then turned up until all I could see was white." Buck struggled to finish. "Then, Skeeter, she just keeled over in the kitchen floor. I took her to the bed and called Doc, but she's already dead when he got here. Lord God, I wish there was something I could have done."

"Buck, please don't even think like that," I said. "There's nothin' anybody could have done. Your sister wanted her mama, I promise you. So now she's with her!" People have told me that you can't will yourself dead, but I've often thought Elsie Mae Osborne did it. A research center in Lexington asked Mr. Osborne to let them do an autopsy, but he flatly refused. Nobody ever knew the exact cause of her death.

It was a horrible day for a funeral. Rain drizzled and dripped off the roof onto our umbrellas as we watched the pallbearers bring the coffin from her house through the wisteria-covered archway to the hearse. Then, of all things, they couldn't get the door of the hearse to open. It was stuck. The men stood there getting drenched while the white-gloved driver wrestled with the door handle.

An old lady standing behind me gasped, "Oh, my gosh, what a terrible omen."

"What do you mean?" someone standing next to the old woman whispered.

"Why Lord! Ain't you heard? A locked hearse is a sure sign of another death in the family within a year."

Someone in the crowd laughed. *You crazy old witch*.

The door finally released and the pallbearers hurriedly slid Elsie Mae's casket in the back. I waved goodbye and softly cried. I'll never forget the love she had for her mother, her dedication and devotion. Elsie Mae Osborne was a strange but remarkable girl.

I couldn't believe it. What I'd told her, "me and you are just too young to die," kept gnawing at me while I cried. It opened my eyes to a new, frightening reality. You had to be eighteen to join the service, nineteen in Kentucky to be able to vote, and twenty-one to drink, but anyone was old enough to die.

On the anniversary of her death a year later, the curse of the locked hearse worked its fatal, evil charm. Elsie Mae's brother Junior came home after visiting his fiancée. The girl told the police that he had acted fine, that they had a nice date, and he seemed to be in good spirits. They had even made some wedding plans. But that very night, Junior rigged a tube from the exhaust pipe to the window of his car and asphyxiated himself.

Beside his body they found a note and a poem. The note stated that he couldn't handle Elsie's death because of the way he had treated her, teasing her about not being sick when she must have been terribly ill. On the poem, he had written at the top, "If anyone ever decides to sing this, use the tune of 'The Old Lamplighter'."

> She made the days a little brighter
> Wherever she would go.
> My sister Elsie Mae,
> Who died just a year ago.

THE BETTY JACK YEARS

One of a Kind

Where's the Class of '49 from dear old Dixie High?
I wish that we could go back, and you didn't have to die.
You were so special, it just had to be.
But you'll always live here in my memory.
Oh, Betty Jack, I wish you could come back.
Life won't be the same with you gone.
I always sang the harmony;
You always sang the melody.
Do you think I'll ever learn to sing alone?
They said we were rebels, but we had a cause.
We had to sing our songs, and we'd die for that
applause.
You were so special, like one of a kind.
And you'll live forever, right here in my mind.

Oh, Betty Jack, I wish you could come back.
Life is not the same with you gone.
I've learned to sing the melody,
And overdub my harmony—
It was the only way I could go on.
But I've been singing sad songs since you've gone.
                                        —Skeeter Davis

Sweet Sixteen

How many people walked on you
Before they left your side,
Never caring that the river holds
The teardrops that you've cried?
Lonely Bridge standing there,
Lonely just like me,
Maybe you can help me
End my misery.
            —"Lonely Bridge,"
            Skeeter Davis

Covington, Kentucky, is an old riverfront town that stares across the Ohio River at Cincinnati. An imaginary state line is all that separates the two cities. They share the same newspapers, the same smog, and the same devotion to the Cincinnati Reds. Nineteenth-century buildings stand like dominoes along the waterfront streets, and they look to me much taller and more narrow than buildings should. To the eyes of a stranger, Covington would probably appear very quaint and beautiful, because most of the skinny houses perched on the bluffs overlooking the Ohio are painted pastel yellow, green, or blue with nice red shingled roofs. Covington wears a colorful coat indeed, but what I remember most clearly was its dismal hidden heart filled with taverns and gambling houses where my kinfolks mixed with other lost souls looking for some meaning to life beyond their poverty and problems. When I was sweet sixteen, Covington glared at me like the dark gate of hell itself, trying to swallow my daddy. I never wanted to live there.

In 1947, however, my father got a job in Covington as an electrician, wiring the suspension bridge across the Ohio. Since we weren't making it farming, the job offer was too good to refuse. I recall Daddy bringing home a work permit that his wife and oldest child were required to sign before he could get the job. I had mixed emotions about signing my name to that paper. I didn't want to leave Dry Ridge, much less move to a place anywhere near the size of Covington. On the other hand, the little girl in me was proud my daddy would be doing such a dangerous job. Besides, I knew we needed the money desperately.

When I drive across that bridge nowadays, I think, *My daddy hung those lights. They're the prettiest lights in the world.* Yet that same bridge inspired me to write "Lonely Bridge," a song of suicide, while on a road trip a few years back. It's funny how old conflicting feelings intermingle and stay with us.

In June before my junior year in high school, my family and I left our friends in Dry Ridge to move into a two-story house on the outskirts of Covington. The house was owned by Villa Madonna, a Benedictine convent and academy. It sat less than a hundred yards from the Ohio River. It was a nice brick building, freshly painted yellow, with high ceilings, and surrounded by shade trees, a banistered porch, and Easter lilies. Supposedly, slave labor built it before the Civil War. Like every other house we'd lived in, it had an outdoor pump instead of running water. In the back yard stood a privy with double doors and double seats. My brother Punkin spotted the outhouse while we were unloading our furniture and came running back to the front yard to tell us, "Guess what? We're rich. We got two seats. Nobody's gonna have to wait no more."

It was the largest house we had ever lived in, and it would have been large enough for all of us if Uncle Jeston and Aunt Helen hadn't lived upstairs. Jeston claimed Helen's chronic gambling is what drove him to chronic drinking. He was an alcoholic, like my father, and I really disliked the fact that he and Helen were going to be living above us. It literally meant trouble on top of trouble. The nine of us were left with the bottom four rooms. All seven kids were stuffed in the same nine-by-twelve bedroom. Mother and Daddy had a bedroom of their own; we also had a kitchen and a living room. That was it.

Our first day there brightened up, however, when I discovered the house was magical. We had moved into a music box. Fifty feet away, beyond a barbed wire fence, was the transmitting tower of WCKY radio. We could hear disc jockey Wayne Raney selling rose bushes and playing country music right through the walls. Raney also wrote "We Need A Whole Lot More of Jesus," which I later recorded. On any given day, we could place our ears against any one of the door facings and hear WCKY broadcasts. If the weather was just right, the very air of the house filled up with music. The Benedictine Sisters who live there today told me it was one of the greatest little miracles of their lives when they put a pot on the stove to boil and it started singing a Merle Haggard song. Thank goodness, they're all country music fans.

When we lived there in Covington, cornfields circled the house. Sister Augusta and Sister Bernhard Gripshover worked those fields dressed in their full black habits. They worked harder than any ten men would have. Sometimes Buddy, Shirley, Boze, Punkin, Doozie, and I pitched in to help. The Sisters never failed to reward us with berries they had picked or something they had cooked in the convent kitchen. We wore sleeveless shirts or little capped sleeve blouses out in the July sun. It bewildered us how they could possibly bear the heat under those long dark habits. The Sisters were always telling us, "You children should learn to wear more clothes."

Besides the nuns, another hard worker was Uncle Jeston. He was an alcoholic, like I said before, always involved in meetings of Alcoholics Anonymous. Jeston was also a workaholic. He was a junk man as well as a Squirt soft drink dealer. In the space of one month he could go from the highest joy to the deepest despair. Jeston had loads of charm. He would work hard, get the top position a company offered, and have the best of everything. Then he'd go on a drinking binge and three weeks later be picking up junk again.

One day I had the kids out on the banistered porch playing Mother May I when Boze laughed and pointed behind me. "Look, Sis! Uncle Jeston should wear more clothes too."

I looked over my shoulder to see Jeston coming up the long driveway toward the house, dead drunk and stripped naked. He later admitted to having lost all of his clothes, except his hat, in a poker game. The nuns were in the cornfield working as Uncle Jeston staggered by; he politely tipped his hat. Like I said, he was full of charm. It's funny, looking back, but at the time it embarrassed me to death. I wonder what those nuns must have thought of us.

Later on in life, Uncle Jeston and Aunt Helen divorced. Until his death in 1987 Jeston ran the largest junkyard in Phoenix, Arizona. Mother's sister Helen, on the other hand, was found dead one morning in 1969 by some friends. She had overdosed on alcohol and drugs. Whether her death was accidental or suicide was never determined. In 1974 I went to the funeral of their youngest son, Jeff. There was no question about the nature of Jeff's death. He had shot himself in the head with a borrowed gun. Another sad ending for another Vietnam veteran.

Daddy kept working on the bridge, bringing home paychecks like we'd never seen. Things were taking a turn for the better. Then one night I heard Mother calling me, "Skeeter, come here. Get your clothes on and help me."

Daddy was on the porch so drunk he couldn't get in. Mother wanted me to help her drag him. I was pulling one arm and Mother the other, trying to get him up. Daddy kept mumbling over and over, "Punzie, I been rolled. I been rolled."

"I'll make you think you been rolled," Mother said, jerking on Daddy's arm that much harder. I was disgusted with my father. Pulling harder too, I asked, "Mother, what does 'been rolled' mean?"

"It means he ain't got no money. He's done lost his paycheck," she said. "But he wasn't rolled."

Daddy had stopped by the Bridge Cafe after work and spent all the money on booze, or maybe he was rolled by some hooker—who knows? I'm sure he didn't. The curious thing was that I was going to be a junior in high school and I didn't know what a city word like *rolled* meant. There were a lot of new words I would learn that year, but at that moment I was feeling a new emotion as well.

"I hate him," I said under my breath, looking at my father lying there in the floor, more helpless than baby Suzan.

"Don't let me ever hear you say that again," Mother said, staring into my eyes. "That's your daddy and don't you ever forget it. Don't say you hate your daddy."

I thought, *Well, it sure is hard to love him when he's like this*. Not a week later Daddy came in drunk again, and my feelings of anger and disgust, which I called hate, turned to fear.

My sister Suzan was only two years old at the time, but she had already learned a cute way of bringing attention to herself. As I mentioned, she was the seventh child; strangely, she had been born with a birthmark that looked exactly like someone had taken a red ink pen and drawn the number seven on her side. We had made such a big to-do over it that Suzan soon learned it was curious and different. She would raise her little dress up and say in her child's voice, "Yanta see my seben?"

On this particular occasion, Mother was sitting on a stool, smoking a cigarette, flicking ashes toward the fireplace, while Suzan bounced on her knee. Daddy arrived on the scene, demanding, "Punzie, give me a cigarette."

"This is the last one." She smiled. Then crushing the butt against the hearth, she tossed it into the fireplace.

In anger Daddy slung the beer he was drinking toward her, but instead of hitting Mother, the beer splashed across Suzan's face. After that incident, Suzan learned a new phrase to say in her little two-year-old voice: "Daddy threw beer in my face."

It hurt Daddy to have done such a thing, but even that incident was not enough to make him quit drinking. He continued to come in from work after he'd been drinking, acting crazier and crazier each time. Many evenings when he came home, Mother wasn't there. Instinctively I would hide my brothers and sisters in the kitchen stairwell that led to Uncle Jeston and Aunt Helen's rooms above us.

One night Daddy came in and began ransacking the house for a cigarette. Jeston and Helen were gone. Mother was gone. He was ranting and raving 'cause he couldn't find a cigarette anywhere. Fearing for our safety, I gathered all of us in my secret hiding place to wait for Daddy to pass out.

One of the truly nice pieces of furniture my family owned was a beautiful hardwood and glass buffet. After Daddy had rifled through all the drawers of the buffet without finding a single cigarette, and as I peeked out from the stairwell door and watched, he took an axe and proceeded to smash that buffet into a thousand pieces of kindling and splintered glass. I was scared to death. Even though he never, ever hurt one of us kids, I wasn't willing to take any chances when he was drunk and had lost his temper.

When Mother came home, I was still hiding in the staircase with the kids. Although I was so glad to see her after all that had happened, I ran right past her out the door to the side yard, where I crouched down among the lilies of the valley. The blooms gave off the only smell sweet and strong enough to erase the odor of the alcohol. I practically had to lie in the flower bed to erase the smell from my senses.

Once I felt cleansed, I went back in the house. There in the kitchen I found Mother holding a bottle of Clorox bleach up to her mouth. "Mother, what are you doing?" I screamed.

"I'm killing myself."

"You can't do that!" I begged. "Mother, please don't!"

"I'm not living with that man like he is, coming in here like a crazy man." She started turning the Clorox bottle to put it to her lips, but I slapped it from her hands, shattering the glass bottle over the kitchen floor. She had only had time to drink a small amount of the bleach. I patted her on the back, while she coughed and spat, and drew her a dipper of water. Sitting down at the kitchen table together as she drank the water, we both put our heads down on the table and cried.

And so I learned early on to hate the stink of alcohol. I hated it then and I hate it now. I keep thinking in one way that I should be able to deal with it or at least learn to tolerate it. But I just don't like it. The slightest hint of alcohol just makes me sick to my stomach: it triggers the worst of memories. I witnessed my own parents getting so sick from drinking that they vomited all over the floor, all over themselves and each other. And of course, I was the one to clean it up.

I can look back and see how frustrated Daddy must have been. It's easier to deal with these memories now because my father gave up drinking in his later years. The night Suzan graduated from high school, Daddy prayed to God to be delivered from the curse of alcoholism. His prayer was answered: my father never smoked or drank again. When I think how proud of Daddy I was, I remember he'd just say, "Give God the glory." So I do.

I share these memories because they shaped my outlook on life then and now. I also want to show others how God can change people. There is hope in the most hopeless of situations. As Daddy would say, "To God be the glory."

That first summer in Covington, Shirley pulled Punkin out of the pond and saved his life. He almost drowned right there in front of our own house. Despite the fact that the situation could have ended tragically if not for Shirley's heroism, both she and Punkin got spankings: Punkin for nearly drowning and Shirley for letting him go into the pond in the first place. Not a soul bothered to say, "Punkin, we're glad you're okay" or "Shirley, you did a good deed pulling Punkin out." Shirley and Punkin just knew that they would never let something like this happen ever again.

Summer finally ended, signaling that the school year lay ahead. All summer long I had seriously considered running away, back to Dry Ridge. The pressure to run away increased when I learned that I would attend Dixie Heights High School. Dixie was a ritzy new school, ten times the size of the Dry Ridge or Mason high school. I knew I was just a country girl, and the idea of going to a fancy city school scared me more with each day that passed.

Ritzy Dixie

Do you want to hear a hillbilly song?
You can even cry or sing along.
The music may seem sad,
And the words might sound all wrong,
But it's me and my hillbilly song.
                    —"A Hillbilly Song,"
                    Skeeter Davis

Fans have said I never wear the same dress twice on the stage of the Opry. Although that's not actually true, it's not far from it. It takes four walk-in closets, as well as two long clothes racks stored in the garage, to hold my clothing. The fact that I'm a renowned pack rat partially explains why I'm overloaded with outfits, but the answer goes beyond that. I believe I'm still reacting to my experiences at Dixie Heights High School.

Like I thought they would be, the girls at Dixie were nothing but the pure cashmere sweater types. The few cotton dresses I owned stuck out among those sweaters like a wild daisy in the governor's rose garden. Although my dresses were not threadbare and were always washed and ironed, it was obvious to anyone that they were purchased at Penney's and not Shillito's, where the well-heeled shopped.

By the time the first week of school was over, I had managed to run through my entire wardrobe twice. In the lunchroom I ate by myself. I clung to the walls and found a seat near the back of every classroom in hopes of not being noticed. And I wasn't. At times I felt

100

ridiculously obvious; at others, completely invisible. Within the week I lost hope of ever finding a friend in the whole city of Covington, much less there at Dixie Heights.

I had been preregistered for college preparatory courses by the teachers, who realized from my sophomore report card that I had been an A student at Mason. I felt suddenly stupid in this fancy school. After only the second week there, I went to the principal's office to change my program from college prep to general education.

In the lobby of the principal's office I saw a girl for whom I felt sorrier than I did for myself. She was a pretty girl and well dressed, but something had happened to her face. Her hair was singed and her right eyebrow seemed completely burned off. The whole side of her face was red as though it had been scorched. I was not aware of having studied her so long, but she shot me the meanest look and said, "What are you looking at?"

"Nothin'," I said, dropping my eyes toward my textbooks.

"Yeah, you were," she corrected me. "My face." Stomping out of the lobby, she slammed the door behind her. I felt so sorry for her, but I thought, *Why should I? She's just as mean as the rest of these rich kids.*

"Are you Mary Frances Penick?" the school secretary asked. I stuttered, "Yes, but call me Skeeter."

"Okay, Skeeter, the principal will see you now."

I pointed toward the door that had just been slammed by the curious-looking girl and asked, "Who was the girl that just left?"

"That was Betty Jack Davis," she answered.

Betty Jack Davis, I repeated the name in my mind along with a word of caution to myself. *Watch out for that one.*

The principal listened to my request to change courses but he disagreed with me. He said I was to report back to the same classes the following Monday.

On Monday morning the first person I saw when I walked into home economics was Betty Jack. The injury to her face had kept her out the first week of school. I found a seat as far away from her as possible and started looking at a scrapbook from Dry Ridge that I had brought with me, hoping to pass time wallowing in those happy memories of when I was a cheerleader and as rich as the next girl. Waiting for the teacher to arrive, I heard somebody yell across the room, "Hey, B.J., what'd you sing Saturday night at Renfro Valley?"

Half the class gathered around the girl I had seen in the principal's office and felt so sorry for, and she began to sing an Eddy Arnold song:

> I'll hold you in my heart
> 'Til I can hold you in my arms
> Like you've never been held
> before.
> I'll think of you each day
> And then I'll dream the night away
> 'Til you are in my arms once more.

I don't know what came over me. I was so scared of her anyway. Where the harmony came from, the Lord only knows. I had always sung like other girls before, a low alto harmony, but suddenly there came this *high* harmony from my mouth, as if someone else had put it there while I was asleep. The girl stopped singing. Suddenly the room was deathly silent and I heard her ask, "Who's singing that?"

Her voice got closer, and I buried my face deeper into my Dry Ridge scrapbook. She repeated her question. "I said who is singing?"

She was right in front of my desk. I could feel my knees knocking together. I wished the teacher would come in and catch her. She tapped me on the shoulder. "It was you, wasn't it?"

"I'm sorry," I whispered without looking up at her. I wanted to die.

"Sorry!" she mimicked. "Ya'll hear that? She's sorry." Then she laughed and said, "You don't need to be sorry for nothin' like that. It was beautiful."

I blushed from head to toe, shocked by the sudden twist. The whole classroom was listening to what she was telling me. I giggled. It was the first time anyone had even noticed I was there, and now the whole classroom acknowledged my existence. She sat down next to me and asked, "Do you like hillbilly music?"

Before I could answer, the teacher came in. Everyone including Betty Jack scurried to find their desks. Later in the period B.J. passed me a note about another girl in home economics who seemed so stuck-up, you would have thought she'd won the Miss America title two times over. Betty Jack's note read, "What do you think about Ruth Foster?"

I tore a corner from a piece of notebook paper and wrote, "I can't stand Ruth Foster," but then I started thinking, *I ain't going to let her trick me like that; that girl might be Betty Jack's best friend.* I scratched through what I had just written and sent her back a note asking her what she thought of the girl.

A minute or two passed before a note came back across the aisle from Betty Jack. It read: "I can't stand her." The truth was, she was one of the rich girls who sang opera. We thought that she thought she was better than us.

Later B.J. sought my company in the lunchroom and asked me what I was going to be doing after lunch. I shrugged my shoulders. "Wanna sing?" she asked.

We got her Martin guitar from the locker and went outside to sit in the grass and share songs we had learned from the radio. That's how I came to know Betty Jack. I learned that her face had gotten burned after her sister Georgia had left the gas running on the kitchen stove without remembering to tell her. When B.J. tried to light the oven, the flames blew up in her face. She told me she was alone at the time and had to drive herself to the hospital.

As we talked and sang, a crowd gathered around us. We sang until the bell rang for afternoon classes. Every lunch period was the same. It was our meeting time. We'd play and sing country songs out on the school grounds. We developed a following of classmates that liked to hear us sing, but in all honesty, most of the kids were cruel and picked on me a lot about my clothes and country ways. B.J. helped me keep what little self-esteem I had.

For instance, not long after we met, she noticed that I was being ridiculed and shunned for wearing the same clothes to school all the time. So she brought a couple of new dresses to school for me to wear. One was pink, the other aqua, and both of them fit perfectly. Needless to say, I was overjoyed.

The next morning I paraded out of the bedroom wearing the pink one, ready to catch the school bus. Finally I would at least look like I belonged at Dixie Heights. "Hold it, Skeeter." Daddy stopped me at the door. "Where'd you get that dress?"

"A girl at school," I answered.

"You don't need nobody's clothes, Skeeter."

I started crying; my brothers and sisters stared at me. They had all been proud of my new dress too. "But Daddy," I begged, "you just don't understand how hard it is."

"I don't care how hard it is," he said, "you ain't takin' charity. Now march right back in there and change, young lady."

With Betty Jack's two dresses folded neatly in my outstretched arms, I stood in the hallway at school choking back the tears as I told her, "Here's your dresses back. Daddy says we can't take no charity."

I soon learned that B.J. was smarter than a fox on a chicken farm when it came to working around things like false pride. She shrugged and smiled. "Then bring me two of yours, Skeeter. We'll just swap."

"Really?"

"Really," she answered. "Take those back and bring me two you don't want no more."

I took the two dresses home again that evening and bundled up my two for her. The next morning I put on the aqua dress and walked right past Daddy toward the door.

"I thought I told you to take that girl's clothes back, Skeeter," I heard Daddy say. I shivered all the way to my toes.

"Well, she's borrowing two of mine," I shouted back as I lifted the two dresses I was taking to Betty Jack. "We're just swapping clothes, Daddy."

"Well, in that case, it's alright," Daddy said, smiling. "You can do that."

Ain't that something? Just a little different perspective on it and suddenly everything's okay. I took my two old dresses to Betty Jack. I can't ever remember her wearing them, but I sure wore my two new ones.

Her family wasn't really all that rich, but it got to where every time Betty Jack got herself a new dress, she'd buy me one, either just like it or with the same pattern but in a different color.

Slowly that would become our style for our stage clothes. As the days went by, we grew closer and closer. Betty Jack and I were together every day. If we weren't talking, we were singing. At first we didn't have any intention of becoming country stars. We were just practicing for the Dixie Heights High School Follies.

The Follies was an annual Broadway-type variety show. The lady who produced it every year was Adeline Rocke. She did all the choreography, the set designs, and so forth. They had everything on that show from classical pianists to ballet. It was the biggest event of the whole school year. The women in the audience came dressed in furs.

Country music was for the most part sneered at around Dixie Heights, but Mrs. Rocke decided that year that she would let Betty Jack and me be "divertissements." *Divertissements* is a fancy word for the acts that perform during intermission. These acts come out on stage while the audience goes out to the lobby for refreshments and cigarettes.

Waiting backstage for our cue, Betty Jack and I were looking over the program for our names. We were so proud just to get a chance to be part of the Follies. There we were on the program: "Divertisse-ments—Betty Jack Davis and Mary Frances Penick." Betty Jack laughed. "What are they calling us, Skeeter?"

I answered her the best I could, one syllable at a time, "De-ver-ties-mints." Everybody standing around backstage just died laughing. We didn't know what was so funny, but we knew it must be us. I laughed too; then my face turned bright red as I felt sweat trickling down the inside of my arms. My thoughts turned from laughter to insecurity. *Maybe we ain't being laughed with, but laughed at.* I stared at Betty Jack for a second and saw her eyes turn suddenly wet. She was dying inside, just like I was. I grabbed for B.J.'s hand just as the emcee called us onto the stage for our very first public appearance together.

Betty Jack was incredible at making the best of a bad situation. "De-ver-ties-mints!" B.J. yelled to the audience as we reached center stage. A chuckle ran through the crowd. She draped the guitar strap over her shoulder and stepped up to the microphone. "What that means, folks, if you leave now you don't miss nothin'. All we gonna do is sing you some hillbilly music."

And so we sang. The audience did stand up, but it wasn't to go smoke cigarettes; they gave us a standing ovation. We stole the show. The audience loved us and we loved them. We curtsied and left the stage with the audience still applauding. I looked at Betty Jack; she looked at me. I know the smile on my face must have been as big as hers.

We spent the rest of the evening at B.J.'s house, staying up all night to relive the experience again and again. That's the night we started dreaming. Kidding her, I said, "B.J., we're gonna grow up and be stars, make records, and everything."

She replied, "I know. That's why God sent you. I know we're supposed to sing together. If we work hard enough, Skeeter, we can do anything. Ain't nobody can stop us. We're gonna be stars of the Grand Ole Opry."

We practiced continuously. We learned every new song we heard on the radio or on the jukebox down at High's Soda Shop. And we always sang at church. By the next year we got to be in the Follies without even asking. And we weren't "de-ver-ties-mints." We were

the headliners, programmed to sing four songs. Mrs. Rocke built us
the craziest backdrop set you've ever seen. There was an old fireplace
that looked like it came out of a pioneer's cabin, standing right next
to an Indian teepee. Betty Jack pointed at the set and told the
audience, "Well, I've heard of country and western music before, but
never country and indian."

Once again the people loved us and we loved them. Thereafter
other kids were more friendly toward Betty Jack and me. We
performed encore after encore. We'd leave the stage with the
audience still standing, and Mrs. Rocke would signal for the emcee to
call the next act out. The kids backstage protested, "Oh, come on,
Mrs. Rocke, let 'em sing another one. Really, we don't mind."

"It's just not fair," she said to me. "These other kids have spent so
much money. Their parents have paid for all those music lessons, and
we just can't let you girls sing all night."

"You're right, Mrs. Rocke, so right." I nodded in agreement. I was
thinking, *Somebody better get out there, because we don't know but
one more song.*

Finally one brave freshman classical piano player, Wayne Rusk,
drifted on stage. *Da-da-da-da-Dum-da-da-da-Dum-da-dum*, the piano
went, and the applause sank into silence.

That night we outclassed the classics. Now I ain't makin' fun. I
loved classical music then, and I love it now. In fact I had always been
determined to see a ballet before I died. That had been one of my
ambitions, to sit all the way through a ballet. In the eighties, I saw
Swan Lake performed by the New York City Ballet and just loved it—
all the way through.

After our first appearance at the Follies, Betty Jack's mother and a
neighbor lady rewarded us with a trip to the Opry. I was so excited.
My whole family was envious. Like most everyone else that came to
Nashville, we took an early morning tour of the Ryman Auditorium
long before the show ever started. Betty Jack wanted to go up on the
stage. I was scared, but when she asked one of the janitors if we could
step on up, he said it was all right. I went right up there with her.

Betty Jack headed straight for the microphones. "Test, one, two.
Testing," she said, grinning at me from ear to ear.

I whispered from behind a curtain, "Betty Jack, you ain't supposed
to be out there." The janitors were out in the aisles sweeping up when
one little guy cupped his hands around his mouth.

"Go on and sing one. You singers, ain't ya?"

B.J. said, "Yeah, okay." I joined her on stage and we started singing. I don't even remember what, I just remember being scared to death because the people who had come down to get their tickets were wandering in and out.

Somebody from a group of tourists yelled up at us, "Hey, tell the people from West Virginia we got here okay." Then someone else piped in, "Tell everybody in Arkansas hello."

Betty Jack yelled back, "Okay, we'll do it."

I poked her in the ribs. "Betty Jack, don't lie. They ain't gonna see us up here tonight."

"They'll never know the difference," she smiled back. "Them folks will be so excited when they see Hank Williams, they won't miss us."

There we were, out there on the stage singing a song at the Grand Ole Opry for stagehands, janitors, and people wandering in. Our dream, in a way, had already come true.

That night we asked Jim Denny, the stage manager, if we could sing. He laughed at us and said, "Girls, you just can't come in and sing on the Opry." We were so persistent with him that he finally asked us if we would settle for just coming backstage and meeting some of the stars.

"Yes!" we both chimed in unison.

We met Hank Williams that night and Chet Atkins, who later would play such a significant role in our lives. With our little Kodak Brownie, we took a picture of both of them standing together. When we developed the roll, a picture I had taken of B.J. in her flannel gown was double-exposed over the picture of Hank and Chet. Both of us were disappointed that Hank's picture was ruined, but we laughed about it.

It's really funny now. I've been offered over a thousand dollars for that picture. Hank and Chet are standing about two feet apart with Betty Jack in her nightgown floating like a ghost between them. I wouldn't take any amount or anything for it.

Sisters

Oh, the Sisters of Mercy
They are not departed or gone.
They were waiting for me
When I thought, I just can't go on.
And they brought me their comfort
And later they brought me their song.
Oh, I hope you run into them,
You who've been traveling so long.
　　　　　——"Sisters of Mercy,"
　　　　　Leonard Cohen

My family stayed on at Villa Madonna my whole junior year. I would see the nuns every day in their habits and think to myself how beautiful they were. I never even saw a Catholic in Dry Ridge, much less a nun, so the first time I saw one I asked my mother what they were. She said, "They're Sisters."

After that when people asked me what I wanted to be when I grew up, I'd answer, "A Sister," which made no sense at all to anyone, since I was already a sister six times over. I don't know if I ever got anybody to understand that I meant that I wanted to be a nun.

Betty Jack would come out to our house at Villa Madonna to spend the night. My family thought she was some sort of a princess, like somebody from another space and time. B.J. had dark hair and dark eyes that made her look like a foreign queen. My brothers and sisters would stare at her while she ate and tell her how pretty she was.

108

When she woke up in the morning, their little faces would be looking down into hers, as if they expected her to perform some magic trick or something. She wasn't used to being made over so much and she loved it. She loved my family.

It's so strange. Betty Jack never felt pretty or loved. She felt like all the love in her family went to her older sister, Georgia. I hadn't known her more than four days before she invited me over to her house. The first thing she did was dig through some old family portraits. Her mother and daddy had taken hundreds of pictures of Georgia from the time she was born, posed in all kinds of different settings. Truthfully, Georgia had been a beautiful red-headed, curly-haired baby.

"She's pretty," I said. "Where are the pictures of you?"

"Here it is." She handed me a picture of herself as a baby splashing around in an old galvanized washtub.

"Where are the others?"

"There ain't none," she answered.

Occasionally my mother and daddy would let me go over to the Davises' after school to spend the night. B.J. and I would sing and talk until the wee hours of the morning, sharing dreams of singing on the Opry someday.

In those days Betty Jack smoked. Since I never did, I would walk between her and her mother, or her daddy, or her preacher, or whomever she was trying to hide the smell of tobacco from. It's funny how B.J. thought she was fooling everybody.

One day she went down behind a hill near their house to smoke while I stayed at the top of the rise to act as the lookout, peeping out from behind a tree to make sure nobody would catch her. So help me, no sooner had I started my watch than Mrs. Mullins, one of the Davises' neighbors, peeped right back at me so that our eyes locked.

"Hi-i-i, Mrs. Mullins," I said. As soon as she passed, I hollered down the hill, "Hey, that was Mrs. Mullins, B.J. I know she's gonna tell your mother!" Betty Jack just kept on smoking. Sure enough, a few minutes later out of the house comes B.J.'s mother, Ollie Davis, creeping up on us. I couldn't even manage to yell down to Betty Jack; I nearly swallowed my tongue.

Mrs. Davis shouted down the hill at Betty Jack, "Okay. You can come up now, girl. Mrs. Mullins done told me you two was down here fixing to set fire to something." Betty Jack came up the hill, and her mother grabbed her by the arm and looked over at me. "Betty Jack didn't smoke till you came around."

I said, "Really?"

B.J. said, "Mother, she don't smoke."

Except for B.J.'s smoking now and then, we were still two innocent girls. At seventeen, B.J. and I were still virgins, and we aimed to stay that way until we found the men we'd marry. If we both had dates, we double-dated. We were inseparable. If B.J. had a date and I didn't, she'd say, "Come on and go with us, Skeeter."

I know it must have irritated the dickens out of the boys, 'cause one of us was always tagging along. One boy I was dating asked, "Do you always have to do everything with her? All I hear is 'we this' and 'we that.' You'd think you got fleas or somethin'."

That was the last time I saw him. Or should I say, that's the last time he saw me. If the boys couldn't understand us, we dropped them. We were determined to sing together and be together as much as possible.

There were two boys that understood, bless their hearts, Frankie Chaney and Merle Mullins. Frankie loved B.J.; Merle gave me my first wristwatch. (Merle and his wife still send me a Christmas card every year.) Merle and Frankie lived over in the DeCoursey area where Betty Jack lived. Betty Jack's house was right near a railroad switching yard and many were the nights those railroad tracks kept me and B.J. out of trouble. On the nights we went out, we were supposed to be home by eleven. B.J.'s floor squeaked something awful, so if we were late, Mrs. Davis would hear us squeaking across the floor, alerting her that we had violated curfew. Then we'd catch it. Sometimes, though, we'd be lucky. A freight train whistle or the noise of cars coupling in the yards would drown out our squeaking, and we would make it safely to the bedroom.

One night Frankie and Merle took us to Lexington to hear Lester Flatt and Earl Scruggs. It was really unusual to get to do something like that. Driving back from Lexington, B.J. and I were praying the train would come by like it had on other nights we had come home a few minutes late.

It didn't. A little past midnight we were tiptoeing as silently as we could across the squeaking, creaking living room floor toward the stairs when the lights flicked on. There sat Mrs. Davis on the sofa, softly tapping a leather razor strap across her knees.

"Now I know you girls have been up to no good, coming in this late," B.J.'s mother said as she started to swing the strap at Betty Jack's legs. As the razor strap sliced the air, B.J. danced away. But Mrs. Davis grabbed her quicker than a striking snake.

I could hardly stand it. "Oh Lord, Mrs. Davis, don't!" I begged. "We weren't doing nothing bad. Oh please don't whip her!" I cried with my hands over my face but I couldn't shut out Betty Jack's screaming or the sound of the biting strap. "Then whip me too!" I yelled, but Mrs. Davis went on and on and on.

I fell to my knees, pleading, "Don't hit her no more. Don't just whip her."

"I can't whip you," she said, "you're not mine—but this goes for you too." Then she whipped Betty Jack again. I hate telling this but it's an important part of what I feel today. I react when I see violence toward a child or an animal that is being mistreated. It's still hard for me to forgive Ollie Davis for treating Betty Jack so harshly.

Betty Jack didn't say anything that night as we fell asleep. I know she must have been totally humiliated. Sometimes that hurts worse than any whipping.

The next morning when we woke up, I packed up the things I had brought over and said, "B.J., I can't stand this. I ain't gonna stay around here and watch the way your mother treats you. She knows who we're with, where we are, and what we are doing at all times, but she keeps on. I can't stay here anymore 'cause you ain't gonna take any more whippings for me. We are good girls and your mother should know that!"

"Please don't leave, Skeeter," B.J. begged me. "You're the only person who loves me. God sent you to sing with me." I felt so sorry for her; her mother's cruelty, I thought, must be a symptom of a mental problem. Although I found her treatment of Betty Jack unacceptable even then, later I would personally experience just how vicious Mrs. Davis could be. I unpacked my things and sat down to console B.J.

If we loved anything more than our music or each other, it was Jesus. We attended the DeCoursey Baptist Church, where we just adored the preacher, Brother Rader. At the morning service there'd be plenty of kids our age, and we had a real good Sunday school class because our teachers were wonderful ladies, Marie Mullins and Ada Ray Proctor. They were in their late twenties, so we thought of them as old maids. We teased them all the time. "When we get to be country stars, we're gonna bring you back a couple of rich old men from Nashville."

Later when we'd come back from road trips, they'd say, "Well, didn't you bring us no good-looking men?"

I gave my heart to the Lord in that little church. So did Betty Jack. As a matter of fact, we did it the same night. I stepped out into the aisle at the same time she did, and we weren't looking at each other either. Both of us had our eyes closed, praying.

Her mother wouldn't let B.J. be baptized again, though. "If you get baptized over, everybody's going to think you've been doing something bad. You accepted Christ once already when you was twelve. Why do you want to get saved again? Unless you've done somethin' you ain't told me about, there ain't no need in it."

The truth is that we didn't feel saved until that night. We joined the church before to stay out of hell, but that night we felt especially close to the Lord. I was not a child influenced by threats of fire, but a young adult accepting Jesus. As begging Mrs. Davis would do no good, I finally went down to the river and was baptized alone, even though Betty Jack should have been with me.

B.J.'s mother always thought about what other people would think. We were trained to think that way too; always we worried about what people were saying.

One night after we had already finished singing our three songs at church, we were getting restless. Although there was no doubting that we loved the church, Brother Rader, and, of course, the Lord, we were young teenage girls wanting to be with people our own age. We were the only young people at the evening service because the adults wanted us singing for them. We didn't mind that, but when we had finished our part, we were ready to go to meet Frankie and Merle and play guitars and sing. This particular night B.J. asked her daddy if we could walk on home. He consented, so we left and started walking up the road. I said, "Betty Jack, your mother'll get us for this."

She said, "For just walking home? We already sang for them. We did our three songs." A few seconds later we heard a car pull up behind us. Sure enough, it was Mr. and Mrs. Davis.

I said, "Betty Jack, I know she's gonna smack you or something."

"Surely not tonight," B.J. replied. "Besides, I asked Daddy if we could walk on ahead."

"To be on the safe side," I said, "you better let me get in the car first."

My strategy didn't prevent Mrs. Davis from hitting Betty Jack. As soon as B.J. was in the car, Mrs. Davis whacked her across the face and said, "You don't leave church till I tell you that you can. Do you hear me, girl?"

How many times did I hear Betty Jack express her desire for her daddy, Tipp, to stand up to her mama just once? He just sat there and let it all happen. Nobody, but nobody, bucked Ollie Davis.

I left Betty Jack's house that night and went back home to stay with my family. I couldn't take any more. She'd call and beg me to come back over.

"I'm going to run away, Skeeter," she'd threaten. This went on for weeks. "You made my world worth living in! You know I'll never be able to sing without you. I have to have your harmony." I finally gave in. I felt sure she'd run away if I didn't stay. Somehow or another we managed to put up with the punishment Mrs. Davis inflicted. And my staying with the Davises meant one less mouth for Mother and Daddy to feed.

B.J. and I held a special, secret ceremony on a hill near her house that was supposedly an Indian burial mound. If it wasn't, it was good enough to fool me. Wildflowers grew there and several of our friends had found Indian relics nearby.

Betty Jack led me to the top of this mound one day through some evergreen thickets into a clearing. She had a knife. Handing it to me she said, "Okay. You've got to cut your thumb."

"Cut my thumb?" I giggled. "Lord, what's this for?"

She was crying. "The Lord sent you to me. He knew how much I wanted to sing. He knew what I had to do with my life and that I couldn't make it by myself, so, He sent you to me—and we're going to be sisters."

I was thinking, *with a knife*? I laughed but something also made me cry, like rain falling on a sunny day. I asked her, "Oh, I believe that too, B.J., but what's the knife for?"

"The Indian custom is to mix blood, Skeeter. Don't you know that?"

"Yeah, sure," I said, but I didn't really know that in 1947. Although I have since seen movies where such rites are performed, I had to take B.J.'s word for it then. I took the knife, nevertheless, and sliced my thumb. She nicked hers, then we placed our thumbs together to mix the blood and stuck them into each other's mouth.

"Now my blood is in you and your blood is in me," B.J. said, "and we're really sisters. Nothing can ever change that."

On the way down the hill she asked me, "You love me as much as you do Shirley, don't you, Skeeter?"

"Yes."

"You love me as much as Doozer, don't you, Skeeter?"

"Yes."

"You love me as much as Suzan, don't you, Skeeter?"

"Yes."

That's how I really felt. I loved Betty Jack as if she had been one of my own family members. That's why it's been hard for me to say no when people ask, "Are you and Betty Jack real sisters?"

"Yeah, we're real sisters."

The Penick family in the early years. From left: Skeeter, Shirley, Mother and Dean, Boze, Daddy, and Buddy.

Skeeter with friends at Dixie Heights High School. From left: Skeeter, Wanda Rose, and Betty Jack.

Skeeter at ten years of age.

The Davis Sisters:
Betty Jack and Skeeter.

Georgia and Skeeter.

Skeeter Davis with a *very* young Elvis Presley and Georgia Babbitt, Betty Jack's sister.

The Davis Sisters in their final performance, in Wheeling, West Virginia.

Skeeter goes solo.

Skeeter as an RCA recording artist and member of the WSM Grand Ole Opry.

A composite photograph of Grand Ole Opry entertainers, 1960-61.

Ralph Emery and Skeeter in their Brentwood home.

First tour after the divorce—to Tokyo, Japan! Skeeter joined Chet Atkins, Hank Locklin, and the Browns, none of whom were aware of her divorce.

Skeeter receives a top award for "The End of the World" as George Marek and Chet Atkins look on.

RCA artists celebrate Steve Sholes's birthday. Left to right: Stu Phillips, Leona Atkins (Mrs. Chet Atkins), Ed Bruce, Steve Sholes, Jim Ed Brown, Skeeter, Dottie West, George Hamilton IV, and Liz Anderson.

Skeeter with pets Tinker, Taffy, Sonny and Cher, plus Prince, Kim, and Melody.

Skeeter joins London, England, tour with, from the left, Nat Stuckey, Bobby Bare, Connie Smith, and George Hamilton IV.

The Davis Sisters

Straight out of Baptist Sunday school
We cannot play the bars
Playing guitar, singing harmony,
Lord knows, we wanna be stars.
Surely folks won't blame us
For wanting things we never had.
God help and keep us good girls,
We promise we won't be bad.
We just wanna be stars!
                                                    —"Stars,"
                                                    Skeeter Davis

I could never spend more than two or three nights at a time at Betty Jack's house before I'd get homesick for Mother and Daddy and my brothers and sisters. Sometimes B.J. would come home to Villa Madonna with me; sometimes she wouldn't. Although I loved her like I did my real sisters, I never really liked staying away from my family overnight all that much. I wanted to be with her and with them. But as my junior year came to a close, my family decided to move. They were going back to Dry Ridge to try to make it farming again.

The old feelings came back. It was like when I first came to Covington, except in reverse. I didn't want to leave. Once again I was torn. I wanted to be with my family, but I wanted to stay there, finish school, and sing with Betty Jack. When I told her we were moving back to Dry Ridge, B.J. became hysterical.

"Oh, no, you can't go, Skeeter! No! Come live with us." Her begging made my confusion even worse, but I knew what I had to do.

"I've got to move, B.J. My family needs me."

"No, you ain't moving," Betty Jack told me, "'cause I'm going to ask your parents if you can stay with us till you finish Dixie Heights."

"Okay," I laughed, knowing Mother and Daddy would never agree to it.

We drove out to Villa Madonna for her to ask my daddy first. I couldn't believe it. All he said was, "Ask her mother." From Villa Madonna we went to Covington looking for my mother in the bingo parlor where she played the games. Neither B.J. nor I had ever been in a bingo parlor.

"We'll find her," a determined B.J. said. "We know your mother and she knows us. We'll just stand there and look obvious."

We spotted her first. We stood near the door for a while, but Mother wouldn't look up from her bingo cards. It seemed she didn't want to take her mind off the game, so it didn't take her long to decide.

"I don't care. Ask her daddy."

B.J. piped up, "He said he don't mind, if you don't mind."

"Then it's okay with me."

"B-seven," the caller yelled.

"Bingo!"

And so I went to live with the Davises while my family moved to Dry Ridge. Betty Jack was happy and couldn't see how hurt I was. As much as I loved her, I remember feeling disappointed and somewhat rejected that my parents let me go so easily. I thought at least they should have considered it longer or put up some kind of a fuss to keep me with them.

There ain't much to yodeling. *Yo'dol lady, yo'dol lady, your ol' lady too…* you know. Just a little hollering and you can do it. Especially if it's harmony, you can fake it.

Whoever yodeled or tap-danced always won the Le Sourdsville Lake talent contest. I can remember so vividly the little tap dancers with their mothers pushing them out onstage. There would be Betty Jack and me standing right in the middle of all these kids, trying to compete to win ourselves a radio.

Harris Rosedale ran the contest. He'd tell us, "Ya'll are definitely the best, girls, but it's hard to take away from these little kids; they're so cute and try so hard."

We'd still get out there and try to win every weekend, competing with some six-year-old in an Uncle Sam costume doing the military tap. The kid would win, which never made sense to us. Later on we found out that Mr. Rosedale ran the tap dancing school. We drew the crowd so that he could show off his tap dancers. I'm learning about all these scams as I go through life, and when I discover one it just tickles me to death.

Betty Jack and I couldn't stand yodeling, but we couldn't stand continuing to lose to those little tykes either. We knew if we yodeled that they'd have to award us the prize. There just would be no way out of it. We finally decided to go against our good taste for one of those radios. So we sang "Cowboy's Sweetheart" and yodeled the fire out of it.

As we planned, the judges had to give us the radio because the crowd went absolutely crazy; it was a ridiculous victory because, like I said, there ain't nothin' to yodeling.

But more important than winning the radio was the other prize that went along with winning the Le Sourdsville Lake contest. This prize was what we were really after—a guest appearance on *Midday Merry-Go-Round,* a WCPO television show sponsored by Mr. Rosedale.

Television was new in 1947 and not many people had their own sets. Most of our friends had to find somebody with a TV in order to see us. When we showed up at the studio for our guest appearance, Harris Rosedale asked, "Okay, girls, what'd you say those names were again?"

"Skeeter."

"Betty Jack."

"Yeah, I remember that," he said. "I mean your last names."

"Penick."

"Spell that."

"*P-e-n-i-c-k.*"

"Naw, that won't do. What's yours, Betty Jack?"

"Davis. D-a—"

"We'll go with Davis," he interrupted her. "How does the Davis Sisters sound until we find something better?"

With no forethought on my part, I had suddenly become Skeeter Davis. The name would stick with me for good. The mail-in response to our performance caused the station to ask us back again and again, until finally we had ourselves a regular spot on the *Midday Merry-Go-Round.*

Since the show was at noon, we had to leave school every day just before lunch, then come back for afternoon classes. The station paid us fourteen dollars a week. Sometimes we did commercials for department stores and the sponsor would pay us in merchandise. For example:

> If it's savings you are after,
> Ben's is packed from floor to rafter.
> Ceiling's high, the price is low.
> Big Ben's is the place to go.

Our reward was to go to Big Ben's Bargain Store and pick out whatever we wanted. I was looking through the dress racks when B.J. called to me from the cash register, "Hey, Skeeter, I done found what we want."

She had a pile of children's clothes on the counter: blue jeans, T-shirts, and little dresses. I said, "B.J., you're crazy. Why would we need that stuff?"

"We don't," she said, "but your brothers and sisters do."

The Davises had a television set. Betty Jack's grandfather, Pappy, had come to live with them after his leg had been amputated and he could no longer take care of himself. He and Betty Jack's grandmother sat in front of the TV all day, every day, and argued. Television was a mystery beyond belief to the old man. I've seen children who understand it the same way he did. Pappy thought not only could he see us on television, but that we could see him as well. Betty Jack just fed his delusion.

"Hey there, Pappy, we see you sitting there in your wheelchair. Hope you enjoy the show."

Betty Jack's grandmother would laugh at her husband, "They're just a-foolin' you. Them girls can't see you."

Pappy argued with her until he'd literally get blue in the face. As soon as we got home from school, he'd bring us into the argument. "Ya'll girls can see me, can't you?"

"We sure can, Pappy. Didn't you see us waving at you?"

Like most teenagers, Betty Jack and I had a place we used as a hangout. It was just a little hamburger joint called High's Soda Shop, run by Mr. and Mrs. Lloyd High. They considered all of us their "kids." We'd go out on dates and head for High's. It was the place to be on a Saturday night. B.J. and I'd take our guitar and fill the place. Sometimes when he missed us, Mr. High would call the house and say, "Why don't you girls bring your guitar and come on down tonight? Let's get this place jumping."

They didn't pay us, but sometimes we'd get a quarter for playing a certain song. Quarters! Betty Jack and I saved quarters. We got quarters from tips, quarters from passing the hat, quarters from the dates who sent us to the jukebox with seventy-five cents. We'd put one of the quarters in the jukebox, knowing our dates would never know that the jukebox didn't stop until somebody unplugged it, and keep the other two.

Those quarters added up. Betty Jack and I bought a brand new automobile in 1953 from the quarters we had saved over the course of four years.

In addition to working at WCPO, playing square dances on the hill, and hanging out at High's, we had regular jobs as waitresses at Mill's Cafeteria across the river in Cincinnati. We got our share of quarters there too. There was never a dull moment. Add church and school to all of that, and you'll realize we never had a spare moment. We didn't have time to get in trouble, but one night we almost did.

We were in High's, of course, and everybody was ranting and raving about this country band they'd heard at a beer joint called the Chicken Roost. All the kids were begging us, "Come on ya'll, go with us."

We said, "Lord a' mercy, we can't go out there. If they found out at church we's at the Chicken Roost, they'd kill us both."

"It's a good band," they said. "Sorry ya'll have to miss it."

This kept up several nights running. We finally decided to go out there and hear this band everybody was talking about. We loaded up in a car and went to the Chicken Roost. Mr. High called it the Turkey Foot. "Ya'll have fun out there at the Turkey Foot, ya hear?"

The band was just as good as everyone had said, and our friends were urging us to get up and sing. "We can't do that," we said. "We don't want nobody to know we're here. We'll really get in trouble."

Suddenly two policemen came in the front door and asked the owner, "You got anybody here under twenty-one?"

Kids scattered everywhere. We all but busted the back door down. B.J. and I lay on the ground in the wet dew out behind the beer joint, praying, "Oh Lord, please don't let 'em find us. We'll never do this again."

We hid in the outhouse for over an hour afterward, wondering, *Did they go?* Finally everything seemed quiet and we got in the car and drove back to High's.

Mr. High was standing there whistling, polishing glasses with a rag. He looked at us and grinned. "Heard ya'll was doing the Turkey Foot out there a while ago." Then we realized he had set the whole thing up. But we'd learned our lesson and we stayed out of honky-tonks for good.

Baptists are supposed to be teetotalers. Betty Jack and I were. I've never had a drink in my life. We vowed to each other that we wouldn't play in nightclubs.

We did play one place, however, that was almost a nightclub. We decided we could play Joe and Eleanor's because they called the place a supper club instead of a nightclub. We were only fooling ourselves, trying to rationalize our way around our convictions. We loved Joe and Eleanor. They were big fans of ours and kept wanting to hire us. Finally we agreed.

If you'd walked in on us playing that supper club, you'd have sworn you were at a prayer meeting. We would sing a song, then I'd preach; sing another song, and Betty Jack would preach. The crowds got larger and larger, but after only a few nights, Joe came up to us and said, "I'm sorry, but I'm going to have to let you girls go."

B.J. said, "Ain't we drawing you a good crowd?"

"Too good," Joe answered. "I'm having the largest crowds I've ever had, but I'm losing money. I love ya'll, but you've just about converted me out of the business. Won't nobody drink anything."

So Joe let us go. The situation didn't change our feelings for him and Eleanor one bit. We continued to drop by to see them whenever we had a chance.

One night Betty Jack said, "Wow, I just had the most awful pains."

"Oh yeah?"

"Yeah, it's strange," she said. "One started on one side of my head and another started on the other, and they just crossed right in the middle."

"Oh, Betty Jack, don't ever do that again."

"What do you mean?" She laughed.

"Just don't ever do that again."

"Don't ever do what?"

"Oh, B.J.," I said, "you need to tell me exactly what it did."

"Well," she started telling me, befuddled, "just this old pain started in my temple and it just went right up and, oh well...They didn't really cross, Skeeter. They just felt like they were going to."

Scared serious, I said to her, "Well, if they were to cross...," but I couldn't finish. I knew what I was thinking, but I couldn't share it with her. I didn't want her to die like Elsie Mae.

"If they ever cross, then what, Skeeter?"

"Oh, it's nothin', B.J.," I said. "Don't even worry about it."

Georgia and B.J. would argue over who was going to wear a certain dress, and B.J. would always lose. Between me and B.J., however, there was never any competitiveness. Sometimes we'd go to the YMCA dances on Saturday night and do the jitterbug. If she was participating in the dance contest, I dropped out. If it was my turn, she dropped out.

Because of *Midday Merry-Go-Round*, everybody recognized us on sight as the Davis Sisters. She was dark and I was fair; I wore black and she wore white. It wasn't a gimmick we were trying, it was just us. We'd try to convince the guys at the dances that we weren't really sisters, but they wouldn't believe us. We'd sing pop songs at those dances backed by a pop band. They'd tell us, "Ya'll can't sing that good a harmony and not be sisters. Ya'll are so good, we can't see why in the world you would want to sing hillbilly songs."

We'd stick up for Hank Williams and Eddy Arnold. They'd say, "Oh, Eddy Arnold ain't country. We saw him on *The Perry Como Show* the other night."

As I said, there was never the slightest hint of competitiveness between B.J. and me, even over boys. If we ended up liking the same boy, one of us backed off. There was never any crowding—maybe some tears, but never a struggle.

Both of us fell in love with Bob Sinex, the steel guitar player on our TV show. He was the first really accomplished musician we'd ever met; he was Nashville quality. Bob Sinex had been around. Boy! Did he ever have a way with words. He'd tell me something about my pretty eyes and have me floating all day. You've got to remember, we girls were both seventeen going on twelve. *Oh! He thinks my eyes are pretty.*

Betty Jack would ask me, "What'd Bob tell you today?"

I'd tell her, then ask, "What'd he tell you?"

"He told me not to believe anything you told me."

He had us going. It wasn't long before both of us went to a movie with him. Bob sat between the two of us. Midway through the picture, he put his arm around Betty Jack. My poor little heart broke a little right there.

He chose her over me, but my love for B.J. overcame my initial shock and pangs of rejection. I was able to say to myself, I love him for loving her. It wasn't a one-way street either. She fell in love with Bob too. It was the first time I'd seen her have a relationship that meant more to her than just a way for us to get to a country show. I remember thinking, *Uh-oh, we ain't gonna sing no more.*

Suddenly Bob Sinex became more important than our singing. B.J. started going out with him and leaving me home. That had never happened before. We had always double-dated. Then one day, the dates with Bob stopped and her interest in our careers and dreams renewed. I let things be and didn't ask questions; then one night a car pulled us off the side of the road. It was Bob Sinex. He wanted B.J. to run off with him and get married, right then and there.

"I can't do that," she said. "I want to sing with Skeeter. That's what God wants us to do. That is our calling."

I graduated from Dixie Heights a year ahead of B.J., but since we had the TV show, I now asked my parents to let me live with the Davises until B.J. graduated. When she finished school, I moved home to Dry Ridge to live with my family on the farm, like I promised I would.

It was mid-summer. I was helping to set out the tobacco and tend the crop. The beating sun burned my neck as I bent down between the rows of tobacco plants. It was hard, dirty work. Almost immediately I began to resent leaving Covington. I wrote in my diary, "I guess doing this and getting married someday is what my life is going to be about. I thought my life would be special at one time, but I guess I was wrong. I've had my time in the limelight. I'm sure glad I got the chance to meet B.J. and sing with her."

One day I saw a cloud of dust coming down the road, trailing behind what looked like Betty Jack's car. It was her. She wheeled into the yard and almost hit our house because her car didn't have good brakes. I was so embarrassed when I realized the guy in the car with her was Roland Palmer, a boy I liked and had been dating. Tobacco worms were stuck to my jeans and my hair was tied up in a bandana. My hands were filthy. I heard her yell at one of my brothers, "Where's Skeeter?"

He pointed out in the field toward me and she threw up her hand. I waved back as B.J. ran up the rows, swinging a pail of water and a dipper, singing just like Bill Monroe.

Hey little water boy,
Bring that bucket here, here, here.
Do you need a mule skinner?

"I could just kill you," I said, looking over her shoulder at Roland, a good fifty yards behind her, and raising my eyebrows. "Look at me, and here you come bringing Roland out here."

"Wash up," she said, handing me the pail. I poured water on my arms, my hands and face, then took a long drink while Betty Jack asked me, "How would you like to move to Detroit?"

I almost choked. "What'd you say?"

Roland joined us. Betty Jack repeated, "How'd you like to move to Detroit, Michigan?"

I thought she'd gone crazy until she explained that somebody connected with WJR Radio in Detroit had seen us on WCPO. The producers of a very popular show called *The Barnyard Frolics* wanted us to join them. Casey Clark and Barefoot Brownie Reynolds, two of the stars, had traveled down to Covington to try to talk us into coming to Detroit. The program would give us almost nationwide coverage.

"Your mother don't mind?"

"She did at first," B.J. answered. "Then Mr. Clark told her that me and you would be living with a woman preacher and we'd only be a block or so from where he and Mary live. They'd look after us."

We both agreed this was the break we'd been looking for. Mother and Daddy said okay, so I packed my things once again. The day before we left for Detroit, we drove over to say goodbye to Joe and Eleanor, the couple who ran the supper club where we got fired.

Joe had a strange look on his face. He said, "I love you girls and hate to see you leave town. I want you to be careful. Promise me that you'll be careful."

We both said we would and laughed, saying, "You know how we are, always careful."

He didn't smile. "No, I'm serious. I had the strangest dream about you two last night."

I said, "You dreamed you had to fire us again, huh?"

"No, Skeeter. I dreamed you had a terrible automobile accident. Both of you were dying," he went on, "and I pulled one of you out, but I couldn't get the other one."

Betty Jack butted in, "Well, if you saved either one of us, I bet it was Skeeter. You always loved her best." We both laughed.

His wife Eleanor agreed. "That's what I told him. I bet it was Skeeter."

We drove to Detroit the next day, very carefully.

His Master's Voice

The rock-a-bye boogie is the latest way
To rock your baby to sleep
Rock-a-bye boogie is guaranteed to put your baby to sleep
But it won't mean a thing unless you sing
the rock-a-bye boogie with a beat
—"Rock-A-Bye Boogie,"
Will Carson

We thought it was really something to receive the offer from WJR, young as we were. But we were scared to death to be moving off by ourselves to Detroit to perform on a fifty-thousand-watt station. *The Barnyard Frolics* was held in the United Dairy Workers Hall. It was a live square dance and singing broadcast. We sang, and I called the square dance. Besides the *Frolics*, we did road shows all around Michigan and even up into Canada. It was a thrilling episode in our early careers. During the days B.J. and I worked in a chili stand as singing waitresses, except we weren't supposed to be singing. We'd sing when the boss left, and customers would leave us quarters.

We lived on chili and Dad's root beer in an attic apartment above Mr. and Mrs. Kemsley. I've never known a nicer or stranger lady. If we had a hole in a sock that she knew about, she mended it. She sewed patches on our blue jeans. We were bohemians, I see looking back, two hillbilly hippies, but we were nowhere near as strange as Mrs. Kemsley. She was a preacher like Casey Clark said she was, but we could never figure out what kind. She intrigued us.

One day when we were taking out the garbage for her, we saw all

125

these books she was throwing away. I read one article to B.J. while she set fire to the trash. It was about this kid who would communicate with his dead grandfather every time his mother locked him in the closet for misbehaving. This book made us even more curious about Mrs. Kemsley. She had enchanted us.

One day we were down in her part of the house socializing when Betty Jack noticed a very pretty vase on the mantel. She walked over to the fireplace and was fingering around with it, saying, "Mrs. Kemsley, this sure is a pretty vase you got here."

Mrs. Kemsley said, "Why, thank you, Betty Jack. That contains the ashes of my late husband."

B.J. released her grasp on the vase. Catching it in midair and delicately steadying it back onto the mantel, she looked at me with her eyebrows raised. Mrs. Kemsley left for the kitchen to make hot chocolate for us, and I laughed. "You just had to bring up the vase, didn't you? Reckon what she's got in them other three vases?"

The week we took out the garbage for her and found the book, Mr. and Mrs. Kemsley had gone to some kind of convention. God only knows what kind of convention it was. We know a lot of traffic came and went from her house. Someone would come for two hours, three hours, and as they left someone else would pull in. We just couldn't stand not knowing what was going on, so we decided to take advantage of her being gone to investigate.

We walked around downstairs for over thirty minutes, looking in drawers, behind closet doors, and so on, searching for clues. Nothing. Finally we sat down at the living room table to rest. B.J. put her face in her open palms and pressed her elbows down on the table. *Whamm!* A door flew open and a golden trumpet swung out of it, playing a melody that made our skin crawl. I thought Gabriel had come for us. B.J. and I almost killed each other trying to see who'd get out the front door the fastest.

Mr. Kemsley always appeared to us to be the picture of health. One day he got sick; three days later he was dead. After another two days, his ashes joined those on the mantel. I guess Mrs. Kemsley preferred talking to her husbands long distance.

B.J. wanted to move. I said, "No, we're safe as long as we don't go down there. We'll just stay up here and be nice little girls."

"Hank Williams is dead!" I yelled through the bathroom door.

"What? I can't hear you," B.J. yelled back above the noise of the running water.

I barged in on her. "Hank Williams is dead. I just heard it on the radio." She didn't say anything. "Hank Williams is dead," I said again and then put my hands together and cried.

"No, Skeeter, no...Bring the radio in here. I don't believe you."

"But they've already said it. He's dead."

We both sat in the bathroom crying as we listened to the radio. We loved him so. Betty Jack just sat there in the bathtub. She wouldn't budge for over an hour. She gazed off into space, looking at nothing, and we both started talking about death for the first time.

She brought it up first. "I just hope if something like this happens to us, that we'll be together. 'Cause we'll take care of each other, won't we? I'll take care of you and you'll take care of me."

"For sure, B.J.," I said, "but it won't happen."

"What if it does, Skeeter? What if it does?"

"Then we'll do like you said. I'll take care of you and you'll take care of me."

Norman J. O'Neil, who ran *The Barnyard Frolics*, loaned us money so that we could make demonstration records of our songs at a studio in Detroit called Fortune Records, owned by Dorothy S. Brown. We also recorded two songs she had written called "Heartbreak Ahead" and "Jealous Love" as a favor to her. (Fortune 45-175A and 45-170A, respectively). She told us they were merely demos to help her sell the songs to other artists. In the weeks ahead we would hear ourselves singing "Jealous Love" on the local radio station. We were so infatuated with having a record programmed on the air and so ignorant of business that we let it slide by and never protested what Fortune Records was doing.

During those sessions at Fortune, we recorded "Kaw-Liga" by Hank Williams and a song B.J. and I had written (later to be on RCA) called "Sorrow and Pain." Fortune Records has marketed those four recordings for the last twenty-five years; we never received a cent from them.

Our little trip to Fortune Records had its rewards, though. At the session we were backed up by a fiddler named Curly Cline. He and his brother, Ezra, were members of a really great bluegrass group called the Lonesome Pine Fiddlers that recorded for RCA Victor. Curly talked to B.J. and me about RCA and how great an A&R man Steve Sholes was. (A&R men and women are responsible for signing acts to labels.) I wrote Mr. Sholes's name and his New York address down on a piece of scratch paper and put it in my purse.

In a month or two we had made enough money from our road shows, plus working in the chili stand, to repay Mr. O'Neil and buy two airplane tickets to New York City to see Mr. Sholes. We left Detroit for New York early one morning in the spring of 1953 with a copy of the demo tape from Fortune. We wanted to record for RCA because we thought it was the top label. I guess both of us loved that little dog listening to his master's voice.

Looking back, I see how country-honest-ignorant B.J. and I were. When we sat down in our seats on the plane, I stopped one of the stewardesses and asked, "Will you be our waitress?"

"Stewardess," she corrected and frowned.

"Well, where's our parachutes?"

She must have thought I was being a smart aleck, because she didn't even answer; she just acted huffy, fluffing up a pillow she was handing to a man across the aisle. She walked rather hastily away from us toward the first-class section. B.J. and I looked under our seats and in the overhead luggage racks for the parachutes. Finally we decided they must hand them out when the plane's going down. It took quite a few flights before I realized that passengers don't get parachutes.

I read Loretta Lynn's book, *Coal Miner's Daughter*, and have heard some other stories about her, and I think to myself, *Lord, Loretta Lynn couldn't have been that dumb*. But I guess she could have been, because we certainly were.

We landed in New York and went directly to RCA with our guitar and tapes. When we entered, people filled every chair in the lobby of Steve Sholes's office. B.J. strutted up to the receptionist and said, "We'd like to see Steve Sholes."

"Names, please?" the receptionist asked.

"We're the Davis Sisters, Betty Jack and Skeeter."

"I don't seem to find your names here. Do you have an appointment?"

"An appointment?" Needing an appointment had never crossed our minds. "Do all these people have appointments?"

The receptionist nodded and grinned.

"Well, we'd like to make one for today, please."

"I'm sorry, we're booked solid for the rest of the week, girls."

"But we've come all the way from Detroit."

"I'm sorry."

I said, "Come on, B.J., I saw a sign down the street that said Decca."

At Decca we had no problem seeing an A&R man named Eddie Kissack. I see what happened that day as part of God's plan. Eddie Kissack was sold on us; he loved our music and harmony. "You're just too good to wait," he kept saying, "too good to wait." We didn't know what he meant, but it sure sounded good. "You girls need to be recording right now, and there's no way I can sign you. My boss, Paul Cohen, is in the Caribbean on vacation, but I'll tell you what. There's a man here in town I want you to see. He's the best in the business. His name is Steve Sholes and he works at RCA."

"We done been there," I interrupted him, "and he won't listen to us. Says we need an appointment."

"Well, you go back over there and tell him Eddie Kissack sent you. He'll listen to you." Decca fired Eddie Kissack for that little mistake he made that day. However, when Decca fired him, RCA hired him.

We walked back to RCA. It was late in the afternoon. A few people were still sitting in the lobby waiting to be auditioned. Finally no one was left but us and a man. He went in and came out. Putting on his overcoat at the door, he turned around and asked us, "What do you girls do?"

B.J. answered for us, "We play guitar and sing."

"Good luck." He laughed. "There's a saying somewhere that the first shall be last and the last shall be the first."

"It's in the Bible," I said. He smiled, winked, and walked out the door.

The receptionist was disgustedly putting things in her purse as she watched the clock. "Well, you girls know you really don't have an appointment, but if somebody from Decca sent you over here, I'll see what Steve wants to do."

We could see a man coming down the hall and overheard the receptionist point at us and whisper, "Steve, those hillbilly girls I told you about are back."

"Well, you are certainly persistent young ladies," Steve Sholes said, peering at B.J. over his horn-rimmed glasses. We stood there in the hall with him as he continued, "What makes you girls think you're so good? I've got a girl duet on this label already, and we can't give their records away."

We had heard the duet he was talking about on the radio. B.J. said, "That's because they're really not very good." He looked at us over the rims of his glasses with piercing eyes. If me and B.J. hadn't talked each other into having nerves of steel that day, I swear his eyes would have burned a hole in my face. I imagine he must have thought we had our nerve to come in his office and tell him that an act he had signed to RCA himself stunk. He sighed, tapped his fingers on his paper, and shook his head, as if to say, *Incredible.*

"It's really a great song they do," B.J. said, "them Beaver Valley Sweethearts. 'How's the World Treating You' is a hit, but they'll never make it one."

He looked at B.J. funny and said, "You both really don't like my duet, do you?"

"Nope," we said together, "we don't sing like them at all."

"Well, how do you sing then?"

"Better," B.J. said in total honesty.

He looked at her and said, "Better?"

"Well, what she means," I tried to clarify, "is we don't sing their kind of harmony." I looked at B.J. with a look that was supposed to say, *Don't push so far that we make him real mad.* I went on, "I sing harmony different than they do. They sing the melody and low harmony. I sing high harmony." (That's all I knew to call what I did at that time.)

B.J. reached for her guitar to show him, but Steve held out his hand and shook it to stop her. "Honestly, I wouldn't know what you're doing, if my judgment was as bad as you say about the Sweethearts." Then he smiled for the first time and said, "I'll tell you what, do you girls ever go to Nashville, Tennessee?"

"Yeah, we go there all the time. We love the Grand Ole Opry. Go every chance we can get," B.J. lied.

I thought to myself, *We've been one time*, but my mouth was saying, "Yeah, we're down there a lot."

"Fine," Steve Sholes said. "If you go all the time, then it won't be putting you girls out any to meet me there in a couple of weeks. I'll be there recording a couple of artists and I'll listen to you then."

"You're not going to listen to us now?" B.J. demanded. I nudged her.

"I don't have time to listen to you now."

"Okay. We'll be there," B.J. said.

I repeated, "Yeah, we'll be there. What do you want us to do, call you in a couple of weeks?"

"No," Steve said. He handed us the oldest line in the trade. "Don't call us, we'll call you."

Back in Detroit, we told Mrs. Kemsley about the call we expected, and her excitement for us helped overcome our fear of her. Every time the phone rang, she yelled up the stairs, "Hey, girls, the phone's ringing."

B.J. and I would jump up and down. "That's them! It's just gotta be them this time!"

But it wouldn't be them. Finally I quit running downstairs with Betty Jack; the disappointment was getting to be too much for me. It was already several weeks past the time Steve Sholes had promised he would call us.

"Skeeter, it's *them!*" Betty Jack came screaming up the stairs.

"Oh," I said sarcastically, "tell me all about it."

She said, "No, Skeeter, it's no joke this time. We're supposed to be in Nashville on the twentieth of May."

"Yeah, sure," I said, acting as if I didn't care one way or the other. We'd played this disappointing joke on each other before. I looked in her eyes.

B.J. quietly said, "I'm telling you the truth. I promise. I'll even swear on a stack of Bibles."

Seconds later the two of us were doing a silly child's dance around the room, knocking over lamps, books, and everything else in sight, including the guitar. We were going to Nashville! It was true; our dreams were on their way to coming true.

We went down to the chili parlor to resign. The boss promised us more money if we returned to work for him after our trip to Nashville. Confidently we replied, "No thanks, we're going to be recording stars now. We don't want to be waitresses anymore."

Faith? Maybe, but it might as well have been that old country innocence and ignorance I told you about. We stopped at service stations on the way down to Nashville where people would ask, "Where you girls headed?"

"We're going to Nashville to cut records," we'd answer.

My earth-level spiritual guide and friend Scott Hammacher tells me, "First there's the idea, then there's the reality; nothing lies between them but time and space." I think that's true. Just get the idea, and believe, *I'm going to do it*, and you will. You'll do it.

We called RCA from the Andrew Jackson Hotel in downtown Nashville to let them know we were there.

Mr. Sholes answered, "All right, if you girls will just stay put for about an hour I want to bring a couple of guys over with me and let them hear you sing."

An hour later Steve Sholes arrived at our hotel room. The two men with him were none other than Chet Atkins and Eddy Arnold. At sixteen we had gotten their autographs at the Opry; now we were preparing to audition for them. We were scared to death.

"These girls are really persistent," Steve told Chet and Eddy. "I've never even heard them but they say they're good. Better than the Beaver Valley Sweethearts." He grinned.

Steve Sholes had never even listened to the demo tapes we brought him. He had a lot of faith in the opinions of Chet and Eddy and wanted to see what they thought about us.

"All right, sing one, girls," he said, and we did. It's well known in the business that Chet Atkins never, or rarely ever, gets excited. Two bars deep into the song we were singing, Chet stopped us. From that day to this, I've never seen him as excited about anything as he was about us. "Lord, Steve! Do they ever have punch!"

Eddy Arnold agreed, "They are really good, Steve, really fine."

What a thrill it was for us to hear these two famous and talented men saying these things. Even though we had been trying to convince Steve Sholes how good we were, we only halfway believed it. We never expected Chet Atkins to say the same thing.

Steve opened his briefcase and said, "I've got some demos here. I want you to listen to them. Practice the ones you like, and I'll be back in about three months. At that time we'll record the ones you do best. I don't seem to have any contracts with me," he continued looking through his briefcase, "or I'd go ahead and sign you today. I'll be back in three months, though."

I butted in, "We'll record anyway."

Steve looked up at me from his briefcase quizzically. "Without a contract? I wouldn't think of it."

"We have to have a contract?" B.J. inquired. "We want to record right now."

"Are you kidding?"

Knowing what I know now, I would never do this again. B.J. and I were lucky that we didn't get ripped off. I'm not advising anyone entering the music business to do this, but we said, "We just want to record."

Steve looked at us, then at Chet and Eddy. Chet spoke out, "You'd better go ahead and record them."

Eddy backed him up. "If they are that gung ho, just mail them a contract from New York."

"Okay, girls. You're on. Let's do it this week." Steve put out his hand to shake on it. "Welcome to RCA."

I Forgot More Than You'll Ever Know

> You stole his love from me one day;
> You didn't care how it hurt me.
> But you can never steal away
> Memories of what used to be.
> —"I Forgot More Than You'll Ever Know,"
> Cecil Null

Like a couple of kids waiting up for Santa Claus, Betty Jack and I were wide awake, talking all night in our room at the Andrew Jackson Hotel. Tomorrow would be the most exciting day of our lives, and our minds were racing with fantasies of what it would be like to cut our very own record in the RCA studio.

After what seemed to be the longest night in history, we pinched each other on the way to the studio to make sure we weren't dreaming. It was no dream, but it was magic indeed. Everyone at RCA appeared to be completely focused on the workings of the studio. As we entered the studio doors, the world outside simply disappeared.

From among the demos and records which Steve Sholes had given us, we selected a song recorded by a young artist named Sonny James.

The song was entitled "I Forgot More Than You'll Ever Know." Betty Jack and I had no idea what *covering a record* meant, even though that was exactly what we were doing. I've had it done to me plenty of times since then. In covering a record, an artist records a song previously recorded by someone else in hopes he or she can do an even better job. We sang our arrangement of "I Forgot More" to Steve, and he agreed that it should be our first release.

We wanted to start the song with the title—cold, with no instrumentation, something that had never been done before. And that's what we did. We started the song with our voices unaccompanied by instruments until we sang the word *more* in the title:

> I forgot more
> Than you'll ever know
> About him.
> You think you know
> The smile on his lips,
> The thrill at the touch
> Of his fingertips...

On this Friday, May 23, 1953, we also recorded "Rock-a-Bye Boogie," which became the flip side of our first release, plus two other songs we had written, "Sorrow and Pain" and "You're Gone." When we finished, we still had forty-five minutes of our session time left. We had expected to record one song and had recorded four. Everyone was amazed—especially B.J. and me.

As we sat there listening to the replay, Steve Sholes kept saying, "Would you listen to that? It sounds like there are three voices instead of two. It's unbelievable."

Betty Jack looked at me and said, "Skeeter, you sing the best harmony in the world."

"Yes, she does," Steve Sholes agreed. "What are you singing, Skeeter? What are those notes?"

"I'm just singing what's in my head."

He nodded. "Well, I see. Can you write that down?"

"Lord, I can't write music," I laughed. "It's just in my head."

Steve said, "Good!"

What does he mean? I thought.

"Then you have no idea what you're doing?"

I felt stupid and happy at the same time. I guess *silly* is the word. "I'm just singing what's in my heart like I've always done. Just hillbilly music."

"Skeeter, you're doing something different to the notes. Isn't she, Chet?"

Chet came out of his thoughts for a second to respond, "Yeah, she's bendin' 'em."

I was so embarrassed. I was used to B.J. bragging on my harmony, but now, with her, Steve, and Chet all going on about me, I knew it was something I'd never forget.

After all the ranting and raving about how great the song was, Chet said, "We've got to do it over."

I knew what he was talking about because I had noticed the grimace on his face when he made the mistake he wanted to correct the second time around. If you ever watched him during a concert, you might occasionally have seen Chet Atkins make that grimace if the notes didn't sound the way he intended them to. On this session for "I Forgot More," he produced that expression just as he went into the lead break. We decided among ourselves to leave the particular boo-boo he made that day as it was because it sounded beautiful. His error actually enhanced the recording instead of diminishing it. If you listen very closely to the original recording (RCA Victor 47-5345), you will notice that just as Chet goes into the break, he leaves the low register he was playing in and goes to a higher one.

Jerry Byrd, who played steel guitar on the session, was considered one of the finest steel players around. He was a staff musician on the Opry. His guitar, like everyone else's at that time, was a one-neck steel that you hardly ever see these days. And the reason you don't see any more of them than you do is because of "the Davis Sisters' sound." Here's how we helped replace the one-neck steel with the twin-neck pedal.

One evening about a year later, after "I Forgot More" had become a bestseller, I lay in bed listening to Nelson King's show on WCKY in Cincinnati, and I heard this beautiful instrumental. I couldn't remember ever hearing an instrument that sounded so much like the blend of Betty Jack's voice with my harmony. I woke everybody else in the house so that they could hear it. "Listen, ya'll. Don't that sound like me and B.J. singin'?"

"Go back to bed, Skeeter. You're sick or crazy, one. That's an instrumental."

I crawled back in bed. Nelson King said, "Well, you folks out there listening probably thought the Davis Sisters should chime in on the chorus of that one. It sounds so much like it's Skeeter and B.J., but actually that was Bud Isaacs playing "The Waltz You Saved for Me."

Somebody agreed with me! I could hardly believe it. I immediately called Nelson King at the station. He told me that he had an interesting story to tell me, if I would hold while he put another record on the air. Once he got back on the line, Nelson said that he had met Bud Isaacs, a young steel guitarist, at a memorial show for Hank Williams on New Year's Day of 1954, the one-year anniversary of Hank's death. Bud had explained to Nelson that he had designed and built this twin-neck, or double-neck, steel with pedals so he could imitate the harmony he had heard on our recording of "I Forgot More."

At first the pedal steel was just a novelty, but its popularity grew and grew. Later I worked an RCA tour with Bud Isaacs and just adored knowing him. I receive a Christmas card from him every year. I wish he had decided to stay and play the Opry and Nashville sessions, but Bud chose to move out west instead. He became a sheepherder by day and a steel player at his brother's club by night.

I think of Bud often when I am listening to Weldon Myrick, Hal Rugg, Jimmy Day, or Buddy Emmons, who are all great steel players. They all, of course, use a twin-neck pedal steel. Everyone I know does, except for Jerry Byrd and little Roy Wiggins. Knowing that Bud Isaacs invented the pedal steel guitar, trying to copy the sound of B.J. and me singing together, makes me proud of the contributions we made to country music beyond our own recordings. Very few people are aware of this fact. If you listen to the recordings which preceded the Davis Sisters, you will only hear the sound of the single-neck steel guitar with no pedal.

Of course, all entertainers borrow from each other and are influenced by so many voices, past and present, that it's hard to say when something new first comes to be. However, I can honestly say that I can't remember where I ever learned the harmony I began singing the day I met Betty Jack at Dixie Heights. It must have come from somewhere.

Another contribution with which I have been credited includes inventing the suspended harmony chord. Phil and Don Everly later told me how much they were influenced by the Davis Sisters' style. Since the Beatles credited most of the influence on their harmony to the Everly Brothers, you might say that B.J. and I indirectly influenced early rock-and-roll groups without being one of them.

When I was in England taping a medley of my hits for a BBC special, a couple approached me after the taping and said, "We knew 'End of the World' was yours. It's one of our favorite songs, but we didn't realize that you had recorded one of Dylan's songs."

I laughed, knowing immediately which song they meant. I told this couple that Dylan was the one doing my song and not vice versa. Like a lot of the younger people they were Dylan idolizers, and I could see they doubted me. So I went ahead and told them the story of how Dylan came to record "I Forgot More Than You'll Ever Know."

Shortly after he came to Nashville to record *Nashville Skyline*, I was in New York City playing Carnegie Hall with George Hamilton IV, Jim Ed Brown, and Eddy Arnold. I turned in one of my finest performances ever that evening; the audience demanded an encore, and my reviews in the *New York Times* were excellent. I admit it was a strange experience for me to sing with accompaniment from a full string section.

Eddy Arnold reminded me that night before I went on stage that I was playing to a New York audience and would probably fare better if I held my hillbilly talking to a minimum and concentrated on singing my hits. But I just couldn't resist having fun with the Carnegie audience. I told them that there was a little girl new to the business named "Sinatrie" who came from a real poor family and had little chance of making it without somebody helping her. And I intended to do just that by singing one of her songs. "I think her name is Nancy," I said and sang "These Boots Are Made for Walking." I was dressed in high-top walking boots, and my hair was fixed in braids with beads woven in them. Hardly what they expected from a hillbilly girl singer.

When I left for Greenwich Village that night after the performance, the musicians were worried about me wandering around that part of New York City by myself, but not one of them wanted to go with me because they had made other plans.

"Aw, she'll be alright," my drummer said. "They won't bother her; she looks just like 'em." He meant the hippies, of course. I took a taxi to the Bitter End. No sooner had I found a seat from which to listen to the Fifth Avenue Band than a man approached my table and said, "Hey, how'd you like to go smoke a joint?"

"No thanks, just finished one," I lied. No longer the ignorant little girl that had come to New York in the winter of 1953, I had gotten streetwise over the years. He left me alone.

As I listened to the band, I noticed a fellow seated in a booth against the wall. Each time the house lights went up, he would slide down in his seat. Each time the lights dimmed, he would ease back up. Obviously he didn't want to be seen. I thought I recognized him. I called the club's proprietor over to my table and asked him, "Isn't that Bob Dylan?"

"Yeah, it is," the man said. "But I happen to own this place, girlie, and if you so much as bat an eyelash at him, I'll pitch you out on your ear." After that warm response, I found myself concentrating on watching Dylan slide up and down in that booth rather than on listening to the band. Finally I could resist no longer. *So what if the owner pitches me out, I'm leaving anyway.*

"Hello. I don't think you know me, but I know you and I just couldn't help but to come over here and tell you how much I like your music like everyone else does."

"I'm afraid *everyone* doesn't." He laughed.

"I know you don't know who I am"—I felt awkward and apologetic—"but my name's Skeeter Davis."

"Sit down, Skeeter. Of course I know you. You know my friends John and June Cash, don't you?"

I explained how I knew them both but was closer to June since I had known her from my first days in Nashville. "June Carter used to come get me in her pickup truck and take me out to her place," I told him. "She helped me a lot when my first marriage broke up."

He listened intently as I sat down in the booth, but before I could finish what I had to say, I felt a hand jerking on the sleeve of my blouse. "I warned you, girl," the owner said. "Out of here. Up and out!"

"Paul," Dylan interrupted him, "it's alright. This is Skeeter Davis, a good friend of mine from Nashville—and a good friend of John and June."

"Oh, I thought she's some kid from the street. Sorry, miss." The owner left us to our conversation, and Dylan started telling me that he planned to come to Nashville and record again soon. I didn't want to bother him further, only to say hello, so I dismissed myself.

As I left he said to me, "By the way, I like your music too, Skeeter. I intend to record a song of yours one of these days."

I told my musicians what he had said, and they laughed at me. "Dylan don't do other people's songs."

"Well, he told me he was," I argued back. I was so happy when Bob Dylan released "I Forgot More Than You'll Ever Know" on his very next album, *Self Portrait* (Columbia C2X30050). Basically he had used the same arrangement B.J. and I had. In fact, he and Tom Petty actually sang "I Forgot More Than You'll Ever Know" as a duet in their tours together. I'm proud of that, needless to say, even when people think I'm doing a song of his rather than the other way around. I only wish I had been there to sing harmony for him too.

As you will remember, B.J. and I had stretched the truth when Steve Sholes had asked us how often we came to Nashville. So when Chet Atkins took B.J. and me to the Grand Ole Opry the evening after our first recording session, you can imagine our excitement. After all, it was only our second time even in the vicinity of the Ryman Auditorium. This time, however, instead of sitting in the recesses of the balcony, we had front row seats, just like regular hotshots. We could see every detail about everything and everyone on stage. Betty Jack pinched me and said, "When we get up on that stage, we're gonna be a main act, not no backup singers."

Chet interrupted our musings by introducing us to the writer of "I Forgot More." Cecil Null told us he had heard our rendition of his song and was delighted with it. It still pleases me when I know writers are pleased with my interpretation of their work.

We left Nashville the next day to return to Detroit to pack our things. Most of what we owned, we stored at Betty Jack's house. We were going to be spending most of our time living on the road, plugging our records, dropping into radio stations, introducing ourselves to deejays, and living out of the suitcases in the trunk of our Ford Victoria. The record started selling like crazy. By July in Memphis "I Forgot More" had outsold the previous bestseller, "All I Want for Christmas Is My Two Front Teeth."

Even with the almost immediate success, Betty Jack and I both were so insecure and uninformed about the business, we thought RCA might not keep us; Steve said, "It's summertime. This record may not make it, but at least it'll get you ready for the next one."

We were scheduled to play the Ernest Tubb Record Shop on Broadway in Nashville on a Saturday night in mid-July. As we came in the front door of the record shop, we overheard a boy and girl standing at the counter asking for "I Forgot More" by the Davis Sisters.

"We're the Davis Sisters," we announced together, overjoyed that we had come upon someone interested in buying our record. The two new fans turned out to be none other than Jim Ed and Maxine Brown. They were not *the* Browns at the time, since their sister Bonnie was yet to join them. They told Betty Jack and I that they were looking for a copy of our record so they could work it up for a show they were doing in Little Rock. Our record was doing so well there, they told us, that the shops had sold out of it.

We ended up doing a live broadcast with Jim Ed and Maxine at the Little Rock station where they were working. We were such clowns. Betty Jack would mimic the lead guitarist during the solo. "Don't let me down, Leroy," she'd say looking over her shoulder at the lead man. The people in the audience would think she was really picking.

I never sang lead. Sometimes she would catch me off guard by yelling, "Take it, Skeeter."

There I'd be, alone at the microphone, singing lead, while she stood off to the side grinning and clapping her hands. We had a good time on and off stage and so did the crowds. We were friendly and comical, I guess, because we knew our songs were sad, but more than anything else, because that's just the way we were.

In Little Rock we went to church and made sure we took a picture of ourselves on the front steps, just in case anyone would ask when we got home, "Have you girls been going to church?" After church we went to lunch with Jim Ed and Maxine, then to see a new movie called *The Snows of Kilimanjaro*. Years later I would be in Africa on Betty Jack's birthday in 1974. As I flew over Mount Kilimanjaro on my way to a performance in the foothills, she seemed to be right there with me too.

We left Little Rock for St. Louis, then from St. Louis we returned to Kentucky. It had been a long time since we spent any time at home. Detroit, and then the road, had somehow taken the place of home for a while. Our next concert would be the *Wheeling Jamboree* in Wheeling, West Virginia. It was still a few days away, so Covington seemed the best place to stay until then.

We were returning home victors. We had done the very thing we had set out to do, the very thing that we had told our friends we were going to do. We had recorded with RCA, and our record was climbing in popularity. A feeling of triumph was in us, but folks have a way of making good feelings like that short-lived.

It was early Wednesday night, July 29, when we got home. The folks were at prayer meeting over at Brother Rader's church. Of course, we just headed straight over there. We expected everybody to be real proud of us. However, instead of the pats on our backs we expected to receive, everyone was warning us, "I hope you girls are living the right kind of life out there on the road. You know there's a lot of men just waitin' to take advantage of nice girls like you."

One lady at the church didn't even bother to say hello before she flipped the cross on my neck with her middle finger and said, "You know you ain't supposed to be wearin' a graven image." Betty Jack and I had bought two identical silver crosses while on the road back to Covington; we had been so proud of being able to buy something nice with our earnings, to show people we were Christians. There was nothing fancy or gaudy about the crosses; they were simple and tasteful.

We were trying to figure this whole situation out. If you didn't wear a cross, you were bad; if you wore one, you were bad. Neither one of us, at that time in our youth, had the wisdom to know that it simply is not possible to please everybody. That's what we were trying to do. Looking back, I can't believe I actually stood there trying to defend my cross against the judgments of that woman, but I can hear myself so clearly saying, "This cross represents my Christ."

While I argued, Betty Jack talked to Brother Rader. She clutched her white Bible in her hands. I could hear her telling him, "Preacher, I just want you to know Skeeter and me don't change the way we live when we get out of the city limits." Poor girl. She was as desperate as I was to prove her innocence. It wasn't the wrath of God we feared; it was the wrath of the congregation. She spent over an hour talking to Brother Rader that night. We had an appointment with Nelson King at WCKY in Cincinnati. I tried to hurry her up, while Mrs. Rader was calling her husband, "Come on, Charlie, the ice cream's meltin'."

Both of them just stood beside the pulpit talking as though they couldn't hear us. By the time they joined us, the heat of the July evening had long since melted the ice cream and Nelson King had long since finished his broadcast. For some reason unknown to me, B.J. felt that it was very important for her to talk to the preacher that night. She seemed to be in some sort of daze.

"Has something happened to you," I asked her, "that you haven't told me about?"

"Why?" B.J. replied, and without waiting for an answer she said, "You know something, Skeeter? You oughta get a driver's license while we're home. It scares me to think we could get caught by the police on the road to Wheeling and you without a driver's license." I had been sharing the driving with her for the last two years without bothering to obtain a license. Frankly, the idea of taking the test was so frightening that I had just put it off. I thought to myself, *Being home in a relaxed place for a change might make it easier; besides, it won't matter that much if I flunk it.*

"Okay, tomorrow."

The next day we were waiting in the Kentucky state patrol station for the examiners to call my name—me biting my fingernails, B.J. teasing me for being so nervous. She parked the Ford Victoria that we had bought with our quarters as tight as she could get it between two other cars.

I protested and begged, "Please, B.J., don't do this to me."

"You're a good driver, Skeeter. Don't worry about a thing."

I thought I would faint, but just as the policeman and I were about to leave for the road test, the car in front of the Victoria pulled out. *Thank God*, I thought. *Now Lord, do you hear me? Don't let anybody park there till I get back.* The palms of my hands were drenched with nervous perspiration and I was having a hard time keeping my fingernails out of my mouth. I felt sure the cop could see the sweat beading on the steering wheel, and that just made me more nervous.

We drove around the block and upon returning to the station, I asked him, "Where do you want me to park?"

"Park in the same place," he said. Betty Jack was leaning against the parking meter with a big grin on her face. The other car had left. Now I had the space of three meters, but I pulled up like there were cars all around and backed in. I parallel parked just perfect. The patrolman stared at me like I was crazy. Betty Jack applauded. "Boy, that's real good, Skeeter. For the first time to ever park, you done real good."

I got my license anyway. Betty Jack snapped out of that daze she had been in the previous night and everything was fine.

On Friday we said goodbye to everyone, and I mean everyone, as was protocol in our community. Then we left for Wheeling, West

Virginia. The *Wheeling Jamboree* was the biggest show we had ever done. It would almost be like being on the Grand Ole Opry. Betty Jack's mother stood on their front stoop as we left and yelled at us, "Ya'll girls let us know where you are, now. 'Cause I ain't a feelin' well and might die before you get back."

"I'll be gone before you," B.J. said. Since I had my new driver's license, I was driving. B.J. leaned out the window and hollered at the neighbors as we drove out to the highway.

"'Bye, Mrs. Miller! 'Bye, Mrs. Mullins! 'Bye, Mrs. Chaney! Goodbye, goodbye, goodbye!"

The End of the World and the Day After

I wake up in the morning and I wonder
Why everything's the same as it was.
I can't understand;
No, I can't understand
Why life goes on the way it does.
—"The End of the World,"
  Sylvia Dee and Arthur Kent

Why did we leave Wheeling, West Virginia, that night? I have asked myself that question at least a hundred thousand times. Our concern about what people in Covington were saying about us made us leave that night. We left to avoid yet another hassle and another guilt trip which would have been initiated by Betty Jack's mother had we waited to return the next day.

People we knew in Covington, especially the churchgoers, thought that we were doing a terrible wrong by singing country music. They considered it utterly shameless and sinful for two young girls to be out on the road without a chaperone. To dispel their gossip, we would bring home pictures from our road trips of Betty Jack and me posed on the steps of the local Baptist church in whatever town we were playing. We faithfully attended services, even when we were on the

144

road. We would go to great lengths just to prove that we were still "good girls." The departure from Wheeling that night would be the last of those efforts.

Patrick J. Hurt, whom everybody called P.J., had always had a crush on Betty Jack. When he came back from the Navy on leave, P.J.'s first thought was to find Betty Jack. So he and a Navy buddy hopped a bus for Wheeling to find the Davis Sisters at the Jamboree.

They found us in the Jamboree Hall dressing rooms. Although Betty Jack hadn't seen Patrick in quite some time, the moment she saw him, she said, "P.J., does anybody know that you're down here?"

"Why, sure," he said and grinned. "Everybody does."

Betty Jack wearily turned from him to me and said, "I guess that means we have to go home tonight."

B.J. didn't say another word until after the show was over. She was furious. We had already planned to stay in the hotel room where we had earlier unpacked our clothes and settled in for the night. B.J. had even mailed picture postcards of the hotel and Jamboree Hall to my family and hers.

It was a great night for us at the WWVA *Wheeling Jamboree*. We sang "I Forgot More" over the network; although our spot was pretimed and planned for only that one song, we were asked to do an encore, knocking another group from their spot. We were truly sympathetic to the other group but equally ecstatic for ourselves. We knew we were on our way to the top of the charts and the top of the world.

Back at the hotel room, however, Betty Jack reiterated the need for us to return home since P.J. had showed up in Wheeling. We didn't want anyone getting notions they could use against us. We began to pack our clothes, which we had hung out just hours earlier in an attempt to rid them of wrinkles.

In the middle of packing, B.J. stopped and sat on the bed. She asked me the question that she always asked, "You do love me, don't you, Skeeter? I mean like a sister. You love me as much as you do Shirley and Doozer and Suzan, don't you?"

I hugged her my most sisterly hug. "Of course I do, B.J., and I always will."

We finished packing and loaded the trunk of the Victoria. We told P.J. that even as mad as we were at them, he and his buddy could ride back with us. The four of us left Wheeling just before midnight.

Approximately thirty minutes west of Wheeling we drove past an

Italian restaurant. Italian food was Betty Jack's favorite. With her coal black hair, many people thought she was Italian; her true ancestry was Cherokee. Italian, Indian, whatever, she still couldn't pass up a spaghetti house. When she spotted the neon sign, she yelled, "Stop! Stop! Stop!"

Patrick was at the wheel, ignoring her command. I said, "Oh, B.J., they're probably closed anyhow."

"No, they're not." Betty Jack insisted, "Stop. Let's go back."

Although I had never really considered myself superstitious, I said, "Don't turn around. It's bad luck if you turn around."

Patrick proceeded to make a U-turn, and we headed back to the spaghetti house. When we arrived, they had quit serving, but they let us use the facilities just the same.

"See, I told you it was bad luck. We still don't get no spaghetti," I said.

As we left the restaurant, Betty Jack stuck her head in the kitchen door. "Haven't you got just one dish left?"

The kitchen crew laughed and so did we. But all the same we walked back to the car empty-handed. We stopped again that morning at an all-night truck stop to eat cheeseburgers and slices of butterscotch pie.

I remember the little old man seated at the truck stop counter who spoke to Betty Jack when we ordered our pie. "You better not eat that stuff, sweetie. You better watch that purty girlish figger."

"Mister, I'm gonna eat this pie," B.J. said. "You can watch my figure."

At first I thought the sensation I felt was a result of eating that butterscotch pie a little too quickly. Something choked me as we pulled out of the truck stop, but it wasn't inside my throat. I felt pressure on the outside of my neck as though hands were strangling me.

I became increasingly frightened, afraid even to speak. Finally I could stand it no longer. I panted, "Something is gonna happen. I know." I gagged. "Something is fixin' to happen."

Puzzled, Betty Jack turned to me. "Skeeter, what in the world's wrong with you? I've never seen you act so crazy."

"Do we have gas?" I shivered. "Are we gonna run out of gas?"

"Yeah, there's plenty of gas." Patrick pointed at the gauge. To satisfy me, he pulled off the road into the next service station. We bought soft drinks and I tried to relax. I still felt no relief. I kept touching my neck and throat, feeling for the hands closing in on me.

"Let me drive," I begged. "I'm so nervous. Maybe my mind will relax if I drive."

They allowed me to drive, but the choking sensation continued. *It ain't 'cause I don't have my license, 'cause that's already been taken care of*, I thought. *I've never worried like this before.*

I must have driven almost all night. We were listening to XERF radio from Del Rio, Texas, when all of a sudden, the disc jockey played a song that B.J. recognized from the very first chord. It was "Rock-a-Bye Boogie," the flip side of our hit. "Turn it up, Skeeter, that's us. Ain't that something?"

The excitement of hearing our song played on such a big station, so far away, seemed to kill the nervousness I had been feeling. When the tune finished, B.J. said, "That's nice for him to play the back side, but why don't he play the other side? That's gonna be the hit."

The disc jockey's voice boomed back on the airwaves. "I don't know about you, but somebody might want to hear the other side of this record besides me. So here they are once again, folks, the Davis Sisters."

"Just pull over here, Skeeter," Betty Jack instructed, slapping my shoulder. I pulled off to the side of the road and we listened to ourselves singing the song that would become the biggest hit of 1953.

Then the craziest thing happened. As soon as our record finished, the radio conked out. I twisted all of the knobs trying to tune it in, turn it on and off, and adjust the volume, but nothing seemed to work. Betty Jack banged the dashboard; P.J. checked for loose wires. Another unsolved mystery; the radio never came back on again.

I drove off with the full August moon overhead. When I next stopped for gasoline, the sun was coming up behind us in the east. The choking sensation was resurfacing. Patrick and his friend got out of the car to stretch their legs, and Betty Jack crawled from the back seat into the front. *That's strange*, I thought. *She usually gets out of the car when we stop. I wonder what's the matter.*

I went into the service station to get a soft drink. The manager was in full display in the window, asleep on top of his desk. He didn't even wake up when we tracked in and out buying our sodas. When I returned to the car, I asked B.J., "Don't you want nothin'?"

"No, nothin'." Betty Jack dangled the keys out in front of her, handing them to Patrick.

"Ain't I goin' to drive?" I asked. "I was driving good."

Without answering me, B.J. said to Patrick, "This is what you're here for; you drive!"

"Boy, she keeps reminding me, don't she?" Patrick looked at me. "She really knows how to hurt a guy."

Climbing into the back seat, I picked up the map to trace our progress. I knew we were on Montgomery Road. Holding my index finger and thumb an inch apart, I said, "Hey, ya'll, we're just this far from home."

With the corn high in the fields, the crows rising up in black clouds behind us, Betty Jack began to sing. I, of course, sang along. She would sing a line or two of one song before moving to another one. Patrick interrupted. "Why don't you girls finish one before you start on another?"

"'Cause I ain't got time. I'm just singin' every song I like," B.J. answered.

The next thing I remember is a man dressed in white pulling the bloodied map from my hands. I knew something terrible had happened when I saw that the handprints that decorated the map were imprints from my own hands in my own blood. I screamed, "Betty Jack!"

I felt myself being lifted up and rolled into an ambulance. My thoughts were dominated by concern for Betty Jack. *I've got to get to B.J. I've got to help her. Where is she? Where is Betty Jack?*

I could sense her presence in the ambulance with me but I couldn't see her. My eyes stung as I tried to open them; each time they filled with something wet. My mind flashed back to the scene in our Detroit apartment on the day that Hank Williams had died. I recalled our promises to each other, "If anything like that ever happens to us, we'll help each other, won't we?"

I heard her voice saying those words over and over again. I tried to fight my way to consciousness, to get to the other side of the ambulance to help her. I was helpless.

I woke up in the hospital. I could see clearly enough to make out that a girl lay in the bed across from me. "Betty Jack! Oh, B.J., are you alright? Oh, you're not Betty Jack. Where's Betty Jack?"

I stumbled from my bed to the window. We were four or five stories up. *Betty Jack's in this place somewhere*, I thought, *and she's wondering if I'm all right. Just like I'm wondering if she's all right.* I spied a tree beneath the window in the hospital courtyard. *If I sit under the tree yonder, she'll see me and know that I'm okay.* I turned to maneuver my way to the door but collapsed face first into the floor before I could get there.

Though she'd been hit by a car herself, the girl in the bed across from me helped me to my feet and back to bed. How she did it with her one remaining arm, I still can't figure out. She called for the nurses to help her as I fought to reach the tree so that I could let B.J. know that I was all right.

Hours passed. I cried with loneliness and helplessness. I wanted my mother and daddy. I hadn't seen them in so long. As I lamented my separation from all those I loved, I could see their forms coming toward me from the door of my hospital room.

Daddy bent down to kiss me. "We don't have no money, sweetheart, but we're gonna get some somewhere and take care of you. You're gonna be alright."

The wreck occurred on Montgomery Road near Cincinnati on Sunday, August 2, 1953, at approximately 7:00 A.M. We were less than twenty miles from home. Betty Jack was killed. I was hospitalized with a brain concussion and a dangerously mobile blood clot lodged temporarily under my left eye. The driver of the automobile that collided with us head-on had a minor laceration across his knee, for which he was treated in the emergency room prior to his release that same day. Patrick J. Hurt received not a scratch, but his buddy was treated for minor injuries and released.

The man who drove the car that hit us was a soldier who had fallen asleep at the steering wheel. I can only recount what I was told, for I have no personal recollection of what really happened. At the time of impact I had my eyes fixed on the road map tracing the route of our journey as I sang along with Betty Jack. Thereafter I lay among the wreckage, unconscious.

To this day I can't be sure about the soldier's first name; his last name, I believe, was Whitmyer. I often wonder about this phantom soldier. Have I ever sung to him, seen him, or maybe even talked to him among the fans who gather 'round? I was told that at the time of the accident, he was having domestic problems and was on furlough to see his wife. The people driving behind him said they thought he was drunk because he had been weaving from one side of the road to the other for miles on end. No one could get around him to pass. Supposedly he met us windshield to windshield on our side of the highway as he rounded a curve atop a hill.

One of the strangest parts of the incident was that our '53 Ford Victoria was completely demolished on Patrick's side, and he was not even hurt. Yet Betty Jack was on the other side and died as a result of her injuries. Some say she was dead immediately; others say she said something before dying. I don't know who to believe. Someone even said that Patrick lifted her head up before help arrived. Betty Jack died of a broken neck. When I start thinking that Patrick's attempt to help her may have been what killed her, I have to remind myself that it's all hearsay. I'll never know.

We were taken to Our Lady of Mercy, a Roman Catholic hospital in Cincinnati. News of the wreck was broadcast ahead of the notification of next of kin, and the local wire services were releasing copy that both of us were dead. All day long on Sunday, the radio stations announced, "RCA recording artists Skeeter and Betty Jack Davis were fatally injured when the car they were driving collided with an oncoming vehicle outside of Cincinnati, Ohio, this morning. The Davis Sisters, as they were known, were pronounced dead on arrival at Our Lady of Mercy Hospital."

A correction of the news bulletin was not aired until the next day. And then the update failed to mention which one of us was killed. You can imagine the distress this caused my family. On Monday my sister Shirley called the morgue to discover that Betty Jack had been killed and that I had been miraculously spared.

Those who knew who we were from television, and those who only knew of us from our records hovered around the wreckage like vultures, scouting for and stealing souvenirs from the remains of the car. It's pathetic that some people live not only their lives but also their deaths through others. The crosses we had been criticized for wearing were thrown from our necks on impact, along with our matching, antique rose silver rings. I recovered only one of each of them, bent and crushed.

It's a nightmare I'll awaken from someday, I've told myself time and again, but I never have. Forty years have passed, yet I cried two solid weeks in 1981 recalling these scenes for this book. It is especially painful for me to remember the point at which Brother Rader told me that Betty Jack was dead.

I know that from the time Brother Rader told me until well over a year later, I fell victim to mental depression so severe that I would have doubted my chances for regaining my mental health. In my confusion I actually thought that we both were dead. I would ask those around me, "Tell me again now, how did we get killed?"

I was not aware of who I was. I was totally disoriented. I felt as if I existed outside of my body and could not comprehend the separation between us. I kept thinking that Betty Jack was desperately searching for me as I was for her, that we were two spirits groping in the darkness for each other. Then I would think, *If we're both dead, then who am I?*

Unfortunately, the inaccurate bulletins on the car radio confirmed what I believed to be true: I was dead. The astute reader may wonder how I heard the radio announcements of my demise when I had been listed in critical condition upon arrival at the hospital. I owe my rapid and physically threatening discharge from the hospital and the rare opportunity to have heard these broadcasts to the cunning deceptions of Betty Jack's mother.

Upon entering the hospital I was tagged Skeeter Davis. After my mother and daddy arrived, they were informed that a portion of my charges would have to be paid before I could be moved to another hospital closer to home. They left in search of a friend who might loan them fifty dollars. Bless their hearts, they finally managed a loan from Beneficial Finance the next day, but they were too late. Tipp and Ollie Davis had arrived at Our Lady of Mercy in the interim and identified themselves to the hospital staff as the parents of Skeeter Davis. The doctors advised them that transporting me too soon could cause the blood clot in my face to reach a major vessel and place me in danger of a fatal hemorrhage; furthermore, the doctors insisted that I be hospitalized until the clot dissolved and that to avert the risk of traumatic shock, I should be shielded from news of my sister's death.

Tipp and Ollie Davis assured the staff physicians that they were indeed taking me to a hospital nearer home where their advice would be followed. Then they paid the fees in full and signed a waiver of responsibility for the hospital. Their very next move was to bring Brother Rader in to tell me about Betty Jack. Just minutes later, I was propped up in the back seat of their car listening to the most credible sources of information in America tell me news I had no reason to doubt. "From the wires of United Press International comes this hour's lead story. Skeeter and Betty Jack Davis...dead on arrival..."

Instead of taking me to a Covington hospital, the Davises took me shopping in Cincinnati and Latonia, Kentucky. As a detached observer, I stood by as they instructed me to choose a burial dress for Betty Jack. *Let's see, what dress should we be buried in?* They chose the casket. Then I was driven to the city morgue to see proof that we had died.

Marie Mullins and Wanda Rose Rader told me the details of the actual funeral. Again I don't remember much. I was either so heavily sedated by this time or completely insane. I do remember, however, Mrs. Davis at Swindler's Funeral Home telling me that I had caused Betty Jack's death by pushing the seat over on her. Perhaps I remember this because it was the first of many times that Mrs. Davis would repeat this particular accusation. Every day for months without end, I heard how I had killed Betty Jack. After a while, even when you know that something just isn't true, you begin to believe it, until you acquire all the feelings and behaviors as if it were the very truth. For a long time, even after I began to regain my senses and realize who died and who didn't, I regretted that she had to be the one to die and wished with all my heart that it could have been me instead.

Marie told me she begged the Davises to take me home, away from the funeral ceremony. More than once I tried to pull B.J. from the casket. Mrs. Davis had installed a promotional picture of the two of us up in the coffin lid. I was jerking her body, screaming, "Come on, Betty Jack, let's get out of this place. We'll go sing. Let's go and sing." Finally I must have collapsed one time too many and someone took me to a bed.

They buried her where I told them that she had asked to be buried the day Hank Williams died—Highland Cemetery. Over four hundred cars followed the hearse to the grave site. God bless B.J., everybody that knew her, loved her.

After the funeral I was taken to the Davises' house, where I remained secluded in the bedroom where Betty Jack and I had lived. In the months that followed, I was not in control of my life. I may as well have been a robot, with someone else pushing my buttons. When I recall this period in my life, I experience feelings that I cannot explain. The pain and suffering of that period rush back to me, inflicting a dose of that old heartache all over again. I always end up in tears, knowing that I was unable to help myself and can never change what happened. Mrs. Davis with her cold, calculating mind took advantage of this tragic situation to suit her own ends.

I remember Mrs. Davis taking me to a doctor whose name I never learned. While I was in his office, he injected an unknown substance into the veins of my arm. Thinking back on these trips, I am inclined to say that perhaps he was a dentist. When I returned to Covington in 1981 to do more research for this book, the building I remember having entered on those trips was a dentist's office. Those I asked said that particular dentistry practice was located in the same building in 1953. I do not know how many of these shots I received, but I do know they were frequent. Each time I was awake during the day, it seemed that I was on my way to get a shot. Logic tells me that the injections were a narcotic or sedative of some kind. When one arm was too bruised to insert another needle, they moved to the other arm.

I view this part of my life as a dense fog in which I seemed to float through the motions of living in a dreamlike state of slow motion. Was I being "fixed" because I was hysterical or to keep me under the smothering care of Mrs. Davis?

I would beg to see my mother but she never came. I know now that my mother, as well as people from our church, tried to get in to see me, but they couldn't get past Ollie Davis. She would tell them I was sick and did not want to be disturbed, that I would see no one, not even my mother.

Eventually, though, Mother was finally allowed in. She said later that I attempted no response to her whatsoever, that I appeared to be in a daze or a hypnotic trance. Mother told Mrs. Davis, "I wish it had been her, 'cause at least I could have buried her and gotten over it. This way I know she's alive but I still don't have a daughter."

Mrs. Davis didn't miss the opportunity to tell me that my own mother wished that I had been killed instead of Betty Jack. "She don't love you. We're the only ones that do. You're a Davis now and you're gonna carry on Betty Jack's work."

"It's only fair," B.J.'s mother would say, "that we have you to continue her work because we only had two children and you killed one of ours. Besides, your mother wouldn't even miss you if you were gone. She's got six more where you came from."

At night the drugs would wear off a bit and I would get out of bed and wander around. I would go to the window of our upstairs bedroom and contemplate. *Reckon where the girls are? They ought to be home by now; it's getting late. It don't take that long to drive from Wheeling.* Other times I would hear a car pull in the driveway; I would jump from the bed shouting for joy, *"It's them. It's them. They're finally home. The girls are home."* But of course Skeeter and Betty Jack would never come home.

Mrs. Davis played our record constantly, morning, noon, and night. I would fall asleep, then wake up to the sound of our voices singing. I'd say to myself, *The girls are downstairs singing. Wonder why they don't come up and visit me.*

Time lost all meaning for me. Yet it passed nonetheless. Gradually the cyclone of craziness in which I had been whirling began to lose its power over me. It abandoned me on a distant, unknown shore, where I scoured the landscape, picking up the scattered pieces of my mind wherever I could find them. Lost and alone, I did the best I could to gather myself together again. Some people may think, *Well, what a mess you made gluing yourself together, Skeeter.* But I wouldn't and couldn't accept me any other way.

When I first was able to walk outside again, I strolled along the railroad tracks behind the house, looking for signs of B.J. I knew in times of trouble that's where she went to be alone so that she could collect her thoughts. I couldn't find her, of course, but I found part of me. It was there in that solitude that I rediscovered myself.

Back in the bedroom, however, Mrs. Davis would dress me in Betty Jack's clothes. I would stare at myself in the mirror, thinking, *From the neck down I guess I could be her.* Was I me or her? Then it dawned on me. I was both of us. Physically Betty Jack had died in the wreck while I lived. I died a spiritual death while her spirit revived through me. There are moments, even today, when I feel this way. I may be in Skeeter's body, but I possess Betty Jack's spirit just the same.

The blood clot slowly went away. Yet nowadays if I get the least bit worried, the eye above where it once lodged bothers me. There's nothing really there, just a memory of pain. Betty Jack, on the other hand, is more than a mere memory.

Out of the Fog, Into the Fire

I take myself to places
Where we didn't go.
I surround myself with faces
That we didn't know.
I think this way
I'll leave the past behind;
Then I look up and see you on my mind.
—"I Look Up and See You on
My Mind,"
Skeeter Davis

Once I realized that I was still alive, getting my life untangled seemed to take forever. It takes a lot of mental wrestling for me to remember those years. They reside in the darkest part of my memory, yet the few things I am able to recall prick my brain like thorns. I have longed to discover the reason I allowed the Davises to govern my every movement, but I have yet to uncover anything plausible.

Friends have encouraged me to fabricate some other version of this interlude in my life or to avoid it altogether. The truth is I was excessively weakened. The fight in me had nearly evaporated amid

155

the shame and guilt cast upon me by Mrs. Davis and her brainwashing sessions. It would be a lie for me to tell anything other than what
really happened. My only attempt at anything resembling living was
survival, and that effort proved only halfhearted most of the time. In
fact, the events that would propel me from Betty Jack's singing sister
to a career as a solo country artist were not by my design. For the
most part, I was running blind.

I have to admit that I inadvertently inflicted injury to my family
during all this craziness. For three years I made little or no effort to
contact my mother and daddy, not even to let them know how I was
doing. I had become a Davis, though I admit, not by my own choice.
With the passage of time my real family came to an understanding of
what transpired and forgave me.

If you have ever felt the anguish of a loved one's death, then you
know what I mean when I say that death can bring out the worst in
people. For instance, I've noticed nearly everyone tries to fill the
empty void death leaves with anything or anyone they can find. Some
turn to the bottle, a few to God, but most simply try to replace that
loved one with someone else. For the Davis family I became the
logical replacement for Betty Jack.

Had that proved the only role I played for them, I could have
accepted the events that were to take place with more understanding.
They had already convinced me that my own family wanted nothing
to do with me and that I should feel fortunate indeed to have them to
fall back on in my grief. However, one thing continues to stand in the
way of my appreciating my good fortune at being taken into the Davis
family. That is that considerable amounts of money from record sales
and an insurance policy began to flow into the Davises' hands. As
Betty Jack's beneficiaries, the Davises were entitled to her share; as
my custodians, they were getting my share as well. Skeeter, the ugly
duckling who Mrs. Davis claimed had been such a bad influence on
Betty Jack, had been transformed into the goose that laid the golden
egg.

Almost immediately after the first royalty check came in, Mrs.
Davis took me to a local bank where we opened a joint account from
which either one of us could withdraw funds. Then she took me to
see her nephew, Ray Hensley, who just happened to be a lawyer. She
had him draw up a will naming the Davises as my beneficiaries. In
1981, after I had begun writing my autobiography, I saw a copy of this
document. I wept as I read each line detailing that the Davises would

be the sole beneficiaries. She had it written so that my family would have received nothing.

The only way I can frame this part of my past into a somewhat healthy perspective is to imagine what would have been my fate had the Davises not taken me into their home. I was most definitely a physical and emotional liability, incapable of fending for myself. My parents, who still drank heavily at the time, would have found it difficult to contend with me at their Hamilton, Ohio, home. Perhaps the ideal situation simply didn't exist. In all fairness to the Davises, whom after much prayer and time I have forgiven for their treatment of me, the bitterness I have harbored against them surfaces only when I lose sight of the grief and pain they must have felt in losing Betty Jack. I did love them because they were Betty Jack's family, but I have to tell it like it was.

Mrs. Davis could hardly wait for her chance to re-create the Davis Sisters. Her designs became clear each morning when I appeared at the breakfast table. "Betty Jack would have wanted you to carry on her work, and you know that, don't ya, Skeeter?"

Why does she always say "her" work, never "your" work?

Mr. Davis, throughout his wife's tirades, sat meekly eating his breakfast. I would stare at my food, pushing it around the plate while tears welled up in my eyes and slowly dampened the tablecloth.

"Why don't you say something? You hear me, don't ya? You've just got to keep singing, and Georgia says she is perfectly willing to sing with you."

Betty Jack's sister nodded as if singing with me would be an act of compassion on her part. I argued with them over and over in my mind. *Georgia can't sing. Betty Jack even said she couldn't. If B.J. had wanted to sing with Georgia, wouldn't she have sung with her instead of me? After all, Georgia's her natural sister. She was around a long time before I appeared at Dixie Heights High School.* No matter what I thought, I didn't dare utter a word of it out loud. I finally managed a hoarse whisper, "No, I don't think it would work."

"Wouldn't work? What on earth do you mean? Skeeter, you listen to me. You owe this to Betty. It's the very least you can do. After all, have you forgotten so quickly who it was that shoved the car seat over on her?"

Pushing my chair from the table, I ran for the bathroom, where I lost what little breakfast I had managed to swallow. I pressed a wet cloth across my face and slipped quietly back to the bedroom. With my eyes turned to the door, I spent the day alone. Occasionally someone would rattle the doorknob and shout my name. I refused to answer.

The same scene was repeated so many times and with so little variation that it's difficult for me to remember the exact day their repetitious brainwashing program actually wore me down, but regretfully it did. One morning at the breakfast table Mrs. Davis began her spiel. I relented. "Okay. I guess I'll sing with Georgia."

Six short months after the accident, I was back on stage again. I've seen pictures of me that fans took from those appearances. I looked horrible. The pupil of my left eye was so severely dilated that it was the size of the iris of my right eye. Expressionless, my face resembled that of a shell of a person. I showed no outward sign of emotion. Inwardly I was hating every minute of my life. I felt I was betraying not only myself but Betty Jack too.

While I drilled Georgia on the art of performing, Mrs. Davis made arrangements for the resurrection of the Davis Sisters on the Ernest Tubb show at a National Guard Armory in Indiana. We had one week to prepare. Like I had thought earlier, Georgia really couldn't sing. She didn't understand meter. I knew the only way we were going to be able to perform was for me to sing Betty Jack's part, and then switch to harmony on the chorus. Even then I had to squeeze Georgia's hand to cue her when it was her time to come in. Being forced to sing Betty Jack's part reinforced in me the feeling that she was still alive inside of me. At times my voice sounded so much like hers that it made my skin crawl.

Mrs. Davis drove us to the show. She always drove. Never once do I remember her allowing Mr. Davis to take the wheel. On the way I fainted. Mrs. Davis stopped at a drugstore where she purchased Miles Nervine and an unlabeled brown bottle full of liquid. It seemed she would let nothing get in the way of "Betty's work."

Much to my surprise, the audience yelled and applauded all the way through "I Forgot More." Still, it wasn't the same. When we finished, I found a corner backstage and hid. When I watched Georgia devouring the attention that rightfully belonged to Betty Jack, my stomach somersaulted. My thoughts were even worse. *This ain't right. She's stepping into this after B.J. and I worked so hard to get here. She doesn't deserve this.*

Fans crowded Georgia backstage. Flashbulbs popped while I kept my seat in the corner. Someone asked, "Which one of ya'll is the sister of the girl who got killed?"

"I am," Georgia smiled.

"Oh, so you sang with her on the record?"

Her smile vanished. Reluctantly Georgia confessed, "No."

"Then who did?"

I volunteered a whisper from the corner, no longer sure of myself. "It was me."

A flashbulb illuminated my corner, burning my dilated eye. Finding the pain unbearable, I covered my face with my hands to keep the cameras and the flashes away and headed for the car.

I could not find courage in me to confront Mrs. Davis. I was intimidated and totally petrified by her accusing stares, her bitter barbs, and when all else failed, she knew an even more effective way of manipulating me. Once Mrs. Davis had my obedience, she praised me for it. For example, I accompanied her to buy new furniture for the house. She had arranged the pieces in a conventional setting, with the sofa against the wall and lamps on either side and the new chairs clustered around it. Then Georgia came and rearranged it. The setting looked great in *Better Homes and Gardens*, but we weren't progressive enough to have seen anything like that yet. Visiting neighbors laughed. "What ya'll doing with your couch out in the middle of the floor?"

"That was Georgia's idea," Mrs. Davis replied, "but isn't this beautiful furniture Skeeter bought us? She's so sweet to think of me and Tipp like she does." The visitors, of course, agreed on cue, and I stood there smiling, conned into feeling proud of something I had no intention of doing.

Georgia told me one day, "If I had your money, Skeeter, I'd have me a mink stole."

Mrs. Davis lit into her. "I'd be ashamed of myself talking like that, Georgia. Skeeter's so good to your mother. She's better to me than you are. She buys me all these things, then you come in here talking about her buying something silly like a mink stole."

When RCA learned that I was performing again, Steve Sholes called from New York. "Well, I'm glad to see you decided not to give it up, Skeeter."

I couldn't tell him that it was not my decision to make. Instead I said, "I'm still not feeling well, Steve."

"We're more concerned with your health than anything else.

You've got all the time in the world as far as we're concerned. I just wanted you to know that we're here when you need us. Just give us a call."

"You mean you're going to keep me with RCA?" I had never dreamed that they would want me without B.J.

"We never thought otherwise. We've considered putting you with Rita Robbins and Anita Carter and calling you Rita, Nita, and Skeeta. How does that sound?" Steve laughed. "We're also prepared to have you do a duet with Hank Snow, or you can even go solo if you like. You call the shots, Skeeter. And the main thing, like I said, is we want you to get well."

"Oh, thank you, Steve. Thank you." It was the most relieving news I had heard in what seemed like years instead of months. The relief didn't last long. Mrs. Davis rounded the corner of the living room as I hung up.

"Was that the man from RCA?"

"Yes."

"And just what did he want?"

I couldn't lie. I told her exactly what Steve had said.

"You get that man back on the phone this minute and tell him you've decided to sing with Betty Jack's sister."

From 1954 through 1956 Georgia and I recorded for RCA as the Davis Sisters. With Minnie Pearl, Hawkshaw Hawkins, Hal Lonepine and Betty Cody, Hank Snow, Charlene Arthur, Bud Isaacs, Chet Atkins, and Eddie Hill, we toured the country as the RCA Caravan of Stars. It was one of the most grueling tours I can remember. We played to packed houses everywhere and started RCA on its way to making the Nashville sound an even more important part of American music.

During those years Georgia and I released nine singles, all of which were either cut in New York or Chicago but none of which ever did anything other than bubble around at the bottom of the country charts. The material was good. For example, we sang songs by A.P. Carter and Felice and Boudleaux Bryant, but Georgia and I lacked the punch and polish that had led *Cashbox* to honor Betty Jack and me as the Most Promising Vocal Group of 1953 or *Music Vendor* to award us the Most Programmed Song. It was a hopeless situation made even worse by the crazy way we had to sing. I was still singing lead, then switching to harmony on the chorus and squeezing Georgia's hand when she was supposed to come in. This was the routine from the beginning of our career to the end of it.

Throughout our entire career I arranged only one appearance of my own accord. I called the Grand Ole Opry and told them that I wanted a guest spot to sing "I Forgot More" as a tribute to Betty Jack. They readily agreed, and I tried to no avail to convince Georgia that I should appear by myself. She went out on the Opry stage and just stood there beside me while I sang. B.J.'s absence robbed me of any excitement my first real appearance on the Opry could have brought me, and the memory of the two of us singing to the Opry janitors at sixteen caused me to break into my ten millionth crying jag as I left the stage.

Later that evening when Georgia and I went down to the Ernest Tubb Record Shop, something happened there that would signal a change in at least one aspect of my life. Ray Price was there, and while the people milled around asking for autographs, Ray pulled me aside and asked, "What you shootin' up?"

I gave him a puzzled look, and Ray pointed to the bruises on my arm. "Hadn't you better hide those?"

"What do you mean?"

"I mean them dope tracks."

I was totally confused. I said, "But that ain't what that is. I go to a doctor…"

"Well, I got a feelin' you better change doctors, sister. You gonna end up like ol' Hank if you ain't careful."

Thereafter I flatly refused to go to Mrs. Davis's doctor anymore. For a week or so I was violently ill, but when it passed, I felt physically stronger. All the while Mrs. Davis kept urging me to resume the injections. "Your nerves can't stand it, Skeeter."

Still it never occurred to me that she was trying to do anything other than help me by taking me to the doctor. I just finally figured I was well and didn't need any more medicine regardless of what it was. Although my physical health was improving, throughout 1954 I was still confused and emotionally wrecked. The only happy times were when Georgia would bring her daughter, Trena Ann, over during the day so that I could baby-sit. The two of us would play with dolls. Little Mary Frances, the child in me, got a chance to come out and be free. I loved Trena Ann like she was my own and she attached herself to me as strongly. Had those episodes been the limit of my activity for a while, I might have gotten well much more quickly.

In 1955 RCA called to ask me to come to Nashville without Georgia for a recording session with Hank Snow. I was delighted—

not so much for the opportunity to sing with someone else, but for the chance to get away on my own for a while. In retrospect I can see that the session with Hank went well, but at the time all I could think, of course, was *It's supposed to be me and B.J., not anyone else; not even someone as great as Hank Snow.*

While I was at the RCA studio that week, Sonny James dropped in to say hello to Chet Atkins. When Chet introduced us, I said in my excitement, "Oh, we recorded your song."

"Tell me about it." Sonny frowned, then smiled to let me know all was forgiven. "I knew from the minute I heard ya'll's record, mine was dead."

That day a warm relationship began between Sonny James and me. There were times when I felt that Chet may have been pushing Sonny and me toward each other, but we've always been just the best of friends with no romantic involvement between us. Sonny and his wife, Doris, are special friends of mine.

As Sonny and I shared our stories about "I Forgot More," Chet interrupted us with a new trick he wanted me to try. "Skeeter, while you're here, why don't you help me with a little experiment. Sing 'Honky Tonk Angels' and let me record you."

I sang "It Wasn't God Who Made Honky Tonk Angels," the song Kitty Wells had recorded in response to "The Wild Side Of Life," while Chet taped it. Sonny James played rhythm for me on his guitar. When we finished the song, Chet handed me a pair of those old bulky headphones and said, "Now listen."

He replayed the tape and I thought as I listened, *How horrible! I still can't sing lead.*

"Okay, Skeeter," Chet said, rewinding the tape, "now I want you to sing harmony over your lead vocal."

"Are you kidding?"

"Nah. Just listen to your lead through the headphones and sing harmony as if you were singing with Betty Jack. Just pretend the other voice is hers."

I did exactly what Chet told me and then listened to the replay of my harmony along with my lead. All I could say was, "Wow! That's amazing."

I couldn't believe it. I was sitting there listening to me singing with myself. He called it *overdubbing*, and as far as I know that was the first time it had ever been done by anyone. In this age of thirty-two-track studios turning out quadraphonic masters, that simple concept may seem antiquated, but at the time it was totally beyond my wildest imagination. To me Chet Atkins has always been, and will always be, a genius. I asked him, "What will you think of next, Chet?"

"I think I'd like to cut a record like that when you're ready for it, Skeeter." He hesitated. "That's what I think will happen next. You're still the best duet around."

It never really occurred to me that overdubbing would ever be done as anything other than a gimmick. Little did I know Chet's prediction would come true. I would become my own duet, my own Davis Sisters. Four years later we would use this same procedure to cut my first solo album, *I'll Sing You a Song and Harmonize Too*. But many things lay ahead for me before a Skeeter Davis album would ever be cut.

On TV Patti Page was selling America a new automobile. "Ummmm...this car has Olds-mobility." Her smooth talking convinced me and a nation of automobile buyers. Years later, I would marvel at the irony of my connection with Patti Page: Not only did she sell me an automobile, but as a pop artist, she released a version of the Davis Sisters' "Everlovin'." Decades later, she would receive the Academy of Country Music's Pioneer Award for her overdubbing recording technique. Ironically, I still have an earlier tape of Chet Atkins's demonstration of the magic of overdubbing harmony on my recording sessions. I have never been one to squabble over awards, but I have always meant to talk to Dick Clark about this one!

Each time I heard Patti, I grew more and more enchanted with the idea of having a car of my own. I had no idea how much money I had. So I asked Mrs. Davis for enough money from my account to buy a new car: a turquoise and white Olds 98. I paid the dealer cash for it.

The Oldsmobile gave me the freedom to drive over to Highland Cemetery every day without having to ask somebody to take me. The cemetery was the only place I ever went, but these excursions were my first step back into a world where my own will was at work.

I would sit for hours in silence by Betty Jack's grave, trying to picture where my life was taking me or quietly telling her what was going on. The grass beneath the tree by her graveside felt like home to me. In a way I belonged there. It was the only place I had found, besides the railroad tracks behind the house, where I could be myself and share my innermost thoughts and feelings. It was a sad place but free from accusations. I could cry there in sorrow instead of fear.

A year before a man had come by the Davises' to discuss what kind of monument we wanted for B.J. I had envisioned a gigantic statue bearing her likeness, with the words to "How Beautiful Heaven Must Be" carved in the base. The man sketched it for us, and everyone agreed that Betty Jack deserved such a marvelous memorial. I gave Mrs. Davis the money to pay for it. The months turned to years, no monument came. I would ask about it, but no one seemed to know the reason for the delay.

One day Ada Ray and Marie, our Sunday school teachers, dropped by the Davises' to accompany me to the cemetery. I know, looking back, that they knew the monument had arrived. When I saw it, it was like a paring knife had been thrust into my heart and twisted. Instead of the beautiful statue I expected to find, her grave was marked by a marble slab the size of a small stepping stone. The only inscription that it bore was her name, date of birth and death, a couple of musical notations, and the words "Our Beloved Daughter. Till We Meet Again."

I fell on my knees, clawing at the tombstone, determined to pull it up and remove it, screaming, "No! B.J., I never meant this!" I choked, "Where's the one I paid for?"

Ada Ray bent down and tried to unwrap my arms from the cold stone. She whispered, "Honey, didn't you know the Davises are building a new house at Taylor Mill?"

I pushed her away from me and pounded the ground with my clenched fists. "You're lying. You're lying to me, all of you. They'd never leave our house! They know Betty Jack's there."

They patiently let me scream until I finally exhausted myself. No one spoke until the caretaker drove by and warned us he would be locking the gates in five minutes. I was like a limp bag of laundry when the two women lifted me from the graveside to load me in the car. Marie said, "Skeeter, believe us. We're not trying to hurt you. We love you. Please come back to church and let us try to show you how much we really care."

Back home I climbed the stairs for the bedroom and sobbed for hours. I begged God to find me a way out of that house.

I hadn't been back to DeCoursey Baptist Church since the funeral, but the Sunday that followed the cemetery scene I found strength to return, due to Ada Ray and Marie's encouragement. I thought I could handle it. As long as the congregation was singing everything went fine, but as soon as Brother Rader began to preach, I heard a whispering sound coming from behind me. I recognized the voice immediately. It was Betty Jack's. She was softly whispering in prayer. Her voice became more and more distinct. "Oh, dear Jesus, please help Skeeter. Lead her away from here."

I thought I was going crazy again. I fought my way to the aisle and ran out of the church, gasping for breath. Outside I walked around trying to regain my senses. Ada Ray and Marie soon joined me. They walked one on each side and without saying a word seemed to understand. What love those two women had! Gradually, through their kindness Sunday after Sunday, I became able to sit through the whole service and take the vivid presence of Betty Jack for granted. I even started taking part in the service, singing specials with Ruby Williams and her niece Wanda Rose. I asked Georgia to join us, but she said, "The Blackwood Brothers get paid for singing, and so should we."

"We're not the Blackwood Brothers," I said. "Me and B J. always sang at church for free."

The very next day we received a call from Colonel Parker. He was interested in booking us on a tour through Alabama and Florida with Hank Snow, Mother Maybelle and the Carter Sisters (minus June), and Elvis Presley. At the time I was trying to coax Georgia into agreeing to sign Colonel Parker as our manager. Just like she didn't want to sing at the church for free, she didn't want Colonel Parker to touch even one cent of her money. I was always glad when the Colonel would ask us to tour. And this time, I was especially glad that I would see the Carter Sisters again.

The first night of the tour, Elvis Presley followed Onie Wheeler in the program lineup. I cannot adequately convey the atmosphere of excitement and absolute hysteria that filled every nook and cranny of the auditorium. Because of the charged crowd Elvis generated, the show's program schedule changed every night. Elvis never knew which spot he had. The only thing he could be sure of was that he couldn't open nor could he perform before intermission. As the tour progressed, he just had to close the show.

Elvis enjoyed my company backstage and would hold my hand to try to keep me from biting my nails as we strolled together in the wings. Sometimes I would hide in a dressing room other than the one assigned to the Davis Sisters just to see if he would come in search of me. He always did. Once he found me, we would head to the backstage entrance of the building, where we'd sit on the steps and sing every gospel song we knew.

From the very first conversation I had with Elvis, he spoke of his love for his mother, Gladys. One of the reasons I believe Elvis liked me was that I reminded him of her. I didn't smoke or drink alcohol, and I always went to church even when I was on tour. I knew the gospel songs too that made him think of home.

Elvis would ask me to go eat with him after the show. My reply would always make him smile. "I'll starve by the time you get through that line of girls waiting to see you." He would come right back at me with a good-natured response, telling me that I would be first in that line if only I would go with him.

We developed a kinship that revolved around a series of exchanges throughout that tour. I would tell him, for instance, that I didn't even watch him during his performances. He would pretend that I had wounded his ego and hurt his feelings. Of course the truth is that I always watched. Once his spot ended I would race back to the dressing room to stick my nose in the book that I had been reading in case he would stop by to see if I had been listening. I had so much fun teasing him, making him think that I didn't consider him to be anyone particularly special.

The truth was, however, I knew that he was very special indeed. An incredibly unique talent. Elvis was the first act that mesmerized young girls, women, and men of all ages and races. Everyone was completely enchanted by him. He was on the scene long before the Beatles and the Rolling Stones affected audiences in a similar fashion. The fans would work themselves into a frenzy over him.

When we played Silver Springs, Florida, on that tour, he asked me to take a ride on a glass-bottom boat with him. Later in the elevator back at the radio station there, Elvis tried to kiss me. I resisted him, saying that I was not going to be another one of those silly girls who fell all over him. The elevator doors opened at just the right moment and I ran out.

Later he told Anita Carter and Georgia that I just didn't like him. He even consulted Onie Wheeler for advice. It seems he told Onie that he liked me very much, but he just didn't understand why I wouldn't eat with him or let him take me out to the picture show on our days off. Feeling for him as they did, they all urged me to accept his invitations, assuring me that he was in earnest.

The night I accepted his invitation to dinner, I was amazed at his appetite. Many Elvis stories have been told over the years, and I can vouch for those that depict him as a voracious eater. That night after the show, he consumed a T-bone steak, two cheeseburgers deluxe, and a banana split. Compared to me with my sandwich and soft drink, Elvis could really put it away. Throughout the course of the meal, he would tease me, saying that the only reason he was eating all of that was to take a long time so that he could have me all to himself.

He told me how he had really loved my record with Betty Jack. He had been driving a truck in Memphis when he heard the record for the first time. He pulled his truck over to the side of the road to listen to the song. After it finished playing, he located the nearest telephone booth to call and request the station to play it again. He just sat in his truck listening to the record. Every day thereafter, he made a song request for our record—the prettiest song he had ever heard.

"Let's have a banana split," Elvis said.

"You already had one!"

The next thing I knew, we were sitting at the table with two banana splits—one for me and another one for him.

"I have another story to tell you, Skeeter, but I don't want you to laugh and think that I'm weak."

I told him that I thought he was going to be more than weak. "You're going to be the fat man in the circus, eatin' like you do."

"Will you come to my circus?" He grinned. "That might be fun."

I was ready to return to the hotel, but he insisted that he tell me his story. "Can't you tell me while we walk back?" I asked.

As we walked back to the hotel together, he told me that while driving his truck on August 2, 1953, he heard the radio news about the Davis Sisters' fatal automobile accident. He stopped his truck. As he slowed to a stop, the bulletin was corrected: only one of the girls was dead, the other critically injured and hospitalized. He said that he began to cry on the spot and reached out to God, saying that he wanted to meet the girl who survived to tell her how much he loved the record and how sorry he was that she lost her sister.

He said, "I'm telling you the truth, Skeeter. Do you think I'm weak? A man ain't supposed to cry."

By the time he finished his story, we had already approached the hotel grounds where Anita, Georgia, and a member of the Carters' group, Becky Bowman, were enjoying the moonlight and the Florida breezes, reclining in lawn chairs as they kept a watch out for me. They were giggling and teasing Elvis, "We thought you ran off with Skeeter since you finally got her all to yourself."

I never revealed to them the conversation I had with Elvis. I kept it to myself and returned to my room. How sad I was that Betty Jack wasn't there. Elvis would have adored her!

The very next day we were scheduled to play Jacksonville's Gator Bowl. Elvis came to look for me before the show as usual. He was particularly excited about showing me the new shirt he was wearing for the performance. I simply had never, ever seen a man wear such a thing. Elvis stood before me wearing a pink lace shirt!

"Skeeter, look at my new shirt. I spent a pretty penny on this one. What do you think? Do you like it?"

"Elvis, that shirt looks like a girl's blouse."

Displaying his disappointment and injured pride, he started to unbutton his shirt. "You take it then," he said.

"I don't want your shirt, Elvis!"

Mae Boren Axton walked by just in time to overhear the end of the conversation. "Elvis, if you ain't going to wear that shirt, give it to me. I'll take it."

Elvis handed the shirt to Mae, saying, "Skeeter don't like it on me, so I'm not wearing it."

Mae and I have laughed about that incident through the years. She held on to the shirt and liked to tease me, "Skeeter, how much would you give me for a good Elvis Presley shirt?" Mae cowrote one of Elvis's classic recordings, "Heartbreak Hotel," and has remained a good friend of mine.

Hank Snow stood under the dugout at the Gator Bowl watching Elvis. The fans stormed the grounds. Elvis hardly made it back to safety. They tore his clothes off him. Hank and I remember that day well and have spoken of it often. No one was quite like Elvis.

Colonel Parker arranged for the whole troupe to go waterskiing the very next day. Since I couldn't ski (and still can't manage waterskis), I rode in the boat as Elvis pulled the skiers. What a fun day! When I told my family about this excursion, my brother Dean and sisters Doozer and Suzan bragged to their friends at school about their big sister who worked with the already legendary Elvis Presley. Dean would later joke to me, "Skeeter, why didn't you like Elvis? We could have all been living at Graceland!"

In July of 1977 Onie Wheeler stood by his locker next to mine at the Grand Ole Opry and blurted out, "Skeeter, let's go see Elvis!"

"Onie, I can't believe you said that. I was just thinking how nice it would be for us to go over. He knows we don't want anything from him. He knows we just love him like always." I explained that I had upcoming concerts through August but that as soon as I finished, we should go.

Onie said, "That would be great. I'll tell him that I finally got you for him." Regrettably, Onie and I never made that reunion visit.

On the morning of August 16, 1977, I woke up with a choking sensation that reminded me of the night of the wreck. I could not shake the feeling of dread that came over me. My band had left in advance of me for the three-day fair date we had accepted in Washington state. I would join them on the seventeenth.

I called Linda Palmer, who was then my secretary, to tell her to stop whatever she was doing because I needed her. I felt that something terrible was going to happen. She thought that I was anxious for the safety of my band and dismissed my anxiety. I knew that wasn't so; I always trusted the Lord to keep them safe.

When Linda arrived, she said, "Why don't you go shopping? You might feel better." Since I didn't need to buy anything in particular, I decided that we could go for a ride instead.

"Linda, I feel that the Death Angel is coming for someone we know." Knowing me like she does, Linda couldn't dismiss my premonitions very easily. She has seen them hold true too many times.

Linda drove as I prayed. As we pulled beside a truck and its driver, we heard the news, "The King of Rock and Roll is dead."

I screamed and then shouted at the truck driver from the open passenger window, "Is that true? Elvis is the King of Rock and Roll. He can't be…Is he dead? Is he? What is happening?"

Linda pulled the car off to the shoulder of the road to try to calm me down as I wept uncontrollably. Elvis was dead.

The Death Angel I had foreseen had come. Linda reminded me later of the parallels between Elvis's experience of hearing the news of B.J.'s death and our experience of hearing of Elvis's death. I was even more saddened that I would be unable to attend his funeral because of my obligation to the fair dates in Washington. Throughout the three sad days spent on that job, my band and I shared our grief over the loss of Elvis by reminiscing and singing gospel songs in memory of him.

When I returned home to the Opry, Onie Wheeler and I spoke with Mae Axton about the funeral service. She said, "Skeeter, I talked to Elvis the day before he died. He asked me if I ever see Skeeter Davis. I told him that I see you all the time. He said, 'Next time you see her, tell her I still love her.'" Onie and I stood together crying; we had waited too long to see our friend ever again.

In August of 1991 Mae Axton met me backstage at the Opry on one of her visits with friends from Oklahoma. "Skeeter, how's your book coming along?"

"It's coming along just fine, Mae."

"You had better tell about that pink lace shirt of Elvis's I got." I was so happy that she still remembered.

And so goes the story of this silly little girl who didn't get in line with all the rest, but who remained a friend to Elvis forever.

The End of an Error, the End of an Era

The wedding was just the kind you planned—
The flowers, the church, and even your love song.
But it was me that reached and took his hand
And the ring you'd waited for so long.
Tomorrow my teardrops will fall,
Though I seem so happy today.
Tomorrow I'll cry and recall
The love that I lost yesterday.
—"Tomorrow I'll Cry,"
Skeeter Davis and
Betty Jack Davis

One Sunday Mrs. Davis drove me to church in my new Oldsmobile. Kenneth Depew, a railroad coworker of Mr. Davis and Georgia's husband, Larry, was standing outside the church doors with the other men, smoking cigarettes and talking before services started. I had seen him there before. When Kenny saw us pull up, he sauntered over and opened the door for me. He gave the Oldsmobile the once-over and said, "That sure is a nice set of wheels you got, Skeeter."

"Why, thank you, Kenny," I said and grinned, not so much because I considered his statement much of a compliment, but because it

171

reminded me of an old saying of B.J.'s from our teenage years. "He's not much," she used to say, "but boy, somethin' about that car of his makes me crazy about him."

Throughout the service I would catch him watching me. That afternoon he came calling. "Where would you like to go?"

"Well, if you really want to take me someplace, I'd like to go to the cemetery."

"I don't mind taking you there at all. Why don't we drive your car, though."

"Sure, that'll be fine with me."

Kenny sprawled out in the Oldsmobile, reading the owner's manual, while I sat out by B.J.'s grave site.

Everybody at church was raving about Kenny—how good looking he was and how cute we would look together. They all wanted to play Cupid. I think they figured a boyfriend is what I needed to pull me out of my grief.

For some reason, the Davises also encouraged me into a relationship with Kenny. They would invite him over, even when I wouldn't. I didn't want him around. First of all, his name was wild. *Kenneth* was a nice name, but *Depew*?

Georgia said, "That's a French name, Skeeter. And the French are such good lovers."

"Well, *Depew* sounds to me like something somebody says when something stinks," I said and laughed at my own joke. Come to think of it, I believe that was probably the first time I'd cracked a joke or laughed since Betty Jack died.

The church began organizing parties for every occasion possible. Valentine parties. Halloween parties. All kinds of parties for things I'd never known Baptists to celebrate before. There was a row at church about it, but I guess as word circulated from Ada Ray and Marie as to their motive—that is, to help Skeeter—things quieted down again.

I wouldn't go to the parties with Kenny and he wouldn't take me home, but the parties were planned in such a way as to ensure that the two of us got paired off together. At the Halloween party, someone came in dressed like Frankenstein and scared me to death. Everybody laughed, including me. The events forced me to participate in life again, to do something besides walk around the hill behind the church and cry.

It is beautiful, in a way, to know people cared so much about me. I suppose they figured that I'd stay in shock forever if they didn't do something. The final outcome of their caring, however, would turn out to be a double-edged sword. On the one hand, it would be the tragic misfitting of two people, me and Kenneth Depew; on the other hand, it would be the answer to a prayer I thought had gone unheard.

Did I like Kenny? It's hard to say. I was almost indifferent. If anything, he often got on my nerves. It was just another one of those times when I acted to please somebody besides myself. There were other guys I had dated who struck more desire in me. But I'd never been beyond hugging and kissing anybody, anyhow.

I had always envisioned that I would be a preacher's wife. I wanted to follow the example of Brother and Mrs. Rader as the role model for the perfect couple. I thought that I could make a good wife for a preacher; I could sing and help with the visiting and everything else preachers do.

When Billy Mitchell came to DeCoursey Baptist to hold a revival, he had been the first guy I looked at with interest since Bob Sinex, the steel player on *Midday Merry-Go-Round*. Reverend Mitchell was a good-looking, young, unmarried preacher. His preaching excited me and I liked him as a person too. But by the time I first saw him, I was already wearing Kenny's engagement ring. Billy Mitchell and I talked and talked. I felt comfortable and at ease and safe, until he looked down at my hand and said, "I see you're engaged." I remember standing there wishing that I wasn't. I had totally forgotten.

Did Kenny love me? Never did I ever hear him once say, "Skeeter, I love you." We seldom shared anything. We double-dated with Georgia and Larry, although they were already married. We went to movies mostly. I don't ever remember having a meaningful conversation with Kenny. We hugged and kissed a lot, but like I said, he didn't thrill me nearly as much as other boys I'd dated. I married him simply because everybody seemed to want me to and because there seemed to be nothing left to do but become a wife. All the other girls my age were married.

But why did he marry me? He was supposed to be in love with another girl when the church folks started pushing us together. I guess he saw me as having good potential. He saw the nice new furniture my money had bought the Davises; he saw the Oldsmobile and knew I had money in the bank. I could be a shortcut to easy street.

Regardless of what our motives were, after a brief, contrived romance, we were married.

Everyone except me had a hand in arranging the wedding. I was looking through the pictures of our wedding to refresh my memory, only to observe that the entire wedding party was made up of Georgia and her friends. Sometimes I feel like I played a role in somebody else's wedding. None of my real family was there, none of my sisters. As a matter of fact, they didn't even find out about it until the wedding story hit the papers. It nearly killed my mother. They tell me somebody found her passed out drunk on Betty Jack's grave and carried her home. Daddy said when mother came to she was screaming, "I've lost my girl. They've stolen Skeeter from me."

I guess they actually had. The wedding announcements read: "Mr. and Mrs. Tipp Davis request the honor of your presence at the wedding of their daughter Mary Frances to Mr. Kenneth Carl Depew on Saturday the Twenty-First of July at three thirty o'clock in the afternoon. DeCoursey Baptist Church, Covington, Kentucky."

I had honestly forgotten my wedding date until I reread that old announcement that had been stacked among the pictures. I do remember Georgia selected the date so that it would come as near as possible to her and Larry's wedding date.

I made no decision of any kind on my own. That's not to say I didn't try. One of the places I could hide and think, besides the railroad tracks and the graveyard, was the bathroom. Even today one of my favorite times is when I'm bathing. I used to think it was because I was so poor as a kid. But I still enjoy it and gosh, I've had a bathtub a long time now. Anyway, I'd lie back in the tub of hot water and ask, "Lord, am I really going to marry this man?"

One night while I was bathing, the Lord directed me to this scripture: "For I would that all men were even as I myself. But every man hath his proper gift of God, one after this manner, and another after that. I say therefore to the unmarried and widows, It is good for them if they abide even as I. But if they cannot contain, let them marry: for it is better to marry than to burn." (1 Corinthians 7:7–9 K.J.V.)

I was certainly not burning with passion. I felt I could easily emulate St. Paul. I took the scripture down to Mrs. Davis and asked her to help me interpret it. She said, "Oh, Skeeter, how silly! The wedding's already set. We don't want to disappoint these folks, now do we?"

The very next day Georgia came over to see me. She had a sex book with her which she gave to me and asked me to read. "Aren't you excited about getting to be with Kenny? Boy, it's good with me and Larry. You'll just love it, Skeeter."

I was so embarrassed. I hid the book as soon as she left and never read it.

Georgia even arranged our honeymoon plans. We were to drive to Miami, then catch a cruiser across the Caribbean to Havana, Cuba. (Obviously, these were the days before Castro.) Kenny drove my Oldsmobile and I begged him not to stop until we reached Miami. I kept reminding him that if he got sleepy, I could drive, but he stopped anyway.

In the motel room I started crying. And Kenny hadn't even touched me. Underneath my new white nightgown, I wore my bra and panties. After about thirty restless minutes of tossing and turning, Kenny rolled over and asked, "Wouldn't you be more comfortable with your bra off?"

I didn't want Kenny to see or touch me. He reached to undo my bra and I scooted as far away from him as I could. "No, I'm going to sleep in it!"

Eight days passed before our marriage was consummated. When it was, the act just about killed me. I simply wasn't prepared for intimacy with Kenny. Hugging and kissing had been the limit until that moment.

As time passed I found myself constantly at the doctor's office with one complaint or another. First I broke out in hives, red ones the shape of roses. *Ain't nobody wants to make love to a woman that looks like a necktie.* Later my period would come on a weekly basis. My doctor thought I was going to be the youngest woman ever to go through the change of life. I drove Kenny absolutely crazy trying to adjust to the role of the good wife.

I wonder whether Kenny actually wanted me any more than I wanted him. He never touched me without a prophylactic. At that time, I thought the only good thing that could possibly come out of sex was a baby. That's the reason I finally relaxed enough to submit to him. I wanted to have a baby. *If I had a baby,* I thought, *I'd settle down for the rest of my life.*

I told Kenny to stop using the prophylactic.

"No way! There ain't gonna be no towheaded brats running around this place."

Our sexual relationship was ridiculous. Kenny never tried to help me through my fears, and he never went to the trouble of making it an enjoyable experience for me. Believe it or not, I was so naive, I didn't even know it was supposed to be enjoyable to the woman. I had constantly heard my mother complain about how much she disliked sex and considered it merely a chore.

In the middle of the night I'd get up, go to the bathroom, and cry tears of frustration. I knew that the coming Sunday the ladies at church would pat my stomach and say, "When we gonna have a baby, Skeeter?"

"Oh, just any day now." I'd smile, hiding my discontent and pain, just like I'd hidden that sex book.

To make matters worse, Kenny and I lived with the Davises up in Betty Jack's room. The only joy I had was when Kenny left each day for the railroad. I had reestablished contact with my oldest sister, who was living nearby. It was probably one of the healthiest things I had done on my own. Every day I'd call Shirley and ask, "Have you given the babies their baths yet?"

"Oh, no. Come on over."

"Okay. Wait till I get there. Let me do it." Shirley had two daughters by this time, Terry and Cheryl. Eventually, she would have a grand total of eight. The two little girls looked like twins because Terry had been premature, a tiny miracle baby, and Cheryl had caught up with her. Shirley let me bathe them both and dress them before we loaded them in strollers and headed to the movies. How I enjoyed those hours with Shirley and the girls. Yet even with a good substitute for motherhood, I kept hoping in some miraculous way I would conceive a child despite the precautions Kenny was taking. In retrospect, I thank the Lord I didn't.

One day Kenny came home from work and announced, "Get packed. We're getting out of here. I've found us an apartment."

It happened so fast. I couldn't believe it. I was so excited to be leaving the Davises. Had they foreseen this development, I am certain that they would never have contrived my marriage to Kenny. Their ploy to keep me under their thumbs had backfired. Kenny was moving me out.

When we started carrying our stuff down the stairs, I witnessed Mrs. Davis losing her composure for the first time. She, who was always so cool, became a raging crazy woman. Another first—Mr.

Davis stood up to his wife. I wish Betty Jack could have seen her daddy. She would have been so proud. As Mrs. Davis screamed, "You can't leave! Skeeter, you can't go!" he grabbed Mrs. Davis, pinned her arms to her side, and calmly started telling her, "Now, Ollie, don't do this. Ollie, you've got to let her go now." She screeched at Kenny, calling him unmentionable names.

Tipp Davis said, "Please don't say things you'll regret later. Kenny's her husband. You've got to let her go with him."

She broke loose from her husband's grip and began hauling everything we had brought down back upstairs. She pulled on my arm and pleaded with me to stay. I jerked away from her and said, "You wanted me to marry him; now let me go with him."

We loaded Kenny's car and left without the Oldsmobile. I never got it back. I also had to leave our awards hanging on the wall. Mrs. Davis managed to snatch away every photograph, but one or two, that B.J. and I had taken on the road. I sneaked one of her dresses down, but only made it out with that one because it looked like one of mine that I left hanging in its place. Our departure was like that of a couple fleeing a fire, grabbing things in haste. As I closed the door, I told the Davises, "If you can live with these things of mine, I can live without 'em."

I left the fire with a man I didn't even love and hardly knew. But I was free from the Davises, thanks to Kenny. But in truth I abandoned irreplaceable posessions. The awards, the photographs and clothing, of course, but other things as well. The footprints the two of us made the day they laid the new concrete porch. The railroad tracks where Betty Jack had roamed. The grove where she sneaked off to smoke. But one thing left that burning house with me, more important than all of that. Something no one saw me leave with, nor could ever take from me. Betty Jack.

Our apartment was half of a white frame house that faced the railroad tracks at the Latonia cherry factory, where Grandma Roberts had worked all her life. From our porch I watched for her, but I never crossed the tracks and sought her out.

Life became routine housework and the unanswered desire for a child. Instead of children, I bought two goldfish for company, and I spent a lot of time away from the apartment, shopping and keeping my frequent rendezvous with Shirley and her two little girls.

For the most part nothing much exciting happened for months, and I was thankful. There had been too much trauma for too long. One day the neighbor lady came over to visit, and while she was there, her child flushed my goldfish down the commode. Other than that, life had become much more settled, uneventful, and easygoing. No hassles, no accusations to defend myself against, and no Davis Sisters.

I had called Steve Sholes on the sly while Kenny and I were still living with the Davises and told him that I didn't want to sing with Georgia anymore. I did it after Georgia became critical of Chet Atkins, claiming that his picking was responsible for our records' not selling. I still can't believe she said that. It was easy for me to defend other people then, but never myself. I told Steve about it, asking him to violate our contract and make it appear as if RCA decided to let us go. He did as I asked. I was grateful for his willingness to comply with my request. The Davis Sisters' career was over.

I always had dinner ready for Kenny when he came home from the railroad. I was trying my best to be a good wife. One day over dinner he said, "Call Steve Sholes."

It was the first thing he had said since he entered the house that afternoon. Stunned, I sat wondering for a minute or two where in the world Kenny was coming from, then I replied, "No sir. I'm through with it. I quit the music business the day I called him from the Davises'. It's over."

"I say you oughta call RCA, Bud." For some strange reason he called me Bud. "You're not gonna be happy till you're singin' again."

"I'm happy enough."

"Bull..."

Deep inside I wasn't happy. I was still afraid. Afraid to try to sing. Afraid RCA didn't want me without B.J. despite the interest expressed by Steve Sholes and Chet Atkins. There was no way I would reveal my insecurities to Kenny. I wanted him to believe that I just had no desire to sing.

In a twist of fate, however, I ran into Justin Tubb in downtown Cincinnati while shopping the next day. During the course of our conversation I mentioned how much I appreciated his father's helping me and Betty Jack by letting us perform on *The Ernest Tubb Record Shop*. Halfway kidding, I said, "Next time you see your daddy, tell him there's a little country singer in Covington named Skeeter Davis who's looking for work."

Justin took me seriously and made sure he had my phone number. In no time at all, Ernest Tubb called. "Did you know, little girl, that of

Skeeter with Roger Miller, 1967 Grammy Night.

Skeeter, a Peace Queen since
World War II.

With Buck Owens on the Mike Douglas Show, in the late sixties.

A pensive Skeeter.

A pleased Skeeter.

With Charlie Pride in the early seventies.

With Gordie Howe, Jr., of the Toronto Maple Leafs. Her first time on ice skates.

With President and Mrs. Jimmy Carter in the late seventies. At right is Zell Miller, present governor of Georgia.

Skeeter and Joey Spampinato, 1987.

With Roy Acuff, 1990.

Skeeter and Joey with Linda and Paul McCartney, 1991.

Backstage at the Opry with Garth Brooks.

With Loretta Lynn . . .

. . . and Sissy Spacek, who played Loretta in *Coal Miner's Daughter* and won an Oscar for Best Actress.

With country music stars Mark Chessnut and Kathy Mattea at AIDS Walk in Nashville, 1992.

With Johnny Cash at Johnny and June's Anniversary Party, 1993.

Skeeter today, with George Jones.

With Joey.

With "Jack."

all the people I've had on my show, you and your sister was the only ones besides Elvis Presley to write me a thank-you note?"

His words warmed my heart, and I thanked him for thanking me for thanking him. He laughed and continued with the reason for his call. "We're just now planning a forty-two-day tour. A bunch of fairs, you know. We're going to work our way toward the West Coast, then over to Hawaii. We sure would like to have you join us."

"Forty-two days? Wow! I don't know if I could be gone that long. I know my husband wouldn't want that, Ernest."

Kenny let the newspaper drop to his lap. His arched eyebrows taunted me, *Are you crazy?* Retrieving his paper, he said, "I don't care how long you're gone."

I asked Ernest, "Is there any way I could meet ya'll, let's say, halfway?"

"I'm sorry, Skeeter, but that'd be too expensive for us transportationwise."

"Well, in that case, I just can't go. Thank you for asking me anyhow, Ernest, and maybe you'll think about me for a shorter tour later. Okay?"

When I hung up, Kenny had a fit. He threw the paper to the floor and thrust his finger at me. "You call Ernest Tubb right back and tell him that you're going on that tour."

"You were serious?"

"Of course I was. What do you mean telling him you can't go 'cause of your husband?"

It was natural for me to assume that two married people shouldn't be separated for such a long time. Once again, someone else was in control of my decisions. I wasn't sure what I wanted, but I did call Ernest back, laughing with embarrassment. "Okay, I talked it over with my husband. And he says...he says he's willing to make the sacrifice. I can go if you're still willing to take me."

"That's great, Skeeter. Glad to have you. Meet us next week in Nashville at the Record Shop."

I asked Ernest one night decades later at the Opry, "Have I told you lately that I love you?"

He grinned. Ernest knew how much I owed him. He helped me to become an entertainer in so many ways. He was my first tutor. He taught me little things that turned out to be big things. From the start of the tour, he could sense that I was nervous. So one night he advised me to spot one or two faces in the crowd and sing directly to them, rather than trying to sing to everybody or nobody. What I had been doing was staring out above the crowd and avoiding any eye contact whatsoever.

I tried his suggestion during the very next performance, and it worked like a charm. My self-confidence was enhanced one hundred percent. I'd step out under the lights and look for that one face that seemed to be really listening, then I'd sing my heart out to that person. I'd move around from face to face, but if I ever got nervous, I'd just go searching for that familiar face and I'd be okay again.

Ernest understood me too. He knew I didn't want to play nightclubs, so he never forced me. The few nights of the tour for which they had scheduled clubs, Ernest left me on the bus while he and the Texas Troubadors did the job.

One night outside a small honky-tonk in west Texas, a drunk tried to get on the bus with me. Scared to death, I kicked the bus door so hard I sent the man sliding across the parking lot. Then I ran through to the stage of that Texas honky-tonk, screaming, "E.T., there's some guy out there trying to get me."

They were right in the middle of a number. Ernest stopped the band and told the audience they would be taking a short break. He turned to Johnny Johnson, one of the Troubadors, and said, "Take this little girl into town and find her a room. We ain't never leaving her on the bus again. We were fools to do it in the first place."

Ernest and the Troubadors were great to me on that tour. We worked Pasadena, Texas, with the Cisco Kid, Duncan Renaldo.

"Ah. Pancho."

"Ah. Cisco."

I sang "I Forgot More" by myself, then a song with Ernest, and then as our finale we all sang "May the Good Lord Bless and Keep You."

Each time we were paid I mailed my share, except my food money, back home to Kenny. And although he knew from our itinerary where I was on any given day, I never got one card or letter from him. When we went to check the general delivery at the post office, Johnny Johnson and I would be the only ones on the bus who never received mail. One day Johnny said, "Well, Skeet, looks like me and you ought to get together, 'cause somebody don't love us enough, do they?"

Bless his heart, I could tell he was kidding me to hide the

disappointment he knew we both felt. I never complained about it, but Ernest overheard Johnny and said, "Yeah, I thought you was the one that was going to have so much trouble getting away from that husband for this tour. We ain't seen no evidence of any husband."

That hurt. I turned away from Ernest, hiding my eyes, which were near tears, and stared out the window as we rolled past the factories and movie marquees toward the next town. We stopped along the way, like we always did, at a little truck stop to eat. Still picking at me, Ernest played a song for me on the jukebox:

Before you leave be sure you find
You want her love much more than mine.
Then I'll just say we never met,
If I'm that easy to forget.

I identified with those words immediately. They captured how I felt so accurately that I jotted down the verses to this Carl Belew tune on a napkin. I told Ernest that his little joke had just given me a new song for our show. We worked it up on the bus and by the next stop I was ready to perform it. From then on, "Am I That Easy to Forget?" became part of my repertoire; later it became a big hit for me.

When we finally returned to Nashville, the scene rivaled that of an ocean liner full of soldiers returning home from war. The musicians' wives were there to meet them, and the guys were delighted to be off that bus and back home.

I waited for Kenny to arrive for well over an hour before I called to make sure he hadn't had car trouble. "Hey, guess who? I'm home. Ain't you coming to pick me up?"

"How'd you get down there, Bud?"

"On a train."

"Then catch a train home."

That year, 1958, Ernest Tubb invited me to become a regular member of his touring show. And at the same time Chet Atkins told me that RCA had kept me under contract despite my phone call to Steve Sholes. "We've kept a file marked 'Skeeter Davis' for a long time."

They wanted me to record again, but this time it would be solo, like Chet had suggested the day I met Sonny James.

I rented a little trailer over in East Nashville so that I would always have a place to stay when I came to Nashville to work. The trailer was parked in the yard of a couple who had bought it for their married daughter before her soldier husband was transferred to Germany. They didn't charge me much rent, and I'll never forget their kindness. So I split my time between two homes: the one in Covington with Kenny and the one in Nashville by myself.

I made my stage dresses by hand. I washed and ironed those old ruffled petticoats I wore underneath my dresses. It was an all-day process. Once when a friend was sorting through my old pictures, she said I resembled Little Bo Peep. But I had no desire for better clothes; I still sent all the money I was making back home to Kenny.

One week when I was back home in Covington, Shirley called me to report that she'd seen Kenny at a nightclub with another girl while I was gone. I asked her why she wanted to start trouble, but she swore it was true.

I waited a couple of weeks, then I mentioned the incident to Kenny one evening. "Who was that girl you was with at the club?"

"Who told you that, Bud?"

"The person that saw you." He didn't say another word.

The very next day I was washing his laundry. (This ought to make somebody a good country song.) When I picked up his shirt, his wedding ring fell out of the pocket and rolled across the floor. The pit of my stomach hollowed. But my brain rallied. *Hey, I may have a way out of this mess after all.*

I kept the laundry incident to myself, but that evening while I washed the dinner dishes, I sized up the situation. *I don't even know this man, even though he's my husband. It sure would be nice to have real love. I don't love him, but the least he can do is love me.*

Kenneth was sitting at the kitchen table drinking coffee and smoking a cigarette. I asked, "Kenny, do you love me?"

"What do you think?"

For some reason I had imagined him rushing over, throwing his arms around me and telling me how dear I was to him. Instead he rose from the kitchen chair and left the room.

The radio perched in the kitchen windowsill transmitted an update on the case of a Cincinnati woman who was on trial for murder. The jury had found her guilty; the judge sentenced her to death. *How lucky that woman is! How nice it would be to lie down tonight, go to sleep, and wake up in heaven.* I fixed myself a cup of hot tea, sat down at the kitchen table, and began scratching out the first words to a song entitled "Give Me Death." Marie Wilson helped me finish it later.

> I'm standing in the courtroom.
> The trial is for my life.
> The jury's found me guilty;
> My crime was killing twice.
> I found him with another;
> I guess he loved her best.
> And in a lover's jealous rage,
> I shot them both to death....
> A lifetime in a prison
> Is what they've given me,
> But in some lonely graveyard
> Is where I'd rather be.
> So, Judge, I beg for mercy.
> Please put my soul at rest.
> Judge, please change my sentence
> From life and give me death.

Of course my despair wasn't due entirely to my unfulfilling relationship with Kenny; I had harbored a death wish for quite some time—ever since B.J. passed away. Deprived of the love of another human being, I felt my wish for death resurface with a greater intensity than I had known for a long time.

Another song I had written with Marie Wilson and Penny Moyer became a big country hit for me that year. It was called "Set Him Free." It not only earned my first Grammy nomination and the award for Most Promising Female Vocalist, but it also provided me with a guest spot on the Grand Ole Opry during the disc jockeys' convention in 1958.

I was so excited. Now I had a reason to bring Kenny down to Nashville to see me perform. I wanted to prove to the Nashville bunch that had relentlessly teased me that I really did have a husband. I called Kenny, pleading, "Kenny, could you just come down here for the convention, where Ernest and these guys can see you do exist? It's embarassing for me to not have you here."

Kenny's refusal made me so uptight and nervous that I forgot the words to my very own song that night. It was the first time I went absolutely blank during a performance. And what a place for it to happen—right there on Skeeter Davis's first solo appearance on the Opry.

The Texas Troubadors were backing me up. I glanced back at them and asked Johnny Johnson, "Oh! Johnny, can you help me?"

He shook his head. He couldn't remember the words either.

I burst into tears right there on nationwide radio. The deejays applauded in sympathy. I managed to pull myself together to finish the chorus before dashing off stage.

I drove out to my little trailer and phoned Kenny. "Did you hear me?" I squalled.

Laughing, he said, "Yeah, you forgot your words, didn't you, Bud?"

He could have cared less that I had just humiliated myself before a national radio audience. I boo-hooed all night, and prayed, *Lord, help me out of this. I've jumped from that fire I was in, into the frying pan. I can't stand it anymore.*

I went back on the road with Ernest Tubb. It was during this tour that E.T. witnessed me mailing my money home to Kenny. He said, "How come you never buy Skeeter anything?"

"Why do you say that?"

"'Cause we all deserve something for ourselves every once in a while. That's somethin' you need to learn real bad, little girl. There ain't nobody buying you nothin', is there?"

"Oh, no." I shook my head. "I couldn't do that."

Deep inside, I guess I felt that I owed my life and my money to everyone else. I was still trying to earn love and acceptance as I did when I handed out my candy at school. I had old-fashioned ideas too. For instance, I thought that if a woman worked, she owed her income to her husband.

Nevertheless Ernest persuaded me that day to spend some money on myself. Even though my face burned with guilt, he and I found a western store where I bought a couple of new petticoats to go under my skirts. I think I even bought a square dance dress that day.

In Wichita we had a three-day layover. E.T. and the rest of the gang had decided to spend it playing golf. Once again I was the only girl on the tour. But they invited me to play too.

"Oh, ya'll don't want me out there taggin' along."

Jack Drake said, "Sure we do. Come on along and walk around with us. The only thing is, though, you'll have to keep quiet!"

Their good-natured laughter rang out. Everyone I had met in Nashville teased me because I talked so fast and so much.

Playing golf with them that day proved good therapy. I even hit the ball a couple of times after receiving these explicit instructions from Ernest: "Keep your mouth shut, your head down, and don't lose my ball."

The next day I said, "Hey, let me go again, and I want to play this time."

"Okay," E.T. said, "then get yourself some golf clubs."

He knew what I was thinking. "Oh, now come on, Skeeter. Remember what I told you. You deserve something yourself. Now let's go get some golf clubs." I bought myself the best set of clubs I could find and had my own golf balls that day out with the guys.

When we got back to Nashville at the end of the tour, once again Kenny failed to meet me. But instead of heading for Covington on the train this time, I returned to the solitude of the East Nashville trailer. Marie Wilson came over to see if I wanted to write songs together that evening. I confessed to her how disappointed I was that Kenny never came to meet me when I came in off the road.

Marie said, "I'll tell you one thing, Skeet. I bet if you don't send that money home just one time, he'd get hisself down here lickety-split."

I said, "Anything's worth a try." I called Kenny from the trailer. "I ain't coming home. We'll just be here three days before we have to go back out again. I'm worn out. Besides, I've got to wash and iron my clothes tomorrow. So I ain't coming home this week."

"But what about my car payment?"

"I guess you'll have to come get it."

When I hung up, Marie laid a dollar on the coffee table and said, "Betcha he'll be here before sundown."

I lost a dollar to Marie but it was worth it. My husband finally came to Nashville. Trouble is, nobody got to see him but me and Marie. I can still see him, plain as day, sitting on the sofa counting the money I handed him. He looked up and said, "Ernest shorted you this time, didn't he?"

"No, he didn't."

"In that case, you're shortin' me, ain't you, Bud?" I stared a hole through him.

"I bought me some golf clubs."

"Sure you did!" He didn't even ask to see them. He didn't hug me, kiss me, say "hello" or "kiss my foot"—nothing. He hopped back in his car, peeling out so that his tires spit gravel against the trailer, and sped back to Covington.

I hollered out the door at him, "You ain't gonna be able to pay for that car, unless you help this time."

But he was long gone. The next week I received my first letter from Kenny. It was a one-liner: "If there's anything up here you want, you ought to come get it."

I returned to Covington immediately after my next tour, but I forgot my key to the apartment. I left a note on the door: "I've gone to Shirley's. Call me there."

By coincidence Mother and Daddy were at Shirley's. We were enjoying a modified family reunion, catching each other up on all that had happened in our lives, when Kenny called. "Come get me. I'm here."

"I'll be right there!"

I bid goodbye to my family, pledging to see them again the next day. I had mistakenly assumed that Kenny and I were headed for home. Instead we ended up sitting silently in the parking lot of the White Castle hamburger restaurant until Kenny finally asked, "Well, Bud, what do you want to do?"

"About what?"

"Well, what do you want to do about us?"

"You mean get a divorce?"

"Yeah, that's what I mean."

"Well, if you do." There was another long pause, then I asked, "Who's gonna get it, me or you?"

"You can."

"Okay."

The scene was executed in such a cut-and-dried, unemotional manner that it still seems more like a bizarre dream. Kenny drove me back to Shirley's house and dropped me off. I waved goodbye. And that's the last time I ever saw Kenny Depew.

I walked into Shirley's and announced, "Guess what? We're getting a divorce, I think."

Divorce was virtually unheard-of in those days. Daddy said in the most somber tone I ever heard him use, "A divorce. Well, how are you, little girl?"

"Fine, I guess." There were no tears. In fact, I was downright indifferent.

"Why, Skeeter," Daddy said, "if your mother was to divorce me, I think I'd die."

I just shrugged my shoulders.

One of the girls from church later admitted that she and Kenny had an affair while he and I were married. She had a baby as a result of her liaison with him. Her confession was the only thing that ever caused the people at the church to forgive me. There was a big uproar about it around DeCoursey, but her confession came long after I had already filed for divorce and moved my things to Nashville. I wouldn't have done anything about it, even if I had known.

Like I said, I haven't seen Kenny since we parked that night at the White Castle. I hear that he married a schoolteacher and still works for the railroad.

Both Tipp Davis and Brother Rader have come by my Brentwood home since then, asking my forgiveness for the role they played in my marriage to Kenny. My mother once said that Kenny did serve a purpose: he rescued me from the Davises and pushed me back into the music business. All I ever really did for him was to buy him a new car every now and then. I guess if he ever had been crazy about me, it must have had something to do with those cars.

PART THREE

THE NASHVILLE YEARS

Bus Fare to Kentucky

I know I'm just a country girl
I hadn't seen much of the world
The day my bus pulled out of old Kentucky
My Daddy waved and Mama cried
I felt all choked up inside
Cause I was leaving everyone that loved me

The first I saw of city ways
Went against how I was raised
This country girl was really out of place
I was set to go back home
But I was broke and all alone
And I couldn't find another friendly face

And I didn't have the bus fare to Kentucky
Or this city would have seen the last of me
I didn't have the bus fare to Kentucky
And that old gray dog won't let you ride for free

I met a boy from Tennessee
And I guess he reminded me
Of someone that I knew
From Ole Kentucky
It was good to have a friend
It was good to laugh with him
And it was good to hear him say he loved me

I never thought he'd do me wrong
So, I gladly went along
I loved him more than any man I'd known
But after he had all his fun
He told me that our love was done
And then he left this country girl alone

Now, I can't afford to go first class
So I make it the best I can
Anything to get my feet on that good Kentucky land
My thumb is in the air
My suitcase by my side
Won't somebody give this poor old country girl a ride?

Kentucky, I'm coming home
I'll never leave you anymore
Kentucky, I don't know why I ever strayed
Kentucky, your bluegrass ridges and your valleys call to me
Kentucky, I'm coming home to stay
Kentucky, I'm coming home to stay

—Ronny Light

Music City

They said to take my music
And go to Tennessee.
The Grand Ole Opry, that's where I belong.
Though I can't believe I made it,
The record that you hear
Is me and my hillbilly song.
—"A Hillbilly Song,"
Skeeter Davis

I moved to Nashville on a train. Betty Jack and I had always wanted to live there. We were going to conquer the world from Nashville. So there I was, standing on the platform at Union Station with a suitcase in one hand and a coffeepot in the other. Not a soul appeared to welcome this perfectly innocent fool.

I didn't even drink coffee. I had left so many things I had wanted at the Davises' that I was determined not to make the same mistake with my departure from Kenny. Nobody was going to take Skeeter for another ride! So there I stood, staring up at the pigeons perched upon the towering Gothic stones of Union Station, with a useless percolator clutched in my right hand.

My mind flashed back to the parting scene at Kenny's apartment. His mother feigned shock at my apparent willfulness, shouting, "So you're even going to take his coffeepot, are you? You don't even like coffee!"

191

"Maybe I'll start liking it," I yelled back. "Or maybe I'll find some guy who does. It's a coffeepot. It was a wedding gift to *me*. And besides, I'm free."

Free? Ha! *Lost* would be a better description. I was trembling there on the platform from the weight of my newfound freedom. To realize that you're absolutely on your own, that it's all up to you, and there's no one else to do it for you is terrifying. If you're not careful, you'll end up racing back across the Red Sea to Egypt, searching for the very chains you kicked so hard to break.

I heard a story not long ago about the Angel of Life appearing to a sleeping woman, demanding her to choose between freedom and love. The woman, after much deliberation, chose freedom. And the angel said, "You are blessed among women. Had you chosen love, then you would have lost both. But since your greatest desire is freedom, you shall attain them both."

That parable has helped me to understand why I felt so lost and lonely standing on that platform. I had no desire for freedom. Down the roads and highways, across the airwaves and the stages, my quest had always been for love. Yet I always found myself ultimately condemned to freedom alone.

Nashville, Tennessee. This was the city of my destiny. Home of the Goo-Goo Cluster candy bar. Home of the only full-scale replica of the Parthenon. To some, a center of learning. The Athens of the South. To others, the promised land for hillbilly singers. I was finally home. And yet...well, there's just a lot of difference between a suitcase and a coffeepot. One's made for pilgrims and the other for settlers.

Who was I fooling? I couldn't seem to decide which one I most wanted to be: a pilgrim or a settler. What did I want more: love or freedom? I had tried to outwit the Angel of Life. In my search for love, I had found neither true love nor a true sense of freedom. It seems that the only one I had fooled was myself. Unfortunately, the time of fooling myself was not yet over.

The Davises had my *Oldsmobile*. Kenny had our *Buick*. I had our coffeepot but no automobile. I hailed a taxi to drive me to my trailer on McAlpine Street, but once inside the cab I changed my mind.

"No, wait," I told the driver. "Take me to the Hermitage instead."

"Oh, how I love this place," I said, thinking out loud as we drove up to the gate. I still remember the look on the cabbie's face when I handed him a five-dollar bill, as if he was thinking, *The more they come, the stranger they get.*

I blushed and tried to explain, "My sister and I used to—"

"Thank you, lady," he interrupted, stuck the five in his shirt pocket, and zipped off back toward town.

I had read every book I could get my hands on about Andrew and Rachel Jackson. They had lived the perfect song of love, and this was the house where they had shared their lives of love. Why should I have expected a taxi driver to share my enthusiasm?

"Maybe someday, Betty Jack," I muttered to myself as I strode beneath the gigantic red cedars down the guitar-shaped path, "we'll live with a guy in a house like this instead of in that trailer."

I must have been a sight to behold walking around among the four-poster beds, the massive paintings and tables, the velvet curtains and canopies, carrying a suitcase and a percolator in my hands. Everyone else must have thought I was some screwball who had come with the intention of moving in.

Rachel Donelson Robards Jackson may as well have been a "lady of the night," considering how people slandered her. She was a divorced woman, a woman who had been married to a man who drank and beat her. Yet people had advised her to stay married. She divorced him despite what others advised and later met and married Andrew Jackson, who eventually became President of the United States. But even then, people wouldn't let the shame of her past die. I believe the humiliation inflicted upon her by others is what finally killed her.

I identified with Rachel Jackson. I truly felt as if those passersby could tell that I too was a divorced woman. That I bore the mark. Yet I also felt as though I belonged there in that age, dressed in a floor-length gown, listening to men discussing politics and planning the episodes of tomorrow while I knitted booties for the baby and swayed in an afghan-covered rocker beside the blazing fireplace. I spent the rest of the day at the Hermitage, living out my dreams of Rachel Jackson. When night fell, I called a taxi to drive me back to reality.

Reality sat on concrete blocks in the back yard of the East Nashville couple. From that trailer I kept abreast of what was happening with the world through radio broadcasts. I was a long way from the Hermitage and the smoke-filled rooms of power, but my home provided warm, quiet, quaint, and healing solitude, which I probably needed more. Although I was without an automobile, I didn't feel trapped. I washed and ironed my clothes. I cooked. And believe it or not, this little girl who had almost flunked home economics when she sewed the legs on a pair of pants backwards was actually fashioning, cutting, and sewing her own stage wardrobe. I was my own mother doing the tough job of raising myself. You do what you've got to do to survive. If it's sorting socks, you sort socks.

The people I liked the most were the clerks in the Nashville stores. While I was making my stage dresses, I often ran into town to buy things that I needed, such as a hook, a certain button, or a zipper. Back in Cincinnati if I'd asked somebody at Shillito's if they had such and such they'd say, "Sure don't." But at Harvey's in Nashville, they'd say, "No, honey, we sure don't. We had that a couple of weeks ago, but we've sold out. I think if you check across the street at Cain-Sloan's you may find what you're looking for at the notions counter." I used to walk downtown just to feel a little of that love and attention these folks showered on me with just a few words of kindness.

The days were not all so dull and undramatic. Beyond my lonely trailer stretched the never ending road to the next gig, truck stop, county fair, and interesting stranger. I'd make the long hauls with Ernest Tubb, June Carter, and Hawkshaw Hawkins.

And I guess I may as well go ahead and confess. I slept in Justin Tubb's bed. Justin wasn't in it, of course. By the time I moved to Nashville, Justin was already grown, out on his own, and probably raising himself too. When we came in off the road, Olene Tubb would invite me to stay with her, Ernest, and the kids rather than go back to the empty trailer. These invitations helped me feel like I had a family. Justin's bed was just my bed away from home.

The Hula Hoop was the rage of 1959. I'd get out in the front yard and Hula-Hoop with the younger Tubb children while E.T. made movies of us. I was still a kid myself. Every time I came over, I persuaded them to let me watch *American Bandstand* on their television. Even in my trailer alone at night I was listening to the pop stations and the rhythm-and-blues broadcast from WLAC: "This is John R from Ernie's Record Rack in Gallatin, Tennessee. What we got for you, friends and neighbors, is a money-back. Now get this! M-o-n-e-y-b-a-c-k, money-back guarantee. A one time only on this long-playing 33⅓ record album, featuring Hank Ballard and the Midnighters, our beloved Ray Charles, Mr. B.B. King himself, and many, many more. All for the low, low price of two dollars and ninety-five cents, plus a small handling charge. Did you get that? All for the incredibly..." I got it.

Ernest knew I had gotten it. I overheard him tell Hawkshaw one day, "If you want to know what the kids and colored folks are listening to, just ask Skeeter. She's a walking, talking *Billboard* magazine."

I wasn't about to change my taste to please Ernest. "Yeah, that's right. Why, I heard a song just last night you oughta record," I told E.T. "If you don't, I'm going to."

At the next stop, I found it for him on the jukebox. The song was "What Am I Living For?" Ernest liked it and covered it country. I had repaid the favor for "Am I That Easy to Forget?" I even found his follow-up song, Laverne Baker's "I Cried a Tear." Those songs were a long way from "Walking the Floor Over You" and the other Ernest Tubb tunes up until that point. Both of E.T.'s next country hits came directly off of rhythm-and-blues radio. Segregated musical boundaries were changing. Black was becoming white; white was turning black. By the mid-sixties, American music would explode and lose virtually all of its so-called boundaries. Little did I know at the time, I would be at the very heart of that blast. As far as I know, I am the only female country artist to have performed with the likes of the Rolling Stones and the Beach Boys and the first to appear on the same stage with the great Aretha Franklin.

I had other friends in the business besides Ernest Tubb and Chet Atkins. Charlie and Ira Louvin both loved me, as did Teddy and Doyle Wilburn. My best friend at this time in my life, however, was June Carter. We were touring together with Faron Young. As a matter of fact, it was on a California tour with June that I first met two other women I would come to love as years went by, Jan Howard and Bonnie Owens. But June Carter was the one with whom I shared my true self.

June was always rescuing me. I remember attending my first disc jockeys' convention. After my first exposure to this group during my appearance at the Opry that time when I forgot the words to my song, I was nervous and out of place. She must have sensed my discomfort, because she quickly made her way over to me and whispered, "You want to get out of here? I'm hungry."

June taught me to eat lobster that day. I'd never had one in my life. June was an absolute contradiction. She dressed immaculately, complete with hat and gloves, yet she drove a pickup truck. On many occasions we would slip away from the crowd in her pickup and end up out at her big old house. I bared my soul to June Carter. She was the closest thing to a therapist I ever had. I was struggling hard with guilt feelings over the divorce, yet I was determined not to let it show.

"You're just gonna have to bury Kenny like I did Carl."

That's when she took me out to the garden spot (about which she wrote the eloquent poem in her own book, *Among My Klediments*), where she had symbolically buried Carl Smith. It was a learning experience for me, but I don't think I ever buried Kenny. Nothing dies that was never alive. The burden I carried was pure, old-fashioned, unadulterated guilt—guilt over being a Christian who had married and divorced. Guilt was my burden, not a corpse of lost love. Later in life, however, June's lesson would be put into practice.

"Set Him Free" lost the Grammy for Best Country Performance of 1959 to Jimmy Driftwood's rendition of "The Battle of New Orleans." I couldn't have lost to a better song (after all, wasn't it about my heroine's husband, Andrew Jackson?) or to a more authentic artist. Jimmy Driftwood's voice had all the archaic rough-ness of a backwoodsman, and that mouth bow he played just intensified the emotion and authenticity of the recording. Coming in second to Jimmy felt just like winning to me.

Besides record sales, "Set Him Free" earned writer's royalties for me and boosted my earnings from Ernest Tubb too. My value as an artist jumped from a meagre twenty-five dollars a day to a whopping one hundred. It also offered me recognition for a song other than "I Forgot More," and it landed me a contract as a regular member of the Grand Ole Opry, a privilege I have managed to keep to this day.

The night before my first appearance as a regular on the Opry stage, a violent battle raged through my brain. I ended up biting my fingernails to the quick and almost called to cancel my spot. The conflict began when I asked myself why I felt so little joy at accomplishing the very thing Betty Jack and I had set out to do over a decade before. The answer came in the form of a harsh, commanding voice I recognized immediately, "You've got to finish Betty's work! Don't you remember who pushed the seat over on her?"

Is that why I'm doing this, I asked myself repeatedly, *because it's Betty's work?* I would imagine myself fulfilling a personal dream one minute; the next I would see myself only as an old mule that had been whipped so hard, it finally caught up with the carrot tied to the stick on its head.

I managed to stop the war, or at least postpone it, by telling myself that no matter what the motive, I was going to be on stage the next night, giving that audience every ounce of energy I had. And I did just that. Like a politician eating 'possum, I forced myself to enjoy it.

One night soon after I had started working at the Opry, I dreamed that I was recording "Am I That Easy to Forget?" Chet and I were using that overdubbing method he had shown me in 1954. But instead of just two parts, I was singing three-part harmony.

I laughingly told Chet about my dream as we recorded "Am I That Easy to Forget?" but I didn't have the nerve to mention the third part I had heard. The master tape had already left for New York the day I found Chet sitting in the studio listening to the mix, talking about how good it sounded. During the playback I started singing the third part I had dreamed. Chet stopped the tape and asked, "What are you doing?"

"I'm singing a part I dreamed about."

"Why didn't you tell me about it earlier?"

I hemmed and hawed. "Well, because I figured you'd think I was crazy—singing from a dream."

"Look," Chet said, almost angrily, "you're the artist. Do you understand that? What I'm saying, Skeeter, is trust your own creative judgment. My gosh!"

As I pondered what he had said, Chet telephoned the New York office and told them to ship the master back to Nashville immediately. Crawling under the control table would have been my first inclination, but I sat there nodding my head in the realization that I had just learned a very important lesson. Chet called engineer Bill Porter to retape the third part. Why was it so hard for me to accept my abilities? I had always thought of myself as a voice that had to be directed by people who knew what they were doing. That day, Chet Atkins helped me to discover that I did know what I was doing, that I had talent in areas other than being just another voice.

When the master arrived, Bill Porter rerecorded the song exactly the way I had dreamed it should sound. The recording was so successful that it crossed over to the pop charts before Debbie Reynolds finally covered it. Debbie Reynolds wisely kept the steel guitar out of hers, and that's what made the difference for the pop audiences. Back then, the pop disc jockeys weren't used to the twang of steel; totally alien to their ears, the sound was unacceptable in the pop arena. All the field men for RCA were telling Chet, "If you had kept that steel off the record, we could've had ourselves a pop hit with Skeeter."

Chet listened to them. Despite my protests, Chet brought in strings to take the place of the steel for our next session. I was bewildered by the orchestration and had to admit in my embarrassment, "Ya'll are going to have to cue me when to come in."

Like the field representatives had predicted, the orchestrated song, "Optimistic," without steel accompaniment, became a territorial pop hit. I remember how scared I felt the night I first heard it being programmed along with all the other pop songs at the drive-in movie during intermission. I remember asking myself, *Skeeter, are you really ready for this?*

At the same time "Optimistic" was being released, Chet and I were busy working on my first album, *I'll Sing You a Song and Harmonize Too*. I'll never forget the pride I felt the day I first held the finished product in my hands. In the upper right-hand corner, in the same block with the RCA logo, someone had had the insight to add the words "Duets by Davis." Maybe it had been Chet's idea. In the liner notes Ott Devine had referred to me as a soloist, but the cover told the truth. I was a duet.

Confucius said one picture is worth a thousand words. Without a doubt that album cover told an entire story. Anyone looking at it today, with any other eyes but mine, would see an outdated record jacket from the late fifties, but I see, even now, all that it expressed. A black line split the front of the cover in two. On either side of that dividing line were pictures of me, dressed in the blue velvet squaw's dress I had bought in Oklahoma to please my Indian blood sister buried deep within my soul. The picture on the right side was me, but the one on the left was her.

As I study that cover now, I notice I had pinned my lapels up to the neck to avoid showing my cleavage. I notice the primitive headset I'm holding to my ear and remember how uncomfortably heavy they became during the hours spent recording. But what glares at me from that cover is my right ring finger. I'm wearing the antique rose ring I recovered from the wreckage of our car.

It was *her* album, pure and simple. Even the songs I selected for it were mostly ones that B.J. and I had done on our WCPO television show: "Just When I Needed You," "Chained to a Memory of You," "Your Cheatin' Heart," and "Let Those Brown Eyes Smile at Me." Of course, it included the two new hits of my own, "Set Him Free" and "Am I That Easy To Forget?", as well as a rerecorded version of

"I Forgot More" by myself. Those three actually were the songs that would carry the album and make it sell.

To me personally, the most important song was the one I had written for my daddy, "Have You Seen This Man?" I had tried my best to convey the emotional conflict I was experiencing over his battle with the bottle:

> See that man there on the corner?
> He can't call his life his own.
> Dressed in rags and eyes so empty,
> He's like a statue made of stone.
> Yet he chose this way of living
> And not the life that God had planned,
> And each day he's sinking lower
> With that bottle in his hand.
> Do you ever stop to wonder
> Have you really seen this man?
> Or do you see just another bum
> With a bottle in his hand?

My family was living in a shack in Hamilton, Ohio, while I stood there on the brink of fortune and fame. I could see success hovering before me. I was living proof of the predictions of those who two years before had voted me the Most Promising Female Vocalist of 1958. What once had been a mere dream was becoming a reality with each passing day. I was going to make it and make it big. One of the most chilling aspects of it all was that I knew it.

I had money enough to leave the trailer. I had spotted an absolutely beautiful ranch-style house in Ridgetop, Tennessee. It had *Skeeter* written all over it; its garden plot and clothesline in the back yard reminded me of Dry Ridge. It nestled on four wooded acres; a small brook ran along beside the property, ready for me to soak my feet. The owner wouldn't let me buy it outright, but he at least allowed me to rent it with an option to buy if he ever decided it was for sale.

I had to share this paradise with someone. As soon as I signed the lease, I called home in search of a family member willing to live with me in Nashville. I figured if anyone deserved or needed to be with me, Doozer was the one. Of all my brothers and sisters, Doozer is the one to whom I feel the most attached. It's not that I love the others less; Doozer still seemed to belong around my hips, where she had become like a warm layer of my own flesh as I lugged her around as a child. Another reason I love her so dearly is that she always got shorted when love and attention were being dispensed. For instance, if Punkin got a new bike, then Doozer got his old one. My youngest sister, Suzan, could get anything she wanted. Doozer never could. I remember one particular time when Suzan wore brand-new shoes and Doozer had cardboard stuffed in hers to keep her toes from sticking out of the soles.

For the longest time Doozer went without eyeglasses although she needed them desperately. Her grades dropped so drastically in school that she finally dropped out. Her behavior baffled all of us until I discovered her predicament. I spotted Doozer walking down the other side of the street in Covington one day and called out. Doozie glanced across the street in the direction of my voice, squinting her eyes. I yelled again. Finally she hollered back, bewildered, "Skeeter, is that you?"

"Doozer. Hey, Doozie." She couldn't see me. There were other things she needed besides glasses. Things like care and attention. These things I could provide.

Doozer came to Nashville on a Greyhound bus in January of 1960. She had packed everything she owned in one tiny suitcase. The first thing I did was buy her a complete new wardrobe. We ran together like two kids through clover as I showed her every square inch of Nashville. Then I took her on tour with Ernest. Her adventures in Nashville even included a much-needed trip to the dentist. And best of all, I convinced her to enroll at Greenbrier High School. She was frightened at the prospect of starting back to school with kids two or three years younger than herself. To please me, she went anyhow. Much to her surprise, she made the honor roll; her report cards were straight A's. She finally began seeing herself as an achiever. Doting on my success as a sister, I also regained some of my own self-esteem, which had vanished upon my divorce from Kenny.

When I wasn't on the road, Doozer and I filled our nights seeing the movies in downtown Nashville with our friends Velma "Vitamin" Simpson, Corky Ellis, and Geneva Foster. Other times, alone at Ridgetop, we wrote songs together. I recorded a few of our collaborations, such as "The Face of a Clown" and "Now I Lay Me Down to

Weep." Ferlin Husky also recorded one of Doozer's tunes. In fact she even sang with me one time on the *Ernest Tubb Record Shop*. For the sake of making a more sophisticated appearance, Doozer asked Geneva to hold her glasses while we sang. She was fine until we finished our spot. Doozer groped her way off stage, managing to right herself after a few moments when a crash landing looked inevitable.

Those were good times. Truly happy, carefree times. However, one of our favorite activities would lead me to make a grave personal and professional error. It would lead me to circumstances that would be my undoing. Circumstances the damaging consequences of which I still endure. Our fun and games led me to commit the one act of will that I would never repeat if I could ever live my life over again.

In our idle moments, Doozer, our friends, and I would go down to the WSM studios in the evening to listen to a homely but perfectly charming disc jockey on the late-night show. As I would enter the studio, he would announce, "Well, well, well. Here comes that little ray of sunshine to brighten up my night—Miss Skeeter Davis."

He was one of the most charming and eloquent individuals I had ever met. In 1960, he was an obscure late-night deejay who pulled hours others refused. Today he is none other than Mr. Country Music Television himself, Ralph Emery.

I had met Ralph earlier, of course. Within Music City business circles, how could I have missed him? During the usual interviews up at the WSM studios, he showed me the charming, considerate side of his character. He treated me like one would a fragile keepsake, attentively and tenderly. No wonder I laughed when friends would warn, "Ralph Emery says he's out to get you."

I honestly didn't consider the first time Ralph and I shared a meal as a date. Doozer and I had joined Ralph and his son, Steve, at his invitation. Ralph, like me, had been married and divorced. In fact he had twice married and divorced Steve's mother, Betty, before I ever met him. I looked on our outing simply as friends sharing a meal together. Between bites of dessert, Ralph caught me totally off guard. "I'm going to marry you," Ralph said.

I almost choked. I hadn't even thought of dating anyone since my divorce from Kenny. I couldn't think of anything to say or do, so I laughed nervously. So did Ralph. I changed the subject. "Uh...I like to go to the Hermitage, you know?"

He nodded, as if he knew.

"Yeah," I rambled on, "Rachel Jackson is my favorite person in history."

"I said I wanted to marry you, Skeeter," Ralph whispered.

"I heard you," I said so loud that I turned around to see if I had drawn attention to our table. I gazed away from Ralph and spoke no more for a few moments. Finally I regained my composure and directed my attention back to him, asking, "And who's your favorite person?"

"You are," he answered smooth as silk.

I blushed. "You know what I mean. Who's your hero?"

He laughed. "Skeeter, you are really funny. You know that? You just don't intend to talk business, do you?"

"Nope," I said, glad that he had finally gotten my point. "Now, who's your hero?"

"Nathan Bedford Forrest," Ralph answered. "Are you gonna marry me or not?"

"I'm not. Why, I don't even know you yet."

He winked, whistling as he strolled to the cash register to pay our tab. He helped Doozer and me into our coats and held the door for us. He was a perfect gentleman, definitely the nicest man I had ever met.

Ralph made up for every letter Kenny never wrote and telephone call he never dialed. When I was on the road with one of the many tours I did then, Ralph would find out where we were, then call to wish me luck before I went out on stage. I was dazzled. I had never known anyone to be that considerate of another person. Ralph would say, "Hope you don't mind, but I took Doozer and Steve out to the movies last night. Doozer said to tell you she still got her homework." Although I discovered later that these good deeds never took place, his technique worked like a charm.

If I had been keeping a scorecard for the brownie points Ralph earned with each little thing he did, I would have exhausted myself. I found it harder and harder to say no to him.

"I don't know what to do," I confessed to June Carter on tour one night. "Ralph has asked me to marry him. He really seems to like me. And what's more, he takes care of Doozie whenever I'm out of town."

June gathered her thoughts for a moment. "Well, Skeeter, I hate to see you marry a man with a child. My friends that have done that always seem to have such a difficult time."

I thought of those words when she decided to marry Johnny Cash and his four daughters. As Roger Miller sang, when you fall in love, you fall "lock, stock, and teardrop."

Since I was scheduled for a personal appearance on the *Buddy Deane Show* in Washington, D.C., Ralph and Steve accompanied Doozer and me to the nation's capital. Buddy's show was similar to *American Bandstand*, with people dancing while performers sang. At the time I had just released a country song in answer to Hank Locklin's "Please Help Me, I'm Falling" called "(I Can't Help You) I'm Falling Too." The song had crossed over nationwide to number twenty-four on the pop charts. From this experience, I began to realize that much of my rising popularity was coming from teenage audiences.

Ghoul Day was the theme of Buddy Deane's show that day. All of those involved dressed like monsters, and the makeup for the celebrities was applied to look like death masks. A casket rolled onto the stage, the lid raised slowly, and out I rose, singing my song. As the song ended, I crawled back into the coffin like Lady Dracula herself. The production team was shocked that a hillbilly singer from Nashville would be so bold and so adept at carrying off the whole gag.

While I performed, Ralph, Doozer, and Steve toured the sights. On the few occasions we were all together, I found myself very satisfied with the present arrangement. Steve and Ralph had a room. Doozer and I had a room. I had the companionship I wanted and couldn't see the point in hurrying to get married. I was loved by someone who was considerate and kind to Doozer and me.

I loved Steve from the beginning. He clung to me like an insecure four-year-old rather than a boy of ten. He once told me he loved me better than anybody in the whole wide world. Doozer and I played games with him when he came up to Ridgetop. We read stories, and when Ralph was there we played basketball. Then Ralph would take Steve home and head to his job at WSM. We had no nightlife because I was doing the *Friday Night Frolics* on WSM, as well as the Saturday Night Opry. The four of us were getting acquainted. I sensed, however, that our times together were quickly turning us into a family. And I loved it.

In September Ralph presented me with an engagement ring that drew contrary reactions from nearly every set of eyes that it flashed before. Faron Young asked me at a weenie roast one night, "Is it true you're taking ol' Lantern Jaws away from his crippled wife?"

Betty had been a victim of polio from childhood. Faron had managed to insult all three of us in one breath. Even though he certainly didn't deserve an answer, I tried to defend myself as best I could. "I saw her out bowling the other night, Faron. Besides that, Ralph and she were divorced before I ever entered the picture. They were even married twice, so she must not want him."

Embarrassed by this confrontation, I turned to leave. Faron yelled out to me, "Maybe you wrote that song 'Homebreaker' for yourself."

I fidgeted with Ralph's ring the rest of the night, thinking of returning it. My thoughts recalled Rachel Jackson and her stubborn determination not to let idle gossip bother her. I bolstered my courage and pushed the ring on even tighter.

Faron's remarks stung, but perhaps the classic statement came from my good friend Teddy Wilburn. He told me, "Skeeter, if I thought it'd keep you from marrying Ralph Emery, I'd tell Ernest to get his tour bus rolling so far and fast you'd never get back to Nashville."

I laughed at Teddy. I didn't listen to Faron or June. I didn't listen to anyone at all but Ralph. I thought I had met my Andrew Jackson. As a matter of fact, I went out and bought the biography of Nathan Bedford Forrest as a birthday present for "the nicest man I've ever met."

God Himself knows how much I wish I'd read that book before I gave it to Ralph. I had no idea who Nathan Bedford Forrest was, other than a Confederate general. If I'd only known more about him, then I might have gained insight into who Ralph would turn out to be. Nathan Bedford Forrest, I learned too late, was a Confederate general all right, but one who turned coward after the war and hid beneath a sheet while he butchered women and children in his loser's rage. That's right, Ralph's idol's most notable achievement was that he was a member of the Ku Klux Klan.

The Only Deejay You Can Hear After Three

He's a drug store truck drivin' man
He's a head of the Ku Klux Klan
When summer rolls around
He'll be lucky if he's not in town.

Well, he's got him a house on the hill
He plays country records till you've had your fill
He's a fireman's friend, he's an all night d.j.
But he sure does make good rent on the records he plays.

Well, he don't like the young folks I know
He told me one night on his radio show
He's got him a medal he won in the war
Weighs five hundred pounds and it sleeps on his floor.

He's been like a father to me
He's the only d.j. you can hear after three
I'm an all-night musician in a rock 'n roll band
And why he don't like me, I can't understand

This one's for you, Ralph
                            —"Drug Store Truck Drivin' Man,"
                            Roger McGuinn and Gram
                            Parsons (The Byrds)

Y ou dream of how it is going to be. He'll kiss you like Clark Gable kissed Vivien Leigh in a romantic ballroom flooded with moonlight reflected from a waterfall. Roses and candles glimmer at the table set for two. You will waltz and swoon to a thousand violins while every problem past or present disappears amid the benevolent bliss of love.

You tell your friends, "Oh, I know we'll have our difficult moments." But you really don't believe a word you're saying because your better judgment has evaporated into thin air as you are swept away with dreams of perfect love. By the time you take the vow "for better or for worse," you're really only prepared for the best.

Then, *BANG!* Reality violently rushes in to snatch away the delusions of a dreamer. The next thing you know, you're in a pitiful, run-down motel room outside of Bowling Green, Kentucky. The mid-afternoon sun still casts its light on the hotel room walls as your sister waits an hour in the very next room for you to finish up between the sheets (shall we call it making love or having sex?). Then you're back out on the road again. At least that's how it happened to me. That was my honeymoon with Ralph Emery.

We were married in Franklin, Kentucky, on our way up to the Penick family reunion. Doozer and I waited in the car while Ralph went to see if the Justice of the Peace was at home. He stood on the front door stoop, knocking. Nobody came. He knocked again. I turned to Doozer and said, "This is the sign I asked from the Lord. If nobody comes to that door, I ain't supposed to marry Ralph. If somebody does, I am."

Doozer was well aware of my confusion. I had already confided my reluctance to her earlier. She lifted a box of Uncle Ben's Converted Rice that she had hidden in the back seat floorboard and giggled. By all rights it should have been a happy day.

Ralph returned to the car enraged. He slammed his fist down on the roof, causing vibrations which rang in our ears like thunder. When I questioned his anger with my eyes, Ralph leaned in the window and swore, "That man told me he'd be here. By God, I'll find somebody in this town who'll marry us."

I begged him to simmer down and think things over. "Maybe it's a sign from God," I said, more to myself than to him. I don't think he even heard me. His mind was set on matrimony. Within thirty minutes Ralph had found another man to perform the ceremony. I don't even remember his name. I do recall his poor little wife, however, offering me tea to calm my nerves.

I'm just making a mountain out of a molehill, I told myself. Then I wavered; *Skeeter, this is not God's will for you.* I shut out the voice, allowing my desire to be with Ralph to win me over. I really loved him and wanted him to be happy.

"I do."

"I do."

As fools rush in, it was over and done. Doozer leaned forward over the seat with her box of rice. "Man, that's what I call quick," she said. "I didn't even have time to throw my rice." She laughed. "Oh well, I guess somebody can cook it when we get to Poppy's place."

Twenty miles up the road from Franklin, Ralph stopped at a roadside motel. He paid for a room for us and another for Doozer. The afternoon sun shone through the paper shades and washed the room a dull brown. Somehow the atmosphere lacked that certain romantic quality I had hoped for, and consequently I couldn't get into the mood for my first intimate encounter with Ralph. Unlike with Kenny, I had expected an enjoyable physical relationship to be an integral part of my marriage to Ralph. I had actually looked forward to it. But my notion of being with someone for the first time didn't match this hurried, almost desperate scene. Throughout our first performance I kept thinking, there's Doozer over there in the very next room, knowing what we're doing right next door. As soon as Ralph had finished, we checked out of the motel and drove on to the reunion in Dry Ridge.

Poppy sat on the porch rocking throughout the reunion. I could tell by the way his eyes followed Ralph and me that he had something he wanted to say. All my uncles, brothers, and cousins were busy playing horseshoes, laughing, hollering, and just generally enjoying each other's company. I encouraged Ralph to join them, but he hung by my side every minute. Finally he went after a soft drink, offering me a minute to myself.

As soon as he was out of sight, Poppy called me over to the porch. He rocked forward to the banister and sent a spray of tobacco juice over the railing into the shrubbery. "Well, little girl," he said, "I'm sorry 'bout your marriage. It ain't never gonna work."

I couldn't believe my ears. I wrestled for words. "But Poppy, we just got married."

"Yeah, I know you did." He paused and leaned toward the banister. Another spray of tobacco darted for the shrubs.

In the silence, I grabbed an opportunity to defend myself. "Well, it's gonna be different this time, Poppy. I love him."

"Yeah, I can see that. I know you do."

"And he loves me too," I added.

"Yep, that's exactly right, little girl. You love him and he loves you. But..." Poppy seemed to take forever getting the next words out. "But this man don't love nobody else."

Poppy took a moment as if to let his words soak into my brain, then he added, "And he ain't gonna want you loving nobody else either. You can kiss your friends and family goodbye."

I could not remember ever disagreeing with Poppy more, but later his words would come back to haunt me. I shook my head in disbelief, becoming almost angry with him, and left the porch quietly to rejoin my husband.

As far as I was concerned, Ralph had already proven Poppy wrong by the time we left northern Kentucky. "You know, Skeeter," he said, "there's one place I've wanted you to take me ever since we met."

"Where is that?"

"To Betty Jack's grave."

We hadn't even talked much about her. All Ralph really knew was that B.J. had been with me at the beginning of my career. With Doozer in agreement, we decided to drive past her grave on the way back home. I broke down crying, of course. Ralph embraced me. I leaned against his shoulder and let the tears go on and flow. I finally had someone strong enough to hold me, so I relaxed my guard and let myself succumb to what I felt was a pure and gentle gesture of genuine love. By the time we left the cemetery and headed back toward home, I had become as willingly vulnerable to Ralph as a stray puppy brought in from the cold.

My warm feelings took a sudden turn on the road home, however, when Ralph asked, "How come you didn't bother to speak to me all day?"

"What are you saying?" I asked. "I was never away from you except maybe to go use the bathroom."

He told me that I lied, that I had acted as if I were trying to run from him during the reunion. In my mind I had given him plenty of attention. Undoubtedly it was not as much as he expected because he badgered me about it for miles. The tension eased somewhat, but by the time we pulled into Ridgetop, I was dog-tired. Nevertheless, Ralph urged me to make love. Afterwards I lay there sobbing, feeling uneasy about what we had done. The sincere feeling of love I'd felt in the cemetery had already vanished.

I confessed to Ralph, "I'm having difficulty with you and our lovemaking because you want me to do things that I have never heard of and don't even know how to do. And because I cannot be the lover you expect me to be, you say something so ugly it makes me think that you don't know me or love me at all. I don't believe the Lord wanted us married at all."

"I don't give a damn what you think or what the Lord wants. You talk crazy," Ralph replied.

"But Ralph, let me talk to you. You don't understand the feelings of guilt I still have over my divorce from Kenny." I told him that I had prayed for guidance in making my decision to marry him but felt that I had done my will instead of what God intended for me to do.

"You talk crazy, Skeeter."

Throughout the night I lay wide awake as Ralph slept. I repeatedly questioned my reason for being, wondering if I was better suited to the single life, doing God's work as a missionary. By morning I had slipped into a familiar mood of depression. The walls seemed to rise so high above me that I resigned myself to this lowly state of mind. I scolded myself, *I am getting what I deserve. If I hadn't married Kenny, none of this would be happening. This time I will just be the best wife I can be and forget about last night.*

When morning came, I cooked breakfast for my man as, I thought, any dutiful wife should. While cooking, I remembered the epitaph on Rachel Jackson's tomb: "A being so gentle and so virtuous, slander might wound but could not dishonor." I leaned on that phrase in expectation of slander from a society that would scorn me as a divorced woman who had entered into another marriage. I never once dreamed that the greatest injustices I would ever endure would arise from the slanderous tongue of my second husband, my Andrew Jackson.

When I married Ralph I had back-to-back hit recordings, "My Last Date (With You)" and "(I Can't Help You) I'm Falling Too." Money literally poured in. Almost immediately Ralph wanted to leave the Ridgetop house which, although I loved it, he never found tolerable. Ralph wanted to move, as he put it, to a "better address."

In spite of his dislike for the house and its location, I finally persuaded him to let me buy it. Because even if it wasn't on swanky Belle Meade Boulevard, it was still a far cry from the East Nashville boarding house where he had lived and stashed his Civil War relics between marriages.

No sooner had I bought the Ridgetop house than another check came. We remodeled everything. We built the largest recreation room I've ever seen underneath the house and stuffed it full of furniture, a Ping-Pong table, and a stereo component system with huge Lansing speaker cabinets. When Ralph's family joined us for Christmas, it wasn't even crowded.

We also built a utility room in the basement for my washing machine, and Ralph constructed an office down there to record the taped programs he marketed to drive-in theaters. When he worked on these programs, Ralph enjoyed playing the music he liked most— pop. Ralph really couldn't stand hillbilly music or hillbillies either. He told me so plenty of times.

In fact, the first time I ever heard the expression "billies" or "billy-bus," Ralph was the one to say it. He was full of snide remarks about every hillbilly singer in Nashville. Whether they were on the very top or the very bottom of the success ladder made no difference to Ralph. They were all a bunch of "billies." To hear him tell it, even the biggest stars were nothing more than "sequins and snuff queens" and all that held the Ryman together was "tobacco juice and chewing gum." The singers he truly respected could have fit in the front seat of a Volkswagen, but he did everything in his power to conceal that fact.

Ralph hated my country image, my JCPenney dresses and petticoats, my bobby socks and shoulder-length hair. My hair had to be cut and styled in a stiff bouffant that I didn't even know how to take care of. My dresses had to come from Gus Mayer or Rich Schwartz, the most exclusive boutiques in Nashville in those days.

I learned important things from Ralph, like *picture* shouldn't sound the same as *pitcher*. He felt that as far as my use of English was concerned, I was a hopeless case. I tried to tell him, "But Ralph, I am a hillbilly. When you say you don't like billies, you're sayin' you don't like me."

"Times are changing, Skeeter. You've got to change with them. If you don't give up that country bumpkin look, you're not going anywhere. To be a star, you've got to look and act like a star."

Patsy Cline had that sophisticated country club look Ralph wanted me to have. One night in the dressing room Patsy herself even commented, "You're still wearin' them gingham skirts, aren't you, cowgirl?"

After a while all the fuss over my appearance and apparel wore me down. I soon realized that if I was going to get along with Ralph, I would have to learn to like things the way he wanted them.

After I finished the Opry on a Saturday night, I'd go up to WSM and wait for Ralph to finish his program. Sometimes I'd fall asleep on the couch. Four in the morning is late even for a night owl like myself. I didn't understand, at that time, how Ralph could tolerate working all night.

I felt so sorry for the guests I'd see come and go from the station, wanting Ralph to play the records that they had cut at some fly-by-night studio in Georgia or Alabama. Most of their records were, in fact, poor quality, but in the end I would feel nearly brokenhearted for those people once Ralph had finished with them. Off the air he was almost belligerent toward the hillbillies. They crawled out of the studio after Ralph had ridiculed and laughed at them, saying, "You really expect me to play that on this station? Look, man, I've got to play quality stuff."

He was right, of course. But I'd say, "Oh, Ralph, why couldn't you have played that little man's record one time at least, even if you never played it again? Don't you know how much that would mean to him?"

That incident demonstrated an essential difference between us. He seemed to be so cold and hard-hearted. And I had not yet learned that mixing sympathy with business can break even the wealthiest millionaire.

I couldn't stand it when I had to watch him treat people so callously. I would often go down the hall to the room where David Cobb put his program together, stretch out on the chairs and fall asleep. I had to get away. I had cried countless times for these folks I didn't even know.

I didn't really want to be up at the station anyhow. But when I would say something about staying at the Opry to talk to Hawkshaw Hawkins and Jean Shepard, Ralph told me, "I get sick of hillbillies. I'm up to here in billies. I don't know how you can stand them either. I play their records all week long, then they come hang around up here and—"

"Them coming by is what makes your show good. That's what

makes people listen," I interrupted, speaking before I realized that I had trampled upon his precious ego with my words. If looks could kill, I could never have written this book.

"That's not to deny that I believe you're the best disc jockey I've ever heard," I quickly added in my attempt to restore his injured pride. But I meant every word of it. As long as I live, I'll never deny that Ralph Emery is the best disc jockey around. He was then, and he is now. He has a talent for extracting the nitty-gritty from his interviews and his probing questions keep his listeners interested and viewers attentive.

Nevertheless, I can honestly say that as good as Ralph was at his job, at the time I was married to him, he could hardly stand the music he played or the people in the business either. He did like Stoney Cooper and Bobby Lord. But as far as I can recollect, they were the only two billies Ralph had a kind word for once their backs were turned.

As far as I know, every profession in the world has its own trade periodicals, from the *Progressive Farmer* to the *Wall Street Journal*. In the music business there were actually three major magazines, *Billboard*, *Cashbox* and *Record World* (alias *Record Vendor*). All three of these combined are called the *trades* by industry insiders. Every entertainer, producer, engineer, promoter, disc jockey, writer, and publisher that I know keeps an eye on the trades. They are like a stock market report for the music business, enabling you to follow the progress of a certain company, entertainer, or record.

Besides the weekly charts, the trades run a listing of the records being programmed most frequently on the major radio stations and a listing of the records that have started selling at a windfall rate in each of the larger metropolitan areas. In the early sixties, it was earthshaking news when a country song started selling in the cities. When a record actually crossed over from the country charts to the pop, it would cause such a stir on Music Row that if somebody had bothered to measure the activity the news generated, I'm sure it would have easily registered on the Richter scale.

Any record that began realizing heavy sales in one of the big cities was called a *territorial breakout*. A record breakout in Chicago would mean forty to fifty thousand copies sold in Chicago alone. Now at that time most country hits were only selling fifty thousand records nationwide at their peak. What was happening to me financially was absolutely amazing. I had records that never made either chart but would break territorially. Suddenly I would have as much money as if I had in fact recorded the number one country song. It always thrilled me, needless to say, to find one of my records had broken out pop somewhere. The next royalty check would be incredible.

One evening I was thumbing through the trades and noticed that "(I Can't Help You) I'm Falling Too" had broken out across the country. Nearly every major station in the United States was playing it. I flipped as fast as I could to the centerfold where the Top 100 pop songs were listed. There it was—near the bottom, but with a bullet. I couldn't have been any happier if Ralph had called and told me that he had struck gold while plowing our garden. I couldn't wait for him to get home that morning.

To my amazement he shared none of my elation. When I showed him the chart, his response was, "I've already seen it. It's great, Skeeter. Great."

I doubted his sincerity, and he certainly wasn't overjoyed like I had expected him to be.

"Doozer's really proud," I told him. "So is Steve."

"Yeah, I am too. I just wonder where it all will lead, Skeet. That's all."

It led to more and more money, more and more bookings, and more and more fans. But with each gain, Ralph appeared to resent me more and more.

Within weeks "(I Can't Help You) I'm Falling Too" had climbed to number twenty-four on the pop chart before it started to descend. Then my very next record, "My Last Date (With You)" made it all the way to number ten.

Ralph couldn't stand me to be out of his sight after that. He insisted that regardless of how many bookings came in, I could work no more than four nights a month. I had to catch the last plane out and the first plane back. As soon as I arrived at my destination, he would call like he used to, but the calls resembled interrogations rather than expressions of concern for my well-being.

"Who's up there? What does the promoter look like? Has he asked you to go to bed with him yet?"

By the time I recovered from the firing line of questions, my nerves would be so rattled that I would be in tears. I can't count the times it happened. Ralph accused me of being with everybody from guitar players to agents to producers to my hairdresser and believe it or not, to my brother and sister. Male or female, it made no difference.

According to Ralph, they were all suspects along with me. I—fool that I was—blamed his mistrust and accusations on the fact that I had been married before. I didn't have a clear, analytical understanding of what was really going on. So I kept my determination to prove my innocence and loyalty to him.

Meanwhile my record sales and popularity continued to increase. Fans began sending me little toys, dolls, mementos, and pictures. All of these expressions of goodwill and admiration were stuffed back in a closet. The awards and plaques from the trades, from BMI and RCA, were stuffed back there too. Ralph even encouraged me to throw them out. He asked, "What do you need with all this memorabilia anyway?"

Yet every gift from one of his fans and each award he won would be prominently displayed along with his Civil War cannonballs. Ralph decorated the house with himself. Reminders of my career were stuffed in the closet and covered in a sheet. I hadn't learned the word *ego* at that time, but I sure had heard my daddy use the word *pride* when I was growing up. I finally figured out that what was going on with Ralph had something to do with pride.

I guess some couples have a hard time dealing with the nontraditional situation of the woman bringing home more money than the man. But that's not the way I looked at it. I loved Ralph. I didn't want to be in a contest with him. I never once asked him how much money he made. I never once saw a check stub from his work at WSM, and I have to this day no idea what he made as a disc jockey. I only know that when we first married, Ralph had difficulty paying child support to Betty for Steve. He had let the payments slide. I refused to let the situation continue, so I made the payments for him. In fact I still have the canceled checks from those years.

When I had first met Steve, he had a hole torn in the knee of his blue jeans where he had fallen at school that day. Overnight almost, that little boy went from denim to cashmere coats with fur-trimmed collars. Seeing how Ralph was dressing him made my mind flash back to those snobs at Dixie Heights. I told Ralph I thought it was ridiculous to dress a young boy so ostentatiously, even if we could afford it.

Ralph interpreted my criticism as a lack of love for Steve, and he told me so. He knew right where to aim the dagger, because more than anything else, I wanted to be a good wife and mother. As much as I wanted my own child, I wanted Steve. In fact, on the road with me Steve would tell my fans that I was his mother as he sold them autographed pictures of me. Steve's real mother, Betty Ethridge, had always been willing to share Steve with me.

After accusing me of rejecting Steve, Ralph would totally reverse his sentiment and express resentment over Steve's being allowed to go on the road with me. "Even Steve is with you more than I am."

Everything had changed because of money. Everything simple, good, and decent became not quite good enough for the Emerys. New suits, new cars, new furniture, you name it—we bought it all. Everything that wasn't new, we replaced. Everything that wasn't immaculate, we changed. We had the house worked on. We had the yard worked on. Finally we had Ralph's face worked on.

Ralph is a completely different looking man today than he was when I met him. At the time he had a malocclusion. Ralph's face was very thin and, of course, his lower jaw protruded from the underbite. Wilma Lee and Stoney Cooper had given us a Pekingese dog named Tinker. Folks would say things like, "You'd better keep that poor little dog away from Ralph. It's beginning to look more like him every day."

Ralph took comments like that one and the nickname Lantern Jaws on the chin (no pun intended!). Deep down I know he must have hated it. He must have been self-conscious about his malocclusion for a long time. A high school classmate of Ralph's told me that Ralph had always been an introvert in those days, and he couldn't understand why Ralph had chosen to be in the public eye.

"Well, actually Ralph's not in the public eye. He's in the public ear," I said, laughing at my own joke.

That was changing, however. Ralph was being asked to make personal appearances more often at conventions, country jamborees, and the like. More than anything else, I believe these appearances were the driving force behind his desire to have something done about his jaw as quickly as possible.

I encouraged Ralph to grow a beard. I have always been partial to men with beards—ever since I saw pictures of Abraham Lincoln, I guess. As everyone who knows me knows, I love a man with a beard. Or maybe I love a beard with a man. But Ralph would not grow a beard as I suggested. Instead he asked Dr. Perry Harris to operate on him. Since Dr. Harris was an intern at the time, two other doctors, Dr. Kirk Todd and Dr. Elmore Hill, were actually considered the attending surgeons. It was a long, painful, and expensive procedure. But Ralph wanted it and I consented to pay for it.

Gradually part of Ralph's lower jaw was cut away in order to move his chin back until it was in alignment with his upper jaw so that his teeth met like they were supposed to. It seemed to me that with each operation it became more difficult to get along with him. Ralph would look at himself in the mirror constantly. To be perfectly honest, I can understand that better now than I did then. He must have had a very difficult time accepting his looks before surgery. Then in a matter of months he felt as though he looked dramatically better. This change in his appearance made him feel better about himself, that's for sure. But all I could see at the time was a lot of self-attentiveness that I called conceit and vanity. "You used to be nice, occasionally," I told Ralph one day. "But boy, the more they chop off that jaw, the more they chop away some of your sweetness. You're never nice anymore."

Soon after the operations were over, Ralph began confessing his frustration to me about never having cut a record. He wanted to have a hit too. These outpourings of his soul always seemed to be followed, however, with self-pitying remarks like, "Aw, nobody's gonna record me. What am I talking about?" Then he'd launch into a tirade about how he could sing as good as any hillbilly.

I listened and took his frustration seriously. I felt that if he did cut a successful record, perhaps it would restore the pride my own success seemed to be taking from him. It's worth a risk, I told myself.

In the evenings I would listen to demo tapes songwriters were sending me. I hoped that I might run across one Ralph could do. Answer songs were a rage in the early sixties. Both of my crossovers had been answers to previous hits. I had written "(I Can't Help You) I'm Falling Too" in answer to Hank Locklin's "Please Help Me, I'm Falling." I wrote "My Last Date (With You)" the very first night I ever heard Floyd Cramer's instrumental "Last Date." I must have called Ralph six or seven times asking him to play it over and over until I had the words just like I wanted them.

Faron Young had a song out at that time called "Hello Walls," written by a virtually unknown writer named Willie Nelson. Someone from the West Coast sent me an answer to "Hello Walls." It was a clever, catchy recitation-type song in which the walls answered the man. Appropriately, it was called "Hello Fool."

The writer had sent it with the intention of my recording it, but it made me think of Ralph immediately. When he got home, I said, "Let's record you doing the thing I got in the mail today." He listened to "Hello Fool" and loved it. He detected the hit potential and began raving about how it could be the break he had been looking for. A split second later, he began complaining that nobody in town would record him and that he could not possibly find the money to back him, and so forth and so on.

"Look," I said, "if nobody else will do it, I'll pay for it. I want you to be happy, Ralph."

Ralph had sized the situation up correctly. Nobody in town would pay for his recording debut except me. I rented studio time at Starday and hired Pete Drake to produce the record. In the end it was worth it. We had a professional product when we finished. As a matter of fact, Joe Allison loved the idea of "Hello Fool" and signed Ralph to a contract with Liberty Records.

Ralph had a hit! It restored his pride and his whole attitude changed. Things sure were nice around Ridgetop for a while. I wish they could have stayed that way.

As long as Ralph programmed my records, he could claim some measure of credit for my success. And of course he said on more than one occasion that he was in some way responsible. But then my recordings crossed over and broke into the pop charts. My pop successes drove a wedge between Ralph and me that we could never overcome.

I recall one incident at summer's end in 1962. A group of vacationing teenagers at Garner State Park in Texas discovered "Something Precious" by Skeeter Davis on the park's jukebox. These enthusiastic fans returned to their homes and began requesting the Houston Top 40 stations KNUZ and KILT to play it. Neither station had the record, so the program directors called RCA, telling them that Skeeter Davis had a hit in Houston if RCA would follow up on it. RCA took their advice. "Something Precious" broke—not as a crossover but as pure pop.

Ralph had been playing the other side of the record, "Where I Ought to Be," and flatly refused to play "Something Precious." Threatened by what was happening, Ralph began threatening me. "See if I ever play another Skeeter Davis song. You listen tonight. All you're gonna hear is Loretta Lynn. She's just another girl on a bucket lid label now, but you watch her, Skeeter. Just listen and watch."

He became possessive again. He tried to dominate my life even more. For example, if I stayed at Ridgetop, he would call from the studio at all hours of the night to make sure I was tuned to WSM. "What song did I just play? Which one before that?"

I felt trapped. Doozer and I loved listening to the music on WLS in Chicago. I began to sneak what little freedom I could. Doozer and I constantly switched our tuner from Dick Biondi back to Ralph to make sure we were never caught.

Between episodes of guilt over not constantly listening to WSM, Doozer and I had good times in the evening when Ralph was at work. We played Scrabble, wrote songs listening to the hi-fi, and enjoyed giggling and cutting up like two teenage kids.

One night Doozer and I were in the kitchen washing dishes and laughing at each other's jokes. Ralph hadn't left for work yet. He called me to the bedroom and without any warning at all demanded, "I want your sister out of here! Tell her to pack her things! She's leaving!"

I couldn't believe my ears. He had always been so kind to Doozer. I said, "You can't mean that."

"I do mean it."

"What for? What has she done?"

"'Cause you're always laughing with her. If anybody's gonna make you laugh, it's gonna be me. Now tell her to get her junk packed up."

Unable to think clearly, I walked in a complete daze to Doozer's room. She was there doing her homework. She looked up at me with tears in her eyes and said, "Don't worry, Skeeter. I heard."

I flung myself across her bed, crying. I said, "Doozer, I don't know what to say."

"There ain't nothing to say. He's just crazy, that's all," she said and started packing her clothes.

As I lay on Doozer's bed, weak and helpless, I tried to muster the courage to confront Ralph, to tell him that he had finally gone too far. Doozer had been living with me when Ralph entered my life. He knew how important it was to me that she finish school. I loved Ralph. Doozer didn't take a bit of that away. How could I reason with an unreasonable man?

I rose from Doozer's bed to find Ralph. I went to plead with him to let Doozer stay. But begging got me nowhere. Unable to accept the prospect of Doozer's imminent departure, I became hysterical.

Within an hour and a half, Ralph, Doozer, and I were in the car on our way to the Greyhound station. I sat stiffly, expressing my grief and frustration by tearing my handkerchief to shreds. Without so much as a word of regret or apology, Ralph loaded Doozer on the bus for Marion, Indiana, less than two months before she would have graduated from Greenbrier High School.

I hated my helplessness and inability to take command of my situation with Ralph. I was left alone in the house at night, alone nursing horrid feelings of guilt and remorse. A black cloud veiled my thoughts, my mood, my very being. I waited a week suffocating in the gloom before I finally gathered the nerve to call Mother.

"What's going on down there? Doozer won't even talk about it."

I couldn't answer her. I couldn't find the words to tell her that my second marriage was failing too. "Did Doozer go back to school up there?" I asked instead.

"No!"

Doozer never went back to school. She started drinking to forget the rejection and heartbreak she had endured. Although she had never had a drink in her life before, reports of her behavior worsened. Finally she returned to Nashville on the bus. But instead of coming to Ridgetop directly, she went to Tootsie's Orchid Lounge, where she met a songwriter named Danny Dill, the author of "Long Black Veil." The abbreviated version of their encounter was that the two of them ran off to California together. Doozer stayed with him there for a while before they both returned to Nashville and later married.

I stopped begging Ralph for anything the night Doozer left. When something doesn't work, why do more of the same? I decided that I would never beg anyone for anything again. I didn't exactly know what to do yet, but I knew begging was one thing I'd never do.

Much later, Ralph said to me, "Skeeter, I know that I pushed Doozer in a corner."

As we sat before Brother Dougherty of Forrest Hills Baptist Church during our marriage counseling session, I replied, "I can forgive you for everything you've ever done to me, Ralph, but I may never forgive you for what you did to Doozer."

Betty Jack and I often talked about how we would buy ourselves a Cadillac when we got to be stars, but we swore to each other never to get one if there was any chance they'd come and take it back. One day when a royalty check from RCA came I decided the day had come to fulfill that dream.

Ralph drove me downtown to Bunch Cadillac. I picked out the prettiest one in the showroom and handed Mr. Bunch cash for it. It wasn't Kenny's. It wasn't Ralph's. It was mine! I had a cash receipt that said nobody could ever come and take it away.

B.J. and I had made another vow as well, concerning my parents. Yet with all the money I was making, I still hadn't made an attempt to buy them their own house as B.J. had promised she would do. By this time my parents were living in Marion, Indiana, in conditions as bad if not worse than they had been in Hamilton, Ohio. Daddy and Mother were both still drinking. They had very little money, and of course the little they did have was going for the wrong thing. The thought kept running through my mind, *I need to get them down here*.

Mother called me from home one day. She told me that Daddy had been laid off from work and that the power company would be suspending their electric service if they didn't pay toward their unpaid balance. It was the dead of winter and snow was falling in Marion.

Mother and Daddy had never asked me for anything before; Mother's voice was choking with the pride she was having to swallow. I had just come in off a road trip. I had money in the bank a foot deep and cash in hand. I wanted to do much more than pay their electricity bill. "Sure, Mother, how much do you need?"

Ralph had a fit about it. I stopped on the way to the bank to buy a money order and Ralph asked me, "What are you buying a money order for?"

I explained my parents' situation to him. He looked directly into my eyes and said, "Why don't you just give your family all your money. What would they do if they didn't have you to fork it over to 'em? What would they do, Skeeter? Tell me. Huh? Huh?"

At that moment the resentment that had been building in me shot up from my stomach to my tongue. Trying to control my anger, I thought, *He doesn't want to share any of my success with anyone. He wants it all for himself. He doesn't mind that I pay for his child support, remodeling the house, his downtown office, his plastic surgery, or his studio expenses, but he minds when I try to send a measly thirty dollars to my very own parents so that they will have heat this winter! What a selfish man!*

I stared him right back in the face and let loose of those stored-up emotions. "Ralph, what would you do if I didn't give you any money?"

He grabbed the cash in the car and tossed it up in the air indiscriminately, sending tens, twenties, fifties, and hundreds flying around the dashboard and backseat as America's happiest couple drove on toward the bank.

The End of the World, the End of a Marriage

My love for you, dear,
Has always been true.
You know there has never
Been no one but you.
I kissed, loved and lost you,
You were playing a game.
Now my heart is filled
With sorrow and pain.
　—"Sorrow and Pain,"
　　Betty Jack Davis and Skeeter Davis

Ralph started coming home later and later and I didn't understand why. Finally he told me that he had been going to his new address. I didn't know what he meant. *What new address?* "Are we moving?"

He told me he would show me what he meant soon. I was really puzzled. *Maybe he's leaving me*, I thought.

One day we went for a ride together, finally ending up in Brentwood. Ralph stopped in front of a house that was under construction but near completion. Ralph pulled the car onto the lot, saying, "Skeeter, this is going to be our new home."

221

"What? We have a house at Ridgetop."

"Well, this is where we're moving just as soon as it's finished." I couldn't believe that he had not even consulted me about such a major decision. With hurt feelings and all of the frustrations of being swept aside as part of the marriage partnership, I felt no joy in knowing that this would be our new address. I didn't even like the house. The living room was too small, as was the master bedroom. I had always dreamed of a house with a huge bathroom, a large dressing area, and lots of room to change clothes. The kitchen and dining area were in no way what I wanted. This was just not the house I wanted no matter what the address was. I meandered from one room to another, showing my disappointment and still feeling upset.

Ralph interrupted my contemplation. "Let's go. We have an appointment with Charlie Mosely to finish the paperwork on this house."

Again I said, "Ralph, I do not want to move."

He told me that he didn't care how I felt, that he had always wanted to live on this side of town away from where he was raised. He was so happy and I was absolutely miserable.

We departed the lot and drove to what I learned was the home of Charlie and Helen Mosely. I barely had time to dry my tears before Ralph handed them the check to complete the deal on the house. I was so proud of that fourteen-thousand-dollar royalty check I had just received. Now it was out of my hands, used as a down payment for a house I didn't even want. Again I was powerless. We moved to the side of town where Ralph had always wanted to live.

After the move I started plans to buy a house for Mother and Daddy. Every time I would mention it, Ralph would have a fit. Despite Ralph's objections, I continued my search for suitable accommodations for my family. Throughout this tumultuous period of my marriage to Ralph, I held fast to this idea.

One day I came upon the perfect place for them. I asked them down to look at the property. They fell in love with it at once. I bought it for them, fulfilling the pledge Betty Jack and I had made. Everyone moved down to Nashville except Daddy. He did not want to give up his job at General Motors' Fisher Body plant in Marion. So he stayed, planning to relocate as soon as he retired. We all missed him and delighted in his visits, but we understood how important it was for him to stay with his job.

I was overjoyed to have Mother close by, especially since things were not going well with Ralph and me. His attempts to dominate me and my life expanded from emotional intimidation to physical threats.

One day I had gone over to Mother's house to hang new kitchen curtains for her. I had climbed upon the counter and balanced myself into a standing position by the sink. Doozer and Suzan held the curtains up to me so that I could hitch them onto the rods. In our revelry I was dancing around on the counter with my back to them when Ralph barged in. "What are you doing?"

"Hanging curtains." Without the slightest warning, I was whacked across the back with a brass curtain rod. I gasped and shouted out with pain. The laughter that had just seconds ago filled the room had stopped, replaced by complete silence. I slowly descended from the counter, leaving the curtains unhung, and sat down in a chair. Mother looked at Ralph, then at my back, and then back at Ralph, without saying a word. A red streaked welt across my back burned, but the biggest pain was in my heart as I silently marched out to the car. Ralph followed shortly thereafter and we went home.

Mother told me later that she asked him why he hit me with the curtain rod. He said he didn't know, that he had no explanation.

Ralph owned a gun. Since his behavior exhibited signs of an increasing tendency toward physical abuse, I couldn't help being a little frightened. In a move toward what I perceived as self-protection, I decided to take the gun to Mother so that she could hide it. Although she didn't want the weapon in her home, she agreed to hide it as I asked.

A few weeks later Ralph asked about the gun. He searched all over the house. I finally confessed to him that I had taken it to Mother. The next thing I knew Ralph was on his way to Mother's. In no time at all, Mother called to warn me, "Skeeter, get out of that house. Ralph found the gun, and he says that now he can take care of you. Please go somewhere, quick!" I could hear Doozer and Suzan in the background, yelling for me to flee.

Not knowing where to turn, I didn't budge. Ralph returned before I could gather my senses and plot my escape. Ralph started acting crazy, holding the gun to my head. I told him to go ahead and kill me because I would just as soon be dead as live the way we were living. The next minute he would kneel on the floor, begging me to forgive him. He would hug me around the knees, look up into my face with tears in his eyes, and beg me to forgive him. He swore that he didn't know why he acted that way, but he refused when I asked him to see a psychiatrist.

"I love you better than anything in the world. I know you are the best woman that ever lived. Please forgive me, Skeeter." I would look at him and wonder what made him go from one extreme to the other. How could he be so mean and aggressive one moment and then so meek and passive the next? I hadn't the slightest clue about all this craziness.

My ignorance of mind-altering substances was rather a disadvantage for me. I knew nothing. But one day I overheard an artist talking about Ralph taking pills—speed.

When I confronted Ralph about what I had heard, he denied that he used it. I believed him. Years later, after our divorce, Ralph confessed to me that he finally had stopped taking speed. The doctor who had been supplying Ralph with the pills was eventually arrested and sentenced to a prison term. Unfortunately for the two of us, the habit the doctor supplied would erode our relationship entirely. The Dr. Jekyll and Mr. Hyde personality that I had come to fear attacked our relationship as its first victim.

Good things were happening to me in the midst all of my marital adversity. "(I Can't Help You) I'm Falling Too" was in the pop charts as well as the country charts. I had received an invitation to appear on Dick Clark's *American Bandstand*.

"The End of the World" became a number one song on all the charts and an international hit as well. It even shot up to Top Twenty status on the rhythm and blues chart. I thought this was a pretty good showing for a country girl from Dry Ridge, Kentucky. It was 1963 and the song had broken in New York City, selling one hundred thousand records in one week. I was so proud to be there! Ralph, however, was not promoting "The End of the World." He instead always chose to play the flip side of the record.

Scott Muni, the pop disc jockey on WABC in New York, had played the record and, I believe, was the one who really should receive credit for the record's dramatic breakout. RCA was hosting a big party for me in New York. I was on my way and Ralph was to fly up and join me later. When I arrived, RCA had reserved a beautiful suite for me at the Warwick Hotel. I ordered room service so that I would not miss Ralph's call. Every time I turned on the radio, I'd hear my record. I would change stations, and it would be playing on the next station as well. I was ecstatic. I called Ralph's Aunt Lorraine and Uncle John, who lived in the city, and made plans with them for the next day to eat at a favorite Italian restaurant of theirs. They drove me to the airport to meet Ralph at Idlewild (which is now JFK). Once there, we were informed that the foggy weather conditions required that plane to land at La Guardia. We rushed over to meet Ralph but we were too late. We could not find Ralph anywhere. Discovering that he had already left for the hotel, we were relieved that he was safe but laughed as we recalled our wild goose chase.

When we got to the hotel, the desk clerk told us that a gentleman had asked for my key claiming to be my husband. In the interest of my safety, they did not give him the key. An angry Ralph took another room. When I called him, he was so mad that he accused me of being with a man from RCA despite my insistence that I had been with his aunt and uncle.

Ralph could only think of himself. In his insecurity and paranoia, he had taken all the joy out of an otherwise pleasant experience. When Lorraine and John and I arrived at his hotel room door, Lorraine arranged with John to throw his hat in the door first. "If he doesn't throw it back," said Lorraine, "we'll leave." When Ralph came to the door Lorraine could see that the situation was no laughing matter. Ralph was absolutely incensed.

John and Lorraine returned home after brief greetings. Ralph moved out of his room and into the suite which had brought me so much pleasure just hours before. My joy faded to sadness as Ralph turned out the light.

Shelby Singleton was in New York at that time and had invited Ralph to go to Harlem to see Dinah Washington. She was Ralph's very favorite singer. So he went off to see Dinah, and our little Pekingese, Taffy, and I went to the stadium to see a Yankees game.

The next night Johnny Tillotson invited Ralph to the Copacabana, where he was playing. Knowing that I would not be comfortable there, Johnny agreed that perhaps I should remain in the hotel that evening. But Ralph insisted that I join him in his ringside seats right by the stage. I will never forget that night. That was the closest thing to a burlesque show I'll ever see. Of course Johnny was great, but when all the girls were out there doing their dances dressed in next to nothing, I was totally embarrassed. Ralph delighted in teasing me about my red cheeks.

The next day we were to meet Ralph's Aunt Lorraine again for a brief sightseeing tour before meeting Uncle John, who would take us to the airport. I carried a small basket for Taffy so that she could be on the plane with us. Lorraine helped me to sneak Taffy on board by walking as close to my basket as she could get. I confided to her as we headed toward the gate, "I'm afraid that by the next time I see you, Ralph and I will not be together." She admitted that she could see Ralph was having problems. She even mentioned that day that his mother had at one time required medication and hospitalization for psychiatric reasons. She added that she hoped Ralph would not have to undergo the same. We hugged each other goodbye and Ralph and I boarded the plane for Nashville.

Things worsened for Ralph and me. We attended Woodmont Baptist Church at the time. Ralph would only attend services at this particular church. This peculiarity of Ralph's was just one more thing about him that I couldn't understand. The church pastor, Dr. West, seemed to be away from the congregation every time we attended Sunday services there, leaving a substitute to serve the needs of the church community.

One Sunday as Ralph and I drove to Woodmont Baptist, we passed new construction for what would become Forrest Hills Baptist Church. "Why don't we go there? Our tithe will help build it. Woodmont is already such a big church." Ralph would not consider making a change.

A short time later I answered the doorbell to come face to face with a man who introduced himself as Robert Dougherty from Forrest Hills Baptist Church. Since Ralph was not at home, I promised that I would come the next Sunday. I'm so thankful that I made that choice. Later I transferred my membership from my beloved church in Kentucky (DeCoursey Baptist Church) to Forrest Hills.

The subject of my tithes and offerings became yet another major battle between Ralph and me. He didn't want me to contribute to the church although I had been a devoted tither since I had been saved. Ralph said, "Well, if you're going to tithe, then give after everything is taken out, not off the top."

"Don't you think Jesus gave His all off the top for us?" Once again I felt the challenge of my traditional Christian understanding that wives should be submissive to their husbands. How could I undermine my allegiance to my beliefs and my obedience to God? I decided that God had to come first in my life; Ralph as my partner on earth would have to come second for things to really work.

One day at church Mother and I noticed that one woman in particular kept looking at us. More than once she turned around in her seat, straining to catch a glimpse of our pew. That's when I recognized her. As we left church that morning, I confided to Mother that I had a strong feeling that she had not been looking at us, but had rather been looking for Ralph. Whether it was intuition, imagination, a lucky hunch, or a sixth sense, I had succeeded in identifying just one of the other women in Ralph's life.

> I guess my lovin' just ain't good enough for you.
> 'Cause every time I turn my head you look at someone new.
> Your kind don't like walking; babe, you want an easy ride.
> What does it take to keep a man like you satisfied?

The words to this song ran through my head over and over again. I came in off the road one morning, exhausted. I bathed, changed into my gown, and crawled into bed. Ralph immediately hurled accusations at me, demanding to know whom I had slept with on this trip. My sister Suzan was sleeping in Steve's room down the hall, and I knew his shouting would wake her up. I said, "Please, Ralph, please don't do this. Don't act that way, especially when Suzan is just down the hall." Ralph's tirade continued. I got out of bed, changed my clothes, and grabbed the keys to my car. Ralph lunged toward me and began yanking my arm and twisting it to make me drop the keys.

"May I please take Suzan home so she doesn't have to hear all of your ugly accusations?"

"Okay, I'll go with you," he said.

I went down the hall to find Suzan wide awake, having heard every slur Ralph had issued. She agreed that it would be best if she went home to Mother's.

When the three of us arrived at Mother's house, I quickly jumped out of the car and dashed into the safe haven of my mother's home. One thing I knew for sure that day, I did not plan to go back home with Ralph.

As soon as I walked into the house, I went straight to the bedroom that Suzan and Doozer shared and locked the door behind me. Ralph followed me, pounding on the door for me to let him in. I refused, telling him to go away, that I had been up all night traveling and simply had to have some sleep. Ralph would not allow me to rest. After a stream of pleas from him, I finally opened the door. At that point I was at the end of the line. I told him I could not take living with him anymore and that I was going to leave him.

Laying his head on my breast, Ralph began to sob. "Mama, please don't leave me. Please, Mama, please don't leave me again." I looked at him and thought, *Again?* I'd never left him before. I simply could no longer listen to his nonsense. I told him that I had no other option but to leave him now and asked him to go. I closed the bedroom door, threw myself on the bedcover, and cried myself to sleep.

Ralph came to see me on his birthday and talked me into going home with him by promising me that he would go with me for marriage counseling from Brother Dougherty. As we entered the foyer of our house, I noticed an opened package and a card on one of the tables. I picked it up and asked Ralph if this was a birthday gift from his girlfriend. He grabbed the box away from me, saying, "That damned woman."

"You shouldn't blame your girlfriend and call her those names. You should just have better timing. Maybe I better go back to Mother's."

He insisted that the present was from one of his fans. Although his behavior simply confirmed to me that he had a girlfriend, I stayed anyway. Running away didn't seem to do any good, so I thought I had better stay and fight my battle the best that I could.

Ralph and I began marriage counseling with Brother Dougherty. After three visits Ralph refused to go again. He claimed, "That preacher is on your side because you give money to the church."

So thereafter I continued to go for counseling by myself. I really had no desire to speak with anyone else. I trusted Brother Dougherty and found solace in crying where only God could witness my sorrow. My conversations with God became increasingly important to me as I could foresee the end of my marriage to Ralph. I looked to God for answers.

One day I came into the house and found a card addressed to Ralph in the foyer of our home. Curiosity getting the better of me, I opened the card. It had been sent by the woman at church whom Mother and I had felt uneasy about. The card depicted a sailing ship on a beautiful ocean. In her own handwriting, the woman had written, "Ralph, someday *our* ship will come in," along with several other lines expressing her intimate affections for him. I knew her as the wife of a well-known entertainer who frequented Ralph's all-night radio show. Some say he traded his wife for his career.

I hid the card in the freezer with all of the other notes from his admirers that I had intercepted from time to time. When I questioned Ralph about the woman, he denied everything.

Several nights later Ralph left for work earlier than normal. He said he had to pull a record and make plans with his engineer, John Riggs, about the program.

Shortly after he had left, within two or three hours, he suddenly returned to the house. Thinking that he had forgotten something important, I was startled at his frantic behavior as he entered the foyer near where I sat.

"Skeeter, I'm really in trouble. I don't know what I'm going to do! I just left Betty's house. She slashed her wrists because she thinks she's pregnant."

"Oh, my gosh! Did you take her to the hospital?" I asked.

"How could I do that? Everybody would know. I would be ruined! I'll have to leave town. My career will be over!" he whined as he paced from room to room.

"Do you love her?" I asked.

"Hell, no!" he yelled. He continued his panic-stricken speech about having to leave town in shame should anyone discover his adulterous behavior.

Of course, I had just found out. My husband openly confessed to me his affair with a married woman who believed herself to be pregnant with his child. Furthermore, in her desperation she had slit her wrists to end her misery. Cowering at home, Ralph only thought of himself as his lover sat in a tub of water trying to stop herself from bleeding to death. What a mess!

I didn't know whom to pity the most. Ralph composed himself and left for work, while I was left alone to pace the floors of the empty house, praying for the other woman whom my husband had abandoned in her time of need. She lived, thank God, to have her daughter, who has since married and moved away from Nashville. Betty, however, underwent a divorce as a result of her liaison with Ralph and still lives alone today.

I was thankful to have my music and the Grand Ole Opry. I thanked God for my hit records. About that time I consulted Ralph about the possibility of my hiring a band of my own. He said that I didn't need a band, that if I was a real professional, I could sing with any local band. Unfortunately the local bands didn't know the chords to "The End of the World," especially if I had no time to rehearse with them.

After an embarrassing incident in Atlanta, I became even more determined to form a band. "The End of the World" was number one, but the band didn't know it. I'll never forget how mortified I felt trying to sing with a band that didn't know my music. The arrangement was so bad, I had to stop singing. The band apologized as I walked off stage. Supportive as always, Ralph scolded me for quitting. He told me that if Marty Robbins had been out there with the band, no one would have noticed that the band didn't know the song. He concluded that a true professional like Marty could have pulled it off. Regardless of Ralph's insults, I knew the next step in my career would be to hire a band so that I could perform with the confidence the audiences deserved.

One Saturday night when I was going in the door of the old Ryman for my Opry performance, a man stopped me. He told me that since the staff rhythm guitarist would not be there that night, he would consider it an honor to play for me. After proper introductions, I learned that Ronny Light was his name. I asked him if he knew my songs and he said, "I sure do. I even wrote a lead sheet on 'The End of the World.'"

He played for me that night and many nights thereafter. Thus began a long and lasting association with Ronny, who would also become my record producer. Ronny introduced me to his musician brother Larry and I hired the two of them. With two musicians backing me, I was on my way to having my own band.

The first date they played with me, Ralph hired Harold Weakley and Spider Wilson of the Opry staff band to go also. Ralph drove all of us. In order for Ralph to go along, we had to depart for the date just after he got off work and return immediately after the show was over to get Ralph back in time to go back to work. This meant I was restricted from talking to the fans and signing autographs. Ralph's style was for me to just sing, get the money, hit the road, and go home.

Folks used to say that Ralph must have had a clock timing me from the time we left until we returned, because the pattern that prevailed was for me to wait until the last minute to leave and to return as quickly as I could travel the distance between performance dates and home. Food and coffee breaks were not permissible. Everything was done on the run. When Ralph would go along, I couldn't even sign an autograph. He told me giving autographs put me on the same level as my fans. He said that I would never be a star because I was just too common—just like the folks that came to see me.

I had two musicians and wanted to add two more. Fussing with Ralph about this hardly mattered because we argued about everything. David McCreery, Frank Evans, and Paul Charon soon joined the band, and David and Paul both stayed with me for several years thereafter.

My bandmembers helped me keep what sanity I had retained. Those were tearful years. I would be in tears whenever I was not on stage. Dealing with my depression must have been difficult for them all. They would bring me flowers and gifts to cheer me up. One of the very first gifts I received from them was small wooden doll that had been painted blue. When the head of the doll was pushed down, a sign would pop up that read, "Don't Be Blue." I still keep it on my shelf.

I would dread returning from each trip. I could predict the accusations Ralph would fling at me upon my arrival. He suspected me of sleeping with each of the boys in the band. When I would speak with them on the telephone to arrange Opry spots and rehearsals, Ralph would monitor my conversations. "Who are you laughing with? I want to be the one to make you laugh!" he would yell.

"Ralph, you're the one who is making me cry."

Finally my nerves were shot. I could no longer sleep at any time of the day or night. I had promised my mother that I would not rely on Ralph's sleeping pills, but the time had come when I needed professional help.

Dr. Sol Rosenblum came to my rescue. Instead of handing me a bottle of sleeping pills and sending me home, he escorted me to a room in the new wing of the Baptist Hospital, where I cried until I could cry no more.

When Ralph came to see me, I told him that he was the reason I had to seek refuge in professional medical help. Brother Dougherty had already arrived to support me in my escape from an emotional battery I could no longer endure.

After my brief period of rest in the hospital, Ralph returned to take me home. As we sat out on the patio in the new furniture he had bought during my absence, I leveled with him. "Ralph, even if the world ended tomorrow, I don't want to stay with you one more night. Besides, you'll be free to marry your pregnant girlfriend."

Brother Dougherty stopped by for a visit later in the day. I informed him of my feelings and of my having said as much to Ralph. In response he advised me that as a pastor he could not recommend a divorce, but as a friend he was afraid it was inevitable.

Ralph and I started divorce proceedings shortly thereafter. Ralph settled for the money. I kept the mortgage and the house I despised and the painful, haunting memories that went with it.

I missed my stepson Steve terribly after the divorce, but it seemed that the separation from him was yet another price I would have to pay. I was so thrilled one day when Ralph's Aunt Lorraine called from New York to tell me that she was planning to visit Nashville to spend time with me. After I met her at the airport, we called Steve's mother, Betty, to ask her if Steve could join us for the day.

Betty met us as we requested and Steve seemed genuinely happy to join us at my home, where we played in the pool and enjoyed the company of one another for the entire afternoon. Even though I was officially out of the family, I had such a wonderful rapport with Lorraine and Steve that I hardly even noticed that we were no longer kin. The three of us were having dinner together when Ralph came storming in to break up the party.

He charged across the patio through the sliding glass doors and into the kitchen. He jerked Steve out of his chair, glaring at me and Lorraine. "Your time with Steve has ended, Skeeter. It's over." That was the last time I saw Steve until he was seventeen years old and independently drove his first car to my house. I was so thankful that he knew I had always loved him and that my love for him would never change.

Steve later had a terrible automobile accident in which he was almost killed. As soon as I heard the news, I called Ralph to ask about him. Ralph informed me that I was not permitted to see Steve under any circumstances.

Refusing to stop there, I called Betty at the hospital. She told me that Steve's wife and she had been praying for me to come. As we hung up the phone, I rushed to get ready to meet her at the hospital.

Upon my arrival Betty greeted me and directed me to Steve's hospital room. With twenty-seven stitches in his head and face, connected as he was to so many tubes and wires, I wondered if he could detect the presence of anything beyond his own pain.

"Steve, I love you," I said, leaning down close to his face.

"Skeeter, is that really you?"

When Steve and I had finished the limited exchange he could manage, I returned to the hallway to speak with Betty and Steve's wife. As I shared with them the good news of Steve's response to me—that he had actually opened his eyes and spoken to me—we cried with tears of thankfulness and hope.

Once again Ralph disrupted the scene. "What are you doing here, Skeeter? You can't see Steve."

Before I could respond, Betty interjected, "She just came out from seeing him, Ralph. He recognized her and talked with her. The doctor is in with him now."

"I don't believe it," he replied and walked away.

After visiting a few more minutes with Steve's friends and other relatives, I told Betty that it was best for me to take my leave because I really didn't like our ex-husband.

Betty laughed. "Well, we'll never encounter anyone quite like him again, will we, Skeeter?"

"I hope not!" I replied in all candor.

Steve survived his ordeal and is a successful dentist today. I see him now and then, delighting in the knowledge that we share a bond of love and friendship that transcended the dissolution of my marriage to his father. That marriage caused me so much pain. I truly regret having ever married Ralph Emery. Surely he knows that he broke my heart a very long time ago, and yet he continues to lie publicly about our years together and my personal and professional life. I had prayed for Ralph's salvation for more than three years after our divorce; then I tried to forgive and forget so that I could go on with my life.

Life After Ralph

Once I chased a pretty rainbow,
Almost found that pot of gold,
But I could not find the treasure
Without your hand to hold.
Once I walked in fields of clover,
That was when you were by my side.
Then you left me for another,
I could not keep you satisfied.
                    —"Once,"
                    Skeeter Davis

F ear is not of the Lord, but perfect peace He gives unto us."
(Tim. 1:7) I knew this Scripture, but it was difficult not to be fearful
and peace was a long time coming. With Ralph gone, the house
seemed huge and empty, its only occupants me and two little
Pekingese dogs, Tinker II and Taffy. I admit that I was particularly
sensitive to every sound I heard inside and out. I became more aware
than ever of happenings in the neighborhood and made sure that I
observed any activity near my house.

Spying my neighbors approaching the front door one day, I arrived
at the foyer entrance just as the doorbell rang. I greeted my
neighbors, who were accompanied by a disheveled-looking man I did
not recognize. "Skeeter, this man is Ralph's father."

During my marriage to Ralph I had never met his father. Ralph had led me to believe that his father had died years before I had met him. Imagine my shock when just a few months after our divorce I came face to face with living, breathing evidence that Ralph's father was very much alive. I certainly hadn't been prepared for the sight before my eyes. Mr. Emery, it seems, had been wandering around the neighborhood in a drunken stupor looking for Ralph's house.

"No, that can't be Ralph's father. The truth is that Ralph's father is dead."

"Well, Ralph may claim that, but I ain't dead yet."

Not quite knowing what to believe in my confusion, I took the man into my home and proceeded to call Ralph at WSM. "Ralph, you'll never guess who's at my house."

"Who, Skeet?"

"Your dead daddy." Dead silence.

"I'll be right out."

"Oh, no, you won't. I'll handle this by myself," I said. "Besides, how could you come right out when you're on the air?"

"I'll put on an album and be right out there," he said.

I pieced it all together at that moment. A tape or an album played in its entirety gave Ralph ample opportunity to do just about anything, leaving the job of disc jockey to the engineer. I couldn't think much more about all of Ralph's clever techniques to appear to be working while he was, in fact, engaged in other activities, when I had his dead father sitting in my living room.

Ralph's father asked me for a drink. Since alcohol had never entered my house, I knew I could not accommodate his request. He began shaking and trembling uncontrollably. The best thing I knew to do was to call my own father for guidance. Daddy advised me to administer lots of tomato juice to Mr. Emery as soon as possible. After a quick trip to the market Mr. Emery consumed mass quantities of liquified tomatoes. Before he passed out, he talked nonstop into the wee hours of the morning, giving even me little time to get a word in the conversation.

Mr. Emery stayed at my house for two nights. During his stay he related to me the story of his life: his tour of duty in the armed services, his return home, his devastation at learning of what he thought were his wife's infidelities, their subsequent divorce, and more recently, his life of drinking. Ralph, he said, would have nothing to do with him, yet his hope was that they could reconcile their differences. He hoped that I could play a role in bringing about their reunion so that he could come to know his grandson, Steve, one day.

I hesitated to inform Mr. Emery that Ralph and I were no longer married. He must have noticed my uneasiness, because he blurted out, "What's the matter? Did he cheat on you?"

The tears began to flow involuntarily down my face. The two of us were a sad sight and an odd couple for sure. However, I felt that a bond formed between us during that short visit. In fact, I asked this lost and lonely stranger to stay in my home as long as he would like. Perhaps I could extend the hand of friendship this man desperately needed.

Yet after our short visit Mr. Emery departed. For some time afterward, however, I would call the Veterans Hospital to check on his progress and visited him on a few occasions. He was later moved to a nursing home facility in Smyrna. I visited him there on Thanksgiving of 1992 accompanied by Phyllis Hill and her son Philip. Phyllis wanted her son to meet his biological grandfather. This first meeting for them all led to several others, including a small Christmas celebration. John died shortly thereafter, on December 31, 1992, with Phyllis at his side.

Until his death, John wished for a reconciliation with his only son, Ralph Emery. I wish that John could have been granted the reunion he desired. I know how important the love of one's family is in one's life. I know what it is to long for love and acceptance from those who find it so hard to give.

I wondered how John Emery's life might have been different if, by chance, his loved ones had been able to look beyond the disease to which he fell victim. In my own experiences with my father and mother, I found that love and prayer can conquer even the most vile afflictions. As my mother and daddy discovered, prayer has the power to change things. And Jesus loves us all unconditionally.

I was fine as long as I traveled with my band. Only as we approached Nashville did the thoughts of that big, empty Brentwood home turn my tranquillity into tears. One night as we came in off the road, we noticed that lights were on in the house. I remembered that my brother Dean was at Doozer's that night, so I thought, *Who could be in the house?*

Ronny and Larry Light went to investigate the garage. They came back to me reporting that they could hear someone walking overhead in the house. We decided the best thing to do was to leave. So we piled back in the car and headed for Doozer's.

Once Dean heard the story, he woke Doozer up so that she could return to spend the night with me. Dean must have thought that the only intruder was one in my imagination. And as Doozer, Ronny, Larry, and I pulled back into my driveway, we found no evidence of anyone inside or out. Finding nothing unusual, Ronny and Larry left us to fend for ourselves.

Doozer headed upstairs. Soon afterward I decided to join her. As I made my way to the staircase, I noticed that the front door was open. I stepped out onto the porch and called Doozer's name. *Perhaps*, I thought, *she forgot something back in the car*. Just seconds later I saw a human form running down my driveway. This person was definitely not Doozer.

"Skeeter, what are you doing down there?" Doozer called down from the window.

I ran inside, slamming the door shut so fast and hard that it shook the whole house. Seeking solitude and safety, I quickly climbed the stairs to my bedroom. Upon entering, I was shocked. The room was a mess. Drawers had been pulled from my chests, and my belongings were all misplaced and out of order.

The police came and went. We found nothing missing. Doozer and I stayed awake all night wondering who had been in my house. Neither of us felt secure for quite some time after that, for this was just the beginning of a series of mysterious invasions.

On several occasions I returned home to find rooms of the house in disarray. However, nothing had ever been stolen. Nothing was missing, which made me even more scared. The police advised me that they could really offer nothing until "something happened." They always responded to my calls promptly and would check on me from time to time when they made their rounds. Sometimes the policemen would meet me at the post office and follow me home to safety.

One day during this string of curious break-ins Ralph called to ask if I had been scared out there by myself. I confided in him about the problems I had been having. He volunteered to spend the nights with me. I refused his offer but his chivalry sure did make me wonder.

Could Ralph be trying to scare me by arranging these break-ins? Once I started thinking such outrageous thoughts, I knew I had to resolve this matter once and for all.

I consulted with my mother about my dilemma. "Skeeter, did you change your locks after your divorce?"

"No, I never thought it necessary." Ralph and I were the only ones with keys to the house. Since our divorce, I never expected that he would want to enter the house without notifying me first. Although I doubted that changing the locks would have any effect on my problem, once I did, the break-ins stopped.

Although my family and I have speculated that Ralph himself or someone he hired may have been looking for remnants of letters, gifts, and other items he had received from the other woman in his life, we have never accused him. Likewise, we never discovered who the intruder was.

If in fact someone had been searching for personal letters, he or she overlooked my favorite hiding place. I had stashed all of Ralph's personal and confidential correspondence in the kitchen freezer for safekeeping.

With new locks on the doors, I was still frightened. I desperately needed someone to live with me in that house. With my sisters and brothers either married, in school, or in military service, I had few choices left. I couldn't return to Mother and Daddy at this stage of my life. I had no boyfriends or lovers although Ralph would have others believing otherwise, so I had to face the prospect of living alone.

That's when the idea of a housekeeper surfaced. Either Ronny Light or my good friend Pennilane suggested that I could hire a live-in housekeeper. That's how I came to know and love Mrs. Pete. She had moved from St. Louis to be nearer to her daughter's family. Her daughter, Catherine, son-in-law, Hal, and grandson, "Bink," became special to me too, once Mrs. Pete established herself as my house-keeper and confidante. She proved to be a lifesaver for me.

One day a young man left a gift for me at the house with Mrs. Pete. The gift was the first of several stuffed toy frogs I would be receiving. Mrs. Pete said that the young man had introduced himself and said that he often saw me at church. He told her that he hoped to pick me up and drive me to church one Sunday morning. I really didn't think of the situation as anything serious at the time, but later this young man gave me reason for great concern.

Days later my brother Dean answered the door to find a little stuffed toy frog sitting on the porch as the young man pulled out of my driveway. Later, I received a letter from him telling me that he knew he was supposed to marry me and take care of me. He continued to send these love letters to me but never approached me directly, although I would see him in church.

Finally, after several letters and more frogs than any one person would ever want, his letters became more intense in sentiment. Actually, the tone of his words became hostile and threatening. In one letter he threatened to kill me if I didn't meet him in Centennial Park by a certain time. I certainly noticed him then. I was scared to death.

Once again the police told me that they really couldn't help me until something happened to harm me or someone attempted to harm me. My first inclination was to contact the family of this young man so that I could discuss the problem with them directly. After calling each listing in the telephone directory that corresponded to the young man's last name, I finally reached his father. I related the content of the threatening letters to him over the telephone and received this reply, "Why don't you go out with him? The boy loves you. What would it hurt for you to go out with him and let him love you up a little?"

"I don't think you understand the seriousness of this situation. Please let me speak with his mother." He and his wife had been divorced for several years and she had since married again. I hung up quickly.

I tracked down the man's mother through various sources. Linda Palmer, my secretary, and I paid her a visit in Franklin, Tennessee. I told her about the letters, the phone call to his father, my fears and concerns for my safety. She told me that her son had been under psychiatric care for some time and that she would not even leave her own daughter alone with him. Her next comment convinced me that I was dealing with a very difficult situation.

"Well, Miss Davis," she said, "if he were to harm you, it could only mean one thing. I know you're religious and a very nice lady and all, but if he kills you, it means that you must have been a terribly wicked woman in your previous life!" We hastily left the premises.

Feeling a complete failure in my attempts to redress the situation, I received a final letter from my would-be aggressor. He wrote that he knew I had contacted the police and his mother. He expressed his anger toward me for having taken this route. He was so angered that he never bothered me again. Thank God!

I told Mrs. Pete that she had better not accept any more gifts from strangers at the door. And you'd be surprised how many come along.

Otherwise my social life was fairly tame. My friends from the band and I would go to see movies together on our days off. Mrs. Pete would cook wonderful meals for all of us after one of our outings or in advance of one of our get-togethers.

When a record of mine would receive a nomination for an award, I would ask Ronny to escort me to the awards show. He became my best friend and companion. I felt safe with Ronny and had no desire to date anyone seriously for years. I will never be able to thank Ronny enough for his friendship and kindness toward me. He is truly one of the special people on this earth, and remains my friend today.

When friends and family would ask me if I had considered marriage again, I replied that I was married to my career. I traveled extensively in those days, enjoying the opportunity to see the country without having to rush away from my fans after performances. All the boys in the band were single too, so we would often turn our tours into vacations. Being on the road was one of the most enjoyable aspects of my life then.

After Ralph and I had been divorced about five years, I returned home from a tour to find him sitting on the patio with Mrs. Pete. I was shocked. "Is something wrong with Steve?" I asked, unable to imagine any other reason for his visit.

"No, I came over to ask you to go to lunch with me. I have just been getting to know your housekeeper, since you weren't home."

I declined Ralph's curious invitation. After he departed, Mrs. Pete told me that he had introduced himself to her and told her how much he still loved me. She was definitely charmed by him and thought that I should have accepted his generous invitation to lunch.

"You just don't know him as well as I do, Mrs. Pete."

Ralph persisted with his invitations. He called several times and stopped by the house and talked to Mrs. Pete, always professing his love for me during their conversations. Finally I consented to accompany him to a basketball game, but only under the condition that Steve would go with us. Because this particular event was one of the tournament games, the media was out in force. What a photo opportunity!

Red O'Donnell, a beloved columnist at the *Nashville Banner* until his death, told me that he wanted to do a story about our reconciliation. I requested that he forget the story, since this was only an attempt to try to be friends and an opportunity for me to spend time with Steve. As I have learned, nothing is ever off the record; Red did the article anyway. I let him know that I was not pleased and that when I decided to get married again, I would let him have the exclusive. He said he was just waiting to hear the good news!

Ralph called again the very next week to invite me to accompany him on a trip to Cape Hatteras. He said it was his favorite place and he wanted to share it with me for a week. Once again I refused his invitation.

Mrs. Pete, however, just knew I was making a big mistake. I tried to make her understand that she didn't know all that there was to know about Ralph. After all, I had lived with him for three years, and that had proved to be enough.

At a 10 P.M. to 1 A.M. RCA recording session one night, Mrs. Pete called me in a state of alarm. "Oh, Skeeter, Ralph Emery just left here so crazy. When I told him you were at RCA recording with Felton Jarvis, he just started acting crazy." She continued to elaborate. Ralph had told her that I must be sleeping with Felton now. She said he became the vindictive and suspicious Ralph I had described to her.

The very next day I had to appear as a guest on Bobby Lord's television show, which aired at 4:00 P.M. each day. Mrs. Pete rode out to the studio with me and stayed with me until the show was over. As we started to leave the studio, Ralph appeared. Running toward us, he said, "Skeeter, you've just got to go away with me. Mrs. Pete, tell her to go with me."

His pleas fell on deaf ears. He had lost his ally.

Once we were alone together, she turned to me. "I can't believe that Ralph fooled me like he did. Oh, Skeeter, what if you had gone and something had happened to you? I'd never forgive myself."

"Don't concern yourself, Mrs. Pete. Ralph has charmed lots of women. You certainly were not the first little lady he fooled!"

On Easter Sunday in 1968 Ralph called me early in the morning. He told me that he had left an Easter present on the porch for me. "It sounds like you are in an airport, Ralph." He was in Atlanta.

Later he called me from Florida. Before dawn the next morning, I was awakened by the doorbell. Mrs. Pete met me at the top of the stairs. "I'll get it," she said. "Wonder who it could be at this time of night?"

It was Ralph. "What's wrong? What are you doing here?"

I was dressed in my gown and robe, so I had no intention of inviting him in. He insisted on talking to me, so I allowed him into the living room. Seated on the couch, he began pulling at me, begging me to let him "have me again." He told me that I was his wife and should submit to him.

"Ralph, we've been divorced for years! What's wrong with you? I am not your wife!"

He attempted again to force me onto the couch. I threatened that if he didn't leave, I would call Mrs. Pete, who was still awake, listening for any sign of distress.

"She'll understand," he said.

"Ralph Emery, you leave or I'll scream for her." I spoke loudly enough this time that Mrs. Pete heard me.

"Ralph Emery, you better leave *NOW!*" Her voice boomed from the top of the stairs. I closed the door behind him and watched as he sped away. I could only imagine what my neighbors must have thought, hearing tires squealing in my driveway at 4:00 A.M. This would not be the last time, however, that Ralph Emery would pay me a surprise visit.

That night I had a dream I shared with Mrs. Pete at breakfast the next morning. The dream seemed so real, it had the quality and clarity of a vision. As I slept, Steve appeared at the foot of my bed and said, "Skeeter, Daddy got married. He married Joy."

"Who's that, Steve?"

"You don't know her."

I told Mrs. Pete that I believed Ralph was already married. She thought I was talking foolishness, but I couldn't change my mind about the intensity of my dream.

A few days later the phone rang, jolting me out of a sound sleep. It was 5:00 A.M. Ralph was still doing his all-night radio show at WSM. He had called to ask me to go to breakfast with him. "What are you doing calling me?" I asked. "You should be calling your wife, not me." He hung up.

Several mornings later Ralph called again when he got off work. I repeated the same line I had given him during our last conversation.

He asked me why I was insisting that he already had another wife. I told him of my dream and said, "So, Ralph, who is going to call Red O'Donnell with the news, me or you?"

He was speechless. Ralph Emery at a loss for words. "Are you still there, Ralph?"

He called me a witch and asked how I knew he had a wife. I told him I didn't actually *know* until just that moment. A few days later, a photo of Ralph and his new bride, Joy, appeared in Red's column in the *Nashville Banner*.

Mrs. Pete never quite got over Ralph. What were his intentions? I never figured him out and neither did she. It has remained a mystery to me. Mrs. Pete would ask, "Why was Ralph trying to get you to go off with him when he had a new wife already lined up for himself?"

I liked to tell Mrs. Pete that perhaps it was all part of a sinister plot. The scenario would have gone something like this: Ralph would lure me up to Cape Hatteras after taking out a large insurance policy on me. Once we were out yachting on the waters together, I would accidentally fall overboard and be knocked unconscious. Imagine the headlines! I would die a premature, accidental death and Ralph would have his private fortune at last! As farfetched as it seems, stranger things have happened to me!

I found out later that Joy was a university student in Florida whom Ralph was on his way to marry the morning he dropped off the Easter present at my door. He had come to my home to try to force himself on me and to ask me to go away with him the very day after his wedding and before Joy could move all of her belongings to Nashville from Florida.

Mrs. Pete left my house to return to St. Louis to attend to her only living sister, who had become ill. I was sorry to see her leave; the void she left was felt by me for a long time. I missed her so very much. In addition Mother and Suzan had returned to Marion, Indiana, to be with Daddy. It would be a while yet before they all moved permanently to Nashville.

I was all alone in the house again. Sometimes I would beg Ronny to stay through the night just so I could sleep. He always refused because he was afraid my reputation would be harmed by idle gossip. I loved him for defending my honor, but his respect for me didn't lessen my fear and loneliness.

Ronny was my avid supporter. He was never demanding and always gave of his time—whether I needed help with songwriting or career advice about things like starting a publishing company. Furthermore, he always provided a shoulder if I needed one to cry on.

We traveled overseas to follow up on my international popularity. Globe-trotting presented me with a new and thrilling challenge, personally and professionally. During these years I appeared on television variety shows such as *The Mike Douglas Show, The Jimmy Dean Show, The Dean Martin Comedy Hour,* and *The Midnight Special.* "One Tin Soldier" was a Top Ten hit that received a Grammy nomination. I even met Tom Laughlin and Delores Taylor in Hollywood, as well as some of the cast members from the film *Billy Jack.* I met my favorite contemporary poet, Rod McKuen, and had dinner at his home. As an independent woman, I found these to be years of intense personal growth.

I was gradually adjusting to being alone at home and learning not to be lonely. Outside of Nashville, either on the West Coast or in New York, I seemed to receive more love and respect within the entertainment industry. I had always felt somewhat of an outcast in Nashville.

Despite the fact that I had been nominated five times for a Grammy and had several Top Ten records, I was never asked to perform or act as a presenter on any of the awards shows. Over the years I came to feel as though I had been effectively blacklisted from the mainstream country music scene despite my efforts to promote the industry worldwide. What had been my crime? I still wonder whose toes I trampled upon, whose feathers I ruffled to warrant this punishment and exclusion. Of course, one name always comes to mind.

I was traveling in Kansas on tour and McGovern was campaigning for President of the United States. It was August 1, 1972. After the show that night I returned to my room with a heavy heart, thinking about that August night in 1953 when B.J. and I had our wreck. I finally fell into a fitful sleep from which I woke with pains in my left arm and chest. I couldn't understand why I felt so strange when my health was fine.

The band and I checked out of the hotel the next morning. I had already boarded the limo when I decided to have the boys wait while I made a telephone call to my mother. Mother reckoned that everything was fine. Suzan, her husband, Jim, and their little son, Charlton, would arrive in Nashville before I returned.

"Great, but is everybody really alright?" I asked. She told me that I was just feeling bad because of the anniversary of Betty Jack's death.

I joined the boys in the limo and we headed for home. Once we arrived, I couldn't wait to get some decent rest before going with Doozer and Suzan's family to Opryland the next day.

I still couldn't shake that awful feeling that something was wrong. I reluctantly went with my family members to Opryland, but I just could not relax. I checked my Code-A-Phone, but no messages of doom could be found. After one more round on the Wabash Cannonball, I checked my Code-A-Phone again. The message had arrived.

Mother's voice, modulating as she fought the tears that choked her words, said, "Please call." Daddy had suffered a heart attack.

Things didn't look so good upon our arrival at the hospital in Indiana to meet Mother and Glenn, my cousin whom we considered a brother. Daddy's condition was critical, the doctors told us, and we would be very fortunate should he survive. Soon thereafter, the entire family arrived from their respective homes: Harold and his wife, Gladys, from Florida, Shirley and Buddy from Kentucky, and Dean from California.

I canceled my concerts to stay with my family. When Daddy was finally released from intensive care, we all heaved a collective sigh of relief. Believing that, despite the doctor's initial analysis, Daddy was on his way to recovery and would soon return home, we all bade our tearful farewells and returned to the lives we had put on hold during Daddy's crisis.

With Daddy well cared for at home, I resumed my life of concerts and touring with my band. On October 4 we arrived in Indianapolis, where we were scheduled to perform. After checking in at the Holiday Inn, the boys headed to look for lunch and I decided to catch a nap instead. Before I could get settled, the phone rang. I was delighted to hear Suzan's voice. "Are you coming to the show?" I asked.

"Oh, Skeeter! Thank God that you're close by. Daddy is in the hospital again; he has had another heart attack."

Soon I was back in Marion, Indiana. Suzan was at the hospital by herself since Mother was away in Covington visiting with her sister Hattie. "Let's look in on Daddy before we go to the chapel downstairs," I said to my youngest sister. The beginning and the end of the Penicks' circle of children, me as the eldest and Suzan as the youngest, prayed for God to deliver Daddy from the grip of death.

We returned to Daddy's floor and were continuing our thoughts in prayer as Mother and Shirley arrived. Mother was clearly over-wrought with pangs of guilt for not having been at Daddy's side when the second attack set in. "I promise you all, he told me to go!" she cried. As her daughters consoled her, she pulled herself together enough to resume her place at Daddy's bedside.

"She needs a rest," I said after she had gone. "We should take her away to Florida once Daddy gets better." My sisters fully agreed.

Daddy rallied once again. Once he was out of the worst of it, I was able to speak with him about his experience throughout this attack. He told me that he had felt that this time had been his time to leave all of us and join God in heaven. He had been ready to walk into the arms of Jesus when he turned and saw the Lord look over his shoulder. Turning around to see what was there behind him, Daddy saw me. That is when he heard the voice of God saying to him, "I'll leave you in her care a little while." Once again, God had answered our prayers.

Upon learning the wonderful news of Daddy's imminent recovery, I made plans to move Mother and Daddy down to the farm I had purchased at Thompson Station, Tennessee. When Mother came to visit, Ronny, David McCreery, Linda, and I drove out to the farm with her to make all of the necessary preparations to make the farm a comfortable place for them to live. Mother was so exhausted, she went to lie down while we went about our business. Realizing that Mother would be better off back in town at my place, we called it quits for the day and hit the trail back to Brentwood.

After I had said my thank-yous and goodbyes, I began to run a bath for Mother. I told her she was to rest, relax, and get a good night's sleep—Skeeter's orders. Once she finished her bath, she called to me as she descended the stairs.

"Skeeter, come quick. I think I feel a lump in my breast!"

Dropping my chores in the kitchen, I rushed to her side. I examined the area myself to check for the lump she had detected. I became even more concerned as I felt the mass in her breast tissue. I was scared.

"Oh, it's probably nothing to worry about, Mother. Just get some rest and we'll look into it in the morning."

As soon as I could hear her breathing deeply, I telephoned my doctor at his home to ask for a referral for a cancer specialist. With his help we scheduled an appointment for Mother right away. Although I was aware of the serious nature of Mother's discovery, I was in no way prepared for the outcome.

Mother was scheduled for surgery within the week. On the morning of her surgery, David accompanied Daddy to the hospital. Shirley and Dean came in, and Doozer arrived from work. It seemed as though we waited an eternity before the doctor emerged, asking to speak directly with me. *Why me, instead of Daddy?* I wondered.

The doctor told me the startling news. It would be my responsibility to tell my family that Mother had undergone a mastectomy that morning. The doctor promised to explain the details another time, but that time never seemed to arrive.

Once Mother was back in her room to recover, we were allowed to visit with her one at a time. None of us could hide the shock we felt. We knew Mother would be devastated with the realization of what had transpired. Yet she had the power to console us in her own time of loss. As pragmatic as she was, she said to me, "Don't cry, Skeeter. After all, God gave me my titties to feed you kids when you were babies. You're grown now. It's okay, now. Don't you cry." I marveled at her courage as I left the room to let another one of her "babies" have their moments with this unusual woman, my mother.

When she was released from the hospital, we took her directly to the farm. The farm would become somewhat of a homeplace for our family. My brother Harold moved his family from Florida to a place nearby, Dean was often able to come around between military assignments, Suzan and her husband purchased a farm in Tennessee as well, and Doozer continued to live and work in Nashville. Only Buddy and Shirley stayed in Kentucky and have until this day.

I rejoiced at having my family members so near me. My solitary days were truly over; the days I spent alone would be by choice from now on. One of the things I enjoyed the most in those days was taking farmland walks with Daddy. Once I asked him if he thought that establishing the homeplace was what God had meant when He spoke to Daddy back in the hospital that day. Daddy said he was sure of it.

Despite the tranquillity of the landscape and the fellowship of the homeplace, Mother didn't sit down at the farm all the time. She insisted on making her runs to Covington to play bingo every now and then. Mother loved her bingo. We all wished she would take her medical checkups as seriously as she took her bingo. Much to our regret, getting Mother back to the doctor proved to be one of our greatest challenges. And although the doctors had cautioned her to discontinue her smoking and drinking habits, she still wasn't ready to stop.

As for me, I was traveling frequently, and international trips were becoming more and more a part of my schedule. Mother would make sure that she was in Nashville for each of my international departures. Before I boarded my flight, Mother would present me with a rose for safe passage.

Although Mother often promised us that she would join us in church, she had yet to make good on that promise. I never questioned Mother's belief in God, but I knew she had not come to know the full fellowship of Jesus in the personal way that Daddy and I had. Since Daddy had given his heart to the Lord years before, he would always go to church with me at the Lord's Chapel. It was hard for me to believe that Daddy hadn't always been a good Christian man. I knew from my own experience that I had only to be patient before Mother would discover the joys of Jesus so that she too would come to know the difference He could make in her life. Until that day came, I would continue to pray for her and love her unconditionally. I relished every moment I spent with her, particularly those Sundays when, although she didn't accompany us to church, she would prepare a big Sunday meal for everyone and have it waiting for us at the farm as soon as services had finished.

In 1976 Pete Drake produced a record for me on Mercury Records. Pete was one of my favorite steel guitar players as well as a good friend of mine. The song, "I Love Us," is still a favorite of mine. Although my career had ceased to be the top priority in my life, in favor of my family, I was still pleased to have a new release. My family, friends, and fans were perhaps even more excited than I was.

Pete had received good responses from his contacts in the business, and he asked if I would personally call the radio disc jockeys to help him with the promotions. Each time I called, the deejay on the other end of the line would ask, "Is Emery on this record?" or "Has Ralph Emery placed this on his playlist?" In all honesty I had to tell them *no*.

I was amazed. They all followed Ralph's lead. It had been that way for a while, it seemed. Pete had asked me to call Ralph myself after we received the same response from one after another of the deejays I was calling. So I dialed up Ralph's number and explained to him that all of the deejays had asked if he was playing my record. I received a typical Ralphian response, "Well, Skeeter, what are you going to do for me if I get on your record?" My response—I hung up the phone.

"What's the matter?" Pete asked. "Did Ralph ask you to go to the Holiday Inn?" Pete Drake knew Ralph Emery too well.

I recalled the earlier days of my pop crossovers, when folks had never heard of Ralph Emery. Thank goodness for those guys who were leaders, not followers.

In 1988, as I was heavily involved in writing this book, an interview with Ralph Emery in *Country Music Close-Up* magazine, the official publication for the Country Music Association, confirmed my analysis of the situation. In the article Ralph said, "A lot of disc jockeys would listen to me in those days. They would listen, I suppose, for information to educate themselves as to what was happening in Nashville. I would jump on a record and the artists would tell me that they (the disc jockeys) would jump on the same record. As a promotional vehicle of national import, the show was important." He also took credit for the success of countless artists. In the same article he says, "I think I had a lot to do with the Nitty Gritty Dirt Band making it in country music. I think I helped break 'Dance Little Jean.' I think I had a great deal to do with Randy Travis's success; I'm going to take credit for a lot of that."

Well, back in 1976 "I Love Us" had been released for just a couple of weeks when Ralph showed up knocking at my door one morning around 5:00 A.M. I was particularly shocked to see him since I was residing at a rented apartment I kept for when I wanted to escape the hectic atmosphere of the Brentwood house. Hardly anyone knew I kept this address. After I opened the door and we exchanged cautious greetings, I asked, "What is wrong, Ralph?"

My thoughts turned once again to Steve. However, once again, my perpetual naïveté prevailed. Ralph had no news. He had come to gloat. "Well, Skeet, you got a new record out, don't you?"

"Yeah. But I haven't heard you play it yet." And I laughed.

"What are you going to give me if I play your record?" he asked.

"Do you know who you're talking to, Ralph?" I shook my head in disgust. "I can't believe you are here asking me that. You can't be serious."

Ralph was serious. Serious enough to issue another one of his (now famous) invitations to go on a trip with him. I asked him whether his wife knew that he was asking me this question.

"You wouldn't tell her, would you?"

"If she stays with you very long, I'm sure she'll find you out. But how do you know I wouldn't tell her? You had better leave." And he did.

The following day I talked to my secretary, Linda, and my parents about the incident at the apartment. Daddy said, "You ought to have called the sheriff to let him run him off."

Linda replied, "Let's wait and see if he plays her record first." Ralph never played the record. After all, I had paid Ralph Emery's price many times before and had lived to regret it.

I know of others who paid Ralph's price. One Saturday night in 1975 I stood in the wings preparing to make my entrance onto the Grand Ole Opry stage. I happened to glance over to my left to catch a glimpse of a young woman holding a toddler on her hip. Hardly believing my eyes, I turned to my boss, Hal Durham, and said, "I don't know the girl, but that baby belongs to Ralph."

"What are you talking about, Skeeter?"

Before I could explain, I had to respond to my introduction and run out on stage. As I did so, I took another look at the woman and her baby; what I saw reinforced my first impression.

My friends Linda and Glennise and I decided to find something to eat between spots, as we often did. I mentioned to them the observation I had made to Hal. I don't know how I knew but I did. I just knew.

A few months later rumors began circulating at the Opry about the connection between Ralph and this woman. Ironically, and perhaps coincidentally, this woman was an employee of the entertainer whose wife was involved in the affair which led to my divorce from Ralph. That entertainer and I have marveled over this situation: Ralph had an affair with this man's wife in the sixties and another affair with one of his employees in the seventies.

I didn't know the woman then, but today both Phyllis Hill and her son Philip are my friends. Never marrying, Phyllis raised her son alone. With the assistance of an attorney, Phyllis filed a suit against Ralph for payment of child support. After court-ordered blood tests proved that Ralph was indeed the father of Phyllis's son, Ralph was required to pay child support until Philip reached the age of eighteen, in 1990.

Today Philip is a very talented musician and recording engineer. In 1992 he received two of the highest honors for his talents: the Owen Bradley Achievement Award for Studio Engineering and the Roy Acuff Young Talent Award.

I am proud to be counted among the many friends that Phyllis and Philip have made in the music business. Phyllis and I often thought that Ralph would come clean and claim his son publicly, that he would take an interest in his son's development and meet his parental responsibilities, as a father should. That day has not come.

The Men in This Little Girl's Life

You're gone, you're gone
And I still love you
I'm hoping you'll come back to me someday.
I'm here alone with only memories.
I'll always wonder why you went away.
—"You're Gone,"
Skeeter Davis
and Betty Jack Davis

Until I met Joey, I had serious doubts as to whether the fairy-tale ending to my quest for love would ever materialize. In fact, within this chapter I tell of yet other episodes in my life when love was but a disguise for something very different. Luckily, God has seen me through it all. For the story that follows, I have chosen to withhold the names of those involved in hope that they have found their own way in life, with God's help.

While on tour in the eastern United States, I met a young man who spent all of one night talking to my band and me about music. We discovered that we all had similar musical tastes. During the course of our conversation, he asked me to dinner. Since it had been my policy to go out only with my band in tow, I declined his invitation, and before I knew it, we were in the limo and on our way to the next date.

A couple of nights later he appeared accompanied by his mother, stepfather, sisters, brothers, and nieces. We were playing a fair, so everybody mingled and talked freely with one another.

A few months later we played a church concert where the young man appeared again. We all talked about religion and God. He wasn't talking about music that night, he was talking to me about Jesus, saying how He had just changed his life. Looking back on those conversations now, I realize that I was as naive as I always was and he was a very clever young man.

He told me he planned to move to Knoxville. Would I see him if he came to Nashville? I played it safe by giving him my office phone number and told Linda that he might be calling. When he did call a few months later, I invited him to the Opry with me. We went out to eat together, talking easily and generally having a pleasant time. I felt good when I was with him. It was good to laugh with him. What wasn't so good was hearing him say that he loved me. I was not looking for marriage at that point in my life. I was resigned to the fact that I would remain single, with my very good friend Ronny Light as my best male companion. Within only a few short months of my association with this young man, however, I realized that he expected much more from our relationship than I was willing to give.

When I hadn't asked him to accompany me to the Opry, I would look down from the stage and see him looking up at me in the audience. He would show up at my house or the farm without any prior notice or invitation. The warning signs of obsession were there, so I decided that putting an end to this relationship was in order.

Since he lived in Knoxville, he commuted back and forth to Nashville to see me. I never knew when he would just show up in town. I decided that prior to leaving for a tour overseas would be the best time to end our association. I wrote him a letter telling him that I felt it was best that we not see each other again. I knew I was doing the right thing for both of us, I told him, as I had no intention of ever marrying.

Although I had ended the relationship with him, I had throughout our association developed a close friendship with his parents. In fact I had promised them that I would visit them upon my return from overseas. Once I had settled back in Nashville following my tour, I contacted his mother to make arrangements for my visit. She said that her son was well and would be seeing me during my visit with them.

As I headed for Philadelphia, I admittedly was uneasy at the prospect of seeing him again. Once I landed in Philly, I followed the signs to the baggage claim. As I joined the throng of travelers crowding the airport corridors, I was startled by someone who jumped out from behind a post in front of me. It was him.

I grabbed my lightweight hang-up bag and flung it over my arm. With my carry-on shoulder bag, I was ready to go. He said, "I'll take you to my van."

Assuming he had parked right out front, I followed his lead. However, as it turned out, we had to board a shuttle bus to the long-term parking area, which seemed miles from the terminal building. While we were riding in the shuttle, I ventured to ask him if he had received my letter.

"Yeah," he replied, "I didn't like it much."

"We've gone as far as we can go with our relationship, you know. You should know that. I don't mean to be unkind, but I feel that it's time for you to find the right girl, a good girl for you to love."

He frowned in response to my explanation, and without a verbal reply we stepped off the bus, which had finally reached his van.

"Do you think you could have parked a little farther from the terminal? What made you park way out here?" I asked.

"Because I spent the night here, and if you look around you'll notice that there is not a soul out here." I began to feel uneasy.

"Why wouldn't you want anybody around?"

He said, "Well, think about it. You could scream your head off and nobody will hear you." As he glared at me, he opened the back door of his van, shoving me toward it. I balked. As I placed my foot on the floorboard, I pushed back rather than stepping inside.

He said, "Get in!"

"Why can't we use the front doors?" I said. I was trying to remain calm, but I sensed danger all around me.

"The door on the passenger's side is broken."

He pushed me in so that I fell with the garment bag piled on top of me. Although he had not offered to help me with my bag before, now he pulled it from me. I was dressed in blue jeans and an embroidered white blouse I had found during my travels in Sweden. He pushed me down as I tried to sit up. He straddled me, pushing my chest back with one hand and pulling at my jeans with the other. I was trying to squirm out from under him, pushing with all my might and trying to talk some sense into him at the same time.

"Why are you doing this? I can't face your folks after this!"

"No, we're going to get married and go to the beach."

How thankful I was that I had worn jeans that day. Maneuvering someone out of a pair of denims can be somewhat complicated, and that is exactly what I was making his attempts—complicated. "Why are you trying to hurt me? Why are you being so mean? You've always been good to me."

He uttered such profanity to me that I shudder as I recall his words. I could not even look at him at this time. I shut my eyes as I held tight to the waist of my jeans. His voice, as he continued his string of expletives, did not even sound familiar to me. I began to deny that this could be happening to me. In a van in a parking lot. *This is not happening*, I thought.

As much as I tried to deny it, I had to fight for what may have been my survival. "Let's talk. Are you on drugs or something? Is that why you're acting so strange?"

Somehow I had hit a chord that distracted him. He said, "I didn't like your letter. You are not going to get rid of me. We're gonna get married and I'm gonna work on your farm with your daddy."

"When my daddy finds out what you're doing to me—" Before I could even finish the sentence he jumped up off of me and hit his fist into a mirror on the wall of the van. Blood spurted everywhere. He quickly pushed me back down, jumped and straddled me again, and started shaking the blood in my face. He started cursing me again, saying that he would kill me, then I couldn't tell Daddy nothing.

He rattled off derogatory names I never knew existed and splattered his blood in my face and over my blouse as he forced himself on me. I could feel the sprinkles of blood and sweat on my eyelids, but I never once opened my eyes. I just started praying, very loudly. "Dear Jesus, I cannot believe this is happening, but if it is meant for God to allow this, for me to die and for everything I've ever said to witness and glorify His holy name just to be lost by this crazy circumstance, no one would be able to make clear just what happened. I am ready to die but God, if you don't will that I die, I ask you to help me now." I opened my eyes then and looked straight into my assailant's eyes and said, "I rebuke Satan in the name of my Lord Jesus Christ. I command you to depart from this van."

He started crying and begging me to forgive him. He said, "I love you, Skeeter, and I just want to marry you."

"Let's go back in the airport or to a restaurant." My tongue and lips issued the words, but my mind and spirit were addressing God.

"No, we're going to the beach." He picked me up off the floor and assisted me into the front seat as he reminded me again that the passenger door was broken. I would not have got out of there anyway. We were still in the middle of nowhere.

I asked him again if he had used drugs. To my knowledge he had never used them before. He said, "No, I just didn't like your letter. I tore it up. You can't break up with me."

Once we started moving, I asked that he stop as soon as possible so that I could use the bathroom somewhere. About fifty miles from the airport, he stopped at a service station, primarily because he needed gas. As I tried to unlatch the passenger door, he reminded me that the door was broken. Through the open passenger window, he asked if I wanted something to drink. "No, I just have to go to the ladies' room, please."

Two young men appeared to be in command of the gas station. I was uncertain as to what I should do. *Should I confess that he had tried to hurt me and would most likely follow through until he succeeded the next time? Or should I wait until we find a restaurant where other people will protect me?* I couldn't think clearly.

The next thing I knew, he was back in the driver's seat and we were pulling across the station's grounds onto the highway. I prayed for help. Lord, Jesus, provide a way for me to escape—now!

Flames of fire shot up between us as we sat in the van. As a reflex action, I tried to unlatch the passenger door, pushing my absolute hardest with all my weight. The door opened; I jumped from the van and ran as fast as I could toward the station. The station attendants were running toward the van with fire extinguishers in hand.

I latched on to one of the attendants, crying, "Please help me. He's trying to hurt me!" I was shaking so badly, my words were barely discernible. The young man helped me into the station, while the other one extinguished the fire. My assailant approached the station after having moved the van safely away from the flow of traffic. When he was within conversing distance of me, he ordered, "Let's go now."

One of the attendants, both of whom were now standing on either side of me, spoke up, "She says you're trying to hurt her. We don't want any trouble here, buddy, so maybe you should go on your way." Standing right in front of the pay phone, I threatened to call the police.

He stalked back to the van, where he waited and watched.

I asked the attendants if they could call me a taxi. "Do you know how far you are from everything? Taxis don't come around here to take anybody to the airport."

Ask and ye shall receive. It was miraculous. A taxi pulled into the station at that very moment. The attendants were stunned as the driver got out of his car to buy a soft drink.

"This little lady needs a ride back to the airport," they advised the taxi driver.

"Do you know how far it is to the airport, miss?"

"Yes, but I can pay you." Luckily I had my purse over my shoulder. The garment bag would have to be counted as a loss on this trip.

I sought refuge in the taxi and looked back to see the young man in his van. I pointed him out to the driver and told him that he was attempting to harm me; under no circumstances were we to stop for anything. "Please don't let him get me."

He reassured me, telling me not to worry. But as soon as we reached the airport terminal, the van was right behind us. The taxi driver escorted me to the American Airlines counter. I asked the airline representative if they had a flight out to Nashville. He was very friendly as he examined my ticket. He remarked that I had arrived earlier the very same day. "Quick stay, wasn't it?"

"Yes, something has happened. I have to go back now. Immediately, if possible."

"I'm sorry, there's not one seat available."

I said, "Oh, there must be. There has to be." As he checked again at my insistence, a cancellation appeared on the computer screen. He quickly processed my ticket, sticking on the changed schedule tag, and I ran from the counter to hide from the young man who had led me on this frightening adventure.

I ran to the phone by the ladies' room and called Linda. "Meet me in Nashville. I'll be on the next American flight from Philadelphia."

"You just got there!" she replied. Without another word, I hung up as I saw him coming toward me. I ran into the ladies' room. I would peek out and see him looking everywhere for me. I was praying and crying and praying and crying.

I heard the flight announcement and dashed to the boarding gate. He was there. He approached me steadily. I told him I would scream and he would be taken away if he laid one finger on me. With each step I was approaching safety.

"Don't leave without talking to me, Skeeter. If you leave now, I know I'll never see you again."

I told him that was the whole idea. I didn't want to see him again, and if I did, I would call the police wherever I was.

The other people in line had to have overheard our heated exchange, but they really didn't pay any attention to us. I know we looked wild and disheveled, with bloodstains streaking our clothing and skin.

At last my ticket was lifted. I was on my way. Before I exited the gate, he pressed his fist into my hand, depositing something as he turned away. When I found my seat on the plane, I opened my palm to see two wedding bands.

I sat there in my seat with blood on my eyes and eyelids, on my cheeks, my blouse and jeans, and in my hair. I whimpered and sobbed all the way to Nashville. No one asked me if they could help me or what was wrong with me, but I couldn't have talked about the ordeal anyhow. My only thoughts were prayers to God, thanking Him repeatedly for saving me once again.

Linda was there with the limo when I arrived in Nashville. I could not even talk to her about my ordeal. She attempted to take me to the hospital, but my only desire was to be home, safe at home.

That night he began to telephone the house. Linda warned him, "I don't know what you've done to Skeeter. She won't tell me what happened. She can't talk now. If you ever show up here again, I will personally call the police."

Later I called his family to explain why I never arrived. They even made a special visit to see me in Nashville and to make amends for the unusually bizarre episode I endured at their son's hand.

In 1978 the young man even sought out my father on the farm in Thompson Station. Although I hadn't told Daddy about the incident directly, Mother had made sure he knew what befell me on that trip. Daddy ordered him to leave and never to return.

I have since talked to the man on the phone and prayed for his recovery from the problems that plagued him. God's love and grace have allowed me to forgive his acts against me. After all, he too is a child of God.

After this horrifying experience, though, I was even more convinced that I would stay away from anything resembling romance. I would find safety in singing, traveling and being happy with my band, and enjoying the security of my family and friends at home.

At a matinee performance at the Opry in the summer of 1984, a man laid roses at my feet as I sang. He repeatedly tried to reach up to me from the foot of the stage to hand me an audio tape. When I didn't immediately reach for the tape, he began tapping the stage floor with it. His tapping was distracting, so finally I communicated to him to take his things to the side entrance where I would meet him at the conclusion of my spot.

When my performance ended, I joined the security guard at the side door, where I accepted the roses and the tape without even extending a handshake to the fan who had brought them. I felt bad vibes from this man and had said as much to the security guard. I couldn't explain why, but my spirit did not address his with goodwill.

I told the security guard to take the flowers to his wife and I took the tape. I didn't listen to the tape and didn't think too much about it.

The next week the man was back, as he was the next week and the week after that. When I didn't go out to see him, he called and threatened the guard and me. On a Thursday afternoon I spoke with Mr. Van Damme, the security guard, and asked him what I should do. He assured me that he would look after me and that I didn't have to go talk to that man. He had brought roses and candy again. He called and threatened Mr. Van Damme again on Friday night, Saturday night, and Sunday afternoon.

A kind and concerned plainclothes policeman, Mark Wynn, accompanied me to the Opry after these incidents occurred. He surveyed the audience, identified the man, and slipped out into the auditorium to stand close to him during my performance just in case he became belligerent. No one knew of this precaution except the Opry management and the security guard. I had already informed the policeman about the tape, which he insisted that we listen to.

The tape consisted of the man singing and playing the guitar to me and talking to me. On the tape he described the clothes I had worn on certain days in certain cities and spoke of the hotels where I stayed. He spoke of my little dog. The more I listened the more shocked and nervous I became. His conversation turned lewd and obscene. When I could listen no longer, I let the police take possession of the tape.

On Sunday night Officer Wynn called to tell me that if I knew Ralph Emery's phone number, I had better call him and warn him that his life was in danger. During the course of this disturbed individual's conversation, he threatened to kill Ralph during his morning television show as a ploy to impress me. He thought that I would marry him for getting rid of Ralph permanently. I called Ralph and told him the entire wild story.

"Oh, Skeeter, don't flatter yourself," Ralph said. "That man probably wrote a letter and gave a tape to all those other Opry girls too."

"Ralph, the police asked me to call you. I believe this man is obsessed with me and wants to kill you. I felt like I should tell you because the police think he means business."

Ralph laughed. "Well, I won't lose any sleep over it."

I hung up the phone, almost wishing I hadn't called.

I spoke with Ralph on a Sunday night. I returned the policeman's call to report on my conversation with Ralph.

"Well, between you and me, Skeeter, I think we'll have someone up there for Mr. Emery, just in case. He'll be thanking you if this man carries out what we think he has planned." He added, "Don't worry, I'll be looking out for you too!" I thanked him, feeling safer now that he had promised to continue to protect me from this potentially dangerous fan.

On Monday morning the police picked the man up as he entered the studio for Ralph's morning television show. Discovering that he was armed, they transported him to the Middle Tennessee Mental Institution to be held there for further examination.

The policeman called to tell me what had happened. Ralph called shortly thereafter. "Well, Skeeter, I don't know what to say."

I said, "Why don't you just try 'thank you'?"

"Well, I owe you one," he said.

After all this time, I have never found Ralph willing to make good on this particular expression of gratitude. Perhaps he'll have a change of heart one day.

Old Wine, New Wine

You're trying everything from drink to drugs
But still you cannot find
The answers to the questions
That circle in your mind.
Let me tell you about Jesus
And what He'll do for you.
He can save your soul from hell
And nobody else can do that!
Except Jesus. Try Jesus!
                    —"Try Jesus,"
                    Skeeter Davis

December of 1973, I believe it was. I had just returned home from the road to work the Grand Ole Opry. My schedule had been particularly hectic, mainly because of the Top Ten record I had out on the charts, "I Can't Believe That It's All Over." As you'll see from what befell me that year, this title foreshadowed one of the most dramatic ironies of my career. Anyway, the record was doing well for me. It was even bubbling under in the Hot 100 chart in *Billboard* magazine, meaning that it was charted at number 101, getting ready to go into the Top 100.

I was looking forward to being home, to being back at the Opry to sing my hit record. The band and I had been on the road for so long that I hadn't even appeared for my required twenty-six weeks at the Opry. When you're hot, you're hot. I was actually checking to see who hadn't made their twenty-six weeks among the Opry artists, in case the management would reprimand me. I found out that Dolly Parton and Loretta Lynn had not made their time either, so I figured if the Opry let me go, they would have to let them go too.

Just prior to coming home, my band and I had played Indianapolis. During the day we spent our time checking out the local shopping and points of interest. On one of our outings we met a group of people that struck a common chord with us. The first of the group I met were B.J. and Anita, a beautiful couple who were witnessing with a street ministry. Their message was that Jesus loved everyone. They were issuing invitations to passersby to come out to a tent meeting that night. Since we had a show to do, we were unable to attend, but we promised that we would try to go by the next day before we left town.

When we stopped by, we told them that we hoped to see them again in our travels; we said our farewells there in Indianapolis as they began packing up their big revival tent. They said that maybe they would come to Nashville and to be sure and look for them if we heard anything about the Christ Is the Answer crusade coming to town. Their team held revivals and got out on the streets to let people know that Jesus is alive and well. We said we'd sure look for them.

Once I unpacked and focused on my schedule back in Nashville, I asked Annie Cooper (secretary to Bud Wendell, who was Opry manager at the time) to schedule me for an early spot and a late spot on the Opry so I could catch up on my Christmas shopping in between performances. It was only two weeks before Christmas and I had so many people for whom to buy presents.

After my early performance I drove out to One Hundred Oaks Shopping Mall, which was the top mall in Nashville at the time. I could scarcely believe my eyes when I came upon the very same crusade I had discovered in Indianapolis. I chatted with members of the team for a while, as we fed our mutual excitement about their work and meeting schedules in Nashville.

I hurried on to complete the shopping I had wanted to do, watching my time carefully so that I could make it across town to the Opry for my late spot. As I found my way back to the entrance of the mall, I witnessed officers from the police department with their paddy wagon parked outside. Upon closer look I discovered that some of my newfound friends had been loaded onto the wagon. Members of the group ranged in age from teenagers to those in their thirties, forties, and fifties. A misinformed public would later believe that these were young "hippies" and "Jesus freaks" instead of individuals of all ages spreading the message of Christ during the Christmas season.

"What's going on?" I asked as I counted eighteen Bible-toting Christians loaded onto the paddy wagon.

The police officer informed me that these folks were going to jail, and the others that they couldn't carry had better get lost before they returned for them too.

I was completely dumbfounded. I said to the officer, "I just came from Sweden, where they pass out all kinds of communist literature on the streets and everywhere. Nobody arrests them!"

I could hardly leave this scene of injustice. I recollected Red Foley's song "Let's Keep Christ in Christmas." Isn't that what these gentle folks were doing?

I went to speak to the mall manager. "Larry, do you know that the police just arrested a bunch of those people?"

"Yes, I called the police, Skeeter, because they're going to hurt my business by scaring away the shoppers. I don't want them here."

"But it's wonderful that they are here. It's in keeping with the Christmas spirit and all!" I coaxed. Larry didn't see it that way.

I began a shopper satisfaction survey of my own. I spoke with shoppers covered in furs and decked with diamonds as well as those dressed in jeans. Each person with whom I spoke expressed outrage that these harmless citizens were run from the premises.

When I returned to the Opry in a state of great agitation, my show business friends said that those people had probably just been there soliciting for money. These new friends of mine had been completely misjudged. Since that time, however, many of these same skeptics have actually become supporters of Bill Lowery's Christ Is the Answer ministry. This in itself has been a reward for the hardships this incident wrought.

Back at the Opry, my band had assumed that I would sing "The End of the World," or my new hit, or one of the many others. My daddy always said that the Opry audience travel hundreds of miles to hear those hits. But on this evening I didn't think I could do my new record. Our spot was about to be called, when I told the band that I wasn't going to sing any of my hits. I went on stage that night leaving my band without a clue as to what I would sing.

After my introduction, I began, "Something wonderful has happened to Nashville. A bunch of Jesus people came and they're holding rallies here in Nashville at a big tent at Second and Lindley. Tonight some of them were out witnessing at the mall and they were arrested. I can't believe that some of my brothers and sisters were arrested for telling everybody that Jesus loves them and to keep Christ in Christmas."

I went on to say that I hadn't talked to the management or anybody about it, but that *my* heart was burdened. "Instead of singing my hit record for you all, I'm going to sing a song that I feel should be the theme of Christianity. Judy Collins had a big hit with it—'Amazing Grace.'" I said, "Jesus may come before Santa Claus."

That is when the band knew what I would sing. As I sang the song, I felt a spiritual bond with the audience. They knew that I had "done as unto the Lord" and that I had spoken out from my burdened heart. I received a tremendous ovation that evening. (Everything is on the tape!) Our announcer Grant Turner said, "I know Skeeter appreciates that, but she's not coming back. Perhaps she'll take a bow." I remember that as I walked off, I was in tears from the warm reception of the audience. Even under normal circumstances that song touches me deeply whenever I hear it, but especially when I sing it.

As I entered the wings backstage, I was met by Lieutenant Ezell, who was the policeman at the Opry, one of our security people. He confronted me, pointing his finger at me and saying, "I'm so ashamed of you!"

"Why?" In fact Lt. Ezell was the reason I didn't go back on stage after the great reaction to my performance. He cornered me. "What do you mean, ashamed of me?"

"For what you just did—getting out there and telling everybody around the country that the police are arresting Christians. How can you do that?"

"Well, they'll read it in the paper tomorrow anyway. I'm sure it will be in the paper. Besides, it hurt me to see that." I asked him if he was a Christian.

"What's that got to do with it?"

"I think if you were a Christian you would have to be hurt by this too. At least you would be softer in your reprimand. I can't believe you would scream at me like that."

It bothered me that he had jumped at me. He ended our conversation on an even more ominous note. "I can't believe that you did that. We'll just see about this." Then he walked away in a huff.

Somehow I knew I hadn't heard the end of this. I told the boys in the band that I was going down to the jail to see what was going on. I was a little frightened because I'd never been down to the jail.

The members of the crusade were all standing inside the police station with their Bibles in hand, waiting for the night court judge to hear them. The scene was a pathetic one. Drunks were disorderly and two men fought openly right outside the station.

Witnesses inside were calling out for the attention of a police officer. I went into the inner offices and announced, "Can somebody come out here? There are two men fighting." Finally a policeman broke up the fight, which had turned into a bloody battle by its conclusion. I tried to stay out of that one; I had my own fight on my hands.

The Jesus people went to jail. The papers carried the story the next morning. Of course they were released the very next day. After all, what could the police really hold them on?

When I returned to my house, I was so disturbed that I couldn't go to sleep. Personally burdened by the whole idea of the arrests, I kept talking to Linda Palmer about it. We decided that we needed a change of scenery and ended up at Denny's Restaurant.

At Denny's two couples who had been at the Opry approached our table and said, "Skeeter, we saw you at the Opry. We love you and admire you so much for what you did. We're going to be praying for you. You really stood up for Jesus tonight. We'll ask our church to pray for you too, since you may get some repercussions from this bold stand for Christ." I wondered why they would think that. What could possibly happen? I mentioned my encounter with Lieutenant Ezell to them, which reinforced their feeling that there could be more trouble brewing. They said, "When you're for the Lord, who can be against you?" I agreed.

A couple of days went by before the magnitude of it all became apparent. The papers were back on the trail of the story. I began to wonder again if there would be any backlash. The papers called me, quoting to me things that I supposedly had said, but I discovered they had nothing right.

Bill Hance, who reported for the *Tennessean* and the *Nashville Banner*, printed many things about me that just were not true. His misrepresentations would cost me lost revenue in the end. He never listened to the actual comments I delivered that night at the Opry. *Rolling Stone* is the only publication that really printed the complete, factual story. They printed the text of the tape word for word. They even sent a photographer to my church, the Lord's Chapel, to take pictures. I appreciated their professional journalistic integrity. Bill Hance could have taken a few lessons from them. Unfortunately the national wire services picked up Bill's stories, from which point they were spread across the nation.

That week and the following week I lost all the fair dates that I had booked into the new year. All current work was canceled and I was suspended from the Opry indefinitely. I would wait fifteen months for them to lift my suspension. It was quite a time in my life, I tell you. Once again I had a hit record and no opportunity to enjoy it.

I would call the Opry each week to ask if I was scheduled, but Bud Wendell would tell me not to come in. I asked if they had fired me. He said they would just call it a suspension. I didn't really know what that meant but I found out. *Suspended* means you just hang in space and wait.

My parents, who lived in Indiana at the time, were calling. All the people who worked at Fisher Body with Daddy were talking about it. I became the talk of the town. The problem was no one had the truth to tell.

Perhaps the unkindest cut of all came from the many Opry artists who used my misfortune to further their own media coverage through their interviews with the papers. Many of them said that I should know the Opry stage isn't for religion or politics. That I should know better. That I shouldn't speak for all of them.

Anyone who heard me that night or listened to the tape of that night's performance would know that I was only speaking for myself. Teddy Wilburn knew what I had said. When he heard the tape, he found it hard to believe that this one incident had been blown so far out of proportion. Teddy said he hoped I could forgive those who had hurt me over this. I've tried to forgive and forget, that's for sure. I love Teddy so much because he did come and talk with me about it; he was not one of the people who relied on hearsay about the doings of others. Teddy was always my favorite Wilburn brother; his love and support did not waver through the hard times I endured at the hands of a misinformed media.

This would prove to be another time in my life when my self-esteem was depleted. Slanderous things were written about me and spread by those who read the articles. A reporter even fabricated something about my having said that I wouldn't work dates anymore without my Bible and my preacher along. I never said anything like that. The whole episode had gotten out of hand and at my expense.

About this time Olivia Newton-John won an award for "Let Me Be There" and later was named the Country Music Association Female Vocalist of the Year. I personally cast my vote for her. I discovered shortly thereafter that her winning irritated many of the country artists. These exclusionists began a group called ACE (Association of Country Entertainers). They were organized to fight the infiltration of pop artists who crossed over into country, as Olivia and John Denver had done. Since I happened to be a big fan of both Olivia and John, ACE members were even more angered with me. Each day the papers carried news of the fight ACE was waging. I recalled my own crossover experiences from country to pop; no one in the pop field had organized to exclude me!

As that battle was being fought, my personal situation was still generating ill will at the Opry and with the police department. Lieutenant Ezell insisted that I apologize to the police department—publicly.

The day I had scheduled my public apology, the papers carried it as a footnote on the front page beneath the caption, "Jesus on the Front Page," complete with a wallet-sized photo of me at the Opry microphone. The headlines of the paper that day read, "Five Nashville Police Indicted on Vice Charges." Evidently these officers had been using their power and official capacity to solicit sexual favors. With this new development exposed, I found it impossible to apologize. I found that I did not owe an apology to anyone. I just held up the headline of the paper, believing that it spoke for itself. My action was not done with malice or bad intent.

I was paying the price for not giving in to the demands of those who would control me. This had become a familiar pattern in my life, or so it seemed to me. The incident with the Jesus people, the police, and the reaction of the media to my stand for free speech and the right of assembly had generated such an uproar that I was chewed up and spat out by those whom I had considered my show business friends. Their Christmas party invitations were withdrawn as they asked me to please not come. The hosts didn't want to make their party guests uncomfortable with my presence. Shunned by my friends and colleagues at Christmas, I found the holiday season particularly oppressive that year.

I had received a gold record from RCA in 1964. A gentleman named Pias Minezez had come over from Kenya to present Jim Reeves a gold record for "He'll Have to Go" and me one for "The End of the World." The ceremony was a splendid one. Chet Atkins and the others who had been so involved in my success were on hand. After the formal presentations, I was asked to come to Kenya—to come to Africa. I was told that the Africans were ardent Skeeter Davis fans. In fact, Jim Reeves and I were the top artists there at the time.

As I considered the invitation, I knew it would be a fabulous adventure. I had always wanted to go ever since I got saved at the little Baptist church in Kentucky. Betty Jack and I had talked about going to Africa as missionaries. The old missionary who was the guest speaker that night advised us to wait until the Lord sent us.

As I considered my situation at home, the betrayal of my friends and my suspension from the Opry, I decided that perhaps the time had come for me to go to Africa.

A major concern, however, was that under my contract with RCA I was supposed to record an album to follow my hit single. I had a big decision to make: record the album or go to Africa. I couldn't do both. I fasted and prayed until I came to my very difficult decision, which I believed was God's will. I decided to leave RCA, my recording company for the past twenty years. I could leave, however, knowing that I had a Top Ten record to my credit at the time and that I wasn't being kicked out of the RCA family like I had been at the Opry.

In order to leave RCA, I hired Jerry Margolis, one of the best attorneys for the entertainment industry. At the time he represented Bob Dylan and Mick Jagger as well. Jerry felt my request was one of the tougher ones, more so than those made by his rock and roll clients.

I asked Jerry to obtain a release from my contract from RCA and to collect the royalties owed me up to that date. The main point was that I did not wish to record the remaining side (songs owed them in fulfillment of my contract). My good friend Connie Smith was also leaving RCA at the time, but she was obligated to record eight sides before she could be released from her contract. So my request appeared to be a tough one indeed, especially since I had a record charted in the Top Ten. I was very serious about my course of action and trusted God to give me the desire of my heart. I wanted to go to Kenya!

Jerry skillfully obtained the release I was seeking from RCA. The company freed me of my obligation to record and paid my royalties to date. Jerry was truly amazed that RCA granted my request. "Somebody up there loves you, Skeeter," he said.

"Yeah, somebody up in New York and somebody up in heaven."

I called Chet Atkins to ask his advice as far as who to contact about going to Africa. I called Michael Andrews at RCA as Chet had instructed, and the wheels started rolling in that direction. In the end we had arranged for Skeeter Davis's tour to Kenya and Nigeria, Africa.

I was in no way prepared for the royal treatment I received there. The people honored me as they honored their president. The experience was inspiring and rejuvenating for me; the full magnitude of the trip is beyond my descriptive talents, but I'll give it a try.

Bill Lowery and members of the Christ Is the Answer team accompanied my band and me to Africa. During this journey to Africa, I realized that my trials were all part of God's well-timed plan for me. I was now an established international recording artist with hit records behind me. Over the years, I had walked with God and grown as a Christian. This was actually a turning point in my life, as I stood up for the cause of Jesus and religious freedom above and beyond my defense of the Christian people who were unjustly jailed. I had learned what meant the most to me, what my priorities were.

I had been a faithful churchgoer since my childhood. I attended services on Sunday morning and was back again for Sunday night prayer meetings. I had always tried to do good deeds and be a good girl. I felt like I was on my way to heaven and enjoying the trip. But without a doubt, my career had taken top priority in my life. So all of a sudden, as my career was being ripped apart, my priorities changed. Jesus became my top priority, followed by my family and then my career.

Our arrival in Africa signaled the beginning of my missionary calling. Once the members of our troupe had settled in, we met in the restaurant for a group meal. Blessing the food before we ate, we were all so happy talking and laughing about our adventures and observations so far. A young waiter who attended other tables walked up to our table. "You pray to Jesus?" he asked.

"Yes, we were thanking Him for our food and everything good that we receive."

"Will you pray for me?" he said. "I want to know about Jesus. How could I know about Jesus if you had not come to tell me?"

We had just arrived in Africa and already we were being asked to share our beliefs with a young man yearning for the good news. As God's disciples, we should go and preach and teach the word so that the people might know of Him. The young man's name was Paul. We all formed a circle around him and prayed for his salvation. The manager came over to find out what was going on, but we assured him that everything was okay. Paul became our first convert that very evening.

As we flew over Mount Kilimanjaro during that trip, I couldn't help but think about those two young girls who got saved decades ago at the DeCoursey Baptist Church in Kentucky. Looking out over the glorious lands below, I thought, *Surely God sent me on this mission.* Later on in the flight I clung to that belief when we had some mechanical difficulties in the air. To dispel fear among members of the group, I said, "Look, God sent us on this mission. I feel sure that I'm in God's will right now. This is what He wills for my life." I felt confident that we all were safe.

I saw many souls saved for the kingdom of God. Wonderful things were happening. Crowds poured into the concerts we played. We had advertised that during my concerts I would sing all of my hit records as well as share my life with them. Then Bill Lowery would deliver a short message, after which I would share my faith, giving people the opportunity to come forward and accept the Lord Jesus Christ as their personal savior.

This is what I am to do! God blessed me with my career and all the hit records so that my success and popularity could be used for God's glory. I had seen a photo of James Brown in the newspaper and read that he left Kenya sad and disappointed because only four hundred fans came to see him. Such news made me prepare myself for a small turnout. Thus prepared, I will never forget my first concert in Kenya at the beautiful ten-story Kenyatta Conference Center. As we pulled up there to the entrance, a huge crowd had gathered outside. RCA's representative went to investigate. "I don't understand this. You stay right here and I'll see what's going on."

He went in and said ticket sales were exceeding his expectations. All of the people outside were being turned away. The fourteen-thousand-seat auditorium was packed to capacity with three hundred additional standing room tickets issued. To accommodate the vast numbers still waiting outside, we arranged to reserve the auditorium for the very next afternoon as well. The announcement was made with a bullhorn to the crowd outside. Only then did the crowd disperse. As I looked out among my audience, I saw beautiful black African faces with about three hundred white faces dotting the crowd here and there.

The response to my concert portion of the program that night was incredible. After a brief intermission, Bill gave a short sermon and asked the people if there was anyone there who would like to come forward to make a profession of faith. Out of that large crowd, only seven came forward that night. For the first time during that trip, I found the results disappointing.

"I know He brought me here to win souls. I know this is what is important right now. That's what I'm trying to do." I wondered why only seven people came forward after God brought us that big crowd. My band and Bill and Michelle, of Christ Is the Answer, were in my suite at the hotel as we discussed the day's activities. The phone rang. The Nairobi news critic had called to speak with me. He said he had been sent to cover the program and to write the review of my concert. A Christian himself, he told me that God had moved him to call me and explain the significance of what happened tonight.

"Because you don't know the peoples here, you won't know who came forward tonight. I must tell you that the seven people who came forward were all of a different nation. They are all of a different religion." He continued telling me that he had talked to these individuals and believed that they really were coming to the belief in Jesus as their savior. He said, "You have come here today telling everyone about your Lord. Perhaps now they will start a good work here that will go on and continue because of your coming here to Kenya." He said that one of those who came forward had worshipped a tortoise. He told me to sleep well and to know that I was doing God's work. When I hung up the phone, tears of joy were glistening on my face.

We all started shouting in celebration of our victory for the Lord. I remember thinking, *How wonderful it is to be winning souls to the kingdom of God. This is a better reward than any gold record on the wall or any awards or accolades from my peers.* To win a soul for Jesus is truly the greatest reward that any Christian could receive.

It was Betty Jack's birthday on March 4. I sat in the hotel lobby that evening talking to the young man who was cleaning up; then I walked out onto a veranda to breathe the night air. I looked up at the stars and the moon, praising the Lord, thanking Him for the strength of His presence. I don't know that I've ever felt more sure of anything than I was of being in His perfect will at that particular time.

Before my tour of Kenya concluded, I toured schools where I sang and talked to the children. I realized why God had never blessed me with a child. These were my children!

Time passed quickly in Kenya; I felt I had much more to accomplish there. But it was time to go. On the airplane from Mombasa to Lagos, Nigeria, the captain invited me to sit with him and the crew. I could see the Masai with their cattle below me, their huts and houses and all the wonderful animals of the Nigerian panorama.

We traveled for two weeks in Nigeria. Every night the response was positively electrifying. One night when we performed in an outdoor arena that was large enough to accommodate the thousands of fans, I hadn't been finished with my concert portion for any time at all when the crowd became hostile.

The crowd was chanting, "We want Skeeta! We want Skeeta! Skeeta must sing! We want Skeeta!"

I bowed my head to pray. I asked David McCreery and Bubba, our guitar player, to pray with me. "We must not let the crowd overturn this wonderful event."

The dissenting fans were trying to turn our touring bus over. I called out to God for the Holy Spirit to fall upon the leader of that group, to bring him to his knees and bring him to God. David and Bubba heard my prayer. The crowd was shaking the bus as the ringleader fell on his knees. He returned to the stadium and heaved himself on the front of the stage as he began to weep. His followers were close behind him. He said, "We have come to the Lord. We came tonight to hear Skeeter sing her songs but something has taken hold of me. It truly must be the Holy Spirit. I surrender to Jesus." I hugged that man who would bring so many others to the Lord. Every night more and more people were saved.

The night before our scheduled departure, Pias Minezez and the Andrews family, representing RCA Victor, hosted a farewell party for me. They had filled galvanized tubs with Pepsi-Cola and prepared lots and lots of food. When they announced that they had killed a special goat in my honor, something in my spirit changed.

I gave up eating meat on that trip to Africa. For health reasons and spiritual reasons, I became a vegetarian. I do not eat meat, fowl, or fish. Serve me mashed potatoes, corn, green beans, and a tossed salad, and I consider it a meal fit for a queen!

When I returned to America and settled back home in Nashville, the situation remained unchanged. I still wasn't scheduled for the Opry. When I called, I was told that they would call me. Many of my fans and friends suggested posting a petition to return me to the Opry. Attorneys contacted me, urging me to sue the Opry management because of the perceived violation against my rights of free speech. I declined the offers to mount a case against my employers. I would place my faith in God, Who would take care of everything in His due time.

I had been away from the Opry for over a year when I decided that a trip to the Old Ryman would do me some good. My bass player, David McCreery, and I turned on the radio as we drove downtown. Speaking from the stage of the Grand Ole Opry was President Nixon. *Am I dreaming?* I decided against going to the Opry that night. But I wonder what people would have said if I had gone on. Policies must have changed in that year since I had been gone. Hadn't the Opry management spokesman told the newspapers that the Opry stage was not to be used for religion or politics?

Never having been a Nixon fan didn't help my sense of outrage any. I had been invited to the White House during his presidency but declined the invitation. My friends said, "Skeeter, you don't turn down an invitation to the White House." If I had accepted that invitation, I couldn't have endured the hypocrisy of it all. If there is one thing I am not, it's a hypocrite. I always remain true to my principles and honest in my actions.

Nixon's dedication of the new Opry House later caused quite a controversy with a lot of people. I personally received volumes of mail from fans who commented on the fact that they "kicked me off" but had Nixon appear after they had issued a statement that the Opry stage wasn't to be used for religion or politics. Years later, when

Ronald Reagan ran for President, Governor Lamar Alexander, our Governor at the time, and George Bush campaigned for more than fifteen minutes right there on the Opry stage. How times had changed. The perception of the public could easily have been that the cast endorsed Mr. Reagan. Since then, of course, the Opry stage has become a platform for politicians from both parties. Perhaps freedom of speech won out after all.

Still suspended, however, when Nixon appeared on the very stage from which I had been banned, I experienced financial difficulties which plagued me for quite some time. I still had a monthly royalty check from RCA—thank God for that—but as I dipped into my savings, I had nothing to put back in.

All my dates had been canceled and never rescheduled. Since I had had a Top Ten record out the year before, the income I lost was quite substantial. As long as the Opry management shunned me, no other promoter would touch me. As my record dropped from the charts completely, I placed all of my faith in God.

After one of the hardest days I could remember, I received a telegram from Dick Ross at NBC in Burbank, California. It read, "Dear Skeeter, Surely God has something wonderful in store for you. Congratulations on your bold stand for Christ. Hold on to your faith!" What timely words of encouragement from a man I didn't even know. Almost immediately after I received the telegram, NBC called me to perform as a guest on an Oral Roberts special, *Oral Roberts and Country Roads*. Roy Clark and the Clara Ward Singers were also guests on the show. Roy and I both performed country as well as gospel songs. At the time this opportunity came along, my funds were at a critical low.

I appeared on the show for a prenegotiated amount of money, actually union scale. The network flew me and my band out to California and paid all of our expenses. Upon returning to Nashville, I learned that not everyone had canceled me out. To my delight, I did have a few concert dates left. God bless them! As I worked one of these dates, my secretary called me to say that I had received a fourteen-thousand-dollar check from Oral Roberts. This money represented my royalty payments from the show's soundtrack sales. It was literally a Godsend. I even made a copy of that check, which now is framed and hanging on my wall. This check is an example of how God kept His word and supplied my needs. This was the first of many checks which followed in payment for the publishing rights to my song on that album.

I continued to sing, doing lots of wonderful things for Jesus during that time. I traveled to Las Vegas to join in a concert with Pastor Sharpe at his church and theater. We were organizing a benefit show to raise funds for a Christian center to help traveling Christians passing through Las Vegas.

After my concerts were over, my band and I were to leave for California. Before I left the city, however, I wanted to stop by to see Elvis at the hotel where he was playing. Pastor Sharpe dropped by with me, but I was told that Elvis was in the shower. He had just completed his performance, so I believed that to be true. Since we didn't have time to wait, I wrote him a note to explain why I was in Vegas. In the note I reminded him that I would keep him in my prayers and that I wished him peace and love.

I know that Elvis read my note. At 4:00 A.M. that very next morning, Pastor Sharpe was awakened by the ring of the telephone. A man who identified himself as Elvis spoke from the other receiver. Brother Sharpe thought it was a crank call until the caller said, "I want to donate some money to that project Skeeter came out here for." Once again Elvis showed his enormous generosity. This was just another one of the many good things that Elvis did without ever asking for recognition.

As we left Las Vegas, I told my band how great it felt to have been working for such a good cause. I told them how I had turned down top dollar offers in 1964 and 1965 to play the top Vegas clubs. They had even tried to get Chet Atkins to persuade me into playing them, but Chet replied, "You don't talk Skeeter into doing something she doesn't want to do."

Pastor Sharpe called me from Las Vegas to tell me that he had a vision and a prophecy. He told me that I would be called back to the Grand Ole Opry in April of '75. His prophecy turned out to be true, but first I would be going back to Africa again.

I left for my second African tour with Dr. E. J. Daniels, John Boss, and the Fairchild Sisters. We were to travel to Nairobi, Mombasa, Tanzania, and Nekuru on a five-week Christian crusade. As it turned out, I did some concerts also, because the people wanted so much to hear me sing the hits they knew so well.

In Kenya I would go to the schools and all the little children would sing "Try Jesus," a record of mine that was doing well there. I taught them Bible verses and once again felt grateful to God for this privilege of sharing Jesus with these young souls.

For three days a Masai warrior I had noticed reappeared at the crusades. Every day he would stand there with his spear, standing above the crowd. The crowd filled the seats of the stadium and every patch of ground as far as our eyes could see.

Dr. Daniels would speak to the people through an interpreter, then the Fairchild Sisters and John Boss would play and sing. Dr. Daniels would introduce me, and I would sing and share my testimony. Dr. Daniels and his interpreter would close the program, but people would keep asking for me to sing. Finally Dr. Daniels decided to announce each day that I would sing after the service if the crowd would stay. And they stayed. This prospect of my performance kept the crowd attentive, and I was thrilled to contribute to the success of the crusade for Jesus by using my successful recording career to bring people to hear His word and receive the true gift of salvation.

I prayed each day for the Masai, *God save that warrior and raise him up to do work for Your Kingdom*. I had been reading a book about the Masai and learned that they serve a god named Eeka and live on the milk and urine of the cow, making their huts from straw and cow dung. When the Masai find a herd of cows, they believe Eeka provided them for the tribe. The strongest warriors in battle keep the cows. I prayed for these warriors to come to Jesus.

On the third day, as I was singing, the solitary Masai came forward to accept the Lord. All of the churches helped to sponsor our crusade, so counselors from every church presented literature to all of those making commitments to Christ. When they talked to the Masai man, he told them he had heard Skeeta Davis sing from his spear. We did not understand what he meant until we saw a small transistor radio tied to his spear. Oh, how wonderful God is!

I sang in every church and college, shared warm milk with Mayor Kenyatta, and even milked a cow for a coffee plantation servant. I visited the animals at William Holden's game preserve and even got to take a trip to the wild. Our hosts arranged for a couple of very small single-engine planes to take us to the jungle where we were met by guides in Landrovers. Our guide was such a fan that he told us that even the lions would stop and listen if I would sing "The End of the World." "Skeeta will sing now and the lion will pose for photo." The guide opened the roof of the Landrover so I could raise my head up through the top to sing while everyone snapped photographs. The lions looked straight at us as I sang.

We saw the elephants, wildebeests, impalas, gazelles, giraffes, baboons, and monkeys of all sizes and colors, hippos and fantastically plumed tropical birds. It was beauty in its truest form. I am not so sure that I can stretch my imagination to consider the hyena beautiful, but it is one of God's creatures just the same.

Darkness fell on our sightseeing. As we boarded our little planes, we decided that we should pray to get back safe. About that time our pilot asked, "Do you mind if I pray?"

Almost in chorus, we said, "Please do!"

What a day we had! It was our only day off throughout the entire five-week crusade, but it was a day we would never forget.

Our crusade over, it was time to say goodbye to beloved Africa again. The captain asked me to be his guest in the cockpit, as had been offered on my very first trip to the continent. As we left the lights of the Kenya airport behind us, I looked over my shoulder till they were out of sight, and in darkness bowed my head and cried silently, asking God to please let me return again. My heart, my soul, my spirit cries for Africa.

On my way back to Nashville to return to the Grand Ole Opry, I had prepared myself for the triumph of my Christian testimony. My return to the Opry stage demonstrated my forgiveness of the Opry management and theirs for me. Mr. Hal Durham was the manager of the Opry now, Bud Wendell having been promoted to another position. Starting afresh, the Opry was transformed. The old Ryman Auditorium downtown had been vacated, and the Opry's new home welcomed me onto the grounds of Opryland U.S.A.

After my first song that first evening back, many of the artists made gestures of welcoming me back. I confessed to them that their negative comments had injured me personally, especially when they spoke without knowledge of what I had really said that night. From them I learned that this was a case of media mania. Reporters turned on the lights and the microphone and the stars talked when they just didn't know what they were talking about. I heard of the positive efforts made to redress the situation by my friends Jean Shepard, Kirk McGee, George Hamilton IV, and Teddy Wilburn. To them I am truly grateful, as I am to others who may have supported me during those long months of loss. I feel close to the Opry artists now, and many of them are my close friends. We have "meet and eat" gatherings often at our respective homes, so that we can be together offstage as well as on.

Lieutenant Ezell, who had caused me so much distress, also told me that he was happy that I was back. He admitted to having done some serious soul searching with the Man upstairs whom I was always talking about after he had been in a car wreck. "Good, you had better start talking to Him. You should get well acquainted!" I replied.

When I was writing this book in 1979, Lieutenant Ezell jokingly asked me if he would be mentioned in it. I told him that he would be a main character in one of the episodes of my life. We joked about it then, and in all honesty, I was compelled to forgive him for the role he played in generating those injurious news stories about me. It saddened me when he died of a heart attack at age fifty-six in 1987.

I love the Opry, love performing there. I hope that I will have the privilege of performing on that stage the rest of my life. After all, I am the only performer besides ol' Hank Williams to ever be kicked off the Opry. Hank for drinking too much of that old wine, and me for talking about the new wine.

Someday My Prince Will Come

Yes, it's you,
And I can shout it out!
And you're all that I think about.
Yes, it's true,
They all fall by the way.
It's all I can say,
It's you.

> —"If I Don't Have You,"
> Joey Spampinato and
> Skeeter Davis

I have always liked all kinds of music. You may recall that Ernest Tubb used to call me the walking *Billboard*. But my favorite rock-and-roll band is undoubtedly NRBQ. I had first heard them play in the early seventies and immediately became a big fan of theirs. NRBQ mix rock, country, jazz, and rhythm and blues for a truly fun and entertaining musical experience. The critics call them "eclectic" and cite them as one of the best, if not the best live band around. Their fans include such notable artists as Paul and Linda McCartney, Eric Clapton, Keith Richards, Bonnie Raitt, Mick Jagger, Elvis Costello, and many, many others.

Since I was already a big fan, you can imagine my delight when Terry Adams and Tom Ardolino (piano and drums) attended a concert I was doing at a park in Massachusetts in 1973. We had such a terrific time talking afterward. Terry really impressed me with his great collection of Davis Sisters records. That very day he asked me when I was planning to write a book to let everyone know where the harmony came from. He explained that he had known about the harmony ever since he was five years old. His father had brought home "I Forgot More Than You'll Ever Know." When he heard it, Terry knew he was listening to one of the prettiest sounds he would ever hear. I was very touched; not many people were talking about the Davis Sisters in those days. He assured me that all of the NRBQ boys thought we were the best. In fact among them, they had a good collection of records, but not near as many as Terry. He had more than I did!

When you meet someone you admire professionally, and then you admire them so much personally, you feel that you've gotten an extra special bonus! That's how it was with Terry and me. We soon became good friends and kept in touch with one another frequently. On one particular occasion I was making a guest appearance on a television show in Cincinnati while NRBQ performed in Louisville. Terry called the television station to reach me and tell me that they would be playing Nashville. Although I missed their performance, we did get to visit with one another briefly before the band had to leave for their next tour stop.

"Why don't you come and meet Joey and everyone else? We are going to be on tour with Carl Perkins in February. You know you don't have to be afraid of us rock-and-roll boys. We all love you and besides, you and Carl are friends. You just have to come and be with us."

I decided to make that tour in February of 1981. I flew up to the first date in Providence, Rhode Island. I met Jack Reich, the band's manager, and enjoyed being with them all so much that first night. (If you've seen NRBQ live, you know how much fun it is!) I traveled on the bus with them for a few days, after which they invited me to sing on stage with them in New Haven, Connecticut. Their fans embraced me, adding to my already wonderful experience with them. Even more wonderful, Joey Spampinato took my hand as I was leaving the stage, saying "I love you."

I said, "You love my harmony."

"No, I love the girl. And someday you'll see that my love is true blue."

Being with Carl Perkins and his band was a rare treat as well. I had always felt that Carl never got his just desserts from the country folks, but he sure received accolades from the rest of the music world.

Throughout my time with Carl and NRBQ, I talked casually to Joey Spampinato and shared a meal or two with him, but my sidekicks were primarily Terry and Al Anderson. Al was a big country music fan, so he was always asking about Wanda Jackson, Connie Smith, the Grand Ole Opry, and Music City, U.S.A.! Terry and I would talk about Thelonius Monk and Sun Ra. He sure was surprised to find out that I had even met Moondog in New York in the sixties and loved his music! There was always a lot for this country girl and those rock-and-roll boys to talk about as the bus rolled down the highway from town to town.

Now and then, Joey would present me with a sack which contained two Granny Smith apples—my favorite! Joey was thoughtful, but we never really became very close because of his smoking habit. I am extremely allergic to cigarette smoke and have to take precautions to avoid it. So most of the time Joey would stand outside the room while the others would be in the room with me talking.

As the tour ended, we said our farewells at the airport. I hugged them each goodbye; as Joey gave me his hug, he said, "When I see you again, I won't be smoking these." He flicked his cigarette to the ground.

Our collaboration during the February tour had been so successful that we had scheduled a recording session for April. I flew to New York to begin on our project. Joey was true to his word. He didn't touch the first cigarette. I was very impressed. Not only did he take the trouble to buy me my favorite apples, he had quit smoking with me in mind. Over a period of months, we recorded our album. Because of their hectic touring schedule, we recorded a few days at a time and then would take a break before resuming the project again.

Our frequent meetings allowed me to become very well acquainted with each of the boys. I knew too that I was beginning to like that bass player too well for my own good.

On one of our breaks in May, I flew to Daytona Beach to join Mother, Shirley, Doozer, and Linda Palmer for a few days. As Doozer and I walked on the beach together, she asked me which one of those NRBQ boys had I fallen in love with. My reply was simple—I loved them all.

"I believe you like one better than the others," Doozer surmised with her sisterly insight. Then Linda began the same line of questioning but was met with my denial of any notion of romantic involvements.

I returned to New York to finish our project. I think that our love and respect for one another showed in the final release.

One of the songs on the album was "Someday My Prince Will Come." As I sang the vocals, I looked through the glass of the vocal room as they played. I have to admit that I knew then that my prince was playing the bass as I sang that little tune. My prince was Joey. He was the one that I had fallen hopelessly in love with. The warning signs were there; I would have to pack my heart along with my other belongings and leave as soon as the album was completed.

We finished in June and once again were saying our goodbyes at the studio. On the way to the airport, I remember looking behind me through the window and waving as I left a little bit of my heart with the bass-playing boy from the Bronx. I didn't know when I would see him again, but it was to be quite a while.

Ours was a long distance romance. We rang up lots of long distance phone calls and met very few times because of our conflicting work schedules. When it's love, it doesn't go away. And although I said that I would never marry again, this love was bound for marriage. So I learned to never say never.

Joey asked me to join him for NRBQ's tour with Bonnie Raitt in November. Soon after we found ourselves in a jewelry store looking for a wedding band. We promised "to love, honor, and cherish each other" as he slipped that gold band on the third finger of my left hand, where it has remained since that day in November 1981.

After the tour NRBQ had commitments for dates in other cities, and I was to leave for a tour of Sweden. That's how it went. We saw each other when possible; either Joey would fly to Nashville or I would fly to New York. Our life together was a revolving honeymoon it seems, with both of us coming and going. Even though neither NRBQ nor I had Top Ten hits then or now, between their club and college dates and my overseas travel and Opry dates, our comings and goings keep us moving at a dizzying pace.

When the joint album was released, it received critical acclaim. Unfortunately, poor distribution made it hard to find. Much later, in May of 1986, we received an award from the National Association of Independent Record Distributors (NAIRD) for that album with NRBQ, which was entitled *Skeeter Davis/NRBQ—She Sings, They Play*. NAIRD voted the album as their favorite for the year.

Not long after the initial release of the album, NRBQ had scheduled a date at the *Exit/In* in Nashville, so I asked Mr. Hal Durham, the Opry manager, if NRBQ could play with me during my spot one evening. My own band were such fans of NRBQ that they didn't mind listening and watching from the wings that night.

In conjunction with NRBQ's Nashville appearances, I contacted the coordinator of the cable television program *Nashville Now* months in advance to inquire whether an appearance could be arranged. I was asked to send over an audition copy. A bit insulted by this response, I overcame my injured pride and I took a tape copy out to them. Although I checked persistently with the coordinator, we were never granted an appearance date.

NRBQ has appeared on numerous national shows, including those of Connie Chung, Johnny Carson, and Dennis Miller, and attracts audiences which include megastars like Jane Fonda, Bette Midler, Christopher Cross, and Jackson Browne.

Finally I called Ralph Emery, since he was the host of *Nashville Now*, but was informed that he was not available to speak with me. Three days before the band arrived, Ralph called me. A friend and I listened to his comments: "Well, Skeeter, I hear you got some band that you made a record with and you want to do my show."

"Yes, Ralph. I wanted to ask you to have us on or at least have them on while they're in town."

"Well, what are you going to do for me, Skeeter?"

"Ralph, there ain't anything that I can do for you 'cause I am not sitting there in the TV chair." This bantering back and forth each time I had to deal with Ralph was becoming ridiculous. I told him that he was the one with the television program, not me.

"Skeeter, do you know what you can do for me?" he said.

"Come on, Ralph. Do me a favor and have my friends on your show." Once again he asked what would I give him in return. Everything was a transaction for Ralph Emery. A debit and a credit. Always keeping tally. He would have made a great accountant.

"Ralph, I ain't going to give you nothing. Stop acting crazy. Not all of the people you have on your show are country, so you can't use that excuse."

"Skeet, I'm not talking about your friends. I'm talking to you about you and what favor are you going to do for me?"

I hung up the phone. Once again I had had enough of Ralph's sleazy power plays. My friend looked at me in awe. "Nobody would believe he would treat you like that, Skeeter." Believe it.

NRBQ played the Opry and Exit/In, but they never made a television appearance on TNN's *Nashville Now* until Carlene Carter was host on June 28, 1993. An NRBQ fan herself, she asked them to appear as her guests on the show. For all of my fans who have never understood why I rarely appeared on *Nashville Now*, I hope this provides some insight into the situation.

As I add the finishing touches to my book, I would add a footnote to the continuing saga of the Skeeter-Ralph stand off. In June of 1991 I played the international, multilabel show at Fan Fair in Nashville. I closed the show, following Jim Ed Brown. As fate would have it, Ralph was the emcee. When it was time for Ralph to introduce me, he threw his prepared notes aside and said, "Folks, I don't need my notes to bring on the next act. I know her real well. In fact, I was married to her once, and I guess I gave her the worst four years of her life." *Wow*! I thought, *a moment of truth*. When he said my name, loud and clear, I made my entrance before the crowd of true country fans. Ralph hugged me and said, "Skeeter, I hope your husband doesn't mind me giving you a hug."

"Well, I don't know if he minds or not, but he's watching."

After my performance, my friends and fellow performers were bubbling with the comments Ralph had made. The Country Music Association's Jo Walker Meador said to me, "Skeeter, that was something seeing you and Ralph out there together. Maybe that will break the ice!"

Laughing, I said, "Well, Jo, it's been thirty years. Don't you think it is time the ice was broken?"

And even if the ice is still frozen solid after all this time, at least the true story will be told with the printing of this book.

Mother

M is for the many things she gave me.
O means only that she's growing old.
T is for the times she fought to save me.
H is for her heart as pure as gold.
E is for her eyes with lovelight gleaming.
R is right—right she'll always be.
Put them all together, they spell *Mother*,
The word that means the world to me.
—"M·O·T·H·E·R"
Howard Johnson and
Theodore Morse

Memorial Day was always a special holiday for my family. Mother packed a picnic lunch as we kids picked roses from our yard to take to the Glencoe cemetery to place on the unmarked graves of Grandpa and Uncle George. Today we place our roses on Mother's grave. And, Mother, how I miss you.

All the kids are here with Daddy except Buddy and Boze. "Where is Glenn?" Daddy asks. Glenn is our cousin, whom Mother and Daddy raised as their own. Once we give Daddy the run-down of where everyone is, he relaxes a little. He says, "Never can get 'em all together in the same place, can we?" Despite the fact that we always miss those who are away, we always manage to have a great time together as though we are all little kids again.

I remember asking Mother and Daddy to go on a tour to Europe with me and Boxcar Willie. Mother said for me to take Daddy; she would rather go to the one place she had always dreamed of going. "Skeeter, will you take me to Las Vegas?"

"Mother," I replied, "are you teasing me or testing my love for you?" She reiterated that she wanted to go to Las Vegas more than any other place. So despite my disappointment that she had no interest in going to Europe, I promised her that I would give her the amount of money I spent on Daddy in Europe so that she could have money to spend however she wanted to. She couldn't have been happier, explaining that after all, Las Vegas had many more games to play than just bingo.

Mother had toured with me before when I played a concert with Slim Whitman in Tampa, Florida. Mother was a fan of Slim's and with a niece and nephew living near Tampa, she found the trip hard to resist. The only hurdle was flying. She didn't enjoy it at all. But with those temptations she made the trip with me anyway. As much as she enjoyed the vacation, she liked being on the ground much better. I kidded her about the trip to Vegas, asking her which mode of transportation we would take. "Maybe we'll go *Greyhound*!" she said.

Mother and I went shopping to buy Daddy new clothes for his trip. Mother picked out a cowboy hat and some boots. Laughingly she told Daddy that folks over there would be calling him J.R. after the popular television series *Dallas*.

Packing was all done and departure was near—October 1981.

Mother, Dean, Doozer, Suzan and her son, Charlton, along with friends came to the airport to send Daddy and me off to Europe. John Rees, my piano player, and Linda Palmer also accompanied us. Mother's eyes filled with tears as it came time to turn loose of Daddy. She was not accustomed to being the one left behind; she had always done the leaving. She told Daddy that she was going to try to stop smoking while we were gone. Then she spoke to him directly. "William, when you get back, I'm going to go to church with you all." Her remark really touched Daddy. We exchanged glances, knowing that something of a spiritual nature was happening to Mother.

"Maybe your Mother is missing me already, 'cause I've always been there and she always left. So maybe that makes her think more of me," he said, smiling. "You know, Punzie must love me after all."

Daddy and I kept Mother in our prayers throughout our three-week tour of Europe. Daddy enjoyed traveling on the coach, talking to Boxcar Willie and the boys. He beamed with pride as I sang to the responsive audiences I always found in Europe. We called Mother often as we sped through our three weeks.

Mother was so thrilled when we arrived home. I was especially pleased that she had successfully stopped smoking. She had been smoking at least since I was in the sixth or seventh grade. And that was a long time ago.

On the first Sunday we were back in the Lord's Chapel, I sat between Mother and Daddy. A sudden burst of emotion overcame me as I realized that the vision I had had nearly ten years before had come true. I thanked God for answering my prayers, allowing Mother and Daddy to be present together with me in the chapel at last.

In preparation for New Year's Eve at the close of 1981, Mother had bought some new silver shoes and a purse to match. She had planned to go with my brother Dean somewhere, but now was talking about going to church. I was scheduled to sing at the Opry, but I told Mother that I knew she would enjoy the watch-care services at church, to see the old year out and the new year in. I hoped she and Daddy would go together.

After my Opry performance, I returned home and called them. No one answered. As I checked my watch, it was just 11:30. I would call later. Snow began to fall, making me somewhat concerned for their safety with the slick roads. Finally at 2:00 A.M. my mother called. She was so excited. She said, "Skeeter, I hope you wasn't too worried. Me and your Daddy just had so much fun, we couldn't leave!" No one was happier than I was.

She told me that she had even prayed for Dean to stay home and forget about his plans to spend New Year's Eve at some bar. "Well, Mother, you must have a good hotline to Jesus because Dean stayed home and went to bed at ten thirty. I talked to him earlier."

Mother continued talking about the joyous singing and the wonderful sermon presented by Brother Moore. She was especially taken by a girl named Cathy Manzer who came at the end of the program singing her own original songs.

Then she sprung the news. "Skeeter, I'm going to get baptized." I shouted in praise! What a wonderful way to leave a year behind and face the new one. Brother Billy Roy Moore baptized Mother on Sunday morning, January 10, 1982. She really became a new woman in Christ. No smoking, no drinking, and no gambling. She said to Brother Moore, "Skeeter was going to take me to Las Vegas, but

Preacher, I've just stopped doing all the things I was going out there to do!"

Instead of the trip she had planned, she announced to us that she wanted to go to Kentucky to see her mother and her uncle Dilver Webster. I said, "Mother, why are you going there?"

"I'm going to see Dilver to tell him that I forgive him for killing my dad and brother." I was so proud of her! She added that she wanted to talk to her mother about her spiritual walk. "I've got some work to do."

She went on the Greyhound and Shirley met her to take her to Grandma's. When Mother returned, Daddy asked her about her trip. She said she did forgive Dilver, but when Daddy inquired about Grandma, Mother said, "I didn't get the answer that I wanted to hear from my mother when I asked her if she was saved."

Mother didn't feel particularly well when she returned from her trip. She asked Daddy to drive her around the Kentucky-Tennessee area. I was thrilled as I watched them falling in love all over again. Mother would go nowhere without Daddy. I was so blessed to be around them.

It had been eight years since Mother's mastectomy. We had taken Mother's health for granted, it seemed. Since Mother just didn't bounce back after her Kentucky trip, she consulted with her doctor, who advised her that she would be entering the hospital for a series of tests. He would check on everything.

Is the cancer back? How can that be? The doctor advised me that if she responded to the treatments, we should have Mother a long time. I believed him.

Mother was in the hospital, and I couldn't really figure out what was going on. I told her that when she was released from the hospital, I wanted her and Daddy to come to my apartment, or to my house, if they preferred.

A few days before Christmas Mother and Daddy arrived at my apartment. I called Linda Palmer and my friends Linda, Dick, and Cheri Stiegele because I was afraid she was actually going to die at my apartment that night. I could not understand why she was this ill. The doctor offered me no understandable explanation. I stood over her all night. Daddy was sleeping soundly thanks to the heart medication he had to take.

I prayed throughout the night and when morning came, Mother told me that she didn't really know what was going on. She would prefer another doctor. We were hopeful that a different doctor, Dr. Lane, would be able to help her.

I started cooking for Mother and Daddy after having not cooked for some time. Mother would ask me if I was practicing for the boy whose gold band I wore on my finger. I just smiled. When Joey would call, Mother would say, "I don't know who he is, but he put that ring on that hand, didn't he?" I just smiled.

Mother was in pain and had to take Dilaudid and morphine. We would talk and share stories and our deepest thoughts all through the night until she could sleep. One night she asked if she could sleep with me.

"Of course," I said. We were awake all night. Mother told me her secrets, and we talked about the whole era when I was a captive of the Davises after the accident. We both cried as we recalled the devastating effects of Mrs. Davis's control, not only on my life but on the lives of my family as well. I asked Mother's forgiveness for the pain I might have caused her; she asked the same of me. When daylight came, Mother and I were astonished that we had talked the night away, but the heart-to-heart discussion was healing for us both.

As Mother became progressively worse, she slept alone so that she would not feel the pain of someone touching her. I gave her her baths. She said, "Ain't life funny. You bathe your baby, and then your baby bathes you."

During these final weeks of her life she gave me the words of praise I had been seeking from her all of my life. She told James, my bass player, "James, I used to go off and leave the kids with Skeeter. She would tell me that she was not going to clean them up or take care of them. Every time I would come back she would have them all sparkling clean and sitting out front on the little gallon molasses buckets, singing to them. You know, Skeeter was a perfect little mother." How I cried when she said this to James. I had always wanted this approval from Mother, and now she gave it to me. I hugged her and thanked her. Money can't buy the feeling of love and acceptance I gained at that moment.

Daddy would read the Bible to Mother because her eyes had failed. I was recording an album at the time, but I would just be away from her for a few hours at a time. I'd bring the tapes and let Mother and Daddy hear them.

Mother was preparing to go to the Opry with me on Saturday, January 29. Mother, Daddy, and I stayed at the Opry for a long time that night. She sat on the bench on stage watching the show for the first time ever. In times past she had always just watched me perform and then we'd leave. This night, however, Mother shook Roy Acuff's hand and said so long to Roy and Bobbi Drusky. "Mother, you'll be back," I said.

"No, I won't, Skeeter." James walked her out to the limo, escorting her on his arm. We all went over to eat breakfast at Shoney's and at 1:30 A.M., we started for home.

The next morning I lay in my bedroom wondering whether I should go to church or not. I went to check on Mother for a minute and found her awake. "I was just hoping you'd come in here. Skeeter, I'm dying."

"Mother, you look good. Don't she, Daddy?" He was reading the Sunday paper, but he said, "I believe your trip to the Opry did you good. You're fine." She started getting up, reaching for Daddy, so I ran to sit beside her. Daddy looked up from his paper, asking what was the matter. She repeated, "I'm dying."

She instructed me to tell all of the kids that she loved them, then she turned to Daddy. "William, I love you more than anything, but I have got to leave you." At that moment, I *knew* she was dying.

Daddy jumped beside her, pulling her back up toward him, crying, "Punzie, don't leave me. Please don't leave me."

I rushed out the door that joined my apartment to that of Margaret Woody, my good friend. She called the ambulance for us.

Daddy rode in front with the driver and I accompanied Mother in back. She did not open her eyes at all during the ride to the hospital. Of course I was squalling and near hysteria. St. Thomas Hospital had never seemed so far away before.

They rushed her into the emergency ward. Minutes later two doctors approached Daddy and me. "I'm so sorry. She is gone. Your mother has gone to be with the Lord."

I refused to believe that she was gone. I was determined to see her and started to walk back into the area where they had taken her. They stopped me before I could make much progress and asked me which mortician we would be using. I did not answer. The lady at the desk asked me to fill out papers. She asked the questions and I was trying to keep enough composure to tell her the answers.

As I responded to the woman's interrogation, Margaret Woody and my friend Lynn Horne arrived. Daddy and I were nearly crazy with disbelief. I told them all that I would not leave the hospital until I saw my mother. Quite some time had passed by now, but Margaret's sister, who was a nurse at St. Thomas, came to our assistance by sending a Catholic nun to talk to us.

Sister Euphemia said, "What is your problem, child?"

"I can't leave here without seeing my mother." She left quickly and returned just as quickly, leading me and Daddy back to where they had taken Mother.

Mother lay there, and I have to admit that she looked dead. Daddy and I were both crying. Sister Euphemia said, "Why don't we say a prayer we all know?" We started to recite the Lord's Prayer. Halfway through our recitation, Mother began speaking in a very faint voice, reciting along with us.

I turned to lift Mother from the bed, but Sister Euphemia restrained me as she held one of my hands and one of Daddy's. She said, "Let's try another that we all know." With each word of every line of "The Lord Is My Shepherd," Mother's voice grew stronger and stronger. The doctors pushed the door ajar as they observed Mother's miraculous recovery. They did not reappear for a while.

After we had prayed, Mother said, "I asked God to let me come back so the kids can see me." She said, "I asked Him for two more years, but He said no."

"Mother, why would God only let you stay for a little while instead of two years?"

"I don't know, but I'll be here till Tuesday." She stated this matter-of-factly.

I said, "That's just three days."

She smiled and said, "Not this Tuesday. Now call the kids and tell them to come and see me, 'cause I'll leave Tuesday."

I had seen enough evidence of God that I was not about to do any less than she asked me to do. I knew that from now till she departed on Tuesday we'd listen to everything she said as if it were coming directly from God.

The doctors asked her what she wanted to do. She asked me for guidance. Sister Euphemia told her, "You are a free spirit, sister. You do as you please."

Mother said, "Skeeter, want me to go back home with you?" I didn't know quite what to say. I was still in shock as I watched her sitting up and talking after the doctors had declared her dead.

"Mother, why don't you stay here for three days, then come home with me?"

She said, "You go call the kids and tell them to come see me."

I went out in the lobby of the hospital and started dialing. I called everyone: Buddy, Shirley, Boze, Dean, Doozer, Suzan, and our cousin Glenn. When I told them that Mother would be with us just a few more days, they all thought I had gone crazy. Particularly when I said, "Mother will be with us until Tuesday—not this Tuesday, but next Tuesday."

Buddy said, "I'm coming down in February. I can't come now."

I said, "Buddy, if you want to visit your mother before she goes, come now!" He was there the next morning. Shirley's daughter Terry drove her down as well. Doozer came by, but as she looked at Mother, she said Mother looked too good to die. Although she had looked bad during her illness, after she died her first death at the hospital, she looked much improved.

Daddy said her improved appearance was a result of her having seen the face of God. "You know, Mother has been with Jesus. She won't be satisfied here no more." I nodded my head in agreement.

We had been at the hospital all day. In the evening Linda Palmer and Cheri Stiegele came by. They found it difficult to believe that Mother was ill. Linda said Mother looked better than either me or Daddy. She said that Margaret had called her to tell her that Mother had died. I said, "Well, she did. God let her come back."

Linda and Cheri left the room to bring Mother a cheeseburger and a milkshake. The way Mother took it all in stride, she seemed to act as though she were at a picnic rather than on her deathbed.

On Wednesday morning Mother returned with me to my apartment. Several of her loved ones came by to see her in the living room, which we had set up as her personal living space. She preferred the fireplace and the living room windows. She could observe the birds and the squirrels that would light on the balcony. God had restored Mother's sight, so she enjoyed all sights she could take in. I placed candles in the windows and hung them from the ceiling. I patterned my apartment after the houses I had seen in Norway and Sweden with their lace curtains and candles. Mother enjoyed the warmth of the fire by day and night primarily because she thought it was pretty to watch.

It was time for goodbyes though. As she spent time with each of her children, she let them go away without asking them to stay longer. She knew her time was drawing short.

When Mother would wake from her short bouts of sleeping, she would describe something she had seen from her glimpse into heaven. She told us how beautiful it was, she told us that we should see all the little babies. "Little cherubs are here," she said. "You should see them."

She had been on strong medication before, but since her release from the hospital she had not needed the medicine to ease her pain. She was not hallucinating or dreaming because of the medication, of that I could be sure. I was continuously testing her, asking her if she was in pain. I decided that God was showing me the credibility of everything that was happening.

She called me to her bed and whispered, "Skeeter, someone is messing in your dresser drawer in your bedroom." I told her she must be dreaming. She was too far away from my room to see or hear what might have been going on in there.

"I'm not dreaming. Go back there and see."

"You're dreaming, Mother."

At her insistence I slipped quietly down the hallway to my bedroom, where I found an individual sorting through my dresser drawers. Taking the person by surprise, I asked, "What are you doing?"

The individual replied, "Just looking at your pretty things."

The shock of it all was that Mother was right! How had she sensed this? It was as if she was already in heaven looking down to protect me. An aerial view is what she had to have had to see what she saw!

Daddy was in bed sleeping. I was seated on the floor by Mother's bed talking to her when she demanded to get up and sit at the kitchen table.

"I hear Buddy praying for me," she said.

I said, "Wait right here. I'll be right back." I slipped into my bedroom and dialed long distance to Buddy's house. Peggy, his wife, answered. I asked her what Buddy was doing.

"He's right here. I'll let you talk to him."

"Buddy, what were you doing right before you were called to the phone?"

He said, "I've been praying for Mother for the last hour. I'm thinking of coming back down there."

I told him what Mother had said and then I walked back to the kitchen and put her on the other telephone extension. Buddy told her that he'd come back, but she told him they had such a good visit and that he should not worry.

After they hung up the phone, she told me that she hated to leave all of us, but it was time for her to be with Jesus. She talked about it with such assurance, I knew she would leave just when she said she would. Before she lay back down, she said, "Skeeter, will you make me a promise? I do not want to hear the sirens, and I do not want them to keep me alive with tubes and machines when I already know that I'm going to be with Jesus on Tuesday."

I began to wail, telling Mother that I could not understand God at all; if she actually asked Him face to face for two years, why would He grant her only a few days? Mother said, "Skeeter, I do not know why God did not heal this cancer in me but I know I'll be healed there with Him." As I continued to sob, she reached for me and hugged me. "I don't want to hurt you or the kids. I love you all so much, and I know that Daddy would be so hurt if he knew that this cancer is all over me. I don't want to hurt your Daddy, 'cause you know I love him more than anything, but I just want to go on to Jesus."

Mother lay down. I got down on my knees, leaning on her bed, and could do nothing but sob. She stroked my hair. "Don't cry. Just promise me I can stay here till I go."

When I brushed Mother's hair, I would take what had come out in the comb and brush and secretly save it away in a little music box in the bedroom. One day while Shirley was still there, she brushed Mother's hair. Mother brought the hair to me and said, "Here, just put this with the other hair you've saved. I know what you're going to do with that." I put it in the music box, wondering once again how she knew.

On Saturday after all of my brothers and sisters and the other relatives who stopped by to see Mother had gone, Mother smiled at me and said, "Now you can lie here beside me and watch your ball game." She knew the basketball playoffs were on. I told her that it wasn't necessary for me to watch the games.

"Skeeter, turn on your ball game and watch it here. You'll love it." So I turned it on, but left the volume turned off.

Daddy was reading the Sunday paper just as he had a week earlier, and he said, "Punzie, you look wonderful! Seeing the kids did you a world of good." Mother looked at me and told me that now all the kids would be away when she leaves, so I could just call them and tell them she'd gone to heaven.

The doorbell rang. Suzan and Charlton had arrived with food for everyone. Five minutes later the doorbell rang again. Doozer and her friend Geraldine had brought even more food. Mother looked up at me and said, "What is this? Now are Buddy and Shirley going to turn around and come back too?"

Suzan said, "What is wrong?"

"Well, Suzan, our mother is preparing to leave and she thought she would just have a quiet time before the final hour, I guess. I don't know."

Suzan went over onto the bed with Mother and said, "I'm not going to let you die, Mother. You can't leave us." I had walked out onto the balcony with Doozer. I said, "Doozer, I think I've given Mother the greatest gift I can." I explained that since Mother had told me three times that she wanted to go on to be with Jesus, that she did not want to suffer with cancer, I told her I would release her. I meant that I would lovingly turn loose of her hand and put her hand into the hand of Jesus. I told Doozer that I had even said to Mother, "Since you are determined to go on, will you please tell Betty Jack hello for me and that I miss her?"

Mother said, "I sure will."

Crying, Doozer said, "I can't let her go yet."

Suzan shot her head out of the door onto the balcony to say she was calling an ambulance to take Mother back to the hospital.

I told Doozer that Mother did not want to go back. I told Suzan as well, but she said, "I'm calling the ambulance." I leaned down and told Mother that I would not be the cause of her hearing the sirens. I went out onto the front porch where Doozer was and told her what Mother had asked me to promise. I prayed, *Lord, this is no longer in my hands. I cannot stop the ambulance from taking Mother away and I know it is not Tuesday yet, but I pray that you'll give Mother the word to say or at least help us all in this situation.*

The emergency medical technicians had arrived and were attempting to lift Mother onto the stretcher. Mother spoke clearly, "Mister, would you please take your hands away? I do not want to go with you because, you see, I am with Jesus now."

The men turned loose of her and Suzan began to speak to Mother, "I didn't really know that you're with the Lord." While Mother talked to the ambulance men some more, I called Dr. Lane for advice. He confirmed that the cancer had spread through to her lungs and that we could give her the choice of staying at home or of being hospitalized. He added that he had not met anyone quite like her.

I asked Dr. Lane to speak with my father. I could tell from Daddy's expression that he had no idea of how far the cancer had spread. None of us really believed that she had been sick enough to die. The doctor spoke with the ambulance attendants after he and Daddy finished their conversation, and they bid us farewell. They shook Mother's hand as they left and she wished them God's blessings.

Doozer too made her peace with Mother. She held Mother's feet in her hands and lovingly told her that she too would turn loose of her so that she could go to Jesus in peace.

On Sunday night Joey flew down from New York to be with me. When I introduced him to Mother, she said, "I've been wanting to meet the man who put that gold band on Skeeter's finger that she won't take off."

He said, "That's me." He met all of my family members who were there at the time: Boze, Gladys, Suzan, Charlton, Doozer, and Dean. And of course Daddy. Everybody loved him. He gave all of us strength, calmness, and comfort throughout our period of sorrow. My brothers and sisters all told me how much he helped each of them through Mother's demise.

I planned to take a ride with Joey after taking him to his hotel so that I could escape from the bustle of the house for a few minutes. But he checked into the hotel and we returned straightaway to the apartment. Doozer and Dean were just leaving as we pulled up into the drive. Joey left soon to go to his room at the hotel for the night.

Mother called me to her side and said, "Why don't you let your friend stay here?"

I called him later and said, "Just check out in the morning and come be with us here."

Monday was a quiet day. I think we all needed it. Daddy was asleep. Mother rested as I kept watch over the two of them. Joey had slipped out to buy me more candles, which I burned constantly. When he returned, he went directly to one of the back rooms, but Mother knew he was there. Although I tested her, her sixth sense was always right.

Mother asked that Joey and I join her in the living room. With Daddy asleep at her side, I sat in the bedside chair next to Mother and Joey sat beside me. Mother reached for Joey's hand and said, "You know, Jesus heals broken hearts, and He wipes the tears from one's eyes. He has done that for some of us more than once." Then she began to pet my arm, speaking softly, "You don't need a wedding dress, just an ordinary dress will do!"

Neither Joey nor I understood exactly what she was really saying. She continued to take control of the situation as she said, "Let's pray," and she bowed her head whispering her prayer.

The next moment she added, "Skeeter, get us a drink!"

"What?" I said.

"A pretty glass of your fancy juice or your water will do." I always keep Mountain Valley water and Martinelli (nonalcoholic) sparkling apple cider on hand. So I brought out bubbly juice and poured each of us a tall glass. "Now let's sing one." So Mother, Joey, and I sang together as was her spontaneous wish.

That afternoon Mother and I talked privately. Although she had described what she wanted before, she insisted on telling me again about her funeral arrangements. Her casket was to be fully open. She should be dressed in a long satin nightgown with lace that provided tasteful coverage of her body. She wanted her hair fixed simply and she was not to wear shoes.

I had hoped that Brother Moore would drop by, although I realized he didn't even know where my apartment was. Before I could say it out loud, Mother said, "Don't worry, Skeeter, I see a man coming, and you'll know when he gets here."

On Tuesday Brother Moore arrived. It hadn't yet dawned on me how he might have found where I lived. He prayed with Mother and sat with the family members all gathered at the apartment that day. Mother began to describe episodes from the Bible that amazed all of us because of the clarity of her descriptions. She was definitely in a spiritual state of being as she saw so many things we could not see.

"William, come here and take my diamond earrings. I see so many diamonds and other beautiful precious stones, I'll never need my diamonds now." She asked for me to take the initial *S* ring that I had custom-made for me in 1964. I had given it to her on her sixtieth birthday. "Skeeter, wear it when you sing so it looks pretty when you hold the microphone." When I wear it, you can be sure that I am thinking of Mother. She dispensed with all of her jewelry except for the small cross I had bought for her in Scotland and Daddy's wedding ring.

Mother had messages for all of us. As she would feel the need to speak with one of us, she would call us to her side. I was the message-taker for those who were absent. She lay quietly without labored breathing or any sign of pain.

I tried to follow Mother's instructions as best I could. I was to tell Shirley that she would go through a dark valley for a while, but that she would be all right as long as she kept her trust in God. Mother said He would bring her through the darkness. Mother's prophecy proved all too true for Shirley, who after eight children and twenty-six years of marriage was divorced by her husband so that he could marry another woman. She waited five years for the final settlement. As Mother told her, her faith in God carried her through.

We were all gathered around Mother's bed when Charlton acknowledged what we all felt. "What's that?" he said.

"She is gone," Boze said. The Death Angel had delivered Mother to Jesus on February 8, 1983.

I had been so strong throughout the ordeal, but those words "she is gone" caused me to collapse. I hardly realized that I was being carried to bed when I actually saw Mother leave. The next recollection I have is of Joey and Boze speaking to me after the undertaker had taken Mother away.

Every detail of her funeral was as she had specified. Daddy had chosen Williamson Memorial Gardens in Franklin, Tennessee, for her resting place, because Mother had asked him to stop there during one of their drives. Although at first we were informed that we would not find a casket like the one she had asked for, the undertaker finally found it in an old storage place in Jackson, Tennessee. At McClures' department store, a little saleslady sensed my difficulties in finding what I was looking for. Joey told her what the gown was for. She went to the stockroom and found the perfect Christian Dior sleeping gown for Mother, almost as if it had been there waiting for her.

Joey had to return to New York to join NRBQ for a show, so I faced the prospect of returning to the funeral home alone. As I drove from the airport, I thought about Mother's cryptic message, "You don't need a wedding dress; just an ordinary dress will do." I still hadn't figured it out as I joined my family at the funeral home.

Mother looked like an angel as she lay there. We had her service at the Lord's Chapel on February 10, 1983, where she had been baptized just thirteen months before. There was preaching, singing, clapping, weeping, and even laughter. The service touched the hearts of everyone who attended. Betty Jean Robinson sang "Ain't No Grave Gonna Hold My Body Down." Teddy Wilburn sang "Because He Lives" and Cathy Manzer sang Mother's favorite hymn, "The Old Rugged Cross," because I was too emotionally distraught to sing.

At the apartment, after the goodbyes were said, I was soon alone again. Just me and God. I became angered. I wanted my mother. I could neither eat nor sleep. I couldn't even cry anymore. The anger and pain over her loss was something I found nearly unbearable.

I think I stayed mad at God for at least two years, until I finally went out to the cemetery, lay across Mother's grave and prayed over and over again, *Lord, I don't want to be angry at You anymore, so please help me*. It was as if God just reached down and lifted me up in His arms.

I felt his words in my heart. "I understand your pain and anger. I see your tears and I feel your heartache." He reminded me that His son Jesus had died for me and for all of us. As I thought of the cross at Calvary, knowing it was God's plan of salvation to give His Son that we might have eternal life, I thanked Him and came to terms with my grief. I sat by Mother's grave until my tears stopped falling. I looked up toward heaven, thankful that Mother had given her heart to Jesus so that she could be with Him in heaven.

Almost four years later, in January of 1987, Joey and I were planning our wedding at the Lord's Chapel. We had our license in hand and a date set when Nashville was blessed with one of the biggest snowstorms ever! In fact, the snowfall broke a record that year. When snow comes to Nashville in a big way, everything stops. The schools close, the churches close, and just about everybody stays at home until the roads clear. Everybody, that is, except our pastor, Brother Moore.

Joey had tried his best to clear the snow from the driveway so we could attempt to meet Brother Moore at the chapel. Joey came into the house, shaking his head and saying, "There's no way we're gonna get out of here right now, unless we walk." About that time the phone rang. Brother Moore called to say, "Skeeter, I had to come to the hospital with one of our church members, and I'll have to be here a while, but would you like for me to just stop by your house on the way home to marry you and Joey?"

Joey said, "Yes, have him do that."

I hung up the phone, not realizing until then that we didn't have a witness. No sooner had the thought reached my lips than Dean came walking in.

At about seven o'clock in the evening on January 27, 1987, I married Joseph Nicholas Spampinato. Later as I lay down to sleep, I remembered Mother saying, "You don't need a wedding dress; just an ordinary dress will do."

Oh No! Not Cancer! Not Me!

Mama, Mama, I need your help today.
Mama, Mama, is there something you could say?
You used to kiss the hurt away
And wipe the teardrops from my eye.
Now, Mama, your big girl's about to cry.
                    —"Mama, Your Big Girl's
                     'Bout to Cry,"
                     Skeeter Davis

Still mourning the loss of my mother, I couldn't believe it when I was diagnosed with cancer. That's right—the big C! I had been busy traveling and performing overseas and singing at the Grand Ole Opry when I was home. The house was running over with company, as it usually does in the summer. With a swimming pool in my back yard and an Opryland pass for my kinfolks, you can believe there's lots of company coming around. I'm always happy to have my friends and relatives, but the summer of '88 seemed to be never ending.

One Sunday afternoon I had come home from the Opry matinee to find the house empty for the first time in days. I had a tired feeling that I just could not shake. I felt as if something was trying to take my breath away. I started to climb the stairs to go lie down, and as I was

301

walking, I was praying, *Lord, please reveal to me what is wrong. Why am I this tired? Rest doesn't make this tired feeling go away. Please reveal to me why I stay tired.*

Instead of going down the hall to the bedroom Joey and I share, I stopped and went into a guest bedroom. As I sat down on the edge of the bed, I noticed on the closet shelf an old colorful purse that I had carried in the late sixties. I pulled myself up from the bed, reached to the shelf, and took the bag, thinking, *Maybe I should start carrying this again.* I opened it. A single item was stowed inside: a letter from my mother. I must have put it there the last time I carried the bag. I began reading: "Dear Daughter Skeeter, How are you today? We are all fine. Me and Suzan played bingo last night, but didn't win any big money—reckon I ever will? Daddy is listening to your tapes. I just walked to the store and am tired. I don't know why I'm so tired. That walk used to not make me feel tired like this."

As I read her words, hot tears were streaming down my face onto the letter. *Oh no, Lord! Do I have cancer?* I looked at the date of the letter: March 10, 1973. Mother died nearly ten years later: February 8, 1983.

The phone rang. It was Daddy. He said, "Why are you crying, little girl?" I told him about finding Mother's letter but nothing about my fears. "You stop crying now and just hang on to that letter. It ought to make you feel good."

After we hung up, I called Linda. I said, "I know now why I'm tired. I know what's wrong with me. I've got cancer."

She said she thought I was just tired from working and having company. She told me not to worry about cancer, just to calm down and get some rest.

Despite Linda's advice, I called Dr. Robert Hollister at his home. He is a good friend and the physician who gives me my yearly physical. I had always made a point of having regular checkups since cancer and heart problems are prevalent in my family. I had my last checkup the previous October, just eight months before. Dr. Hollister told me that I should come to the office on Monday as the last appointment of the day.

I spent the rest of that Sunday alone. I put Mother's letter in my little prayer book and cried intermittently most of the day. Yet I felt some sense of relief that I would see Dr. Hollister soon. When Joey called and found me in tears, I told him everything. But he, like

Linda, felt that I had absolutely nothing to worry about. I knew better.

When Dr. Hollister examined me, he did not detect a lump. He said, "You know, Skeeter, I could say that you're okay, but knowing how spiritual you are and how strongly you feel that the letter from your mother is God's way of revealing something to you, I have to act. I could not forgive myself if I didn't check further. I'll make you an appointment for a mammogram."

The mammogram showed a suspicious lump. As I went to the Opry for a matinee performance, I did not tell anyone about my fears. I only requested prayer from the audience and my friends and band members (and their friends, too!).

Joey was on the road with NRBQ. They were in the middle of a Bonnie Raitt tour, and I did not want the news to affect the whole tour. Too many people would have been affected by Joey coming home, so I decided to wait a few more days. I would perform at the Opry as scheduled, and before I knew it, Joey would be on his way home. Each night as we talked on the telephone, he'd ask me why I sounded so troubled. I'd laugh and tell him that "my jet lag was still jettin'."

I was actually happy to enter the hospital. Since Joey was away and my daddy and sister Suzan both were ill, Linda Stiegele took me to St. Thomas. A good and faithful friend, she called everyone to let them know about me.

On August 1 I had a biopsy which showed a malignancy. By the time I awoke from the anesthesia, Joey was with me. Shortly after I woke up, I was informed that I would be going under again. Although the cancer was very, very small, Dr. Jacobs said that I would lose my right breast.

On August 2—that day of days—Linda Palmer took the calendar off the wall, but I knew what day it was. This was the day we were supposed to have spaghetti for Betty Jack and a bouquet of daisies for the anniversary blues. But not today.

Joey was supportive, loving, and caring—wanting me to know that he loved me *anyway*. I remembered how Daddy had told Mother when she lost her breast, "It's okay, Punzie. I love you *anyway*."

After I had undergone the mastectomy, Joey, Dr. Kenneth Jacobs, Dr. Glenn Buckspan, and I were to discuss whether I should consider reconstructive surgery. I couldn't think about anything, it seemed.

My sister Shirley called and told Joey that she recommended reconstructive surgery for me. She advised him that if I didn't go ahead with the procedure, my mental health was likely to suffer as I faced a constant reminder of Mother, who didn't have reconstruction as an option.

I don't remember how long I was in the hospital. It has been four years now since my reconstructive surgery, and I feel safe and well. Originally I had decided not to write about my cancer in this book. I felt like I might be embarrassed or feel ill at ease on stage, thinking someone in the audience would be seeing me in a different way. In the end, I reconsidered and decided to do what I felt was more important. Perhaps in sharing my experience, I can help to save a life. My cancer was detected early by a mammogram. I urge all women who have reached the age of thirty-five to schedule regular annual checkups that include mammograms. A mammogram could save your life.

Minnie Pearl had told all of us Opry girls to get checkups. A spokesperson for the American Cancer Society, she had long since given me her home number, telling me to call if I needed her. I did more than once. During my days of reconstruction and healing, she checked on me continuously. I had loved Minnie since those RCA Caravan tour days of 1954. She and Henry are both dear to me. Throughout her own battle with cancer and throughout mine, Minnie has been an inspiration to me.

I had often thought that I should volunteer to be a spokesperson for the American Cancer Society. After I prayed about it, God spoke to my heart, telling me to do what I was called to do. So I just keep on singing and sharing—doing what I believe I am called to do.

Daddy

Roses on my shoulder,
Slippers on my feet.
I'm my daddy's darlin',
Don't you think I'm sweet?
—"Roses on My Shoulder,"
Skeeter Davis and Joey Spampinato

It was November 1988 and Daddy had come to visit me for a few days. He and Joey Spampinato did that often during my recuperation, as it was still difficult for me to drive to see him. He planted grapes and a couple of Granny Smith apple trees in my yard. At the end of his visit with me, my brother Harold (Boze) took Daddy back down to his home in Columbia, Tennessee.

A couple of days later, an almost hysterical Boze called from the hospital. Daddy had been rushed to the hospital with a fever of 107 degrees. The doctor diagnosed pneumonia. I sped to the hospital despite the fact that I had still not recovered from the final stages of my reconstructive surgery just three months earlier. As I entered Daddy's room in the intensive care unit, I could not help but recall the familiar feeling of hospital walls.

Several days later his fever had subsided so that he could be released from the intensive care unit to one of the regular hospital rooms. On Thanksgiving Day all of us gathered at Daddy's house to cook food to take to him. But it was easy to see that Daddy was tired. It is sad to look back on that day. Holiday times were family times. We were always missing the ones who weren't there. Since Mother had passed on, Daddy was particularly sad on holidays.

To make matters worse, I was not at my best. I was still not as strong as I wanted to be. I wanted to be able to take Daddy home to my house once he was out of the hospital, but he felt that he would be a burden to me since I had not completely healed.

As the days passed, Daddy got better, and we all celebrated Christmas in Brentwood. The year before I had spent the holidays in New York with Joey's family, so I was especially glad to be in my own home that year. It was to be our last Christmas with Daddy.

I had gradually gotten stronger and had planned a tour with my good friend Teddy Nelson for January in Norway. The crowds were great. As a result of the enthusiastic reception of our tour, we made plans to record an album (which we did in December of 1990). While I was touring with Teddy, Joey went on the road with NRBQ, and Daddy was house-sitting with my dogs and cats.

Daddy seemed strong and healthy upon my return home. I thought that sickness at last was behind us. I was mistaken. In April 1989, Daddy entered the hospital again with pneumonia.

Day and night I stayed by his side. One night as I sat in attendance, the nurse exclaimed to me that his temperature had risen to 107 degrees. Out of his head with fever, he mumbled, "Skeeter, I don't want to die in this hospital." Instinctively I laid my hands on him. I appealed to God in prayer, asking Him to take Daddy's fever away and to return him to his place at home with us.

Moments later the nurse returned to check his temperature. His fever had broken and dropped to 99 degrees. Two days later Daddy came home.

In the midst of Daddy's second bout with pneumonia, I had received a booking request from Jamaica. Joe Taylor, the booking agent, insisted on having an answer quickly. I asked that he give me a couple more days, but I knew I could not put him off for very long. I would be filling in for Percy Sledge, who as a result of his playing to segregated audiences in South Africa had been canceled by the Jamaican promoter. Because of my popularity in Jamaica, the promoter would go ahead with the concert only if I would agree to appear with the Drifters. My staunch refusals to play to segregated audiences began in the sixties, when I first began turning down jobs in South

Africa. Most people who know me, including the Jamaicans, know how I abhorred apartheid.

Despite my reluctance to commit to Joe Taylor, Daddy urged me to go. He said, "Skeeter, I'll be fine. You go on and sing pretty for the people." When he saw that I still felt uneasy about the situation, he told me to let the Lord show me the way. I trusted his advice and went to my bedroom to pray for guidance. Less than twenty minutes later, I uncovered three two-dollar bills—Jamaican dollars, that is—in my bedroom. I raced down the steps to find Daddy.

"Look, Daddy! Is this the answer?" I asked.

"Looks like an answer to me."

"Daddy, if God really wants me to go, He'll give me a perfect rainbow today. Only then will I have peace." I ran back upstairs. A few minutes later Daddy called for me to come down.

"Well, little girl, you wanted a rainbow. God has given you one." He proceeded to open the front door to reveal the most beautiful, perfectly formed rainbow, stretching from end to end across the Harpeth Hills. It took my breath away. "Now call Joe Taylor and tell him you're going."

And so I left for Jamaica. Daddy didn't go with me to the airport as he usually did. He told me that morning that nobody else liked to stay until my plane was out of view. He said, "I'll just say 'bye at the door and watch you until the car rounds the curve at the end of the road here." I laughed at him, telling him that it wasn't the same, but he replied that it would have to do.

I telephoned him when I arrived at my hotel. I told Daddy to tell Joey where he could reach me. I had arranged with Joey to check on Daddy each day as to my whereabouts. Joey was recording an album, so using Daddy as a go-between served two purposes: my calls would not slow Joey's recording sessions down, and Daddy would be getting a daily call from each of us. Dean brought him his meals every day and Suzan, Charlton, and Doozer had all promised to visit him regularly as well.

With my cancer behind me now, and the reconstructive surgery beginning to feel more like me, I felt good again. Singing "Under the Boardwalk" with the Drifters each night was a pleasure. My voice was better than it had been in a long time. Reviews of the show attested to that.

I called Daddy on Mother's Day, telling him that Jamaican radio shows were dedicating my songs to the mothers of Jamaica. I told him that things were much better for me now. Remembering Mother, I asked him to place flowers on her grave for me. He assured me that Dean had already taken care of that.

"Skeeter, I miss your Mother so much. You kids just don't know how bad I feel sometimes without her." I assured him that I understood. I tried to divert his thoughts by telling him that we would all go to Florida when I returned, that the salt water would do us good. "I expect we've waited too late," he replied.

Discouraged by his silence when I asked for an explanation of that comment, I said, "Daddy, I was just reading the little Bible book you gave me. I found the best scripture verse for me. It's Psalm one hundred four, verse thirty-three and thirty-four: 'I will sing unto the Lord as long as I live: I will sing praise to my God while I have my being.'"

"That's a good verse, alright."

I told him that I loved him and that I would be home in just a couple more days.

"I love you, hon. Sing pretty for the people." Those would be the last words Daddy spoke to me.

The next morning my telephone call went unanswered. My tour had finished, so I gave up the opportunity for a few extra days in the sun to return home as soon as possible. I tried not to worry but I could not help but feel concerned. I tried to call again in Miami. When this attempt failed, I called Joey at the recording studio.

Joey said that he was glad I was on my way home. It seemed strange to me that he should be glad about my early return, since he would not be there anyway. Days earlier he had told me that he was glad that I would be relaxing in sunny Jamaica. I decided that he figured my return would be the best thing for Daddy.

I called both Dean and Suzan, but again I received no answer from either of them. Where was everyone? I reasoned that since no one expected me that day, they had all gone out together to eat. Not entirely satisfied with this explanation, I grew increasingly restless during the flight from Miami to Nashville.

My arm started to bother me. I began to feel as I had that time in 1972 when Daddy experienced his first heart attack. Noticing my discomfort, John Rees, my piano player, asked what was wrong. I told him of my fears.

Landing in Nashville, I was surprised to see Dean and Charlton there to meet me. Dean said that Joey had called to give them the word to meet me. "Why didn't Daddy come?" I asked. Dean said hastily that we had company at the house and diverted my attention by asking about the huge doll I held in my arms. I explained that a girlfriend of one of the Jamaican musicians had given it to me. "Daddy will have a fit over this one, won't he?"

Dean's eyes welled up with tears. He told me that the previous night, Doozer, Suzan, Charlton, Daddy, and he had the best time talking about old times. As Dean prepared to leave the house, Daddy looked at him and said, "I'll tell you something, Dean. You all have to find somebody to take over for me as the head of this family. Keep it together. I am getting ready to go on home to be with the Lord." On their way out the door, Daddy's children protested that he just couldn't leave. They went to their respective homes, leaving Daddy alone in mine.

We finally arrived at my house on the way from the airport. Seeing unfamiliar cars in my driveway, I was disappointed at having to contend with company upon my return. I asked Dean about the company, only to see him burst into tears. The front door of the house opened. Brother Billy Roy Moore appeared from within.

"Where's Daddy?" I asked.

"Your daddy's gone to be with the Lord, Skeeter."

"No! No! No!" I collapsed on the floor of the foyer. Even now I find it hard to recall from memory the events of that seventeenth day of May. As I held fast to the Jamaican doll, Brother Moore and Boze lifted me onto the couch. Over and over in my mind, I heard Daddy's words telling me not to grieve for Mother. He had said that it was time for me to sing again, to go forward with my life and be fruitful for the Lord. I remember thinking that now he had gone, it was time to grieve again.

Brother Billy Roy Moore preached at Daddy's funeral. Having known Daddy so well as his brother in the Lord, he compared him to great men of the Bible. Then Daddy was taken to his resting place beside Mother, his beloved Punzie. Now they would be together with Jesus and their loved ones who had gone before in that place called heaven. They cannot come to us, but we can go to them.

"In my Father's house are many mansions....I go to prepare a place for you...that where I am, there ye may be also." (John 14:2–3)

> No more sickness, no more sorrow,
> No more tears to dim the eye.
> No more troubles, no more trials,
> Joy everlasting in their home beyond the sky.

Wake Up, Little Suzie

> Come morning, I'll be crying
> If you leave me tonight.
> Come evening, I'll be dying
> Way down deep inside.
> My misty, tear-filled eyes
> Will have no one to see
> Come morning if there is only me.
> —"Come Morning,"
> Suzan Marley and
> Michelle Dawn

What a fun little song by the Everly Brothers, and how crazy that I should have been thinking of it as I stood over Suzan's hospital bed watching her die. Wake up, little Suzie! Wake up!

Suzan had been fighting kidney disease since her teenage years, but after Daddy's death she seemed unable to fight anymore. She didn't smile, she didn't laugh, because life just wasn't fun anymore. She was in and out of hospitals many times with related illnesses and was riddled with pain. A Christian who loved the Lord, even in her suffering, she praised Jesus. Her faith was unshakable.

On the first Thanksgiving without either Mother or Daddy, Buddy and Peggy decided to come down to be with the rest of the family and to visit Suzan at the hospital. The only time before this that they had ever been present for one of our Tennessee Thanksgivings was in 1981

310

at Suzan's. That year I was involved in one of my Jamaican tours. Despite their joining us, this year's celebration lacked the joy and gladness we had always experienced. Of course we were all thankful for God's goodness and that Suzan was still with us. However, visits to the hospital increased our awareness of just how sick she was. The tears flowed upon our return home as we feared Suzan was too frail to fight much longer.

When Buddy and Peggy returned home and Joey left town on tour, I was overcome with sadness. Suzan worsened in December, and her doctors at Maury County Hospital in Columbia transferred her to Vanderbilt's Medical Center. The move coincided with my plans to record an album with Norway's Teddy Nelson. As time drew near for the recording session, my daily visits with Suzan left me with virtually no remaining strength, energy, or desire to record.

Teddy and his wife, Heidi, had already arrived in Nashville. The studio had been booked and the musicians hired. So Teddy recorded without me. Suzan urged me to go by the studio to see them even if I couldn't record as planned. I took her advice and headed for the studio for a couple of hours.

Ronny Light, my friend and one-time record producer, was engineering Teddy's session. Once there, I was persuaded to try to sing at least one song. I had not even heard the song before, but I sang one verse and harmony with Teddy for "Millions of Miles." Ronny made a tape of that session for me to take back to play for Suzan.

When Suzan heard the tape, she smiled and said, "Skeeter, it makes me happy to hear you singing a new song. You have just got to record again." She started to cry. I assured her that my heart was there with her and that if I trusted God, he would afford me the opportunity to record again. Over and over Suzan listened to "Millions of Miles." The song was eventually released in Norway, where it reached the top of the charts. Teddy and I recorded an album together later in 1991. Looking back on it, I know I did the right thing by spending those weeks with Suzan. Although I didn't know it then, our time together would be short.

At her request I brought her stamps and Christmas cards, which she insisted on addressing herself, saying, "Skeeter, I have to send my cards this year." Unlike in previous years, Suzan sent cards to every friend, relative, and acquaintance—including a Dairy Queen employee who had served her on occasion.

Christmas was coming. I would be heading for New York to meet

Joey as he was finishing a tour and to spend the holidays with Joey's family. I told Suzan that I was inclined to stay in Nashville since it would be our first Christmas without Daddy. I knew Doozer and Dean, both of whom lived alone, would be lonely. Shirley and Buddy both had their own families in Kentucky, Harold would be in Chapel Hill, Tennessee, with his family, and our cousin Glenn would be with his too.

Joey had been touring almost without a break, so I missed his being there for me with a shoulder to cry on. Suzan knew how tired and heart-saddened I was. She insisted that I go to be with Joey. "Skeeter, you need to be with him and to be out of this hospital for a while." Doozer and Dean would be visiting her regularly at the hospital in my place. Another thing intensifying our emotions that year was the pressure we felt in concealing our grief for the loss of Daddy in our efforts to remain strong for Suzan.

From New York I called each of the kids to check on how things were going. When I spoke with Suzan herself, she was so excited. "Skeeter, the doctor is going to give me a pass to go home! Charlton is coming to spend Christmas with me."

"Suzan, are you sure you're strong enough to be out?" I asked in surprise. I was glad that she sounded so happy, but in retrospect I wonder if the events which followed would have been any different had she declined the doctor's pass and had I stayed in Nashville to keep her in the hospital. I do not blame the doctor for releasing her, but it saddens me to think of what might have been.

I discovered from Suzan's neighbor and friend Patsy that she was the one who set up and decorated the Christmas tree that year, because Suzan didn't have the strength to do it. In the end Charlton, who had been visiting his father in Indiana, never made it to Nashville due to worsening winter weather. The disappointment was too much for Suzan. She had managed her Christmas shopping from her hospital bed via television home shopping. She faced her decorated Christmas tree, presents, and heartbreak alone.

I returned home on December 27. Joey's tour schedule resumed until mid-January. I called Suzan to tell her I would be coming out to see her before her pass expired and she returned to the hospital. We also had planned a family get-together to celebrate my birthday on December 30, but we just couldn't rouse our spirits enough for such an undertaking.

On January 5, I called Suzan at home again to tell her that I was on my way to see her. She would be returning to the hospital in just a few more days. We hadn't been speaking long when Suzan began to cry about Charlton's absence due to the lingering snow and ice that prevented him from being with her.

"I am going to hang up and just come on out there, Suzan." I said.

"No—Skeeter. Don't hang up. Something is wrong. I see a bubble in my tube and I have pains in my chest. I feel like I'm having a heart attack."

Knowing that a provision of her home leave from the hospital was that during her dialysis treatments a nurse would monitor the machine and sit with her throughout the process, I asked, "Where is your nurse?"

"She had to go to Mount Pleasant for a minute," she answered. "The bubble is moving, Skeeter!"

"I'm coming, Suzan!" By the time I threw the phone back on the hook and grabbed my car keys and purse, the phone rang again.

The voice on the other end of the line said, "Miss Davis, your sister is being taken to the hospital." I started out the door to find Dean standing there. I hurriedly related the situation to him, and within a few minutes we were on our way to the country hospital where the ambulance would deliver Suzan.

Dean and I found Suzan near death and once again hooked to the dialysis machine. She had suffered a heart attack but was strong enough to tell us, "I told them not to hook me up on these machines. Please get me out of here."

We were thankful that she was alive and tried to quiet her. She continued to cry. And so it began—the night that would lead to an ordeal that would become the most horrifying experience of our lives.

I called the kids: Shirley, Buddy, Boze, and Glenn. From near and far, our brothers and sisters and their children assembled to show their love and support for Suzan and each other. Joey arrived the next day, lending a tremendous amount of strength to all of us.

Suzan attempted to gain Joey's cooperation, pleading with him to take her away from the hospital. He patiently consoled her, saying that when the machines made her well, we would be taking her home with us. His sentiment came from the heart, but it would never happen.

As Suzan slipped in and out of a coma, she said goodbye to us all. We watched as her vital signs weakened, leaving a rare smile upon her lips. She spoke to us, saying that she would tell Mother and Daddy hello for us. We knew that she was slipping away.

Suddenly a nurse rushed in the room, pushing us aside. Using an apparatus that was intended to shock Suzan back to life, the nurse transformed a calm and peaceful scene into one of confusion and hysteria. Suzan actually revived, saying, "What happened?" From the expression on her face, we sensed her anger as she found herself still lying in a hospital bed, hooked up to an assortment of life support machines.

When we confronted the doctors about Suzan's right to die peacefully, we were told that consent was not required for the nurse to perform shock treatments to revive a patient in these situations. Evidently she planned to obtain at least an X on the consent form by Suzan's own hand. We all wondered how Suzan could manage this task without help. At this stage of discussion, Suzan had suffered a stroke which had caused paralysis, she was severely diabetic, her kidneys had completely failed, and her flesh was actually separating from her frame.

What were Suzan's rights in all of this? Although sharing Suzan's plight is difficult for me, I hope that her story may help my readers should they ever have the misfortune to face similar decisions or circumstances related to the patient's right to choose.

Suzan was subjected to many unwanted blood transfusions. She emerged frightened and covered with bedsores. Her arms were completely bandaged to conceal her splitting flesh. I can only imagine that dying with AIDS could not be much worse than what I witnessed during my own sister's fight to die with dignity.

What were these doctors doing? At wit's end, I confronted Suzan's doctor and asked if she was a Christian. She was not. My reason for asking this question was that I saw no compassion in her treatment of Suzan. The doctor's words were, "I saved your sister, not God. I saved her from dying."

"Well, that helps me understand what is going on," I said. "Jesus will have His way. He will not knock you down to come to Suzan, but I believe He will walk past you. His will and not yours will be done with my sister's life." I have never expected all people to believe as I do, but from that day forward I asked our prayer group to pray for this doctor.

Although it was not my wish for Suzan to die, I could no longer bear to witness her horrible suffering, particularly as a victim of this doctor's self-proclaimed heroics. I told Suzan that God would grant her the desires of her heart. She had served Him well. At her side day and night, I understood when Doozer could no longer bear to visit. My faith was put to the ultimate test throughout this torment. I prayed with Suzan as I stroked her forehead and played the gospel recordings she loved by George Hamilton IV and Cathy Manzer, a singer from our church. I quoted Scripture and sang to her.

Suzan's body was literally falling apart. As soon as I came to the realization that we would not be able to care for Suzan at home should she ever be released from the hospital, I attempted to explore nursing homes which might accept her. After I described Suzan's condition to representatives from two facilities, both refused to consider offering her admittance.

A couple of nights before she died, she was in such pain that one of the nurses said to me, "Miss Davis, I know you are a Christian and your sister is a Christian. If I was you, I would be down in the chapel praying for the Lord to come quickly."

"But she's the baby of our family. She's only forty-four years old," I pleaded.

"Yes, but the baby of your family is really suffering. She cannot live like that, can she? Would you want that for your sister?" was her reply.

I continued to pray for Suzan and requested that all of my prayer partners at the Opry and within my church and family pray with me for God to grant Suzan the desires of her heart. As I prayed quietly at her side, Suzan asked, "Skeeter, what is the date? Not day, date."

I told her it was the night of February 7. She smiled, asking me to stroke her forehead with my fingers. I asked her what she was thinking. She replied simply, "You know." In the early hours of the next morning, I asked Suzan if there was anything she needed to do or if I could help her with something. She turned her face to the wall just as Brother Bob Colville came into the room.

On his previous visits he would tell her that the church was praying for her new kidney. This visit was different. "Suzan, I have come to tell you goodbye. Please forgive us for our selfish desires. We had wanted you to stay because we love you. I understand now that you want to go on. We love you, Suzan." She looked so happy, she smiled at him. He delivered a short prayer and said he would return in a little while.

"Dear Jesus," I prayed, "please let me have peace about Suzan. I don't want her to leave. Please show me that she's at peace so that I can live with this." I asked Suzan if there was anything blocking her peace and whether she had forgiven her ex-husband. She frowned. "Lord, help us to forgive those who trespass against us, as You forgive us. Oh, Suzan, let me see that you forgive all who have hurt you."

Suzan looked at me and smiled. This time when I asked, "Is all well with your soul?" Suzan nodded her head and gazed at me with her blue eyes glistening like crystal, becoming bluer than blue. "Is this the veil of death, Lord?" I asked.

No sooner had I finished my words than Suzan's arms lifted twice from under her bedcovers. Her paralyzed arms moved as if she were in flight. I fell into the arms of two nurses who had come running in response to the monitors, which indicated Suzan's vital signs had stopped. Suzan had died.

They removed me from Suzan's side and deposited me in another room where I cried for hours. My faithful friend Pennilane drove me to my home. How appropriate for Penni to be with me, I recalled, for she had been with me that day in Kentucky when I learned that Suzan had only one kidney. I remembered too Ralph's angry response as I became so upset over the news, "Skeeter, your sister won't die!" God had been good to us, sparing Suzan for all those years, and we all thank Him for that gift.

Suzan was the seventh child, born with the birthmark on her side shaped like the number seven. She had lived with her transplanted kidney for seven years, and she went to be with Jesus on the seventh anniversary of Mother's passing. Suzan fought the fight, ran her course, and now she is free from her suffering. I know that the sufferings of this present time cannot be compared to the glory revealed to us when we see Jesus. She was the baby, and a baby needs its mother and daddy. I guess there is some peace of mind in that, but I sure do miss her.

Agape (God Love)

I've got the joy, joy, joy, joy
Down in my heart
Down in my heart
Down in my heart.
I've got the joy, joy, joy, joy
Down in my heart.
It's down in my heart to
stay.
   —"Down in my Heart,"
   Traditional

In the Bible we read that God says He will not leave us nor forsake us. He promises to meet our needs. He tells us we will have joy unspeakable if we believe in Jesus and trust Him. Well, I do believe, and I was trying to trust Him. But after Suzan's death I thought I would surely lose my mind. I could see only black as I would try to think and sort things out. The words to my songs escaped me. I could not finish a sentence when I was engaged in conversation. I would just stop talking and start to sob. I could not understand God at all in this.

Here I was—the oldest child—having to bury the youngest. Somehow this made absolutely no sense. If you have had a similar experience, you may understand some of the strange feelings that accompany it. It would have seemed only natural that the oldest would be the first to leave. Is that what He means when He says, "The first shall be the last, and the last shall be the first"? And "Lean not unto thine own understanding, but in all thy ways acknowledge Him, and He will direct thy path"?

For a couple of weeks I fasted and prayed. I finally decided to sing at the Opry the following week. Debbie Logue, Hal Durham's secretary at the Opry, had called, encouraging me to come back. She thought it would help me to sing my songs. Maybe she was right, I thought. But that first night back I started singing "The End of the World" and broke down in tears on stage. As I looked out into the audience, I could not see faces—only darkness, black. My band kept playing, and the Carol Lee Singers sang the words as I stood crying in front of all of those people.

George Hamilton IV was scheduled to follow me that night; I was told later that he explained to the audience, "Skeeter is a brave girl, folks. She and her brothers and sisters just buried their youngest sister Suzan a few weeks ago. Skeeter came out to sing to you all, but we can understand, can't we? Let's all pray for her and the Penick family." He sang a gospel song that night. He told me later that he and his wife, Tinkey, prayed for me on their way home from the Grand Ole Opry that night.

Linda Palmer had accompanied me that night since Joey was on the road. She said, "I'm taking you to the hospital." I told her that I needed to go home first. Once there, I told her to wait while I went upstairs to pray about what to do. I knew I was going to have to fight the devil to keep in control of my mind. I believe that if I had gone with Linda to the hospital that night, I would have been admitted. I was dangerously close to having a nervous breakdown.

From my bedroom I yelled to Linda that I was going to give God the chance to help me. I told her that I was going to have to fight a spiritual battle to overcome the forces of Satan that were trying to destroy me, weakened as I was with grief. I knew my faith in Jesus assured me of victory!

Linda, a nurse by training, knew the symptoms of emotional collapse and felt that I needed professional help. She also knew of my faith and had seen me exercise its power before. She agreed to stay with me to give me the opportunity to pray and trust God.

In one of the rooms in my house I have a collection of angels, some pictures of Jesus, and some crosses on the wall. It is a very special room. Special and spiritual. I entered the room and called out to God with all of the authority He gives me, in the name of Jesus, and demanded that the spirit of depression leave me. I commanded Satan to take his tools of sadness, sorrow, depression, and anger and depart from this place! I looked up to Jesus and asked Him to let me feel His presence by turning my depression and despair into peace and joy. I asked Him to replace my anger with acceptance.

I prayed, sang songs, and quoted Bible verses for almost four hours. I asked the Lord to please restore my mind. I asked Him to bring to my memory words to songs that I could not sing. I proceeded to sing one song after another. I don't know how long I spent, but soon I was feeling better and better. I praised God as I fell to sleep.

That night I dreamed I was in heaven with Mother, Daddy, Suzan, and Jesus. Jesus had his hand on Daddy's shoulder. I was so excited! I was looking around at everyone. I saw some familiar faces, but none were so familiar as those seated in golden chairs in front of me. Daddy pulled a chair in front of me, saying, "Here, Skeeter, sit down. I know you want to ask Jesus something."

"Yeah, I do. How come He didn't fix her?" I said. "Why didn't He give her a new kidney and fix her body?"

"He did," Daddy said. "Look at her. He gave her a glorified body." I looked at Suzan.

"It's true. You look beautiful. I love you and I miss you," I said.

Suzan replied, "I love you too, Skeeter." The same exchange followed with Mother and Daddy.

Then Daddy said, "Now you have to go back."

"Daddy," I said, "Jesus wouldn't bring me here to heaven and then send me back."

"You've got to go back and do what God called you to do," he replied.

I opened my eyes to see the clock face registering 7:00 A.M. I felt close to God and thankful to feel His presence. I was grateful for all I was sure that He had done to heal me in these trying times and I was sure that He must have more for me to do.

I called out to Linda, "I'm okay now!"

She advised me that she had not slept a wink. She had heard talking in the room and had looked in on me. I told her that I knew I could return to work at the Opry and asked her if she would go with me again that afternoon for the matinee and the Saturday night shows.

When we arrived at the Opry, all of my band members were justifiably anxious. They expressed their concern for me and registered their doubts about whether I would be back. They sought out Linda for an explanation of the change they detected in me from the previous night. All she could say to them was that they should never underestimate the power of prayer.

The following week Joey was still on the road and I was alone. As I fed my big dogs out in the back yard, I decided to stay outside even though the air was chilly. I looked up into the sky, asking God to open a new door for me. Would He send me somewhere for special healing? I recalled the words from the Bible, "Let your requests be known to God" (Philippians 4:6–9). I spoke, "Lord, this is my request. I do not feel like singing yet, but if I could just go to a new place to find peace and tranquillity—a new door which You would present to me for this purpose—I would really appreciate it. Thank You, Lord. Amen."

Hal Durham's secretary, Debbie Logue, called later that day, asking me to please come to the Opry that weekend. She said that Leigh Wieland and Sharon Bell, both of whom worked for the State of Tennessee, were working with a gentleman from Korea who was undoubtedly my number one fan. He had made a special trip to Nashville just to hear me sing. I told Debbie that I would rather not work and hung up the phone. Shortly thereafter she called again.

"I told Ms. Bell that you didn't want to work, but she insisted that I call and ask you again." I told her no. A few minutes later she called for the third time. "Skeeter, I know this may sound crazy to you, but the Korean gentleman wants to meet you. You have been his favorite singer for more than twenty years, and he is coming all the way from Korea. You know Suzan would be happy about that, and she would want you to come and sing."

Of anything Debbie could have said, that got me. I told her that I would do the 6:30 show only and that the gentleman would probably forget all about me once he heard that Loretta Lynn, Crystal Gayle, and Peggy Sue would be there. They would be making their first appearance together on the *Opry Live* that night.

I arrived at the Opry at six o'clock. I had just arrived at my locker, and there they were: Leigh Wieland, Sharon Bell, Mr. Cho Kyoo-Ok, and a young lady named Joanne Park, a Vanderbilt student who would serve as interpreter. After a brief hello I arranged for chairs to be placed in the auditorium for them so that they could see the show. As soon as I sang my song, which I dedicated to my number one fan from Korea, I was surprised to see Mr. Cho and the translator back at my locker!

Since Mr. Cho spoke only Korean and I speak only English, we really needed Joanne's interpretation skills. Still worried about my state of mind, Linda Palmer had accompanied me to the Opry that night. The four of us sat in the Opry's backstage lobby beside Mr. Van Damme's desk to carry on our conversation. It was certainly a spectacle to behold!

Although Mr. Cho spoke no English, he could sing all of my songs. Through the interpreter, Mr. Cho told me how much he loved one of my very first albums, titled, *Here's the Answer.* I must say he blessed my heart with his stories of my songs and the significant meaning each held for him. He told me that my songs were known among every generation in Korea, young and old alike.

Sensing my sadness over the loss of Suzan, he asked if I would like to come to Korea to visit his family and friends, who would receive me with love and affection. I asked for further clarification. Did he mean for me to come to do a concert? He replied that his offer was for me to come so that he and his friends could console me over the loss of my young sister. Joanne interjected that it was her opinion that Mr. Cho was sincere in his invitation and that his motives were pure.

His kind offer touched my heart. In a few minutes Leigh and Sharon returned to us, asking Linda and me to join them for dinner. I really did not feel like going, so I declined and bid them all farewell. Linda and I returned home.

Later that night when Joey called, I told him about meeting this kind man and his genuine offer. I told Joey that I felt the friendship and the invitation extended with it might be a gift from God. Hadn't I just asked the Lord to open a new door? I had never been to Korea.

On Sunday morning when Joey returned home, we sorted through his collection of Skeeter Davis albums (he has more than I do) to find a couple to present to Mr. Cho. We decided that I would go the airport to say goodbye to Mr. Cho. I arrived at the airport just about the time his plane was scheduled to depart. I ran as fast as I could with all of the albums and posters in my arms. To my relief I spotted Leigh Wieland and Mr. Cho Kyoo-Ok outside the very last departure gate.

I rushed over to meet them. They were clearly surprised to see me. Mr. Cho was very happy to receive the albums from Joey. Using creative body language and a smattering of English words, Mr. Cho told us how on a previous business trip he had searched for days in New York record shops for an album of mine. By the time he found the one he was looking for, he had spent two extra days in New York and more than two hundred dollars for one Skeeter Davis album.

At the conclusion of his story Leigh handed Mr. Cho an envelope and said, "Mr. Cho, perhaps you would like to give this to Skeeter now that she is here." I didn't know what to expect. As I opened the envelope, I discovered the contents to be an unrestricted first-class, open round trip ticket from Nashville to Seoul, valid for two years from date of issue. I hardly knew what to say!

I felt in my spirit that this truly was a new door opening for me. A gift from God delivered expressly for my consolation. As Leigh and I waved our goodbyes to Mr. Cho, Leigh, who had already visited Korea and had even visited Mr. Cho's home, said, "Skeeter, you've got to go." We walked to the airport entrance together, and I approached the car where Joey waited for me. I was overwhelmed by it all. You just don't receive a gift like that every day from a fan. I believed it to be a blessing!

Joey agreed that this was something very spiritual and that I should make plans to go. He had been gone so much lately that I felt that I was married but living single. He had been touring with REM when I was grieving over Mother's death; he had been on tour with Bonnie Raitt during my mastectomy, reconstructive surgery, and recuperation; and he was recording albums when both Daddy and Suzan died. Although he telephoned consistently, I had been living in a valley of tears. It was time for me to go to the mountaintops. I did not know when I would go to Seoul, but that day I would go with Joey's blessing.

March 4 is Betty Jack's birthday. For all these years since her death, I have celebrated her birthday. I always would eat B.J.'s favorite meal and have her favorite flowers—old-fashioned daisies—around the house. I am thankful for my friends who have been so kind, attentive, and understanding in sharing this special date with me through the years. Joey had even persuaded me to sing the Davis Sisters' songs that I had not been singing for so long.

On B.J.'s birthday in 1990 I looked at the airline ticket, looked at the calendar, and chose the date for my trip. I would leave May 12 and return May 20. I planned to be away from home on Mother's Day and also on the first anniversary of Daddy's passing. I felt good knowing that I would be walking through the new door God was opening for me.

I never go anywhere alone. I always make sure that Joey or one of my band members—John, Jim, James, or Brannan—goes with me. This time I was to be alone. Just me. Faith—that's what it takes. If you have traveled outside of your own country before, then you know it's always a thrill. This trip would take me from Nashville to New York to Anchorage, Alaska, to Seoul!

I was met with greetings of welcome from the immigration officers and others who had been alerted about my arrival. Mr. Cho Kyoo-Ok and our interpreter, Mr. Kwak, met me, and Mr. Cho's driver, Mr. Kim, escorted me to the Shilla Hotel where they had reserved a beautiful suite for my visit. How happy I was that I had come! Left to refresh myself after the long flight, I could not be still. I found myself praising God for this time and place.

Several hours later Mr. Cho returned to take me on my first sightseeing tour of Seoul. We drove to the foot of a big mountain, parked the car, and began to walk. As I rattled on, I felt sorry for Mr. Kwak. My fast talking must have been quite a shock after the slow and quiet manner of Mr. Cho and the driver, who said nothing. Not expecting that long walk after my long journey, I felt the jet lag set in. I was ready to collapse on the spot. My host was trying so hard to please me that in my excitement I had quite forgotten that I must take time to rest. We decided that returning to the hotel would be in my best interest, and we would resume the sightseeing the next day.

Each day brought greater enjoyment than the previous one. Mr. Kwak had studied at Kansas University, so his English was excellent. He was such a nice, gentle young man. He related bits of Korean history to me as we toured the country. I saw the mountains and the boat-populated rivers. One night, during a cruise on the Han River, three of my recordings played. Having no knowledge of my presence, the disc jockeys who selected the music for the cruise were as delighted to meet me as was I to hear them playing my songs.

I was treated to a Korean folk dancing performance and a traditional Korean restaurant, where I learned to love the food. I gazed upon fields of ginseng and basked in the beauty of the Buddhist temples. I entered these holy places without shoes and sat on the floor, bowing to God and thanking him for this privilege. Having met so many people of different cultures, customs, and religions, I respect them all for their beliefs. Their styles and ways appeal to me as Christlike, and I often feel that we Christians can learn valuable lessons from them. Good manners and gentle ways are inspiring to those who hold Christian values. Jesus is the way for me. I know there are those who have ways that are not mine. I do not sit in judgment of them. I love them all. One of the lessons in which I truly believe is "Judge not, lest ye be judged." I am thankful that God is our judge—not you or I.

On my fourth day in Seoul, we traveled by car to a towering mountain with a temple on its peak. Although getting to the top required a lot of hard walking, I made it to the very top. After taking in the spectacular view, we started down the series of steps that led to the foot where we began. Every so often a level plateau area was available for those who needed to rest. As we came to one of them, I stepped out onto a huge boulder protruding out from a stream of water. I sat there in prayer and praised God for giving us His son Jesus. As I sat here, Mr. Cho Kyoo-Ok stepped out onto the rock and sat down beside me.

Mr. Cho spoke to me. Mr. Kwak interpreted, "Skeeter, Mr. Cho says to leave your sadness and sorrow here."

I told Mr. Cho that he had a very good idea. Although I felt that I had really been delivered of my depression during the night I prayed in my home, it seems that I had picked up some of that which I had cast out. So yes, it was a good idea to leave my sorrows here. Symbolically, I reached my hands to my heart, moving them upward as if to offer them to Jesus. I let go, releasing all of my sadness and sorrow into the stream of water where, I believe, it flowed to the heart of God.

I felt His presence so strong in my spirit. He was replacing my sadness with a sweeter song. My anger was no longer depression turned inside out; God's love and guidance was changing anger into acceptance. I don't think we'll ever understand it all, but if we can accept things, we will become whole again and life can become sweeter.

As we drove away from the mountain, I looked out the window thinking, *I'll never pick up that sorrow again.* That night we went to the home of Mr. Cho's friends. We were invited to stay in their home that evening instead of in a hotel. In their beautiful home was a room that held antiques which had been excavated from ancient tombs. The family made a gift to me of a vase which now graces my home in remembrance of them.

The next morning Mr. Cho took me to the Sam Dong Industrial Company, his factory, to meet his employees. They held a dinner in my honor and presented me with so many gifts that I felt very much like a little princess. I felt so much love and genuine affection radiating from their faces, I cannot adequately express it.

Later that day Mr. Cho's wife and many helpers prepared a dinner for me in their home. The meal was indeed fit for a king. They had purchased some very expensive beef in my honor, only to discover that I was a vegetarian. Accommodating beyond belief, my hosts presented me with a fare consisting of so many vegetables and fish that the other guests could not have felt deprived in the least. It was great!

I loved visiting with Mr. Cho, his wife, and two sons. Before I knew it, the time had come for me to return to Nashville. As we bid farewell to one another at the Kimpo International Airport in Seoul—me with five bags now rather than just the two I had come with—I wondered if I would ever see them again.

When I returned home to Joey and my family, I couldn't sleep for several days. It seemed as though I were flying. Happiness and excitement intermingled with jet lag and fond memories. I could hardly contain myself from sharing my experiences with everyone I met. I had found my joy again.

As I wondered if I would ever see Mr. Cho and his family again, I received word that Mr. Cho was organizing an effort to promote a Skeeter Davis concert in Korea. In December of 1991 my band and I had the pleasure of going to Seoul in concert. Sandy Posey came along to sing backup. It was an extraordinary pleasure to sing to the Korean people.

During a taping of a television special that week, my throat showed signs of strain. When I asked the producer if I could rework the performance of one of my spots, he told me that it was okay as it was. He said, "Skeeter, it is okay if you have crack in voice. People will think we are trying to deceive them because you look younger than your age, but we know you have been singing music for many, many years." He continued with what, I think, may be my favorite compliment, "You are old like mother, but young like Michael Jackson." I laughed and told him to leave the tape as it was, even though I did sound like I had a frog in my throat.

After our shows were finished, we were saying an airport goodbye again. We had to rush like mad to the airport because a miscommunication about our working visas detained us, so our departure was rather nerve-wracking. In fact, having never been detained for any reason whatsoever, I found this experience to be one of the most unusual in my career! We can laugh about it now as we reminisce about our memories with one another.

We didn't know it then, but we would see Mr. Cho again very soon. Leigh Wieland called me on December 28 and said, "Skeeter, guess what?"

Of course I could not imagine what was coming next. She told me to get ready for a birthday party—mine! She asked me to supply a list of friends to invite. Mindful of the expense involved, I did not want Mr. Cho to spend another dime: he had just done so much for me, my band, and Sandy. I chose the Opryland Hotel because I think it is so beautiful with all of the lights and decorations at Christmastime. Having a birthday so close to Christmas has a lot of disadvantages, but it proved to be an advantage for my party decor.

Mr. Cho flew in on the thirtieth. Leigh and Roberto, her husband, picked him up at the airport and brought him directly to the hotel. I will never forget celebrating my sixtieth birthday. *Crook and Chase* sent a television crew to film a segment for their show. My Opry pal Billy Walker performed a miniconcert for us with his wife, Betty, acting as sound engineer. I love them! I had a great time, as did everyone else who came to help me celebrate. I can hardly wait for the next sixty years!

Looking back over my life, I feel that it has been a good journey. Without the valleys, I could not have enjoyed the mountains. There has been a balance, I suppose, with the ups and downs, tears and laughter, joy and sorrow. Keeping my sense of humor has been an important factor in the process. But above all, having faith in God has carried me through as I realized so many of my dreams. Few country music entertainers have had the widespread international success my recordings have enjoyed in more than thirty countries across the globe—particularly in the more exotic markets of Korea, Indonesia, Malaysia, Thailand, Singapore, and Borneo.

I thank God for His guidance. Even though I am far from perfect, He showed me love unconditionally. I will be the first to admit that I have made mistakes in my life, but I can also say that I have learned from these errors in the process. And I learn new things about myself and this glorious gift of life every day. In coming to terms with my experiences, I realized that I do not have to be the victim any longer. I have God's approval and guidance, and ultimately that meets my needs above all.

God tells us that the truth makes us free. I am free indeed. Seekers of freedom also reap love. I now have both. My marriage to Joey Spampinato is the best part of my life. I thank God for Joey. He makes me happy by being the best boyfriend and husband a girl could have. He loved me at first sight, and I will love him until the last.

Sharing the story of my life has, in itself, been a healing journey of soul searching. I wanted to share it with those of you who have remained loyal fans and friends, and with my brothers and sisters who all came after me. Since I'm the oldest, they'll just have to take my word for it.

In 1993 I celebrate the fortieth anniversary of my career in the music business. Forty years of singing and entertaining folks. I have done what I believe God called me to do. I will sing as long as I have my being. And I will sing praises to my God.

Weeping is but a night, and joy comes in the morning. I've got the joy, joy, joy, joy down in my heart, and it is down in my heart to stay!

Discography

*Indicates Grammy Nomination
**Indicates Gold Standard

Gonna Get Along Without You Now b/w Now You're Gone	47-8347
Let Me Get Close To You b/w The Face Of A Clown	47-8397
What Am I Gonna Do With You b/w Don't Let Me Stand In Your Way	47-8450
A Dear John Letter b/w Too Used To Being With You (With Bobby Bare)	47-8496
I Can't Help It b/w You Taught Me Everything That I Know	47-8543
*Sunglasses b/w He Loved Me Too Little	47-8643
I Can't See Me Without You b/w Don't Anybody Need My Love	47-8765
If I Had Wheels b/w If I Ever Get To Heaven	47-8837
Goin' Down The Road b//w I Can't Stand The Sight Of You	47-8932
Fuel To The Flame b/w You Call This Love	47-9058
*What Does It Take b/w What I Go Through	47-9242
*Set Him Free b/w Is It Worth It To You	47-9371
For Loving You b/w Baby It's Cold Outside (With Don Bowman)	47-9415
Instinct For Survival b/w How In The World	47-9459
There's A Fool Born Every Minute b/w I Can't See Past My Tears	47-9543
Timothy b/w I Look Up And See You On My Mind	47-9625
The Closest Thing To Love b/w Mama, Your Big Girl's Bout To Cry	47-9695
Keep Baltimore Beautiful b/w Baby, Sweet Baby	74-0148
Teach Me To Love You b/w Bobby Blows A Blue Note	74-0203
I'm A Lover Not A Fighter b/w I Didn't Cry Today	74-0292
Your Husband, My Wife b/w Before The Sunrise (With Bobby Bare)	74-9789
It's Hard To Be A Woman b/w What A Little Girl Don't Know	74-9818
We Need A Lot More Jesus b/w When You Gonna Bring Our Soldiers Home?	74-9871
Let's Get Together b/w Everything Is Beautiful (With George Hamilton IV)	74-9893
Bridge Over Troubled Water b/w How In The World Do You Kill A Memory?	74-9896
Bus Fare To Kentucky b/w From Her Arms Into Mine	74-9961
Love Takes A Lot Of My Time b/w Love, Love, Love	74-9997
*One Tin Soldier b/w Rachel	74-0608
Sad Situation b/w All I Ever Wanted Was Love	74-0681

A Hillbilly Song b/w Once   74-0827
The End Of The World b/w I Can't Stay Mad At You   447-0709
I Can't Believe That It's All Over b/w Try Jesus   74-0968
Don't Forget To Remember b/w Baby Get That Leavin'   74-0188
  Off Your Mind
One More Time b/w Stay A While With Me   APBO-0277
Lovin' Touch b/w Come Mornin'   PB-10048
The Rose b/w I Love You (Bigger Than Texas)   NR12083-2

MERCURY RECORDS

I Love Us b/w It Feels So Good   73818
It's Love That I Feel b/w If You Loved Me Now   73898

SINGLES by the Davis Sisters

FORTUNE RECORDS

Jealous Love b/w Going Down the Road Feeling Bad (by   45-170
  Roy Hall)
Sorrow and Pain b/w Kaw-Liga   45-174
Heartbreak Ahead b/w Steel Wool (C. Hartfield)   45-175

STAR RECORDS

Jealous Love b/w Firecracker Stand (by Jimmy Lane)   45-1630

RCA VICTOR RECORDS

I Forgot More Than You'll Ever Know (About Him)   47-5345
  b/w Rock-A-Bye Boogie
You're Gone b/w Sorrow And Pain   47-5460
Gotta Get-A-Goin b/w Takin' Time Out For Tears   47-5607
Foggy Mountain Top b/w You Weren't Ashamed To Kiss   47-5701
  Me Last Night
Show Me b/w Just Like You   47-5843
Tomorrow I'll Cry b/w Christmas Boogie   47-5906
Everlovin b/w Tomorrow's Just Another Day To Cry   47-5966
I've Closed The Door b/w I'll Get Him Back   47-6187
It's The Girl Who Gets The Blame b/w Baby Be Mine   47-6291
Blues for Company b/w Don't Take Him For Granted   47-6409
Lying Brown Eyes b/w Lonely and Blue   47-6490
Fiddle Diddle Boogie b/w Come Back To Me

ALBUMS by Skeeter Davis

RCA VICTOR RECORDS

I'll Sing You A Song And Harmonize Too	LPM-2197
Here't The Answer	LPM-2327
Porter Wagoner And Skeeter Davis Sing Duets	LPM-2529
The End Of The World	LPM-2669
Cloudy With Occasional Tears	LPM-2736
Let Me Get Close To You	LPM-2980
Tunes For Two (with Bobby Bare)	LPM-3336
The Best of Skeeter Davis	LPM-3374
Written By The Stars	LPM-3382
Skeeter Sings Standards	LPM-3463
Singin' In The Summer Sun	LPM-3567
My Heart's In The Country	LPM-3667
Hand In Hand With Jesus	LPM-3763
Skeeter Davis Sings Buddy Holly	LPM-3790
What Does It Take	LPM-3876
Why So Lonely	LPM-3960
I Love Flatt and Scruggs	LPM-4055
The Closest Thing To Love	LPM-4124
Mary Frances	LPM-4200
A Place In The Country	LPM-4310
Your Husband, My Wife (With Bobby Bare)	LPM-4335
It's Hard To Be A Woman	LPM-4382
Skeeter	LSP-4486
Love Takes A Lot Of My Time	LSP-4557
Bring It On Home	LSP-4642
Skeeter Sings Dolly	LSP-4732
The Hillbilly Singer	LSP-4818
The Best Of Skeeter Davis, Volume 2	APLI-0190
I Can't Believe That It's All Over	APLI-0322

RCA CAMDEN RECORDS

I Forgot More Than You'll Ever Know (About Him)	CAL-818
Blueberry Hill	CAL-899
Easy To Love	CAL-2367
Foggy Mountain Top	CAL-2514
The End Of The World	CAS-2607
He Wakes Me With A Kiss	CAS-0622

ROUNDER / RED ROOSTER RECORDS
(On Compact Disc)

She Sings/They Play (With NRBQ)   3092/108

INTERNATIONAL RELEASES
(On Compact Disc)

You Were Made For Me (With Teddy Nelson)   Norway
I'll Sing You A Song And Harmonize Too   Japan
Best Of Skeeter Davis   Japan
Skeeter Davis (Lassoes 'N Spurs Series)   Canada
Best Of Skeeter Davis   Singapore

BEAR FAMILY RECORDS
(On Compact Disc)

The Davis Sisters: I Forgot More Than You'll Ever   15722 BH
   Know: 1 & 2

Index